Joseph Bonaparte.

Bonaparte

New York. D. Appleton & Co. 346 & 348, Broadway

THE CONFIDENTIAL CORRESPONDENCE OF NAPOLEON BONAPARTE WITH HIS BROTHER JOSEPH,

SOMETIME KING OF SPAIN.

SELECTED AND TRANSLATED, WITH EXPLANATORY NOTES, FROM THE 'MEMOIRES DU ROI JOSEPH.'

IN TWO VOLUMES.

VOL. II.

NEW YORK:
D. APPLETON AND COMPANY,
346 & 348 BROADWAY.
M.DCCC.LVI.

CONTENTS OF VOL. II.

CHAPTER XII.

(CONTINUED.)

CHAPTER XIII.

CHAPTER XIV.

CHAPTER XV.

CHAPTER XVI.

CHAPTER XVII.

LETTERS

OF

NAPOLEON BONAPARTE.

CHAPTER XII.

(Continued.)

[467.] NAPOLEON TO JOSEPH.

Benevento, Jan. 1, 1809.

My Brother,—General La Romana has less than 1000 men pressed into the service, naked, and dying of hunger; he no longer dares trust his army in the field, exasperated as it is against him. Marshal Soult attacked him on the 26th with 2 cavalry regiments, and took 1500 men and 2 standards. He entered Leon on the 30th, and found 2000 sick in the hospitals. The army of Gallicia cannot be said to have really existed after the affair of Espinosa, and now less than ever.

This first day of the year Marshal Soult is at Puente-de-Orvigo. Marshal Bessières slept at La Banesa, and is marching on Astorga, where we shall be to-day. The English have abandoned on the road 1500 tents, 4000 blankets, all their rum, an immense number of waggons, and many stragglers. I have not yet done with them; I shall pursue them vigorously. I shall reach Astorga this evening. I sent you word that Dessolles's division was on its way back to Madrid: the communication by way of Valladolid, Burgos, Segovia, and Guadarrama, will thus be secured. Order posts to be placed on the road to Villa Castin, and on the roads between Madrid and Segovia, and Segovia and Valladolid. Ask for returns, and take all the soldiers that can be spared, in order to strengthen the garrison of Madrid. By my returns it appears that you have received 2000 or 3000 men in marching companies belonging to the different corps. The Dutch brigade which is at Aranda should proceed to Madrid. The army of Castaños is in the same state as that of Romana. Each of them was called a week ago from 15,000 to 20,000 men; I am sure that neither now amounts to 4000. The weather is bad, the season severe, but this will not stop us; we must endeavour to have done with the English. You will no doubt send agents to Leon. Try to establish a correspondence between that town and Madrid; above all, spread printed papers. We have taken by the bayonet Montetorrero, before Saragossa, and the siege operations are carried on vigorously. General St. Cyr reached Barcelona on the 19th, and went and took all before him. I have there 30,000 men, whose influence is felt to a distance of twenty miles round.

Reding has been taken.

[468.] NAPOLEON TO BERTHIER.

Astorga, Jan. 2, 1809.

My Cousin,—Give orders to the 30th, 31st, 32nd, 33rd, 34th, 35th, and 36th marching companies, which are on their way to Burgos, to remain there on the 3rd and 4th, and to leave it on the 5th for Valladolid. Give the same order to the 39th, 40th, 41st, and 42nd marching companies, the same order to the first company of the 3rd regiment of foot artillery, also to the Nassau detachment, as well as to the 168 horse soldiers belonging to the 10th, 15th, and 22nd chasseurs; all are to go to Valladolid. In the dispositions made this morning for the organisation of the Duke of Dalmatia's corps I forgot to say that the battalion of the 31st light infantry should join its own regiment in Mermet's division, in order that the regiment may consist of four battalions. Desire the 17th light infantry and the 27th horse chasseurs to proceed to Valladolid, and give the same order to Heudelet's division; if from Burgos it went to Leon, let it go on to Valladolid.

[469.] NAPOLEON TO JOSEPH.

Astorga, Jan. 2, 1809.

My Brother,—The Dutch brigade, 1600 men strong, ought to reach Madrid on the 6th of January. It marches by Aranda, together with the 31st, 32nd, 33rd, 34th, 35th, and 36th marching companies, composed of soldiers formerly belonging to the 1st corps.

The 39th, 40th, 41st, and 42nd marching companies, composed of soldiers formerly of the 4th corps, forming altogether 1800 men, were to arrive at Burgos on the 2nd of January. At Aranda is General Treilhard with a battalion of the 118th and 2000 men from the cavalry depôts; and, besides these, the third battalion of the 43rd and 51st infantry, the Irish and Russian battalion, the Westphalian battalion, and the third battalion of the 5th light infantry, all under the command of General Treilhard.

[470.] NAPOLEON TO JOSEPH.

Astorga, Jan. 2, 1809.

My Brother,—I reached Astorga yesterday. Marshal Bessières is now near Villa Franca. He has taken 2000 Spaniards and 500 English, and burnt a great quantity of baggage and magazines. There have been found on the roads more than 800 dead horses and a considerable amount of ammunition and baggage. Terror reigns in their ranks. The Duke of Dalmatia is pursuing them. The guards are to return to Benevento. I am myself drawing near to the centre of my army. I can make nothing out of the Duke of Dantzic's letters. I hope that Merlin has rejoined him. It is probable that more than half of the British army will be in our power; the English themselves think so. As to Romana, his corps has been almost destroyed; 2000 men were taken prisoners at Leon, and 2000 in this place. For this last fortnight they have received neither pay nor provisions, and they are almost entirely without clothing.

On the 22nd the position of Montetorrero, which protected

Saragossa, was taken, and 1000 prisoners. I believe that I told you that General Saint Cyr had arrived at Barcelona, and joined General Duhesme.

Order the guns to fire a salute in honour of our successes over the English. By the time this letter reaches you, General Dessolles ought to be half way to Madrid.

[471.] NAPOLEON TO JOSEPH.

Benevento, Jan, 4, 1809.*

My Brother,—The Chief of the Staff sends you instructions for the manœuvre to be made by the Duke of Belluno on the left bank of the Tagus. Dessolles's division will be at Guadarrama on the . . .† at latest. The Polish battalion which is intended for Segovia ought to have arrived; if it should still be at Somo Sierra, you may desire it to join you, leaving two companies at Somo Sierra.

I have ordered the third battalions of the 43rd and of the 51st to repair to Madrid. After resting eight or ten days, Dessolles's division ought to amount to 9000 men. General St. Cyr arrived at Barcelona on the 17th. On the 15th he had an action with the Spanish Generals Vivès and Reding, whom he beat completely; he took from them six pieces of cannon and 1500 men. I have had Zamora and Toro occupied by brigades of cavalry. A brigade of infantry is to remain at Leon. Send intendants to these provinces. Print 12,000 or 15,000 copies of the 'Gazette de Madrid;' let it be circulated in every direction. It would be well to reprint the gazettes which have appeared since your entry into Madrid. I think that I sent you word that on the 2nd two Spanish regiments belonging to La Romana, two standards, and two Spanish generals, who were preparing to

* Napoleon received, on his road to Astorga, despatches which induced him to expect a war with Austria. He altered his plans, and, instead of superintending in person the pursuit of Sir John Moore, he left it to Marshal Soult, and returned to Benevento, and from thence to Valladolid, in order to communicate more rapidly with France. The French historians of course attribute to this circumstance the escape of the English army.—TR.

† Illegible.—ED.

enter Gallicia, were taken. The cavalry was not able to advance on Villa Franca on the 3rd, as the defile was occupied by English infantry. On the evening of the 3rd, Merle's division arrived and charged the English rearguard, which held a fine position on the heights of Pierros. The English were routed. Several hundred prisoners were taken. We had forty men killed and wounded. General Colbert, who was in advance, burning with impatience to charge the fugitives with his cavalry, was hit in the forehead by a ball, and killed. At Villa Franca the English had immense magazines; every place is filled with them. We shall find there the greater portion of the English sick. I am very anxious for news of the Duke of Dantzic. I cannot understand his having made such an eccentric manœuvre* without orders. If you want him, give him the requisite orders; but if you do not want him, let him remain where he is, and I will find him employment. I shall probably sleep to-night at Medina de Rio Seco.

[472.] NAPOLEON TO BERTHIER.

Benevento, Jan. 4, 1809.

My Cousin,—Write word to General Loison that there is a printing office at Leon, and desire him to print 6000 copies of the Emperor's proclamation, and of every newspaper which has appeared at Madrid since our entry, and to send 3000 to Marshal Soult, 500 to Marshal Ney at Astorga, and 500 to General Lapisse at Benevento. Give orders at Vittoria to have 3000 copies of the Emperor's proclamation printed and distributed all over the province, and in Navarre. Order General Darricau to proceed to Valladolid to take the command of all the battalions and marching companies which pass through.

[473.] NAPOLEON TO BERTHIER.

Benevento, Jan. 4, 1809.

My Cousin,—You will make General Lapisse aware that he is under the orders of the Chief of the Staff; that he is to stay at Benevento, where he will form a corps of observation; that

* Towards Avila.—TR.

he is to canton his troops in Benevento and in the environs, to give them rest, and to re-establish order and discipline; that he is to have a flour-store containing flour for 100,000 rations of bread; that he is always to have 20,000 rations of bread ready; that he is to collect all his carriages and make biscuit, so as to be able to start whenever he is wanted; that he is to repair his carriages, and take the [horses*] of the soldiers, to increase the means of conveyance. He will have under his orders the brigade of dragoons of General Davenay, who is at Toro, and that of General Maupetit, who is at Zamora. It is the business of these two brigades to disarm those provinces, to reduce the towns and to publish my proclamations. They are to correspond with the Chief of the Staff and with General Lapisse, in order that, if necessary, he may support them with infantry. You will let Marshal Ney know that I wish him to remain at Astorga, to administer the country, and establish magazines, in which he should always keep 100,000 rations of flour and 20,000 of bread; and that he is to order biscuit to be made for . . .*; and that I desire that a depôt of cavalry may be formed at Astorga, to receive all the lame horses belonging to the corps in Gallicia; that he should find a place in which this depôt may be established; that he should undertake to guard the defiles which connect Gallicia with the kingdom of Leon, and establish posts, so as to have rapid communication; that some of his staff officers should always be with Marshal Soult ready to proceed whithersoever they may be required, if the English, instead of re-embarking, were to land fresh troops.

[474.] NAPOLEON TO JOSEPH.

Benevento, Jan. 5, 1809.

My Brother,—Seven marching companies, forming . . .* men, ought to have reached Madrid on the 4th of January; . . . * marching companies, 500 men strong, were to arrive there on the 5th, as well as the first marching battalion, which is composed of 900 conscripts. Therefore, between the 4th and the 5th, nearly

* Obliterated.—ED.

3000 men, old soldiers and conscripts, ought to have reached you, some belonging to the divisions at Madrid, and the rest of them to those which remain at the Retiro. These men must be reviewed when they get to Madrid, and those who belong to the division of Villate allowed to rest before they start.

P.S.—On the 3rd our advanced guard had an action before Villa Franca with the English, and beat them. During the last week we have taken ten standards, 2000 or 3000 men, and several Spanish generals belonging to La Romana's corps; we have nearly 1500 English prisoners.

On the 4th the Duke of Dalmatia's head-quarters were four leagues from Villa Franca, on the Lugo road. I start to-morrow for Valladolid.

[475.] NAPOLEON TO JOSEPH.

Benevento, Jan. 6, 1809.

My Brother,—I thank you for your new-year's day wishes.* I have no hopes of peace in Europe for this year at least. I expect it so little, that I signed yesterday a decree for raising 100,000 men. The fierce hatred of England, the events at Constantinople, all betoken that the hour of peace and repose has not yet struck. As for you, your kingdom seems to be settling into tranquillity. The provinces of Leon, of the Asturias, and of New Castile, desire nothing but rest. I hope that Gallicia will soon be at peace, and that the country will be evacuated by the English.

Saragossa must fall before long, and General St. Cyr, who has 30,000 men, ought to settle the affairs of Catalonia.

[476.] NAPOLEON TO JOSEPH.

Valladolid, Jan. 7, 1809.

My Brother,—I arrived yesterday evening at Valladolid; the roads are horrible. Marshal Soult ought to reach Lugo today. I found here one of your intendants, who appears to me

* They were wishes for peace.—TR.

to be possessed of considerable zeal and ability; he has been very much hampered by the people of the country. I will execute severe justice upon them. Send to me, by a deputation from Madrid and the councils, the record of the oath which has been taken: when I have received it, I will give my decision.*

The Duke of Dantzic is at Avila. I cannot conceive such folly. I have given him no orders, and, if you on your part have sent him none, let me know, in order that I may give him something to do. At any rate there is no objection to his corps resting a few days at Avila. All the men who are at Guadarrama and Villa Castin belonging to the foreign regiment must fall back, as in future the route of the army is to be through Segovia. I think that a battalion of this regiment would be of great use at Avila to hold the province, and that you may send thither an intendant to be put at the head of the administration.

It seems that Lasalle's division and some of the Poles were not able to fall back on Talavera; but Dessolles' division, and 3000 or 4000 men in marching regiments and companies, composed of conscripts, as well as of old soldiers, ought, by this time, to have reached Madrid. I suppose that Marshal Victor has commenced operations.

It is of great consequence that the Madrid newspapers should be sent hither, and that they should contain much intelligence about the army, and letters from Lugo, Corunna, and all those parts. Perhaps it would be well to create some Spanish regiments. You might form one in the north, at Palencia, another at the Escurial, and in different directions. They must be commanded by several inferior officers, Spaniards on whom you can rely; you should add a few French officers, give ensigncies to many of your old serjeant-majors. There exists, in truth, no longer even the shadow of a Spanish army. The 4000 or 5000 men who were taken prisoners from La Romana were in a horrible state; still worse than those taken by the Duke of Dantzic in Estremadura.

* As to Joseph's return to inhabit Madrid. He was at this time residing in La Florida, a country house near Madrid.—TR.

[477.] NAPOLEON TO JOSEPH.

Valladolid, Jan. 7, 1809.

My Brother,—War with Austria seems imminent, and her troops are already encamped upon her frontiers. My army and that of the Confederation are also in motion. I asked you for General Merlin or General Lasalle. Send back to me Bordesoult likewise. If you are not actually in want of Belliard, send him back to Paris, and give the command of Madrid to one of the two generals of division Pacthod. However, as General Belliard has had much experience in preserving Madrid, I think that it would be foolish to deprive you of him as yet. His services in the army are not so valuable to me but that I can do without him. Send me back the cadres of the 3rd squadron belonging to the 24 dragoon regiments in Spain, first taking every available man to reinforce the first two squadrons. I wish you to send me back the brigadier-generals of cavalry, Bron, Lagrange, and Davenay; the generals of infantry, Gautier, Puger, and Roger; the general of division Grandjean, who is before Saragossa; and the brigadier-generals Bron and Razout. As these three last are before Saragossa, I have addressed direct orders to them to return. I have also ordered the Duke of Istria to return; he will be replaced by the general of division Kellermann.

[478.] NAPOLEON TO JOSEPH.

Valladolid, Jan. 8, 1809.

My Brother,—I have received no letters from you since the 2nd of January. The orderly officer Germain started yesterday with letters from me to Madrid. I suppose that your couriers have gone by Benevento.

You will find annexed a copy of my letter of yesterday, in case any accident should have delayed its delivery. You will also find the packets which have come for you by the express.

It seems that the English, on hearing of my entry into Madrid, re-embarked the artillery which they had brought for Spain and Portugal.

I have received no letters from Marshal Soult, whom I suppose to be at Lugo. I sent you word that Toro, which had revolted, had been subdued; there was a charge of cavalry, which killed 60 of the rebels. General Maupetit is before Zamora, whence a few shot have reached him. As he has only 500 horse, he has taken up à position where he is waiting till General Lapisse sends him some infantry.

I have arrested here 12 of the worst characters, and hanged them.

I wish you to let me know if the 30th, 31st, 32nd, 33rd, 34th, 35th, and 36th marching companies, which left Burgos for Aranda on the 31st of December, have arrived; and to give me similar information respecting the 39th, 40th, 41st, and 42nd marching companies. The whole of the 1st marching battalion, composed of conscripts, which left Burgos on the 31st of December, ought to have arrived at Madrid by way of Aranda.

Let me know if all these troops, who ought altogether to form a body of more than 3000 men, have arrived.

The Vice Queen of Italy has given birth to a daughter.

[479.] NAPOLEON TO JOSEPH.

Valladolid, Jan. 9, 1809.

My Brother,—I have received your letter of the 6th. I wrote to you from Benevento on the 4th, to desire you to send the Duke of Belluno, with 2 divisions, to meet the Duke of Infantado.

I wrote to you from Benevento on the 5th and 6th. Since then I have written to you from Valladolid, on the 7th, by my orderly officer Germain, and on the 8th by an officer of gendarmes. The Duke of Dantzic arrived on the 5th at Avila. I have given him no orders. I am waiting to hear whether you have given him any; there is no objection to his resting for a few days. That Marshal commits nothing but follies; he cannot read his instructions. It is impossible to intrust him with the command of a corps, which is a pity, as he shows great bravery on the field of battle.

I told you that I was waiting to receive the addresses before

I made my proclamation. Arrange everything for your entry into Madrid. Try to make it imposing, and to secure a good reception by the inhabitants. Assemble afterwards all the councils, and let your ministers make every preparation to administer as well as possible.

I suppose that in the course of the day Victor will have beaten the Duke of Infantado. Talavera de la Reyna must be occupied. You may send thither General Valence, with a regiment of horse and his 1500 Poles. That division is to be assembled as soon as possible.

[480.] NAPOLEON TO JOSEPH.

Valladolid, Jan. 9, 1809, 9 P.M.

My Brother,—I wrote to you this morning. I take advantage of Battaglia's departure to send you a few more lines. On the 5th the Duke of Dalmatia was three leagues from Lugo. He had taken from the English 7 pieces of cannon, 2000 prisoners, and stores of every description; they even found a convoy carrying silver, which the dragoons shared among themselves. It is valued at two millions. The English fly in the most frightful confusion. The barns of all the villages in Gallicia are full of English, hanged by the peasants in revenge for their horrible depredations. As for La Romana's Spaniards, we have taken 4000 or 5000 of them, 9 standards, and, at different times, a dozen pieces of cannon. The Duke of Elchingen has carried his head-quarters to Villa Franca. Zamora closed its gates against General Maupetit's brigade of dragoons. On the 7th the general fell in with two columns of about 800 men each, charged and routed them, killed 100, made 20 prisoners, and carried off their guns. Lapisse's division has marched upon Zamora. Spread all this news, and put it into the newspapers. A deputation from Astorga, composed of the bishop and principal magistrates, and a deputation of the principal magistrates and inhabitants of Leon, are on their way to Madrid. Send deputations also from Avila and Segovia.

Prepare your entry. I hope that before that time the Duke of Belluno will have encountered and beaten the Duke of Infantado.

[481.] NAPOLEON TO BERTHIER.

Valladolid, Jan. 9, 1809.

My Cousin,—Give orders that the Prince of Castel-Franco, the Duke of Altamira, and the Marquis of Santa Cruz, may be sent to Fenestrelles, where they are to be detained as prisoners of state. Acquaint the minister of police with this arrangement.

[482.] NAPOLEON TO BERTHIER.

Valladolid, Jan. 9, 1809.

My Cousin,—Write to General Belliard, to express my displeasure at the want of firmness displayed by his government: every day Frenchmen are assassinated in Madrid, and he does nothing. Tell him that 30 of the worst characters in the town must be arrested and shot; that this is what I have done at Valladolid; and that I shall hold him responsible for the first assassination committed on a Frenchman, if the arrest of a Spaniard does not immediately follow. The behaviour in Madrid is absurd.

P.S.—Desire the depôt at the Carthusian convent at Burgos to proceed to Valencia.

[483.] NAPOLEON TO JOSEPH.

Valladolid, Jan. 10, 1809.

My Brother,—Send back the Duke of Dantzic to me at Valladolid; he shall no longer command the 4th corps. By puttting it under the command of Marshal Jourdan, who may continue to be chief of your staff, it may be retained as a distinct corps, and will be under your hand. The duty of this corps will be to guard the centre; it is composed, first, of Sebastiani's division, which consists of 4 regiments, or 16 battalions, and in the whole of nearly 12,000 men; 3000 are at Leon, and 4000 at Bayonne, on their way from Paris. You will keep this fine division, composed of my best regiments, at Madrid, as a guard for the town and for your person. The general of division is excellent; the two brigadiers are the very best in the army. As the depôts of these regiments are in Paris, I shall always keep them up to their full numbers. The 2nd division of the 4th corps is Leval's; it is composed of one regiment from Baden, one regiment from Hesse Darmstadt, and another from Nassau, one battalion from the Prince-Primate, and a Dutch brigade. All these together amount to 4000 men. Take care to provide this division with ten pieces of cannon. Let it start for Talavera de la Reyna; and send General Lasalle with his 4 cavalry regiments to the bridge of Almaraz to scour the country as far as the other side of Truxillo. General Leval commands as senior general of division; he is to correspond with General Valence, whose division you are to assemble at Toledo, allowing it to spend a couple of days at Madrid, to get the clothing which it requires. The Polish lancers are to remain at Toledo, which will carry the division of Valence to 5000 men; take care that it has 8 pieces of cannon. The divisions of Sebastiani and Milhaud are to remain at Madrid. Milhaud's division requires reconstruction: detachments of it may be posted at Toledo and at Aranjuez, and be ready to proceed in any direction. This will enable you to send back to Marshal Victor the 2nd hussars, and all that you may have of the division of Latour-Maubourg. Dessolles' division, which was to reach Madrid on the 7th, must want rest. As it belongs to the corps of Marshal Ney, who is in Gallicia, you may address your orders to it directly. Therefore, the divisions of Sebastiani, Leval, and Valence, forming the 4th corps, will be under the immediate orders of Marshal Jourdan, as commandant of that corps. General Milhaud's division of cavalry, and Dessolles' division, will receive their orders from you, and from Marshal Jourdan as the chief of your staff. The division of Latour-Maubourg, the 26th chasseurs, and the 2nd hussars, which will make 8 cavalry regiments, and Marshal Victor's 7 infantry regiments, will receive their orders from Marshal Victor, and Marshal Jourdan, as chief of the staff, transmitting your commands. If Leval's division were to require support, you would send the division of Valence to its assistance, and keep by you the divisions of Milhaud, Dessolles, and Sebastiani, at Madrid.

You must employ yourself in completing the guns belonging to Sebastiani's division to 12, those of Dessolles' division to 12, and those of Milhaud's division to 6. It is a point of great importance that Lasalle should soon be at the bridge of Almaraz, and scour the country on the other side of Truxillo.

Marshal Lannes started to-day to join General St. Cyr before Saragossa. General Lapisse is at Zamora; 4000 or 5000 men are wanted at Avila to pursue Pignatelli. Appoint an intendant for that place, and support your agents. The Duke of Elchingen is at Villa Franca; the Duke of Dalmatia ought to have reached Lugo long ago; my guard is concentrated in this place. Heudelet's division, which is here, is about to march upon Astorga. Loison's division is at Leon. On entering Madrid it is desirable that you should have as many troops, and in as good a condition, as possible. I think that you ought to create a battalion of Royal Irish; many of the prisoners are anxious to serve: they might be sent to the Escurial. By adding to them a few good officers of their own nation you would attract all the Irish who were in the service of Spain. Order General Leval to construct a small tête-de-pont at Almaraz, and to put into it a battalion to support the cavalry. The season is very bad: with the exception of Marshal Victor, who ought now to be in the midst of his operations, I wish all the others to be at rest, at least as much as circumstances will permit.

I believe that I told you to form a Spanish regiment. You have a colonel from Murcia who is an excellent man, you have officers on whom you can rely; it can be done therefore; at any rate they would do for police. General Valence may detach a battalion to hold the bridge of Aranjuez. I am not satisfied with the order which is kept in Madrid; Belliard is too weak; with the Spaniards it is necessary to be severe. I have arrested here fifteen of the worst characters, and I have ordered them to be shot. Arrest thirty at Madrid. When I left it there had been an inquiry, and the police were on the point of making a seizure. If you treat the mob with kindness, these creatures fancy themselves invulnerable; if you hang a few, they get tired of the game and become as submissive and humble as they ought to be.

I send you an account of the revolution at Constantinople; let it be inserted in the newspapers.

[484.] NAPOLEON TO JOSEPH.

Valladolid, Jan. 11, 1809.

My Brother,—I wish you as soon as possible to give me information:—1st. As to the roads between Bilbao and Valmaseda. 2ndly. As to those beween Valmaseda and Villercayo; through what towns they pass, the population of those towns, and over what hills they pass; can the artillery travel by them? 3rdly. Between Villercayo and Orduna. 4thly. Between Villercayo and Burgos. 5thly. Between Villercayo and Miranda, or any other point along the Ebro. 6thly. From Villercayo to Santander. 7thly. From Villercayo to Reynosa. Can all these roads carry artillery? I must have details about them all. Let this information be furnished either by the Spanish Minister of War, by practical men of the country who are also officers, or by French officers who have seen and know the country. Let me have a map of the high road from Tolosa to Pampeluna, and from Pampeluna to Vittoria. This information is necessary for me. 2ndly. I also require the following information, but to-morrow will be time enough. Describe the road between Pampeluna and Madrid; is it a paved road? Let me know through what towns this road passes, what is their population, and what rivers, gorges, and other natural obstacles have to be encountered. I wish to have similar information as to the road between Saragossa and Madrid by way of Daroca. These statements ought to be written with every detail; time may be taken for the purpose, so that I have them to-morrow in the course of the day. I wish the scale of all these maps to be in French leagues, or, at any rate, that the number of toises be specified.

[485.] NAPOLEON TO JOSEPH.

Valladolid, Jan. 11, 1809, noon.

My Brother,—I have received your letter of the 8th of January. You must have seen by my letter of yesterday, and by the orders which were sent to you on the day before, that I wished

Dessolles' division to rest at Madrid. If Marshal Victor need assistance (which I cannot think possible), he may be supported by General Valence; but with the infantry which he has, the division of Latour-Maubourg, the 26th chasseurs, and the 2nd hussars, he has ten times as many troops as he wants. It might, however, be useful to place 1000 men at Aranjuez, to hold the bridge and keep up the communication. I had intended the Dutch brigade for this purpose, but it has since been ordered to Talavera de la Reyna with Leval's division. One of the regiments of General Valence, which arrived a few days ago at Toledo, when they have rested, may therefore with 300 or 400 horse follow in the rear of Marshal Victor, and keep his communications open. I think that you were right in not joining the expedition against the Duke of Infantado, as its object is uncertain. The duke will retire upon Valencia, and no result will be produced; you would have done wrong if you had joined it. As you very naturally wish to be engaged in some expedition, you should select that into Andalusia; but it cannot be undertaken for the next three weeks. You can then, with 2 good corps composed of 40,000 men, surprise the enemy by taking a road which they little expect, and beat them. This operation will put an end to the war with Spain, and I intend you to have the glory of effecting it. Order a tête-de-pont to be constructed at Almaraz. Procure a sufficient number of oxen and mules to draw twelve 24-pounders.

Send to Somo Sierra for the 6 pieces which are still there. Put the mortars upon carriages: you will require this amount of artillery in order to take Seville.

M. de Fréville's letter would be right if this corn were meant for sale; but as it is intended for food for the army, it must be seized immediately.* I am writing to the intendant to this effect. I shall see with pleasure all that is taken from the rebels applied to the wants of the army. I am forced to stay at Valladolid to receive expresses from Paris, which reach me in 5 days. The events at Constantinople, the present state of Europe, the recon-

* Fréville's letter does not appear.—TR.

struction of my armies of Italy, of Turkey, and of the Rhine, make it necessary that I should not be farther from Paris. I was sorry to leave Astorga.

One thousand men belonging to my guard are at Madrid: send them to me. Here is the last news from Gallicia : nothing is known of La Romana; most of the colonels have dismissed their troops; some have escaped to Andalusia; the rest have joined the English. On the 8th the enemy's rear guard occupied Lugo. The Duke of Dalmatia has been in presence of the enemy ever since the 6th. The infantry reached him on the 7th. Marchand's division was half-way between Villa Franca and Astorga, proceeding to support the Duke of Dalmatia. You may make your entry into Madrid whenever you think proper. I suppose that to-day, the 11th, the Duke of Dantzic will have arrived; that on the 13th Talavera de la Reyna will be occupied; and that by that time Victor will have put an end to the absurd fears inspired by the Duke of Infantado. If this takes place you may make your entry on the 14th. Put all the troops under arms, and let the inhabitants receive you beyond the gates with the usual ceremonies. Establish yourself in the palace; keep an apartment in it for me, if it does not inconvenience you. Engage in no military operation, except the Andalusian expedition, which cannot be undertaken till after the rains. What must you prepare? Some biscuit and the equipment of your 24-pounders and mortars. Occupy yourself with these arrangements every day; this expedition will be brilliant. You must have 300,000 rations of biscuit. Have some made at Toledo and at Talavera. I have here 300 carriages belonging to the military transport service, which will carry them. As soon as Lapisse's division has put an end to the disturbances at Zamora, I shall order it to march upon Salamanca, where there are 3000 or 4000 men still in revolt. Pray hang a dozen people at Madrid; there are enough bad characters there. Unless you do this, you do nothing. The 3000 Spanish prisoners at Valladolid have considerably cooled the ardour of the inhabitants by their behaviour and conversation. The English prisoners arrive in troops. I recommend the province of Avila to your attention: send thither an intendant.

That wretched Pignatelli has not 10 men. A battalion of 400 men of the royal foreign regiment would do there admirably. They would likewise be of use in keeping up the communication between Madrid and Salamanca on the arrival of Lapisse's division. It seems that your Spanish chargé-d'affaires has left Vienna by way of Trieste. Your ministers should not throw away money in paying agents abroad, except the one in Russia, who behaves well.

[486.] NAPOLEON TO JOSEPH.

Valladolid, Jan. 11, 1809, 11 P.M.

My Brother,—Zamora would not submit; it was necessary to enter it by force. General Darricau arrived before it on the 10th with 4 battalions, breached it, and carried it by assault, with a loss of only 10 men. He is disarming it. General Davenay is disarming the province of Toro. They are both desired to reconnoitre up to the frontiers of Portugal and Salamanca. As soon as you have an intendant at Avila, desire him to correspond with the commandant of my troops when they reach Salamanca.

[487.] NAPOLEON TO BERTHIER.

Valladolid, Jan. 11. 1809.

My Cousin,—Let General Davenay know that you have shown me his letter of the 11th;* that he must not be talked over; that he must arrest thirty of those who have behaved the worst; that he must announce that the estates of all those who do not return will be confiscated; that he must be active; that he must appoint a corregidor for the town of Toro, leave only one battalion there, and send all the others to Zamora. Say in answer to General Darricau that he was right in taking Zamora, but that he ought to have left the 16th there; that one battalion is enough at Toro; that he must assemble all his forces at Zamora, and march upon Salamanca; and that I have granted all the favours for which he asked. Write to General Maupetit that he

* This letter does not appear.—TR.

must reconnoitre as far as the frontiers of Portugal and Salamanca, but in force, so as to be in no danger of a check. You will take care to direct the marching battalion formed here this morning, and belonging to Lapisse's division, upon Toro, and from thence to Zamora. Advise Generals Maupetit and Darricau to procure cloaks and shoes at Zamora, and to collect information upon all that is going on at Salamanca and on the frontiers of Portugal. Besides the prisoners whom Generals Davenay and Darricau will make at Toro and Zamora, desire them to take hostages, and to send them to Segovia, and to send numerous deputations to Madrid. Send to them proclamations from Valladolid and from Madrid, to be made public. Desire them to have addresses from the principal magistrates and clergy, and to print and put them up everywhere.

[488.] NAPOLEON TO BERTHIER.

Valladolid, Jan. 11, 1809.

My Cousin,—See that in every post from hence to Miranda 3 gendarmes d'élite are placed, and order General Kellermann to put into each post at least 50 dragoons, so that my couriers may be escorted and travel safely by night. Express my displeasure to the paymaster-general of the forces at his having left the paymaster at Burgos without funds. Send from hence 20,000 francs to Burgos for current expenses till the proper funds are transmitted. I wish this sum to be sent off this night. Send a courier of the country to Aranda to obtain a return of the troops in that place, and news as to what may have occurred there since the 20th of last month. I see that a 1st marching battalion has been formed at the Retiro, and that the 2nd and 3rd companies are included in it under the name of 1st company of voltigeurs. I conclude that in these companies there are no men belonging to the divisions of Dessolles, Sebastiani, Ruffin, or Villate: if there be, they must be sent back immediately to their regiments. I do not wish to form new cadres; we have too many already.

[489.] NAPOLEON TO BERTHIER.

Valladolid, Jan. 11, 1809.

My Cousin,—Let General St. Cyr know that two regiments of the Grand Duke of Berg, one regiment from Würtzburg, and one battalion of the contingent furnished by the petty sovereigns, foming altogether nearly 6000 men, are on their way to Perpignan, under the orders of a brigadier-general. This corps will reinforce General Reille and enable him to besiege Girona. I wish this siege to be commenced about the 15th of February. You must protect this operation by marching some troops to clear the neighbourhood.

You will tell General St. Cyr that Marshal Lannes is before Saragossa with the 5th and 3rd corps; that they ought to endeavour to correspond; that one of the first things which he has to do is to take Tarragona, and put a garrison into it, and to victual fully Barcelona. If it were possible to take possession also of Tortosa now, just at the beginning, when the enemy cannot expect us, it would be a great step gained towards concentrating all our movements upon Valencia. This despatch must be sent to General Reille, who corresponds by cipher with General St. Cyr, and who will have three or four copies made, which he will send by different opportunities. Inform, likewise, General Reille of the march of these troops to Perpignan.

[490.] NAPOLEON TO BERTHIER.

Valladolid, Jan. 11, 1809.

My Cousin,—Order 500 pairs of shoes to be given to the 17th light infantry, and 80 great-coats to the detachment of the 32nd which is here. Divide the remainder of the great-coats among the five marching battalions which were formed at Valladolid this morning. Desire the 17th light infantry to start to-morrow at break of day for Astorga. Order Heudelet's division to march to-morrow for Medina de Rio Seco. Direct the 1st marching squadron of Valladolid to proceed to Madrid, and the 2nd to Villa Franca, where it will be joined by the men belonging to Marshal Ney's corps. Send orders to the 1st, 2nd, 3rd, 4th, and 5th marching battalions of Valladolid; let them take bread for two days, and appoint for them to-morrow a short march of three leagues to some place whence they may proced to join their respective corps. The men belonging to Lapisse's division will take the road to Toro, and from thence to Zamora. The battalion of the 51st will remain here to do duty as garrison. The general of division Claparède will take the command of the province of Valladolid till I have a division for him, which will be before long. Desire the commissary-general to find means of making 4000 great-coats, 4000 jackets, 4000 pairs of trousers, and 8000 pairs of shoes. Order the battalion of the 32nd which is at Leon with General Loison to repair to Madrid. Let every one know that the following changes have taken place: that the 8th corps is suppressed; that all the men belonging to the 12th, 2nd, and 4th light infantry, and to the 58th, 32nd, and 47th, have rejoined their regiments, and that therefore all detachments should be forwarded to the corps of which these regiments form part. Make known that the 17th light infantry belongs to Delaborde's division, which forms part of the 2nd corps, commanded by the Duke of Dalmatia.

[491.] Napoleon to Joseph.

Valladolid, Jan. 12, 1809, noon.

My Brother,—I have received your letters of the 10th of January. I told you yesterday of the capture of Zamora. My troops march on Salamanca. You were quite right in dissolving all the marching battalions, and in sending to the divisions of Villate and Ruffin the detachments which belong to them. You will see whether it be necessary to send the 2nd hussars to Aranjuez, to scour the country. As for the disembodied men of the infantry regiments belonging to Marshal Victor's corps, collect them together at Madrid, and, when they have rested for a couple of days, send them to Aranjuez, as soon as their numbers amount to 300.

I suppose that at the present time Leval's division is marching upon Talavera, and that Valence's division holds Toledo and Aranjuez. Some marching battalions, consisting of several thousands of men, which belong to the corps of Marshal Victor and to the 4th corps, start to-day for Madrid. I have sent word to you to make your entry into Madrid, and to assume the government, all with as much pomp as possible. I am anxious that it may be on the 14th, 15th, or 16th. I think these things now necessary and important. I have as yet heard no news of the English; our army was in presence of their rear-guard on the 8th. I have ordered a battalion of 600 men, which is at Soria, to repair to Madrid as soon as it is relieved. You may incorporate it in your guard. Numerous detachments of conscripts are on their way. Belliard did admirably.* You must hang at Madrid a score of the worst characters. To-morrow I intend to have hanged here seven notorious for their excesses. They have been secretly denounced to me by respectable people whom their existence disturbed, and who will recover their spirits when they are got rid of. If Madrid is not delivered from at least 100 of these firebrands, you will be able to do nothing. Out of this 100, hang or shoot 12 or 15, and send the rest to France to the galleys. I had no peace in France, I could not restore confidence to the respectable portion of the community, until I had arrested 200 firebrand assassins of September, and sent them to the colonies. From that time the spirit of the capital changed as if by the waving of a wand.†

[492.] NAPOLEON TO JOSEPH.

Valladolid, Jan. 13, 1809.

My Brother,—On the 8th the enemy stayed all day on the heights of Castro. The Duke of Dalmatia resolved to attack on the morning of the 9th, his artillery and infantry having arrived on the 8th. The position of Castro could be attacked only on

* He appears to have arrested between 300 and 400 persons in Madrid, on suspicion that they had evil designs.—TR.

† This was one of Napoleon's earliest and worst crimes. He took advantage of the excitement produced by the infernal machine to transport to the mortal shore of Cayenne, without trial, 130 of the heads of the republican party. Some of them were men whose only fault was the having been members of the Convention or of the commune of Paris, and not one of them was proved, or really suspected, of having had anything to do with the conspiracy.—TR.

the left, as the river protected the right. The Duke of Dalmatia ordered a movement to turn the left flank of the enemy, who, on becoming aware of it, left their position at nightfall, and continued to retreat all through the night of the 9th. 300 English sick and 18 pieces of cannon were found at Lugo. The English have destroyed the greater part of their ammunition. In the course of the 9th, 500 prisoners were taken. We have now, therefore, 3000. 700 horses were found killed by them at Lugo, which makes their loss in horses amount to 2500.

The Duke of Dalmatia hoped to arrive on the 10th at Betanzos, a few leagues from Corunna. The English have 400 ships at Corunna. The inhabitants of Gallicia appear to be animated by the best spirit. The bishop and clergy of Lugo have remained there. The English sacked the town; they commit every possible excess. Let this news be put into the newspapers. Make arrangements for the Madrid papers to reach Valladolid, and desire your ministers to write to your intendants. Two of my gendarmes d'élite, belonging to the post, have been assassinated at the junction of the Guadarrama and Escurial roads. I had requested 25 or 30 of the Royal Foreign regiment to be sent thither. I see no objection to your taking prisoners who may be trusted to form your regiments, but you must take no officers.

[493.] NAPOLEON TO BERTHIER.

Valladolid, Jan. 14, 1809.

My Cousin,—There must be at Valladolid a paymaster, and a commissary-general, who will have under his direction the whole service from Zamora, Astorga, and Leon as far as Segovia, Valencia, and Burgos; and a clothing establishment, with a director at its head. Materials for clothing must be sent thither from Segovia, Valencia, and the neighbouring towns, in order that it may be always supplied with shoes, great-coats, and coats.

[494.] NAPOLEON TO JOSEPH.

Valladolid, Jan. 15, 1809.

My Brother,—I have received no news from you since the 11th. The state of Europe forces me to spend three weeks in Paris. If nothing should prevent me, I shall return towards the end of February.* The chief of the staff will remain ten or twelve days longer, to make sure of your thoroughly understanding the state of affairs. I have ordered my guard to be assembled at Valladolid. I leave it under the command of Marshal Bessières, who will take his orders directly from me. I have told him that I wish the guard to be allowed to rest, in order that it may be fit to be despatched, if necessary, to another frontier. I beg of you to write to me every day, sparing no detail, and even to send me the different reports of the generals, that I may be well informed as to the state of things. The chief of the staff will tell you of my project for entering Portugal simultaneously by Oporto and Gallicia. When you are thus master of the frontier of Portugal, you will be able to assemble all your forces to attack Andalusia, striking your first blows on Seville and Merida. You must not think of Valencia till Saragossa is taken, which ought to be effected in the course of February. When Saragossa is yours the army there must not be diminished without my being informed of it, for much will depend upon circumstances. I have left the command of the provinces of Leon, Old Castile, Biscay, and Santander to Marshal Bessières, who will reside at Valladolid. He has, for the purpose of holding these provinces, the division of Lapisse, which is marching on Salamanca, the garrisons of the different posts, and, besides, a division of dragoons.

I think that I wrote to advise you to make your entry into Madrid on the 14th. Denon is anxious for some pictures; I wish you to seize all that you can find in the confiscated houses and suppressed convents, and to make me a present of 50 chefs-d'œuvre, which I want for the Museum in Paris. At some future time I will give you others in their places. Consult

* He remained in Paris two months, and never revisited Spain.—TR.

Denon for this purpose. He may make proposals to you. You are aware that I want only what is really good, and it is supposed that you are richly provided. I think that as soon as you have settled yourself in Madrid, you ought to form two or four regiments, one of which should be placed in the north. They should not be allowed to approach within 10 leagues of Madrid. If you have officers enough to form the cadres, I think that you will be able to obtain privates. These regiments are indispensable as a refuge for numbers of people who would otherwise become bandits; at the same time they will be useful as police. I believe that I have a cipher for corresponding with you when you have anything very important to say; at any rate, you have that of Laforest. I expect to be in Paris on the 21st of January. I shall ride post the greater part of the way. If you like you can keep my absence secret for a fortnight by saying that I have gone to Saragossa. You will, however, act as you think best. I have had no further news from Gallicia. The Duke of Elchingen had already crossed the mountains and joined the Duke of Dalmatia, who was eight leagues from Corunna.

[495.] NAPOLEON TO JOSEPH.

Valladolid, Jan. 15, 1809, noon.

My Brother,—I sent Montesquiou to you this morning with a letter, in which I told you that I intended to start to-morrow for Paris. The chief of the staff will send you to-morrow by an aide-de-camp the instructions for my army of Spain. He will outstay me 10 or 12 days. This letter will be taken to you by the courier who has brought your packets from Paris, and whom I am sending on. Pay attention to your newspapers, and have articles written from which it may be inferred that the Spanish people is subdued and submits itself. The Spanish chargé-d'affaires who was at Vienna has had the folly to start for Trieste on receiving a letter from the Junta. The court of Vienna is behaving very ill, she may have to repent of it. Do not be uneasy. I have troops enough, even without touching my army of Spain, to go to Vienna in a month. I have few cavalry generals. I wish you to call General Montbrun, who is with

General Lasalle, to Madrid, and a week afterwards to send him to join me in Paris. He is a general whose bravery I esteem, and who will be of use to me. He must not know for what purpose I want him. If I require any other officers I will ask you for them, and yon will send them in the same manner with your despatches. You must tell every one, and let it be generally believed in the army, that I shall return in three weeks or a month. In fact, my mere presence in Paris will reduce Austria to her usual insignificanee; and in that case I shall come back before the end of October. I shall reach Paris in five days. I shall ride post, night and day, as far as Bourdeaux. During all this time Spain will be settling down gently. I have here, under the orders of Marshal Bessières, Kellermann's division of dragoons, which I received to-day, to hold the north of Spain, from Burgos to Gallicia; he will take up his position at Tudela, on the Douro, which will secure the communication with Valladolid. I think that, as soon as Saragossa surrenders, you may send for the Queen and your children. I have written to desire the King of Naples to send an ambassador to Madrid. I have mentioned the person whom I wish him to send. I entreat you to write to me at length and frankly. You ought to do so; it is the only way of acquiring my confidence, and my correspondence will then be of use to you. I think it advisable in the present state of affairs in Europe that the Queen should repair to Marrac after the carnival; she might get there by the 25th of February. The preparations for her departure may produce a good effect. Write to her to be ready to start when I tell her to do so. By that time Saragossa will be taken. There is no reason why the Queen should not rest for a fortnight or three weeks at Marrac.* I think, therefore, that your family may reach Madrid towards the end of February. The news from Russia is good. Pardo is conducting himself well at St. Petersburg. Do not leave him in ignorance; write often to him, and send your letters to Champagny.

P. S. You will find annexed the letters intercepted by General Lapisse between Zamora and Salamanca. You will see

* Napoleon's villa near Bayonne.—TR.

that on the 20th of December the Junta was at Seville. You are aware of the importance of occupying Talavera de la Reyna and the bridge of Almaraz.

INSTRUCTIONS FOR THE HEAD OF THE STAFF.

Valladolid, Jan. 15, 1809.

After the departure of the Emperor the King will command the army.

The Chief of the Staff will leave Valladolid as soon as he hears that the English are embarked; if they have not done so within eight days, and nothing has occurred which appears to him to render his presence at Valladolid necessary, he will go to Paris. While at Valladolid he will continue to give orders in the name of the Emperor.

If Marshal the Duke of Dalmatia should meet with a check, which is not to be expected, and the corps of the Duke of Elchingen cannot remedy it, Lapisse's division may be moved. He will try to communicate with Santander, by sending thither a party of 100 foot, in order to give news to General Bonnet, who has long been without any. The Chief of the Staff will renew at Santander and at Burgos the order to send away the wool and the English merchandise by way of Bayonne.

The Emperor's departure must not be mentioned in the general orders. The Dukes of Dalmatia, Elchingen, and Montebello, must receive direct information of it. The King should be informed that it ought to be concealed as long as possible. A report should be spread that the Emperor is at Saragossa. General Camus will remain at Valladolid as a detached member of the Staff. He will correspond directly with the King and with the Chief of the Staff in Paris.

The Emperor leaves the command of his guard to the Duke of Istria, who will have his head-quarters at Valladolid. The guard is no part of the army. When the Emperor sends for his guard and his equipages, the fact that his Majesty has ceased to command his armies in Spain will be mentioned in the general orders. If circumstances render the services of the guard indispensable, the Chief of the Staff may employ them.

As the corps of the Duke of Dalmatia, such as it now is in Gallicia, supported by the 2 divisions of the Duke of Elchingen, is strong enough to drive off the English, the Emperor wishes Heudelet's division not to pass Villa Franca until the Duke of Dalmatia is on his way to Oporto; one of the Duke of Elchingen's regiments must then go to Astorgo to keep up the communications.

The Chief of the Staff, while at Valladolid, will attend the parade as usual, and see to the unembodied men. He will send off on the ——* the carriages of the 3rd company of the 6th battalion of the waggon-train, loaded with the baggage of the Duke of Dalmatia's corps. He will give them a new escort; if necessary, they may be delayed a day for that purpose.

While the Chief of the Staff is at Valladolid, he will send a courier every day to the King.

On the Emperor's departure the express will be thus arranged:—

There must be at Madrid, and also at Valladolid, a director of the post. The director at Madrid will not send off the express until he has received directly the despatches of the French ambassador; they must be put into the bag by the director himself, without being seen by anybody. He will also receive the packet of the Maître des Requêtes, Fréville, and that of the Intendant-General of the army. The most important packet is that of the King.

The director at Valladolid will not let the express go until he has taken the packets of the Duke of Istria. He will order those of General Darmagnac to be taken at Burgos, and those of General Thiébault at Vittoria. The Chief of the Staff will give instructions for this purpose to the director, and to General Nansouty.

The Chief of the Staff will direct General Thiébault to correspond with himself at Paris, and with the Duke of Istria at Valladolid. A similar order must be given to General Darmag-

* Illegible in original.

nac at Burgos; to General Bisson, who commands in Navarre; and to the Duke of Montebello, in command before Saragossa.

While the Chief of the Staff is at Valladolid, he will send every day to the Duke of Dalmatia an aide-de-camp, to be sent back to himself as soon as there is anything important. At least every other day these aides-de-camp will carry the despatches of the Duke of Dalmatia to the Duke of Istria, and even to the King, by way of Madrid, if anything should press.

While the Chief of the Staff is at Valladolid, he will send to Paris in succession his aides-de-camp as they return from Gallicia; and after he has left Valladolid they will continue their route towards Paris, having previously delivered the despatches addressed to the Duke of Istria.

The Chief of the Staff will send nearly every day, and whenever it may be requisite, an aide-de-camp to Saragossa, in order to enable the Duke of Montebello to send one to Paris whenever it is necessary, and at least once in three days. While the Chief of the Staff is at Valladolid he will send every day to the Emperor one of his officiers d'ordonnance with the different reports.

The Chief of the Staff will leave Valladolid eight or ten days after the Emperor, using his Majesty's relays. When this journey is over, all the relays of the Emperor will be collected at Vittoria under the guard of the chasseurs, and of one half of the gendarmerie d'élite, which is to be placed there for that purpose.

The Grand-Marshal will furnish the Chief of the Staff with a return of the orderly officers and the aides-de-camp. The Chief of the Staff should begin sending to Saragossa to-morrow.

When the Chief of the Staff goes he will advise the Duke of Istria to have a parade every day, as the Emperor used to do, to examine the soldiers who pass, to let them rest, and then join regularly their different corps.

[496.] NAPOLEON TO BERTHIER.

Valladolid, Jan. 15, 1809.

My Cousin,—Tell General Treilhard that you have shown to me his letter of the 11th of January. It was absurd in him to deliver the banditti to the civil authorities; he ought to have brought them before a court martial, and had them hanged. He is right in asking for a battalion of infantry; he should not have parted with the men belonging to the 128th. I have ordered a battalion of the 5th light infantry to join him. Write to General Darmagnac to express my displeasure at his having withdrawn the 118th from Aranda before the battalion of the 5th arrived. Order him to correspond twice a week with Marshal Bessières at Valladolid. Write to General Bron to correspond in the same way with Marshal Bessières by Aranda; and write to General Treilhard to the same effect.

I suppose that the 30 carriages belonging to the 6th battalion were sent off to-day to the corps of Marshal Soult, and have carried the clothing and shoes for that corps.

[497.] NAPOLEON TO JOSEPH.

Valladolid, Jan. 16, 1809, 3 P.M.

My Brother,—I have received your letter of the 13th. The letter in which you ask me to send back 3 prisoners to Madrid has not reached me. You may employ Prince Masserano as you please, provided you do not send him to Paris or to any foreign power. In Paris a safe man is necessary; and at the foreign courts it is better to have no minister at all, unless you have one on whom you can rely. I have sent to the Chief of the Staff the papers relating to the Commandant of Vittoria; the custom-house officers must not be permitted to stop the stores intended for the army.* As yet I have not heard of the arrival of one member of the deputation.† I suppose that it will arrive in the course of the day; I shall receive it immediately. I have ordered all the towns whose population exceeds 2000 to send deputations to Madrid, to present you with a record of those who have taken the oath of allegiance. The more considerable towns

* Joseph complained that a system of smuggling was organised and protected by the French officers under the pretext that the smuggled articles were intended for the French army, and pointed out the commandant of Vittoria as engaged in it.—TR.

† A deputation from Madrid taking to Napoleon a list of the persons who had sworn allegiance to Joseph.—TR.

will send to you proportionably numerous deputations. These deputations will include the bishops. Deputies will likewise be sent to you from the chapters, and from all religious communities.

[498.] NAPOLEON TO JOSEPH.

Valladolid, Jan. 16, 1809.

My Brother,—I have received your letter of the 14th. I suppose that the deputation will arrive to-day, I shall receive it immediately. Your letters are dry, and tell nothing. I think that you ought to have written to me when this deputation started, and told me the names of its members. I sent you orderly officers, and you sent me back three at once. It would have been better to have sent them one after the other, twenty-four hours apart; by this means I should not have been left sixty hours without news, which made me for a moment fear that our correspondence had been interrupted by banditti. You must not write to me that you have received such and such a letter of mine, and that the orders contained in it have been executed; you must repeat to me in detail the order, and state point by point its execution. I shall thus have at once before me the orders which have been given, and the manner in which they have been performed, and I can see whether they have been understood. Montesquiou must have reached you. You will receive immediately the instructions drawn up by the Chief of the Staff. I hear from Gallicia that the Duke of Dalmatia continues to advance, and is constantly picking up some remains of the English. There is no news from Saragossa; we must, however, receive some before long. The place was invested on the 22nd; they have therefore had nearly a month to prepare mines. Mining is a very slow operation. The Staff of the engineers and artillery started yesterday for Madrid; they take with them sappers and miners and tools. The regiment of Aremberg, which is the 27th chasseurs, will rest for a few days at Rio Seco, and afterwards proceed to Madrid. This regiment consists of 1000 men and 1000 horses; it is almost entirely composed of Belgians. The court of Alcades at Madrid has acquitted, or only sentenced to imprisonment, thirty rascals whom Belliard arrested; a court-martial must be appointed to try them over again and shoot the guilty. Give orders immediately that the members of the Inquisition, and of the council of Castile who are detained in La Porcelaine, be removed to Bayonne, as well as the hundred wretches arrested by Belliard. Five-sixths of the population of Madrid are well-disposed, but they require encouragement, and that can only be done by protecting them against the populace. Here they moved heaven and earth to obtain pardon for the condemned bandits. I refused, I had them hanged, and since then I have found that in reality the very people who solicited were glad that I did not listen to them. I think it essential that your government, particularly at first starting, should show some vigour against the mob. The mob loves and respects only those whom it fears; and it is only by being feared by the mob that you will acquire the love and esteem of the rest of the nation. I send you duplicates of my two letters of yesterday, and of several intercepted letters.

As soon as we have entered Salamanca desire all the letters and packets to be sent to you. I have heard many reports of the death of Florida Blanca,* which is supposed to account for the letters of the body which calls itself a Junta being signed only by a secretary. As soon as I am gone, and you have received letters from the Chief of the Staff, I think that you would do well to send one of your officers to Gallicia to be with the Duke of Dalmatia, and report to you all that takes place. I do not think that Marshal Victor ought to go too far from the Tagus. You know that the way to Valencia is through Almanza, turning to the right. Desire the works ordered on the heights above the palace, on the right, to be immediately begun. They ought to protect the palace, the guards' barracks, and indeed all the other barracks; for good sense and experience show that the people of Madrid will never behave well till they are properly held in check. Order some 24-pounders and mortars to be placed in the Retiro; this measure will make the inhabitants manageable and

* President of the Junta of Seville.

docile, which will be an incalculable advantage to everybody. There should be twelve 12-inch mortars in the Retiro, and as many upon the heights above the palace. The capture of Saragossa will put many at your disposal; and, at any rate, you may send for some to Gallicia. Every day will increase the numbers of my cavalry; the roads are covered with detachments coming from the depôts in France to reinforce them. You will receive besides 4 regiments from Germany, 700 or 800 strong.

Above all, do not allow yourself to be in want of money; if necessary, raise loans from the towns, corporations, and provinces. There is abundance of money in Spain; they would find plenty if they wanted to revolt. If my presence became indispensable, I think that I might return by the 30th of February, and that I might even spend the months of March and April here. You know that I hate living in towns. Desire Chamartin to be kept for me, both the house in which I lived and that which is opposite; let persons be put in to take charge of them, that I may go there immediately on my return.

[499.] NAPOLEON TO JOSEPH.

Valladolid, Jan. 16, 1809.

My Brother,—Carignan has just arrived with your letters of the 11th and 13th, so that I received to-day first your letter of the 14th, then that of the 13th, and lastly your letter of the 11th. It seems that Carignan had a fall on the way. I have ordered all the officers whom you ask me for to be sent back to you. There is Pignatelli, who has done us much harm in the province of Avila.* Some conscripts have left France to enter your guard. The deputation has arrived; I am to receive it in an hour. I then intend to ride for nine hours in order to reach Burgos by three in the morning. I have given orders to the Chief of the Staff that all the men belonging to the regiments of hussars and chasseurs who form part of the provisional regiments in Aragon, may, with their consent, on reaching Madrid,

* Charles Pignatelli was one of the Spanish officers whom Joseph wished to be sent back to him.—TR.

be incorporated in your guard. For instance, there are some of the 1st and 2nd chasseurs, and of the 9th, 7th, and 8th hussars; you may take all these detachments. General Belliard ought to have a list of them. I am going to order five mounted conscripts to be taken from each of the different depôts in France, and forwarded to Spain. This will make 400 or 500. However numerous the Spaniards may be, you must march right on them and resolutely. They cannot stand. You should use no manœuvres or strategy, but go straight at them. Print immediately the speeches made to you by the deputations, and the record of the oaths taken, and, directly afterwards, make your entry into Madrid. I believe that I told you to keep for me the little villa of Chamartin and the house opposite, just as I have left them, in order that I may know where to go, if on some fine morning I find myself again in Madrid. I think that the best way of governing Spain is to appoint a junta for each province, to be called a royal junta, and to put a governor at its head. Captain-generals must not be thought of; they would have neither influence nor authority. I am only speaking now of the first three months.. I beg of you to write to me often and at length. Everything that is printed, reports, returns of the army, everything that you send me, I shall be glad to receive.

P.S. The Chief of the Staff has this instant shown me Marshal Jourdan's letters of the 14th.* The enemy must not be suffered to establish himself at Madridejos. Marshal Victor may move towards the right, as it is probable that the enemy will retire upon Valencia. Besides, the division of General Valence would be sufficient. The siege of Saragossa seems to advance. The Polish battery which was at Segovia must have reached Madrid; send it to join its division at Toledo. General Valence ought to receive instructions to push forward strong parties beyond Madridejos, and to clear the whole country.

* These letters do not appear.—TR.

[500.] NAPOLEON TO BERTHIER.

Valladolid, Jan. 16, 1809.

My Cousin,—Give orders to confiscate all prohibited goods in Gallicia, especially those which came from England during the rebellion.

[501.] NAPOLEON TO JOSEPH.

Valladolid, Jan. 17, 1809, 6 P.M.

My Brother,—I received the deputation yesterday evening at 9 o'clock. Put their addresses to me into the newspapers, and make your entry into Madrid. I desired the deputies to report to you all that I said to them. The fog last night was so damp and thick that I deferred my departure till this morning. It is nearly 6 o'clock, and I am going to mount my horse. I leave here my guard, my baggage, and my household. The news from Gallicia is still that my troops continue to advance and pick up remains of the British army. If the enemy appears in any direction within six or seven days' march from Madrid, do not suffer it, fall upon him immediately. I reprimanded the alcades for not condemning to death the wretches who were arrested. They justified themselves not very intelligibly, by saying that they required some sort of permission from the king. Everything must be done to ensure a proper termination of these trials and to make striking examples. Great robberies are committed towards Las Rosas: you cannot allow this so near Madrid. You must send in pursuit of the criminals 2 or 3 columns of 50 men each, and a detachment of cavalry. As the towns of Toro and Saragossa were in arms when captured, I have levied a contribution of 500,000 francs upon one province, and 1,000,000 on the other; this will help to pay the army. All colonial and British goods have been confiscated in Gallicia. It is a general measure, and has taken place at Leipzic, at Hamburgh, in short, everywhere. I have directed the regiment of Aremberg to rest for five or six days at Rio Seco; it comes from the farther end of Denmark; but my orders allow it to proceed to Madrid, if you think that you will want it. I have left in my house plate to the value of 1,000,000 francs, and in the Dominican convent about 150,000 francs' worth; I have ordered it to be converted into specie, and it may be employed in paying the army, but it had better receive your stamp; order a die to be prepared immediately, and 1,000,000 francs' worth of your coinage to be struck. To save time, you may leave the piastre unchanged both in weight and fineness, reserving to yourself the power of altering the . . . .* at another time. If you thus circulate a coinage of your own, I will send to Spain the pay of the troops in ingots. Your coinage will be increased,† and that always has a good political effect.

[502.] NAPOLEON TO BERTHIER.

Jan. 19, 1809.

My Cousin,—I have desired the 10th marching battalion, composed of conscripts whom I found at Irun, to proceed to St. Sebastian, and to wait there for further orders. I have ordered the battalions of the 28th, 58th, and 32nd, 3000 men strong, to proceed to Madrid by way of Aranda. When they reach Madrid, the battalions are to be equalised, and a few old soldiers put into the 4th. The companies have marched 180 strong, in order that some part of them may be spared. I have ordered a detachment of 400 men of the 32nd, and an equal number of the 12th, to proceed to Madrid to be incorporated in the 4th battalion of the latter regiment. If the cadres of the 5th battalions are there, send them back. An equal detachment of the 2nd and 4th light infantry is to join the Duke of Dalmatia. Let them remain for a week at Valladolid, and then send them by the shortest road whithersoever the Duke may be.

These are the changes to be made in the route.

Arrange these things so as to allow another day between Bourdeaux and Bayonne; let them rest for two days at Bayonne; take two days to go from Bayonne to Irun. Let the troops rest at Tolosa, Vittoria, and Burgos. Whenever a detachment is intended for Madrid, it should go thither straight by way of Aranda,

* Illegible.—ED.

† By coining them.—TR.

where it should halt; these detachments should consist of at least 400 men, and take three days between Burgos and Aranda. It is essential to spare the detachments going to Madrid the great détour by Valladolid. For this purpose, a staff-officer should be established at Burgos, where he will be better placed than at Valladolid. The route from Vittoria to Irun seemed to me to be well arranged: not so that from Burgos to Vittoria. I remarked that there were many both horse and foot soldiers in all the towns. It would be well to send an adjutant to oblige every man to join his regiment.

Let General Thouvenot know that I have sent to him another battalion, and that he should occupy in force the post of Passage, and let his conscripts be exercised twice a-day. This battalion, added to the one he had before, will enable him to send back to their regiments all the men who do not belong to him, but he must be particularly careful that they want neither clothing nor arms. He must apply to Kellermann for whatever is required. You will order Kellermann to supply him.

CHAPTER XIII.

THE letters in this chapter extend from the 24th of January 1809 to the 12th of April. During this time Napoleon was in or near Paris, engaged first in the negotiations, and afterwards in the preparations, which preceded the war with Austria of 1809.

[503.] NAPOLEON TO JOSEPH.

Paris, Jan. 24, 1809.

My Brother,—I send you a letter from M. Champagny, containing some details concerning the affairs of Spain. I arrived here on the 23rd at 8 o'clock in the morning in excellent health. All is going on well here.

[504.] NAPOLEON TO JOSEPH.

Paris, Jan. 25, 1809.

My Brother,—You mentioned having sent me a large cargo of quinine. All that has arrived does not amount to more than 468 arrobas or 2450 lbs., gross weight. This is not the tenth part of what you announced to me. Let me know if you have sent some in other ways.

[505.] NAPOLEON TO JOSEPH.

Paris, Jan. 27, 1809.

My Brother,—I received your letter of the 15th at 11 o'clock at night, and also one from Marshal Victor. I am waiting to hear the consequences of the battle of Alcazar, and that he has overtaken and dispersed the rest of the Duke of Infantado's army. The Emperor of Russia has written to you a letter which M. de Romanzoff will send to you. M. de Strogonoff has received his letters of credit.* He has reached Vienna, and he is coming to Paris, whence he will return to Madrid; you may announce him in your newspapers. I have ordered a Spanish regiment to be formed, and I have given the command of it to General Kindelau. It is being assembled and trained at Nancy. Send the prisoners to France; keep only those whom you can trust. As a general rule it is best to form regiments in France, which can be sent to you, but this need not interfere with your forming those which I have already recommended.

My prompt arrival in Paris has already changed the tone of Austria, and fear has succeeded to her arrogance and her extreme confidence. The conscription continues to be levied with rapidity, and numerous detachments are marching towards Italy and the Rhine. Let Marshal Victor know that I have granted the favours which he asked for General Villate, Colonel Meunier, Chef-de-bataillon Reyeau, Colonel Mouton, Jamin, Rouzié, of the engineers, Adjutant-commandant Aymé, the Chefs-d'escadron Château (Auguste), Leroy (François), Leroy-Duverger, &c. &c Among the 12,000 balls found at Zamora with other ordnance, of which I send you a list, there may be some 24-pound shot which is wanted for the guns at Madrid. The four mortars are also necessary for arming the fortifications of Madrid.

[506.] NAPOLEON TO GENERAL DEJÉAN.

Paris, Jan. 27, 1809.

M. Général Déjean,—The provisional adjutants who have been appointed in Spain are poor creatures. I think that it is better not to send all the commissaries to Spain; there are enough there. The rest must be kept for the armies of the Rhine.

* To Joseph. He had been Russian Minister at the court of Charles IV Joseph thought him friendly to the Bourbons.—TR.

[507.] NAPOLEON TO JOSEPH.

Paris, Jan. 28, 1809.

My Brother,—I have received your letters of the 15th and 16th. Pray number your letters in future; so the first which you write to me after the receipt of this letter will be No. 3; I have ordered the same thing to be done with my letters. We may thus be sure that we have not lost any.

The suppression of your apanage was part of a general measure; remarks were made about it, and I did not choose it to appear in the accounts: but you need not be in the least uneasy.*

[508.] NAPOLEON TO BERTHIER.

Paris, Feb. 3, 1809.

My Cousin,—Draw up yourself a list of what will be required by the 5th and 6th corps, the fortress of Burgos and that of Valladolid, in order that the money may be sent thither straight from Bayonne. It must not be sent first to Madrid, to be brought back again to Saragossa, which might be difficult.

Order 200,000 rations of biscuit to be sent from Bayonne to Pampeluna, and ask for exact returns of the state of the fortifications and provisions; if you have them, send them to me. Desire the 4 mortars and other ordnance at Zamora to be forwarded to Madrid for the defence of the Retiro. Give this order directly to Marshal Bessières, and give notice of it to the king. As to the castle of Zamora, it must be furnished with ammunition, a small garrison, and a commandant. This castle will serve as a basis of operations, as 200 men are sufficient to defend it. A convalescent hospital should be established within its walls for Lapisse's division.

[509.] NAPOLEON TO JOSEPH.

Paris, Feb. 6, 1809.

My Brother,—I have received your letters of the 24th and 25th. I wish the confiscated estates to be mine; to make sure

* Napoleon continued in fact to pay this pension of 1,500,000 fr. out of his own privy purse to the Queen of Spain, who never quitted Paris.—ED.

of the allegiance of the Spanish families it ought not to be in your power to restore them.* I am sorry that you are changing the system of government at Madrid, and becoming too indulgent. Nothing could be worse than to allow the prisoners to remain there and have intercourse with the people, and to take 3000 of them for your regiments. O'Farrill committed a great error when he allowed the dispersion of the Spanish army. Do you wish for a repetition of what took place at this time last year? The prisoners ought to be sent to France. You may fill the cadres of your regiments, putting safe officers at their head, not with prisoners, but with deserters, and with men who wish to quit the insurgent army. I am raising a regiment of prisoners in France, composed chiefly of those who have been here for some time. You must show some severity, and excite no false or premature hopes; or the men whose arms you restore will assassinate the French, and turn those arms against you on the first hope of success. It is a pity that when the members of the council of Castile were arrested they were not permitted to come to France. A residence of two or three years in France would have changed their ideas, and they might have been turned into useful citizens.

[510.] NAPOLEON TO JOSEPH.

Paris, Feb. 7, 1809.

My Brother,—I am waiting to speak to the Queen of her departure, till I hear of the fall of Saragossa. I wish Belliard to retain the governorship of Madrid, and Fréville the management of affairs relating to the confiscated estates which I take for myself. It is more important to destroy these ten families than to get rid of the Bourbons. My aide-de-camp Lacoste was killed on the 1st of February before Saragossa. We were masters of part of the town.

According to the rules of war, the movement on Merida should not be unmasked until the Duke of Dalmatia reaches Oporto, and he cannot be there before the end of the month.

* Joseph wished to keep for himself the houses and furniture of the ten families whom Napoleon had selected for confiscation.—TR.

You ought not to allow the enemy to establish himself either at Cuença, or in the plain of the Manzanares. Keep Sebastiani's division at Madrid, and provide in every way for their comfort. They are your best troops in an emergency. If I had money I would willingly send you some; but my expenses are enormous. My cavalry amounts to more than 100,000. The new conscription which I am levying costs me an immense sum.

[511.] NAPOLEON TO JOSEPH.

Paris, Feb. 17, 1809.

My Brother,—I have received your letters. Marshal Ney has more troops than are wanted for Gallicia; his notions are absurd: when he wants 3000 men for Corunna and 4000 for Ferrol, he requires what is impracticable. Give strict orders for the complete disarming of these two towns. Subdue them by making examples of the worst characters. Construct an intrenchment or species of citadel in which the French garrison may take refuge and hold the town. Never think of weakening your main force by keeping up garrisons.

[512.] BERTHIER TO NEY.

Feb. 18, 1809.

I have laid before the Emperor, M. le Duc, your letters of the 29th and 30th of January. His Majesty does not approve the plan of placing a garrison of 3000 men in Corunna or in Ferrol.

This is the Emperor's view of your position:—

Gallicia is a peninsula with more than 100 leagues of coast. If you cannot guard the whole, you can overlook the whole; if you cannot occupy the batteries which keep off the English, you can require the inhabitants to man them. By making expeditions with moveable columns you can punish any misbehaviour. As a general rule, you should have many troops in motion and few stationary. In order to follow out the Emperor's plans, the first thing to do is to choose a centre of operations, which ought to be on the road between Ferrol and Astorga. You should select a small town, protected by its situation from a coup-de-main; such, for instance, as Lugo. You should collect there your magazines, your hospitals, both for the sick and for the convalescent, your park of artillery, and your means of transport, so that the columns which you keep watching the coast may be able to unite at Lugo without losing a man, a hospital, or even a waggon. Thus, if even the whole province were in insurrection, you need lose nothing, all your resources being collected in your depôt, the centre of your operations. You will take care to keep there well-provided magazines and a reserve of 200,000 rations of biscuit. This being done, you may garrison Ferrol with a regiment of infantry, two squadrons and four guns, commanded by a brigadier-general. In Corunna you may place one battalion, one squadron, and two guns. You will place at Betanzos a brigadier-general, the two other battalions, and 100 horse with two guns, which will render safe the communication with your general depôt. The two points of Ferrol and Corunna will thus be occupied. You will order the commandants of these places each to raise a redoubt, where, under unforeseen circumstances, they may defend themselves until you come to their assistance. Ferrol and Corunna will thus be advanced posts: in neither of them ought more than 100 sick to be left; all above this number should be sent to the general depôt. Their garrisons should always be ready to retire to the general depôt on twenty-four hours' notice.

The moveable column, consisting of a regiment of infantry, a few hundred horse, and two guns, may be charged with watching Vigo and Tuy, and should be ordered to be stationary nowhere, but to present itself frequently at the important points of the coast to make examples. The commander of this column will avoid having any incumbrances by sending them all to the general depôt: its action may extend even as far as Santiago. You will thus, M. le Maréchal, find yourself at the head of six regiments of infantry, collected in your central point of operations for the purpose of marching wherever it may be expedient, and even to assist the Duke of Dalmatia if extraordinary unforeseen circumstances should make it necessary.

Your first operation, M. le Duc, is to select your central point of operations where your magazines, parks, hospitals, and means of transport are to be collected.

Your second is to disarm the inhabitants of Ferrol and Corunna, taking especial care to seize their fire-arms, to arrest the most disaffected, and to send to Valladolid thirty hostages; you may then leave the duties of police to the Spanish authorities.

Your third business is to reduce to submission all who are in arms towards Orensa.

Lastly, your fourth object ought to be to make use of March and April, when nothing is to be feared on the coast of Gallicia, to subdue the Asturias.

The marching battalions belonging to your corps will hold Benevento, Astorga, and Villa Franca, will rest there, and be relieved successively by the new-comers.

Such, M. le Duc, is the manner in which you should conduct your operations. Look for no reinforcements; think it more probable that one of your divisions may be called away. Organize the province and make examples; severe and well-chosen examples do more than garrisons. Lastly, until the Duke of Dalmatia is in Lisbon, and in communication with Madrid, watch what happens to him and support him.

[513.] JOSEPH TO NAPOLEON.

Feb. 19, 1809.

Sire,—It grieves me to infer from your letter of the 6th of February that, with respect to the affairs at Madrid, you listen to persons who are interested in deceiving you. I have not your entire confidence, and yet without it my position is not tenable. I shall not repeat all that I have frequently written on the state of the finances. I devote to business all my faculties from 7 in the morning till 11 at night. I have not a farthing to give to anybody. I am in the fourth year of my reign, and my guards are still wearing the coats which I gave to them four years ago. All complaints are addressed to me; all prejudices are opposed to me. I have no real power beyond Madrid, and even at Madrid I am every day counteracted by people who grieve that things are not managed according to their own system. They accuse me of being too mild; they would become infamous if I were more severe and left them to the judgment of the tribunals.

You thought proper to sequester the property of ten families; more than twice that number have been thus treated. Officers are in possession of every habitable house; 2000 servants belonging to the sequestered families have been turned into the streets. All beg; the boldest try to rob and to assassinate my officers. All those who with me sacrificed their positions in the kingdom of Naples are still billeted on the inhabitants. Without any capital, without any revenue, without any money, what can I do? This picture, dark as it is, is not exaggerated. I am not dismayed; I shall surmount these difficulties. Heaven has given to me qualities which will enable me to triumph over obstacles and enemies, but what Heaven has not given to me is a temper capable of bearing the opposition and the insults of those who ought to serve me, and, above all, a temper capable of enduring the displeasure of one whom I have too much loved to be able ever to hate him.

If, then, Sire, my whole life does not entitle me to your perfect confidence; if you think it necessary to surround me by poor creatures who make me blush for myself; if I must be insulted even in my own capital; if I am denied the right of naming the governors and the commanders who are always before me, and make me contemptible to the Spaniards and powerless to do good; if, instead of judging me by results, you put me on my trial in every detail—under such circumstances, Sire, I have no alternative. I am King of Spain only through the force of your arms; I might be so through the love of the Spanish people, but for that purpose I must govern them in my own way. I have often heard you say, every animal has its instinct and ought to follow it. I will be such a king as the brother and the friend of your Majesty ought to be, or I will return to Mortefontaine, where I ask for no happiness but to live without humiliation and to die with a good conscience.

Only a fool remains long in a false position. In forty years of life I have learnt only what I knew almost the beginning, that all is vanity except a good conscience and self-esteem.

A Spaniard has let me know that he has been ordered to give to Marshal Duroc, day by day, an exact account of all that I do. I am complained of for having allowed five councillors of Castile to return, while fifteen more were free. Why did I do so? Because advantage had been taken of their absence to pillage their houses. Sire, my misery is as much as I can bear; what I deserve and what I expect from you is consolation and encouragement; without them the burthen becomes intolerable: I must slip from under it before it crushes me.

If there is on earth a man whom you esteem or love more than you do me, I ought not to be King of Spain, and my happiness requires me to cease to be so.

I write to you my whole thoughts, for I will not deceive you or myself.

I do not choose to have an advocate with you; as soon as that becomes necessary I retire. During my whole life I shall be your best, perhaps your only, friend. I will not remain King of Spain unless you can think this of me. Many illusions have left me; I cling a little to that of your friendship; necessary as it is to my happiness, I ought not to continue to risk losing it by playing the part of a dupe.

[514.] NAPOLEON TO JOSEPH.

Paris, Feb. 20, 1809.

My Brother,—I have received all your letters. I believe that Rœderer has asked the senate for leave of absence in order to join you. I am most anxious to hear that the country between Badajoz and the Tagus has been conquered, and that your king dom is tranquil.

[515.] NAPOLEON TO JOSEPH.

Paris, Feb. 21, 1809.

My Brother,—The chief of the staff has sent to you his military instructions. I am sorry to see that you have dismissed the chief commissioner of police from Madrid. I had already sent one to Lisbon. You astonished me by giving as a reason that the constitution forbids you to retain him.* Tell me whether it is forbidden by the constitution that the King of Spain should be at the head of 300,000 French troops, that the garrison of Madrid should be French, that the governor of Madrid should be a Frenchman? Does the constitution say that the houses in Saragossa are to be blown up one after the other? It must be owned that these views are narrow and pitiful. You must not give way to temper and to petty passions; your views should be calm and suitable to your position. The regiment which was formed at Leon has deserted with its arms and baggage; † the other regiments will do the same. Assassinations already take place in the streets of Madrid; if a commissioner of police were established at Madrid on the French system this would not happen. You will not be able to govern Spain without vigour and energy. Your pretensions to indulgence and clemency will do no good; you will be applauded as long as my armies are victorious, you will be abandoned when they are beaten. Some of the members of the council of Castile whom you set at liberty have rejoined the rebels. Considering the time that you have been in Spain and the events which you have seen, you ought to understand the Spanish nation. As for police, employ people who will be of use, whoever they may be, and accustom yourself to consider your mere royal authority as worth very little.

[516.] NAPOLEON TO JOSEPH.

Paris, Feb. 27, 1809.

My Brother,—I have received your letter of the 17th of February in answer to my letter No. 2,‡ of which you think that you have a right to complain, as well as of the advice given to the commander-in-chief of my armies in Spain. My letter does not justify or even account for many passages in yours. I think

* Joseph had sent away from Madrid to Lisbon a M. Lagarde, sent to him by Fouché as head of the police.—TR.

† It was formed by the Emperor's orders.—ED.

‡ The letter of the 6th February.—TR.

that if you were to read it over again calmly you would share my opinion. I earnestly hope that events may not oblige you some day to acknowledge that there were many things in my letter requiring consideration.

[517.] NAPOLEON TO JOSEPH.

Paris, March 4, 1809.

My Brother,—I have received your letter of the 22nd of February. You were wrong in sending reinforcements to Saragossa, there were quite enough troops there already; sappers and miners were more wanted. Generals are always making fresh demands—it is in the nature of things: there is not one who can be trusted in that respect. It is natural that a man who has only one duty to perform should think only of that; the more troops he has, the more he ensures success. It is a great mistake to consider their requests when they cannot be granted.

[518.] NAPOLEON TO JOSEPH.

Paris, March 6, 1809.

My Brother,—I have received your letter of the 25th. Why does not Marshal Ney carry the Asturias? What is the use of his lining the coast? If the country is not impracticable on account of the snow, he ought by this time to have conquered it.

[519.] NAPOLEON TO BERTHIER.

Paris, March 9, 1809.

My Cousin,—Order the portion of my guard which is left at Valladolid, namely, the infantry, cavalry, and artillery, to proceed to Vittoria, where it will receive further directions: so that not one man belonging to my guard may be on the other side of Vittoria. Give the same orders with respect to my horses, and everything belonging to my stables which may be still at Valladolid.

[520.] NAPOLEON TO DÉJEAN.

Paris, March 9, 1809.

M. le Général Déjean,—I send you back your return, that you may make in it the changes necessary in consequence of two decrees which I have issued this week ordering the incorporation of the provisional regiments which are in Spain into different corps, and the men and horses to be struck off the lists of their former regiments. By one of these decrees several detachments from the depôts in Spain are to be sent to the armies of the Rhine. I have decided on making the infantry return from the depôt of Niort to their respective depôts. It is useless to send horses to Spain. Considering our present circumstances, there is too much cavalry in Spain. This measure will reduce the expenses.

[521.] NAPOLEON TO JOSEPH.

Rambouillet, March 11, 1809.

My Brother,—I have read an article in the 'Gazette de Madrid,' giving an account of the fall of Saragossa. The defenders of the town are covered with praise; of course in order to encourage those of Valencia and Seville. This is indeed strange policy. There cannot be one Frenchman who has not the most thorough contempt for the defenders of Saragossa. Those who make such blunders are more dangerous to our cause than the rebels. I do not think that O'Farill had any bad intentions, but this is his second offence of the kind.

In one of his proclamations he has most improperly alluded to Saguntum.

[522.] NAPOLEON TO JOSEPH.

Rambouillet, March 13, 1809.

My Brother,—I have received your letter of the 2nd of March. I am impatiently waiting to hear that the Duke of Belluna has swept all before him, and that he is marching upon Andalusia. Everything here is warlike, and my armies are being assembled and prepared in Germany.

[523.] NAPOLEON TO BERTHIER.

Rambouillet, March 14, 1809.

My Cousin,—Order the three companies belonging to the principal battalion of artillery-drivers of my guard which were at Saragossa to start for Paris twelve hours after they receive your order. They will transfer their horses to the other battalions if wanted, if not they will bring them with them. Desire these troops to make as much haste as possible.

Order the sixteen waggons containing tools at Saragossa, and a company of sappers and miners, to be sent without delay to Bourdeaux, where they will receive further orders.

[524.] NAPOLEON TO BERTHIER.

Rambouillet, March 14, 1809.

My Cousin,—Write to the general in command of the artillery of the army of Spain, and to the general in command at Saragossa, and desire them to arm and fortify the citadel, to place mortars upon it, and to let the park of artillery be put under its protection. When you send me Marshal Jourdan's correspondence, let an abstract be made of it, in order that, in the midst of my various occupations, I may see what is important. Send me a summary of what you have written to Saragossa. Repeat the order for all the dismounted men in the cavalry depôts of Aranda, Madrid, Palencia, Pampeluna, &c., to proceed to Bayonne. Ask Marshal Jourdan for a return of the army of Spain on the 15th of March. I get no returns from that army, and I do not know in what state it is. Write to General Kellermann for a list of the troops in the depôt of Bayonne.

[525.] NAPOLEON TO JOSEPH.

Paris, March 16, 1809.

My Brother,—I have received your letter of the 7th March. I cannot imagine how the pay should be in arrear. I have large funds at Bayonne; how is it that the paymaster-general does not remit? He must be a fool.

I am giving orders. Everything is warlike. Russia is on

my side against England, Spain (as it is called), Austria, and Turkey.

[526.] NAPOLEON TO DÉJEAN.

Paris, March 17, 1809.

M. Déjean,—No Spanish prisoners must be kept at Bayonne or Bourdeaux. Order all those who are there to be forwarded to Saintes and Angoulême. Take measures to prevent any Spanish prisoners from passing through Bourdeaux.

[527.] NAPOLEON TO BERTHIER.

Paris, March 17, 1809.

My Cousin,—Write to Marshal Jourdan and to the Duc de Valmy, and to the different general officers, that they are in future to correspond with the minister of war, as you are appointed head of the staff of the army of Germany. Repeat the order that all the men at Santander and Bilbao, belonging to the 1st and 2nd provisional regiments at Bayonne, join their respective corps.

[528.] NAPOLEON TO JOSEPH.

Malmaison, March 21, 1809.

My Brother,—I have received your letter of the 11th March. All that is taking place in Gallicia is in consequence of the Duke of Elchingen's error in establishing his head-quarters at Corunna instead of a more central position, at Lugo for instance, or even still nearer to the frontier. Corunna and Ferrol ought to have been occupied only by heads of columns. I presume that as soon as the Duke of Belluno has commenced his measures you will support him with all your available troops. You have at Madrid the division of Sebastiani, of Dessolles, and the Poles. You must take care that the Duke of Belluno has his three divisions and that of General Leval quite complete. He will want much cavalry in Andalusia, especially as the enemy will have very little; for though the English may have some infantry, they cannot have any cavalry. All my troops are in Germany. The

Duke of Auerstadt is at Würzburg with the army of the Rhine; the Prince of Ponte Corvo is at Dresden; the Duke of Rivoli is at Ulm with the army of observation of the Rhine; General Oudinot is with his corps upon the Lech; the Bavarians occupy the Inn; my army of Italy is assembled on the Tagliamento. An inconceivable warlike fury has seized Austria; she has taken subsidies from England; but in the middle of these warlike preparations our two cabinets continue to communicate amicably. One would think us the best friends in the world. Russia supports me in every way. The court of Vienna has no voice in the matter, and, like the court of Aranjuez, is carried away by a faction stronger than itself. My carriages are gone, but I am not yet quite determined upon starting myself. I have been forced to furnish a fresh supply of artillery carriages and military transports, and to remount part of my cavalry, to make up for the deficit caused by the affairs of Spain. All this throws me into enormous expenses. Push on your operations with vigour, for the hot weather will soon set in. The fortifications of Madrid ought soon to be ready; therefore, should the worst happen, 2000 men will soon be in perfect security within them.

[529.] ORDERS OF NAPOLEON.

March 24, 1809.

M. le Général Clarke,—All the infantry of my guard, coming from Spain, is to travel post to Paris. It is composed of three parties,—one of 1000 chasseurs and grenadiers, who are to reach Poitiers to-morrow; a second of two regiments of fusiliers and the remainder of the grenadiers and chasseurs, altogether 5000 men, who ought already to have arrived at Bayonne; a third of three battalions belonging to the rear-guard of the chasseurs, grenadiers, and fusiliers, in the whole 1200 men, who will reach Bayonne in a few days.

Desire General Walther to send an officer of my guard to superintend the execution of this order. Let the troops make three days' march every day, and reach Paris as soon as possible.

Order the cavalry, the artillery, and other detachments of the guard, to hasten their march from Bourdeaux to Paris without too much tiring their horses. I trust this to the superior officers.

Order the surgeons belonging to my guard to travel hither by post.

[530.] NAPOLEON TO JOSEPH.

Paris, March 25, 1809.

My Brother,—War appears imminent; I have sent off my carriages. One of my couriers has been stopped by the Austrian police at Braunau. I wish to have General Lasalle. Generals of cavalry in Spain do not require much experience. Put whomsoever you like in his place, and send him to me without delay.

[531.] NAPOLEON TO JOSEPH.

Paris, March 27, 1809.

My Brother,—I cannot understand what you mean about M. Fréville's correspondence.* You imagine me to be much more occupied with that subject than I really am. I take for myself the estates of twelve proscribed families, and I have no other pretensions. I read to-day five numbers of a newspaper called the 'Courier Espagnol,' written in French; I do not know what purpose it is intended to serve. If it is to act upon the army, ought I not to have known who the editor was, and how far he could be trusted? If it is intended to influence France and Europe, that matter might have been very well left to me, at least as far as France is concerned. This paper indulges in literary discussions on Paris, and is the Don Quixote of Spain against France. If it were written in Spanish, and for the Spaniards, this would be only absurd; but in French it is also improper. France, engaged as she is in so cruel a war in Spain, ought at least to hope to regenerate and liberalize that country. They must be ill disposed who, at such a time as this, publish in French that Spain was well governed under Charles III., and

* Joseph had complained that M. de Fréville, who managed for the Emperor the estates confiscated from certain Spanish families, corresponded directly with the Emperor and disobeyed Joseph.—TR.

give a pompous eulogy of a man like Jovellanos, who is unknown in Europe, and who is our bitter, unrelenting enemy. This newspaper must be suppressed, or published in Spanish. I have ordered all copies of it to be stopped. The Minister of War is writing to you about your military operations, which appear to me to be very feeble. You must re-establish at any price your communications with the Duke of Elchingen and with the Duke of Dalmatia. It seems that a month has elapsed since letters have been received from the Duke of Elchingen, and that La Romana has been permitted to place himself between Gallicia and the Castiles. If this should continue, the affairs of Spain will get rapidly worse. Those operations must be conducted with great care and activity. The Prince of Neufchâtel is just starting. I am assured on all sides that Austria will attack Bavaria in a few days.

[532.] ORDERS OF NAPOLEON.

March 27, 1809.

M. le Général Clarke,—Some intriguers are publishing at Madrid a newspaper in French, called the 'Courier Espagnol,' which may have the worst effect. Write to Marshal Jourdan that no French paper is to be allowed in Spain, and that this one is to be suppressed. I do not intend any French paper to be circulated where I have troops, unless it is published by my orders. Besides, do not the French receive newspapers from France? As for the Spaniards, they should be addressed in their own language. Your letter on this subject should be a positive order.

[533.] ORDERS OF NAPOLEON.

March 28, 1809.

M. le Général Clarke,—Write to General Kellermann, who is in command at Valladolid, that I am sorry to see that the hospitals in Biscay and in Old Castile are in need of necessary articles; that it is his duty to furnish them with mattresses, blankets, sheets, &c., and to take care that his requisitions are obeyed in the country.

Give the same orders to the commandants of Pampeluna, St. Sebastian, Burgos, Vittoria, Bilbao, and Santander, and stimulate their zeal in this respect.

[534.] ORDERS OF NAPOLEON.

March 31, 1809.

M. le Général Clarke,—Order the Duke of Valmy to place a column on the borders of Aragon, towards . . . .* to keep up the communication with Jaca. You will let him know that I order Adjutant-commandant Lomet to collect his moveable column in that fort; that it is to be victualled; that a company of artillery of the line and two engineer officers are to be placed there; and that it is to be made capable of keeping the communication open between Saragossa and France.

You will order the general who commands in Aragon to place 1000 men in Jaca, under Adjutant-commandant Lomet, with a company of artillery, two engineer officers, a superior officer of artillery, and a commissariat officer; to victual the place for six months, in order to keep the valley quiet, and to maintain the communication direçt and uninterrupted between Pau and Saragossa. Desire the commandant of Aragon to open a shorter communication by that road.

[535.] NAPOLEON TO JOSEPH.

Paris, April 2, 1809.

My Brother,—Things are going on very ill in Spain. How is it possible that you should be so long without news of the Duke of Elchingen, and that, in spite of La Romana's manœuvres between Gallicia and Castile, combined with the insurrection of the Asturias, you should march the division of Lapisse upon the south, instead of employing it in the north? I cannot understand all this, and I foresee nothing but misfortunes. The north will again rise, and the losses which I shall sustain in quelling

* Illegible.—Ed.

these partial insurrections will be equivalent to a great defeat. You are deceived by false reports and by hopes of La Romana's submission. During this time the fragments of his army are re-organizing themselves, and for the last month they have been left to do so without interruption. In Spain the north is all-important. The first thing, therefore, to be done is to re-establish communications with the Duke of Elchingen.

[536.] ORDERS OF NAPOLEON.

April 5, 1809.

M. le Général Clarke,—Order General Suchet to repair to Saragossa and to take the command of the 3rd corps. The Duke of Abrantès is to return as soon as he is replaced by General Suchet.

[537.] ORDERS OF NAPOLEON.

April 5, 1809.

M. le Général Clarke,—Write to the Duke of Abrantès that before he leaves Aragon he is to settle three important points:—

1. To fix, in concert with the commanding officer of engineers, upon a plan for a fortress at Tudela, and for a redoubt upon the heights, with detached lines to keep up the communication with the river. These works are to be for the present of earth, but to be capable of being faced with stone, so as to become a good fortress.

2. To make the castle of Saragossa capable of sustaining a siege, and to place in it six mortars commanding the town.

3. To let all the artillery return to France.

It is necessary that there should be a colonel of engineers at Saragossa to superintend and keep up the fortifications of Jaca, and the details of those of Tudela and of the citadel of Burgos. There must be another at Burgos to superintend the details of the fortifications at Burgos and Miranda, and of everything relating to Passage and to St. Sebastian.

Desire the works which I have ordered at Miranda to be

begun without delay, and those at Burgos to be carried on with the utmost diligence.

Attend from time to time to the correspondence relating to the fortifications of Tudela, Miranda, Burgos, and the fortress of Jaca. It is necessary that Jaca should re-establish quickly, and keep up, the communication with France by way of Pau.

[538.] NAPOLEON TO JOSEPH.

Paris, April 10, 1809.

My Brother,—I have received your letters of the 2nd, containing the news of Marshal Victor's victory: two days before, I received the news of General Sebastiani's success. The Minister of War sends you word of all that passes in Catalonia. It seems that the want of provisions made General St. Cyr think that he ought to draw nearer to Barcelona. The King of Sweden has been beaten. The Duke of Sudermania has written to ask me for peace; he is regent of the kingdom. Austria is hastening her movements. I have reason to think that she will make an attack on the 15th. To-morrow, or the day after, I shall start for the army. Do not engage the enemy imprudently, and, above all, prevent La Romana from stirring up the north. The position of Lapisse's division seems to fit it for this operation. I want cavalry generals. General Lasalle has been ordered to return: I do not know why he has not been sent. There are four times as many cavalry generals in Spain as there ought to be, and Spain is the country which requires them least, as cavalry cannot manœuvre there. I do not know how General Junot can march upon Valencia, unless the 5th corps be sent thither; * however, I have sent for it to Biscay, that it may be directed either on the north or on France, according to circumstances. The Asturias and Gallicia will at last play you a trick if you neglect them.

* Joseph had proposed that Marshal Junot should marcn on Valence. —Tr.

[539.] NAPOLEON TO JOSEPH.

Paris, April 12, 1809.

My Brother,—It seems that the English have not been able to enter Cadiz, and that since the 15th of March they have occupied Lisbon with between 10,000 and 12,000 men. It is, therefore, of great importance to know what has happened, or is likely to happen, in that quarter.

CHAPTER XIV.

The letters in this chapter extend from the 12th of June to the 10th of October, 1809.

During the two months which separate the first order in this chapter from the last letter in the previous chapter, Napoleon had entered Ratisbon after a succession of battles which lasted five days, and ended on the 23d of April. He had entered Vienna on the 13th of May, had fought on the 21st and the 22nd of May the undecided battle of Aspern, and he was now in the Imperial palace of Schönbrunn, master of Vienna, and preparing for the battle of Wagram.

In the mean time Sir Arthur Wellesley, having landed at Lisbon on the 22nd of April, had marched with the English and Portuguese army against Marshal Soult, then occupying Oporto, had surprised him on the 12th of May, and driven him out of Portugal, and was advancing towards Talavera. At the date of this first order Napoleon was not acquainted with Soult's surprise and retreat, nor of his bitter quarrel with Ney, which made it peculiarly imprudent to place Ney under Soult's command. To this order, and to the jealousies which it excited among the French authorities in Spain, the French historians attribute the ultimate defeat and expulsion of Joseph.

The battle of Wagram, fought on the 5th and 6th of July, 1809, was the last of Napoleon's great military triumphs, as the peace of Vienna, signed on the 14th of October, 1809, was the last of his diplomatic triumphs. During the three months in which the letters contained in this chapter were written, the greatness and the power of the empire rose to their highest point, but the vast edifice already gave signs of weakness. Among the most striking were the surprise of Oporto and the battle of Talavera, which showed that an English army and an English general could be formidable on the Continent.

[540.] ORDERS OF NAPOLEON.

June 12, 1809.

M. le Général Clarke,—You will send a staff officer to Spain to order the corps of the Duke of Elchingen, of the Duke of Treviso, and of the Duke of Dalmatia, to be formed into one army, under the command of the Duke of Dalmatia. These three corps are to manœuvre together, march upon the English, pursue them without stopping, rout them, and drive them into the sea.

Putting aside every other consideration, I give the command to the Duke of Dalmatia, as senior officer. These three corps ought altogether to consist of from 50,000 to 60,000 men.

If this junction takes place quickly, the English will be destroyed, and the affairs of Spain brought to a close; but it is necessary to concentrate and not to march in small bodies. This is a general principle in all countries, but above all in a country without the means of communication. I cannot point out the place of junction, as I am not acquainted with the events which have occurred.

Despatch this order to the King, to the Duke of Dalmatia, and to the other marshals, by four different channels.*

* This unlucky order was sent from Germany by the Emperor at the very minute when the conduct of Marshal Soult at Oporto, and his failure in the agreement made with the Duke of Elchingen at Lugo, rendered its execution impossible. How could it be hoped that the two marshals, Ney and Mortier, would obey a colleague who, by his obstinacy in remaining at Oporto, had just compromised the fate of the Peninsula? Further on it will be seen what mischief this measure, on which Napoleon depended, did to the affairs of Spain.—ED.

[541.] NAPOLEON TO CLARKE.

Schönbrunn, June 21, 1809.

M. le Général Clarke,—I have received your letter, with the Spanish correspondence. You must write word to the King that the north is the first object; that if Saragossa is carried and he loses Aragon, he will find himself in a most unpleasant position. How is it that nothing is attempted from Madrid? You must write to General Sénarmont that the demands made by the artillery are all absurd; that I see by his return that he has 6000 horses, and that he can at any rate replace them with mules of the country.

[542.] NAPOLEON TO THE MINISTER.

Schönbrunn, July 18, 1809.

It is of great importance that the Duke of Castiglione should advance beyond Barcelona, and put himself into communication with Aragon, which will cover Aragon and Madrid on that side. Tell the King that, if the English should land in Spain, he is not to engage them till all his forces are assembled.* He has the 1st and 4th corps with the garrison of Madrid, which makes more than 50,000 men; the 2nd, 5th, and 6th corps form altogether about 60,000. The English know all this and will not run such a risk. . . . . . † Send some one to visit the fortress of Burgos to ascertain in what state it is. The fortress of the Inquisition, ‡ and that of Tudela, are equally important.

[543.] NAPOLEON TO THE MINISTER.

Schönbrunn, July 18, 1809.

The Duke of Castiglione and General Suchet must be informed that immediately after Girona is taken I wish Hostalrich to be attempted, in order to secure the communication with Bayonne, and to commence the siege of Lerida. Half the artillery for the siege is to be furnished by Barcelona, and half by Sara-

* The battle of Talavera showed the wisdom of this advice.—TR.

† Illegible.—ED.

‡ At Saragossa.—TR.

gossa, and the two armies will join in this important operation. The abundant provisions with which I have supplied Barcelona, this year's harvest, and the plenty which exists generally in Aragon, ought to render its accomplishment easy. Order the works of the fortress of the Inquisition at Saragossa, and those of the fortress of Tudela, to be gone on with. It seems possible to besiege Lerida and Hostalrich simultaneously. Transmit these orders to the King, to the Duke of Castiglione, and to General Suchet, by two different officers. Ask General Suchet what troops he can furnish to invest Lerida on the Aragon side, while on the other side it is invested by the 7th corps, and while he occupies a position in front to hold the enemy in check towards Valencia, and to protect the siege.

[544.] ORDERS OF NAPOLEON.

Schönbrunn, July 29, 1809.

M. le Général Clarke,—General St. Cyr must not leave the army till he is replaced by the Duke of Castiglione.

Write word to Spain that no attack is to be made on Portugal during the month of August (it is much too hot there), but that they are to prepare to make this expedition in February.

Ask the King and the Duke of Dalmatia for a report on the opening of the campaign in the month of September. Before that period there will be time enough for them to receive my orders.

If, however, General St. Cyr is so ill as to be obliged to leave the army, he must first re-establish the communication with Barcelona, and he will leave General Duhesme in command of his troops.

[545.] ORDERS OF NAPOLEON.

Schönbrunn, Aug. 7, 1809.

M. le Général Clarke,—You send me no news from Spain. I learn by a letter from the King, of the 25th July, that General Wellesley has arrived at Talavera de la Reyna with 25,000 English, and has joined Cuesta.

It is very unfortunate that Marshal Soult should have manœuvred so ill as not to have joined the King. I hope that the King, with the garrison of Madrid, the 1st and 4th corps, forming 55,000 men, will have placed himself so as to prevent the enemy from attempting to attack Madrid, and will have effected his junction with Marshal Soult. He will then have more than 100,000 men. It will be an excellent opportunity for giving the English a lesson, and finishing the war.

[546.] NAPOLEON TO CLARKE.

Aug. 15, 1809.

M. le Général Clarke,—I have received your letter of the 8th.* I cannot understand the affairs of Spain, nor what has taken place there. Where was the French army on the 29th and 30th ? and where was the English army during these two days ? The King says that for the last month he has been manœuvring with 40,000 men against 100,000. Tell him that it is his own fault, and that it is the very thing of which I complain. The bringing Marshal Soult to Placentia is wrong; it is against all rules; it is open to every objection, and has no advantage. 1st. The English army may cross the Tagus, support its rear on Badajos, and from that moment need not fear Soult; † 2ndly. It may beat our two armies in detail. If, on the other hand, Soult and Mortier had proceeded towards Madrid, they would have reached it on the 30th; and the army, assembled on the 3rd of August, and 80,000 strong, might have given battle, and conquered Spain and Portugal. I advised a battle to be avoided unless the five corps, or at least four of them, were assembled. At Madrid they know nothing of great military operations.

[547.] ORDERS OF NAPOLEON

Schönbrunn, Aug. 21, 1809.

M. le Général Clarke,—Express to Marshal Jourdan my extreme displeasure at the inaccuracies and falsehoods in his report of the transactions on the 26th, 27th, 28th, and 29th of July. Tell

* The battle of Talavera was fought on the 28th of July, 1809.—TR.

† This is what happened.—TR.

him that his despatches do not describe events as they took place, and that it is the first time that the Government has been so trifled with.*

He says that on the 28th we were in possession of the British army's field of battle—that is to say, of Talavera and of the table-land on which their left flank rested—whilst his subsequent reports, and those of other officers, say the exact contrary, and that we were repulsed during the whole day.

Make him feel that this dishonesty towards the Government is a real crime, and a crime which was nearly having fatal results; for as I was told that the English had been beaten, and that half our troops had been enough to rout them, I had settled my plans in consequence, when I fortunately heard in time that it was my army that was beaten—that is to say, that we had taken neither Talavera nor the table-land. Tell him that he might have put what he pleased into the Madrid newspapers, but that he had no right to disguise the truth to the Government.

In a separate letter you will let Marshal Jourdan know that the whole affair has been ill managed; that Marshal Soult ought to have marched from Salamanca by way of Avila to Madrid; and that, if the corps d'armée had started separately by the 27th or 28th, the head would have arrived in time; that the army ought then to have retreated by short stages, and not have offered battle under the walls of Madrid till all our forces were assembled; that the march of Marshal Soult and of his three corps d'armée upon Placentia was dangerous, and, above all, useless—dangerous, because the other army might have been beaten at Talavera without receiving from him any assistance, so that the safety of all my armies in Spain was compromised—useless, because the English had nothing to fear, for in three hours they might gain the opposite bank of the Tagus; and whether they crossed the river at Talavera or Alamaraz, or at any other point, their line of operations on Badajos would have been protected.

That my best troops and the fate of Spain were therefore endangered through ignorance of the rules of war, and without a chance of obtaining a result even in case of success.

* The battle of Talavera was fought on the 28th of July.—TR.

That at any rate, though the great fault had been committed of dividing the army into two portions of 50,000 men each, separated by mountains and by a large tract of country, neither corps should have attacked the enemy except at the same time, or nearly at the same time, as the other.

Now it was evident that Marshal Soult could not reach Placentia before the 4th, as he was not so unwise as to arrive without the 6th corps, which was at Astorga, and could not at soonest have reached Placentia till then; but the other army of 50,000 men might have manœuvred near Madrid, and have gained a few days before coming to an engagement. The English would certainly have run no risks if they had found our army in a good position.

That, when at length Talavera was reached, it was well known that we were in presence of the English—it was known from the prisoners taken on the preceding days; that it was therefore utterly absurd to attack without having reconnoitred them; that as they had rested their right on Talavera, where were the Spaniards—who, if they are worth nothing in the field, are nevertheless good troops when they can entrench themselves behind houses—and their left on the table-land, it ought to have been ascertained whether the table-land could not be turned; that this position of the enemy therefore required previous reconnoissances, and that my troops were led blindly as if to slaughter.

That, when at last it was resolved to give battle, it was done without vigour, since, though our arms were disgraced, a reserve of 12,000 men did not even fire a shot; that a battle should never be risked unless the chances are 70 per cent. in favour of success; that, in fact, a battle ought always to be the last resource, as from the nature of things its result is always doubtful; but that, when once a battle is resolved on, one must conquer or perish, and that the French eagle should never stoop to retreat till all have done their utmost.

That this sort of generalship excites my displeasure the more, as I know that it was the Duke of Belluno's opinion that, if the reserve had been placed under his orders, he would have carried the English position.

That, for 30,000 English to have defied such an army as mine, it was necessary that all these faults should have been committed; but that as long as they continue to attack good troops, like the English, in good positions, without reconnoitring and ascertaining whether these positions can be carried, my men will be led on to destruction, and to no good purpose.

[548.] NAPOLEON TO CLARKE.

Schönbrunn, Aug. 25, 1809.

M. le Général Clarke,—You will find annexed a report from General Sebastiani, which the King has sent to me.

As soon as I receive that of the Duke of Belluno, which he tells me is coming, I shall see whether it ought to be put into the 'Moniteur.'

In the despatch of the English General Wellesley you will see that we have lost 20 guns and three standards. Express to the King my surprise, and to General Jourdan my displeasure, at not being made acquainted with the real state of things, instead of receiving from them schoolboys' stories; I wish to know who were the artillery men who abandoned their guns and the infantry regiments that allowed them to be taken. In your letter to the King hint that I disapprove his order of the day; that it tells the soldiers that they are conquerors; that this is ruin to the troops; that I am in want of correct information; that I wish to know the number of killed and wounded in each regiment, of guns and standards taken, &c. Say that in Spain affairs are undertaken without reflection or knowledge of war; and that on the day of action there is neither union, nor plan, nor decision. Write to General Sebastiani that the King has sent to me his report; that it is not the report of a soldier describing what has been and what is; that it is full of nothing but fine speeches; that I had rather that he had told me his real opinions, and had given an exact and faithful account of what happened. In short, I have a right to be told the truth; it is necessary for the good of my subjects. Let every one know that it is wanting in respect towards the Government to attempt to hide from it facts which it learns from the letters written to their friends by all ranks in the army, and that even the falsehoods of the enemy are thus in danger of being believed.

[549.] NAPOLEON TO CLARKE.

Schönbrunn, Aug. 29, 1809.

M. le Général Clarke,—I see in the newspapers more news from Spain than I have received; it seems as if some of the King's couriers had been intercepted.

Write word to the King that, if he can spare Marshal Ney, he may send him to France, where he will be of use.

[550.] NAPOLEON TO JOSEPH.

Schönbrunn, Sept. 2, 1809.

My Brother,—I have received the letter which you wrote to me on my birthday. I thank you for all your good wishes.

[551.] NAPOLEON TO CLARKE.

Schönbrunn, Sept. 4, 1809.

M. le Général Clarke,—I have seen the details which you have inserted in the 'Moniteur' on the affairs of Spain; they are not sufficient; this manner of bestowing information on the public will not counterbalance the long narratives of the English. Letters from the different generals must therefore be put in, suppressing all that is intended only for the Government; for instance, there are some letters from the Duke of Dalmatia, the Duke of Treviso, and General Sebastiani which would bear publication. Ask the Duke of Belluno for the account which he ought to send me of his operations. You must also tell General Senarmont that he did not send a correct account of his artillery; that the English took more than he acknowledged; that I approve of his putting what he likes into the newspapers, but that when he writes to me I must have the truth. Desire têtes-de-ponts, strong enough not to be carried by assault, to be constructed on the left bank of the Tagus. The information which I possess is not sufficiently precise, sufficiently clear, or sufficiently true to admit of my giving orders. Ask General Sebastiani for a return of the losses in his corps, similar to the one sent by the Duke of Belluno.

[552.] NAPOLEON TO CLARKE.

Schönbrunn, Sept. 7, 1809.

M. le Général Clarke,—I see, in a letter from General Jourdan, that you have written to him that nothing is to be attempted in Spain until February. I said that nothing was to be attempted until the heats were over. The heat is over at the end of September.

[553.] NAPOLEON TO CLARKE.

Schönbrunn, Sept. 11.

M. le Général Clarke,—Write to Marshal Jourdan that I am surprised that, as the Duke of Treviso had reached the Tagus, the English were not pursued for four or five days, their stragglers taken, and as much harm done to them as possible.

[554.] NAPOLEON TO CLARKE.

Schönbrunn, Sept. 26, 1809.

M. le Général Clarke,—Tell the King of Spain that I am sorry to see that the works on the Retiro are suspended; that it would have been good policy to have worked at these fortifications night and day for ten years; that, if the works already planned are finished, he should trace out others to increase the outworks, and render it capable of sustaining a longer defence; that I should also have liked the fortifications of Somo Sierra to be gone on with without interruption, as they are required to protect the communication between Aranda and Burgos.

Give to General Jourdan the permission, which he asks, to return to France, and tell the King that I have appointed the Duke of Dalmatia chief of the staff, and General Delaborde to command the 2nd corps.

If the Prince of Ponte Corvo is in good health and inclined to serve, send him to Catalonia to command all the troops; those at Barcelona and belonging to the corps of General St. Cyr, as well as those which are besieging Girona. In this case you will recall the Duke of Castiglione. Tell the King of Spain that, in appointing the Duke of Dalmatia chief of the staff, my intention is that he should command all the marshals in the army of Spain, and that, if necessary, he should put himself at the head of one or two corps, and proceed to manœuvre against the enemy.

[555.] NAPOLEON TO CLARKE.

Schönbrunn, Oct. 3, 1809.

M. le Général Clarke,—Write to the King of Spain that a strong tête-de-pont must be constructed and occupied on the left bank of the Tagus, and several bridges built so that we may manœuvre easily on both sides. Let the King know that my troops in Spain are in want of everything, because my generals have no power over the provinces, and the feebleness of the Spanish authorities enables the junta to obtain money through its agents; that therefore the administration of the country must be put into the hands of the military commanders; that in the present season, which in Spain is the good season, he ought to prevent the enemy from approaching within several days' march of the Tagus, falling upon the first comer; that this is likewise the way to obtain provisions, and to cut off the enemy's supplies in men and in subsistence; that it is against all the rules of war to allow the enemy to place himself so as to divide the different corps, when our army holds such a place as Placencia; that the enemy must not be allowed to approach within several marches of Almaraz; that the position occupied by the army is weak, bad, and can occasion only misfortunes; that if, on the other hand, there were bridges across the Tagus, with good têtes-de-ponts to secure a retreat, by scouring the country perpetually he would know what the enemy is about, prevent them from assembling their forces, and be able to collect his own when necessary; that his present position is absurd and contrary to all military principles. Why, as soon as 7000 or 8000 men were bivouacking before Velvin de Monroy, were they not attacked and beaten? Write to Generals Kellermann and Thiébault, and to the general in command in Aragon, and tell them not to suffer themselves to be betrayed by the Spaniards, and to set to work to supply the magazines, provide themselves with provisions, means of transport, and everything which the troops require.

[556.] NAPOLEON TO CLARKE.

Oct. 7, 1809.

M. le Général Clarke,—Order a marching regiment to be formed at Bayonne, taken from the depôts of the 34th, 114th, 115th, 116th, 117th, 118th, 119th and 120th. This regiment is to remain at Bayonne till it is well clothed and drilled, and its strength amounts to between 3000 and 4000 men. General Hédouville will review it on the 1st of November, and will make me a report of its condition.

You will review in Paris the two battalions from the Vistula and the 200 lancers; you will forward all the men who can be spared from Sedan to these two corps, completing them to 1500 infantry and 300 cavalry; you will let me know on the 20th of October the state of these two corps, that I may settle their destination; you will send towards Orleans the Irish battalion, and the other troops which you intend for Spain.

After you have completed the six provisional regiments of dragoons up to 6000 men, collect in Paris all the rest that the depôts can furnish, and try to make the number 3000. You may form these 3000 men in two or three marching regiments, which will await at Tours, or in other places where there is abundant forage, the arrival of the provisional regiments which are to join them; in this way I shall have nine provisional regiments of dragoons, composed of the 3rd and 4th squadrons, and forming a body of 9000 cavalry.

I propose to assemble 80,000 infantry and 15,000 or 16,000 cavalry by the beginning of December, and to enter Spain with these reinforcements. I conclude that the enemy will by that time have evacuated the island of Walcheren. I think that this corps of 100,000 men may be formed thus:—

9000 men, consisting of the 26th, 66th, and 82nd, of a Hanoverian battalion, and a battalion of the southern legion; 6000 men belonging to the 47th, 15th, 86th, and 76th; 3000 men from the 22nd of the line; 8000 men of the 9th battalions of the corps of the Duke of Abrantès and of the regiment of Berg; 3000 men of the marching regiment which is being formed at Strasbourg; 3000 men of the marching regiment which is forming at Maestrich; 14,000 men of the six provisional half-brigades belonging to the army of the north; 3000 of the marching regiment which is forming at Bayonne; 19,000 furnished by all the available troops in the depôts of all the regiments in France, which will be directed on Bayonne, and incorporated in regiments belonging to the army of Spain; 10,000 of my guard; altogether 80,000 infantry, 4000 allied troops. As cavalry: 9000 dragoons of the nine provisional regiments; 2000 from the depôts of chasseurs and hussars whose regiments are in Spain; 1000 of the provisional regiment; 600 of the regiment of chasseurs from the grand duchy of Berg; 3400 from all the depôts of chasseurs and hussars in France, to be incorporated in the regiments of the army of Spain, including 100 men taken from the depôt of the 13th regiment of cuirassiers; total, 16,000 cavalry, which, with the 80,000 French infantry and the 4000 allies, will make the 100,000 men whom I propose to have assembled between Bayonne and Orleans in the month of December in order to enter Spain.

I wish you to have a memorandum, based on these instructions, carefully drawn up in your office, in order to rectify my estimates; and I also wish for a statement of the materials for a reserve of 100,000 men, including no part of the army of Germany except the corps of the Duke of Abrantès.

[557.] NAPOLEON TO CLARKE.

Schönbrunn, Oct. 10, 1809.

M. le Général Clarke,—I wish you to write to the King of Spain to impress upon him that nothing can be more contrary to the rules of war than to publish the strength of his army, either in orders of the day, in proclamations, or in the newspapers; that when he has occasion to speak of his strength, he ought to render it formidable by exaggeration, doubling or trebling his numbers; and that, on the other hand, when he mentions the strength of the enemy, he should diminish it by one-half or one-third; that in war moral force is everything; that the King deviated from this principle when he said that he had only 40,000 men and the insurgents 120,000; that to represent the French as few and the enemy as numerous, discourages us, and gives confidence to them; that it is publishing his weakness throughout Spain. In short, to give moral force to the enemy is to take it from oneself; for men naturally believe that in the long run the small number will be beaten by the greater. The most experienced general finds it difficult on the field of battle to estimate the enemy's numbers, and the instinct of every one is to imagine them greater than they really are. But when a man is so imprudent as to allow such ideas to circulate generally, and to authorise exaggerated accounts of the enemy's strength, every colonel of cavalry who goes on a reconnaissance sees an army, and every captain of voltigeurs discovers battalions. I see, therefore, with regret, the bad influence which has been exercised over the spirit of my army of Spain by repeating that it opposes a force of 40,000 men against 120,000. The result of these announcements has been to lessen our reputation in Europe, by making people believe that it rests on no foundation, and to give moral force to the enemy and weaken our own; for, I say again, in war feeling and opinion are more than half of the reality. The art of great captains has always been to make their numbers appear very large to the enemy, and to persuade their own troops of the enemy's great inferiority. This is the first time that a general has been known to depreciate his own resources and to exalt those of the enemy. The private soldier does not judge; but officers of sense, whose opinion is worth having, and who have knowledge and experience, pay little attention to orders of the day or to proclamations. I trust that no more such blunders will be made, and that on no pretext whatever orders of the day or proclamations will be made tending to make known the real strength of my armies. I desire that all means, direct and indirect, be taken to spread the highest opinion of our numbers. The French troops which I have in Spain are twice as good, three times as good, as regards steadiness, bravery, and even numbers, as those that I have in any other part of the world. When I conquered the Austrians at Eckmühl I was one to five, and yet my army fancied itself at least equal to the enemy; and even now, although we have been so long in Germany, the enemy has no idea of our strength, and we try to make it out greater and greater every day. Far from owning that at Wagram I had only 100,000 men,* I try to prove that I had 220,000. Constantly, in my Italian campaigns, when I had only a handful of men, I exaggerated their numbers; this served my purpose without diminishing my glory. The skill of my operations, including that of exaggerating my strength, was afterwards recognised by generals and intelligent officers. With paltry motives, petty vanities, and small passions, nothing great has ever been done. I hope, therefore, that faults so great and so mischievous will not be repeated in my army of Spain.

* Thiers maintains that the French army at Wagram amounted to between 140,000 and 150,000 men.—Tr.

CHAPTER XV.

THE letters contained in this chapter extend from the 30th of October to the 21st of December, 1809.

During this period Napoleon was in Paris or in its neighbourhood, employed in preparing and effecting his divorce, and in arranging a second marriage.

[558.] NAPOLEON TO CLARKE.

Fontainebleau, Oct. 30, 1809.

M. le Général Clarke,—I have written to you three letters:* the first on the organisation of Loison's division, the second on that of Reynier's division, and the third on the organisation of the 8th corps, or the corps of the Duke of Abrantès; and lastly, one on the formation of the 4th corps, or a third division of reserve. I have supposed Loison's division to consist of 12,000 men; Reynier's of 20,000; the Duke of Abrantès' corps of 50,000 or 60,000; and the 3rd division of reserve to be completed to 20,000. In the midst of the occupations which besiege me, I was forced to make these calculations very hastily. It is urgent that you should give orders in accordance with my letters; but if, on consideration, you think that means can be found to make this corps more numerous, you must suggest them to me. In Spain we must proceed step by step. The first thing wanted is a corps to proceed to the rear of the army. As it is now November, it would be impossible to collect all our resources, especially powder and artillery, before the beginning of January; and in a peninsula

* These letters do not appear.—TR.

like Spain, intersected by lofty mountains, nothing can be attempted at that season. The reinforcements which I intend for Spain may therefore be sent in the following manner: first, the 12,000 men of Loison's division—I hope that they will be able to enter Biscay before the 1st of December; next Reynier's division, which will arrive, I hope, in the beginning of January; the Duke of Abrantès' corps in the beginning of February; and lastly, the third division of reserve, which will enter Biscay towards the beginning of March. I wish your chief secretary to prepare his arrangements on this plan, and when he has finished his work, to bring it to me himself, that I may discuss with him the formation of the divisions and other details. But what I care about just now is, that you should not lose a moment in sending off Loison's division.

[559.] ORDERS OF NAPOLEON.

Fontainebleau, Oct. 30, 1809.

M. le Général Clarke,—I told you that I wished Loison's division, which will consist of 12,000 men, horse and foot, to enter Spain as soon as possible, and before the 1st of December. I told you that I wished Reynier's division, which will be composed of 15,000 infantry and 4000 cavalry, to be assembled at Bayonne towards the end of December.

Lastly, I told you that I wished the 8th corps to be directed on Paris and Huninguen, and to arrive before the 30th of November.

The divisions of Loison and Reynier are to be incorporated successively into the regiments in Spain, as the corps of which they are composed belong already to the army of Spain; but I must also tell you* . . . . respecting the organisation of the 8th corps, which I wish to enter Spain towards the end of January.

This corps is to be commanded by the Duke of Abrantès. The first division is to be composed of 4 battalions of the 22nd of the line, and of the 8 battalions at present with Rivaud's division, in the whole 12 battalions. The number of each of

* Illegible.—Ed.

these battalions is to be filled up to 840, by the incorporation of what they have in the 6 provisional half-brigades in the north. For instance, the 19th has 360 men in the 6th half-brigade, the 25th 300, the 28th 400, the 36th 200, &c.

I imagine that by the 1st of December I shall have part of these provisional half-brigades at my disposal. I intend to withdraw as many as possible. The first division is therefore to be composed of 10,000 present under arms, forming 2 brigades.

The 2nd division, commanded by General Lagrange, will be composed of 3 battalions of the 65th, one of the 46th, and of the 8 battalions of the 8 regiments in Paris; in the whole 12 battalions or 10,000 men.

The 3rd and 4th divisions will be composed of all that the depôts in France are able to furnish on the 1st of December; if we estimate the numbers to which each of these divisions may be brought as 10,000, it is speaking within the mark. The Duke of Abrantès will thus have a corps of about 40,000 men under his command. That it may be properly organised, I wish your chief secretary, who drew up the memorandum which you sent to me for the formation of a reserve of 100,000 men for Spain, to come to Fontainebleau. He will announce his arrival to M. Monnier, my cabinet secretary, bring with him as many returns as possible, and draw up the plans under my superintendence. Among the materials and information with which he ought to be provided, there must be returns of all the existing provisional half-brigades and marching regiments, of the available troops in the different depôts in France, of all the 1st, 2nd, 3rd, and 4th battalions, and of the 1st, 2nd, 3rd, and 4th companies of the 5th battalions. By working for a couple of hours with M. Monnier he will understand how I wish this to be done.

I shall make your secretary draw up a scheme for the cavalry. I wish it to be composed of all the 2nd and 4th squadrons of the 24 dragoon regiments; and I think that I shall thus be able to collect 10,000 horse towards the 1st of December. They will bring the Duke of Abrantès' corps up to 50,000. Loison's division ought to amount to 12,000, Reynier's to nearly 20,000: altogether, therefore, there will be an army of 85,000 men ready to be sent to Spain. When we have done with the 8th corps, there remains the formation of a third division of reserve, to consist of 20,000 men, both horse and foot. This division should enter Spain at the beginning of March, and will complete the 100,000 men who, I think, may be easily brought together there.

[560.] NAPOLEON TO GENERAL DÉJEAN.

Fontainebleau, Oct. 31, 1809.

M. le Général Déjean,—I have received your two letters. I do not know what is meant by sending three ships to Barcelona: who gave the order? Send me a copy of it.

[561.] NAPOLEON TO JOSEPH.

Fontainebleau, Nov. 11, 1809.

My Brother,—I send Tascher to you. We hear nothing of what goes on in Spain. Yet, how is it possible that with so large and so good an army, opposed to enemies so little formidable, so little progress should be made?

[562.] ORDERS OF NAPOLEON.

Paris, Nov. 20, 1809.

M. le Général Clarke,—Order General Loison to be at Bayonne on the 28th of November; from thence he is to start on the 29th, with the first brigade of his division, and repair to Vittoria. He is to collect there his 2nd brigade and all his cavalry. He will take the chief command of the three provinces of Biscay, and correspond directly with the King, but especially with you. I depend upon his occupying them by the 4th of December. You will give notice of this to the commandants of the provinces and of St. Sebastian, and you will desire them to obey General Loison in every respect. All the unembodied men in these provinces, all the detachments joining the garrisons of St. Sebastian, Bilbao, and Vittoria, in short, all the troops of every kind, who on any pretext have retired into Biscay, are to be sent off immediately by General Loison to the interior of Spain, to join their respective regiments.

[563.] NAPOLEON TO BERTHIER.

Paris, Nov. 28, 1809.

My Cousin,—I have just ordered that from and after the 1st of December you are to have nothing more to do with the army of Germany, but that you are to keep up the correspondence of the army of Spain. From that time you are to undertake the duties of chief of its staff. Set about organising your staff and your offices. Send your baggage and that of your aides-de-camp to Bayonne. You will send me an account of the formation of a reserve for the army of Spain, to be composed of Loison's and Reynier's divisions, and of the 8th corps; and of the execution of my dispositions for sending a reinforcement of 100,000 men to Spain, and of every detail relating to the artillery. Many of these corps have neither a general nor a staff. Obtain information on this subject. I think that you should send one of your aides-de-camp to Madrid to-morrow, to give notice all along the line of the present dispositions, and that you ought to have sent to you by express the returns from Navarre, Aragon, the three Biscays, Burgos, Valladolid, and Bayonne, in order that I may shortly resume the direction of the Spanish affairs.

[564.] NAPOLEON TO BERTHIER.

(Returning a Report on Spain.)

Paris, Dec. 9, 1809.

Returned to the chief of the staff, to express to General Suchet my satisfaction at the good condition of his corps; to impress upon him the necessity of having a million of biscuits at Saragossa, to enable him to march on Valencia the day that I enter Spain,* and to prepare the means necessary for besieging the town. The chief of the staff is to ask General Suchet for a plan of it, and to let him know that the 13th cuirassiers and the 4th hussars are to be increased to 1500 men; that before the 20th of December the 2nd cavalry regiment belonging to the army of

* It appears from this letter and the previous one that Napoleon contemplated returning to Spain.—TR.

Spain will have reached Saragossa, and reinforced his cavalry; that 1500 men of the Vistula regiment are at Vittoria on their way to Saragossa to reinforce his 3 Vistula regiments; and that, in fact, in the month of January detachments will be sent to his corps to increase its numbers to 30,000 men present under arms.

[565.] NAPOLEON TO BERTHIER.

Paris, Dec. 9, 1809.

My Cousin,—Pray order without delay the 2nd marching cavalry regiment of the army of Spain, which will reach Bayonne on the 14th of December, to be forwarded from Bayonne through Tolosa and Pampeluna to Saragossa, where it is to be broken up and incorporated in the following manner: the detachments belonging to the 4th hussars in that regiment, and those belonging to the cuirassiers in the 13th. You should desire the officers and quartermaster-generals to return by post to their depôts. By this means General Loison's cavalry will consist only of the 1st marching regiment and the regiment of Polish lancers. I beg of you to let General Loison know that I am most anxious that all the troops in Biscay should be incorporated into either the battalion at Vittoria, or that of Bilbao, or the battalion of unembodied men at St. Sebastian, and that all other unembodied men join their own regiments, in order to increase the companies, so that his may be the only corps in the three Biscays. You will tell him also that I wish him to send columns to pursue sharply the banditti in the environs of Logroño and Santo Domingo, on the frontiers of Navarre, and on the roads between Vittoria and Burgos; that he is authorized to send expeditions of even 2000 or 3000 men, and to direct them towards Navarre and Castile as far as 3 days' march from Biscay, in order to dissolve insurrectionary meetings, disarm the towns, and restore obedience; that he must make the parts of Navarre and Castile which are nearest to Biscay sensible of his influence, of his authority, and of his presence at Vittoria. Simon's brigade belonging to Loison's division, 6000 strong, was to reach Vittoria on the 5th of December; the 2nd brigade, commanded by General Gratien, also 6000 strong, ought to be there on the 8th. Write to the commandants of St. Sebastian and of the three Biscays to desire them to send all their troops back to their regiments. Beg General Loison to send you a report on the condition of the three provinces, and on the way in which they are governed. Tell him that I depend upon his taking all the measures requisite for keeping the country quiet, and arresting ill-disposed persons; that he must refer these measures to me; that in other respects his division of 12,000 men ought to rest, drill, and perfect themselves. Let him know that he is not to dispose of the troops under his command without your order; but that on an emergency he may act on his own judgment, but without leaving the provinces of Biscay; in short, that he is not to venture farther into Spain.

Let me know when the 1st brigade of General Reynier's corps will be able to enter Spain.

[566.] NAPOLEON TO BERTHIER.

Paris, Dec. 13, 1809.

My Cousin,—I send you the last despatches from Spain. Acknowledge the receipt to the King and to General Suchet. Intimate to the King that the colours taken by my troops at the battles* of Medellino, Ocaña, &c. &c., ought to be sent to France to be presented to me, and to adorn our public buildings. You will repeat this to the Duke of Dalmatia. Write also that the prisoners must be sent to France, retaining the Germans, Swiss, and French to serve in my army, but that no Spaniard must be employed; they are habitual traitors.

Order the Irish who belong to Loison's division to repair to Burgos to join their regiments.

[567.] NAPOLEON TO BERTHIER.

Paris, Dec. 14, 1809.

My Cousin,—I see by your letter of the 13th of December that the 2nd brigade of Reynier's division, under the command of General Valentin, and the 3rd brigade under General Lamar-

* In the original, bataillons is inserted, by the error, probably, of the copyist, for batailles.—TR.

tinière, both of which are preparing at Bayonne, may be ready in the beginning of January. Order the 1st provisional regiment of chasseurs to leave Saintes on the 18th to continue their march, and let me know when they reach Bayonne. They must enter Spain immediately.

The 5th marching regiment of horse, which is to reach Tours on the 14th, will leave it on the 16th, and proceed on its way to Bayonne, in order to enter Spain as soon as possible. I approve of the 3rd, 4th, and 5th marching regiments of the army of Spain proceeding to their destination as soon as they are ready. The detachment of the 4th hussars which is in the 3rd marching regiment should be put into the 2nd, as the 2nd is intended for Ara gon, where the 4th hussars are.

[568.] Napoleon to Berthier.

Dec. 15, 1809.*

My Cousin,—General Loison ought to have reached Vittoria on the 4th; I am surprised that to-day, being the 15th, you have as yet no news of him. He was to occupy St. Sebastian and Bilbao, and to send to the army of Spain the battalions of unembodied men and the marching battalions, with the exception of the battalion of the national guard which is to remain in Biscay. Write to the Duke of Dalmatia that I am anxious to see all the corps brought together; that he is to order all the men belonging to the 32nd, 15th, 66th, 26th, and 82nd to repair to the north, to Benevento, and to Valladolid to join General Loison's corps; that all belonging to the 51st, 43rd, 55th, 58th, 47th, and 12th of the line are to join their respective regiments at Madrid; that the 2nd corps is to be composed only of the 2 divisions under Generals Merle and Heudelet, consisting, as at present, of the 2nd, 4th, 17th, and 31st light troops, and the 15th, 36th, 47th, 70th, and 86th of the line. Tell him that in General Loison's corps there are 6000 men belonging to the 2nd corps, and that an equal number are on their way from France to complete these 9 regiments.

* This letter was written on the day on which Napoleon and Josephine announced to the imperial family their divorce.—Tr.

You will repeat to him that he is not to touch General Loison's corps, of which I reserve to myself the disposal. There are many unembodied troops at Madrid, such as the 10th marching battalion and several detachments from different corps, which he must order to join their regiments.

You will let him know that I am going to order General Loison's corps to occupy Burgos; this will set at liberty the 118th, with which I intend to reinforce Bonnet's division. To recapitulate: you will give him orders that all men belonging to the 15th, 32nd, 26th, 66th, 82nd, 122nd, 120th, 119th, 118th, to the legion of the South, to the regiments of Westphalia, Prussia, and the guard of Paris, are to remain in the north to keep Castile quiet, restrain the Portuguese insurgents, and the enemy in Gallicia; that all men belonging to the 6th corps are to remain near Salamanca, where they are to be joined by all the troops of the 5th, 1st, and 4th corps, that they may be ready to receive reinforcements on my arrival, and to finish at last the conquest of Spain. There is also a battalion of the 2nd light infantry, which must be sent to join its regiment, as well as many detachments from cavalry regiments.

[569.] NAPOLEON TO JOSEPH.

Trianon, Dec. 17.

Monsieur mon Frère,—I send your Majesty the 'Moniteur,'* which will inform your Majesty of the step which I have thought it my duty to take.

I received your Majesty's letter of the 4th of December by the aide-de-camp entrusted with it.

[570.] NAPOLEON TO BERTHIER.

Trianon, Dec. 17, 1809.

My Cousin,—Send positive orders to Spain that in the newspapers and returns the Polish division is not to be called the

* The Emperor is alluding to his divorce from the Empress Josephine.—ED.

Polish division,* but that of the Grand-Duchy of Warsaw, and that the German division is to be called not the German division, but the division of the Rhenish Confederation.

[571.] Napoleon to Clarke.

Trianon, Dec. 18, 1809.

M. le Duc de Feltre,—I intend to countermand all the remounts, in order to diminish my expenses. I have advised the Minister of War to direct upon Niort all the horses already on their way to Italy; for I am no longer in want of horses there, and a thousand more in Spain will be of great use to me.

I write this letter to ask you for a general report on the cavalry; my expenditure is enormous, and I must think seriously of reforms. My army in its present state would devour three times the revenue of France. I want therefore, in the first place, to know the number of men, horses, and saddles in all my cavalry regiments on the 1st of December; and 2ndly, what are the reductions which must be made as to men and as to horses to bring the cost of these regiments within reasonable limits. A further advantage of such a reduction will be that I shall be able to withdraw from the cavalry depôts many conscripts, and put them at your disposal to form battalions of artillery-drivers for the army of Spain.

All the budgets must be made on the footing of peace as regards Germany, and of war in respect of Spain.

The men, horses, and harness of my cavalry are divided into two parts, one with the army, and the other in the depôts. Fourteen of my cuirassier and a great many of my chasseur and hussar regiments are in Germany. Whatever may be my peace establishment, my squadrons on service in Germany may be immediately reduced by getting rid of the dismounted invalid men and the unserviceable horses; but the important thing is to reform my depôts, that I may not leave in France a useless horse, and that next year I may save much on forage. I intend,

* Alexander had just extorted from Napoleon an engagement that the word Pole should not be used officially in France.—Tr.

therefore, that there shall not be more than 50 horses on an average for each regiment in the depôts of my regiments in Germany. Supposing there to be 30 depôts, this will make only 1500 horses to be fed in France for my army of Germany. At most, there ought to be in the depôts twice as many men as horses.

After the cavalry of Germany, comes that of Italy. I have regiments of horse in my army of Illyria, and likewise in my army of Italy. I wish my cavalry depôts in the Alps to be, generally speaking, on a higher footing than those in the interior, and my squadrons to be more numerous in Italy on account of the difficulty of obtaining remounts; but I do not choose to pay dearer for forage in Italy and Piedmont than elsewhere. There is abundant forage in Italy; it can therefore be only an abuse to charge so highly for it. I shall authorize the prefects to procure it at the rate of 18 sous or a franc at most, and even to levy it by requisition, if necessary.

I am inclined to place in Normandy the four depôts of my cuirassiers in Piedmont; they will be nearer their remounts, and, besides, I am always in want of cavalry and other resources on the coast.

I have 25 dragoon regiments in Spain; I do not intend them to have more than from 25 to 50 horses apiece in their depôts in France. The same with respect to the 12 regiments of chasseurs and hussars which are in Spain; and as in that army the horse's keep is not at my expense, it ought in general to be proposed to me to send thither all the available horses in the depôts; in Spain they will be of use, yet cost me nothing, and my finances will, in consequence, be much relieved.

I have 80 cavalry regiménts, therefore 80 depôts, which, at the rate of 40 horses, one with the other, will not make more than between 3000 and 4000 horses to feed; the whole amount of forage will thus be reduced from 15 millions to less than 4 millions for the year 1810, a great and important saving.

I believe that I have added a 9th company to all my regiments of dragoons and of light horse. I think that next year these 9th companies had better be suppressed, for four squadrons will be sufficient for my cavalry regiments in Germany, as they will be upon a peace establishment, and the regiments in the army of Spain are so full that three squadrons apiece will be quite enough. I think that the 5th squadron in the cuirassiers should also be reduced, which will bring us back entirely to a peace establishment.

Send to me therefore a report on the additions which the war has made unavoidable, a general return of the state of my cavalry as respects men, horses, and harness, and, lastly, the draft of a decree which may carry out the views which I have indicated to you.

[572.] NAPOLEON TO BERTHIER.

Trianon, Dec. 19, 1809.

My Cousin,—I see by your letters of the 18th that you allow the 1st brigade of the 1st division of my guard, under the orders of General Roguet at Tours, to remain there only on the 23rd and 24th; let it stay at Poitiers on the 27th and 28th. The 2nd brigade may rest on the 27th and 28th at Châtellerault; I wish to give it an additional halt. Order quarters for this division to be prepared at Bourdeaux, that it may stay there at least a week, in order to recover itself completely. Write to General Reynier that, as soon as he enters Biscay, he is to set about destroying the parties of insurgents. Let General Loison know that I am sorry that he has left so few troops about St. Sebastian, and that he has taken no measures for getting rid of the gangs of banditti which are there.

[573.] ORDER OF NAPOLEON.

Dec. 19, 1809.

M. le Duc le Feltre,—Express to the Duke of Castiglione my satisfaction at the capture of Gerona, and my regret that my troops were not long ago placed under his command.

Tell me what is the state of his health, and whether he is fit for active service. Let your messenger be an officer who will report to you on the state of the army, and bring back information about everything of interest to me in the country. Direct the Marshal to proceed to Barcelona to raise the blockade, supply the town with provisions, and exercise a general influence.

It is of great consequence to take Fort Hostalrich, in order to ensure a safe communication between France and Barcelona.

[574.] NAPOLEON TO BERTHIER.

Trianon, Dec. 20, 1809.

My Cousin,—Write to General Suchet that he does not pay sufficient attention to the banditti in Navarre; that I am sorry to see that he has allowed them to take Tudela; and that, although they only momentarily occupied the town, it was a great misfortune, and that such a post as Tudela ought not to have been in danger of an attack.

[575.] NAPOLEON TO BERTHIER.

Trianon, Dec. 21, 1809.

My Cousin,—Among the prisoners taken at the battle of Ocaña there are some officers who were included in the armistice, and who, since then, have served against the King. Order them to be arrested at Bayonne. Desire the Duke of Dalmatia to send such offenders to Bayonne, in order that severe justice may be executed upon them.

CHAPTER XVI.

THE letters contained in this chapter extend from the 11th of January to the 26th of December, 1810. Napoleon passed the whole of this year in the French empire.

He met Maria Louisa at Compiègne on the 27th of March, and married her at St. Cloud on the 1st of April.

On the 1st of July he annexed Holland to France.

These were the principal events of the year.

[576.] NAPOLEON TO BERTHIER.

Paris, Jan. 11, 1810.

My Cousin,—I sent to you by one of my pages this morning a despatch containing orders for the movement of various troops in my armies in Spain.

I have thought proper to make the following changes :—

Provinces of Valladolid and Leon.—General Loison is allowed to fix his head-quarters at Benevento or at Astorga. The principal object of his division is to hold in check all the troops in Gallicia, and to bring into order and defend the whole kingdom of Leon. His division will be composed according to my former orders, except that General Féret, who is already at Leon, is to command one of the brigades. In this position General Loison will rest his right on General Bonnet, and his left on the Duke of Elchingen, who is at Salamanca. Communicate these dispositions to the Duke of Elchingen. General Kellermann is to retain the command of the province of Valladolid. Write to

General Kellermann for information as to the amount of artillery belonging to Féret's brigade, which is at Leon, and repeat the requisite orders for providing General Loison with eight or ten pieces of cannon.

Navarre and Biscay.—General Montmarie is to command the brigade of Reynier's division which is intended to enter Navarre, and the other brigade, which is in Biscay, is to be commanded by General Lamartinière. The brigade intended for Navarre, instead of being directed on Logroño and Tudela, will be assembled at Pampeluna, and General Montmarie, who is energetic, and who will be under the orders of General Dagout, will command the province and take all necessary measures for the destruction of the bands of insurgents. By this means Suchet, having no longer anything to do with Navarre, may withdraw all his troops thence to strengthen himself. All the detachments from the regiments of the Vistula, all those of the 14th and 44th regiments, and all others which are at Navarre belonging to General Suchet's corps, will receive orders to join their corps in Aragon.

Province of Santander.—Desire General Reynier to send General Valentin to occupy Frias and Pont-di-Lara, and to send you constantly the correspondence of General Bonnet. You will express to General Bonnet my approval of all that he has done during the past year. You will let him know that I am sending the 118th and the 122nd to reinforce him; that General Loison is on his way to Astorga with 12,000 men; that I leave General Bonnet at liberty either to enter the Asturias or to undertake the expedition on Gallicia in concert with General Loison; that I wish to know what he thinks about this expedition; that perhaps at this season the snow is an obstacle; but that, if he can enter from his side, it may be useful to attack Gallicia by the coast, while General Loison threatens it from Astorga, for, after all, it is better to carry the alarm home to the enemy than to allow him to make a diversion and take the offensive. Tell General Bonnet that he has the fullest powers to take all proper measures for obtaining the money and clothes which he wants in order to put my troops into the best condition possible.

I also wish him to provide for their pay. Santander is a rich province; it ought not to be difficult to obtain from it a million. I only stipulate that all be done according to rule and without any kind of peculation.*

Aragon and Catalonia.—You will let General Suchet know that he must have 500,000 rations of biscuit in Saragossa, and 100,000 in Alcaniz; that he must also collect a reserve of cartridges and other ammunition at Alcaniz; that I wish to know whether he prefers to lay siege to Lerida or to march on Tortosa; that I estimate his corps, when joined by all its detachments, at 16,000 infantry and 2,000 cavalry; that I wish him to hold himself ready to go to the assistance of Barcelona, and to promote the arrival there of the 7th corps, which is advancing under the command of the Duke of Castiglione; that he must put himself as soon as possible in communication with the Duke of Castiglione, who has just obtained great successes, and is in possession of Gerona and of the greater part of Catalonia. Send to General Suchet a copy of the last return which you have of the 7th corps. Let him know that he ought to supply his troops abundantly with all that they want—clothing, shoes, cloth, &c., as well as pay; that Aragon is rich enough to afford large resources, and my expenses are becoming so considerable that I shall in future find a difficulty in providing for them all.

Old Castile.—I wrote to you that Solignac was to command a French division of from 8000 to 9000 men. Send him word that, as soon as Gratien's division reaches Burgos, he is to collect together the German division and forward it to Segovia, where it will be under the orders of the King. Let the King know that I think that he had better reorganize this division, and let it garrison Madrid or else Segovia, and keep quiet all the environs.

8th corps and Biscay.—General Reynier will continue to hold his head-quarters at Vittoria, to hasten the formation of his three brigades, and to direct all the movements necessary for restrain-

* That is to say, that all that was taken from the Spaniards was to be accounted for to the French authorities. No limit whatever is set to the amount which General Bonnet might take. But he was not to keep, or allow others to keep, any portion of it unaccounted for.—TR.

ing the insurgents in Navarre and Biscay, and keeping up the communications with Santander, through Frias, with Burgos, Tudela, and Pampeluna, between Tudela and Burgos, &c. You will give notice that I propose to assemble the whole of the 8th corps at Logroño. For this purpose General Lagrange, with the 1st brigade of his division, will enter Spain on the 14th, and proceed straight to Logroño. The commissary-general and the chief of the staff will repair thither as soon as possible. The commander-in-chief and all the staff will be there on the 8th of February. Every order shall be given to enable the divisions formerly belonging to Rivaud and Lagrange to reach Logroño with the utmost expedition, as well as the commissariat and the artillery; this makes between 16,000 and 17,000 men who are to be at Logroño in the first ten days of February. The 10th provisional baggage battalion will leave Pau for Logroño on the 21st. On passing through Bayonne it will take charge of clothing and biscuit for the 8th corps. Order General Lagrange and the chief of the staff to have 200,000 rations of biscuit made at Logroño. Order General Reynier to complete the supply of biscuit at Vittoria to 500,000 rations. Give the same order with respect to St. Sebastian and Burgos. Let the supply of biscuit at Madrid be completed to 1,200,000 rations. The cavalry of the 8th corps is composed of the 1st brigade, which includes the 1st, 2nd, and 3rd provisional regiments formed out of the 3rd and 4th squadrons belonging to the regiments of the division of Latour-Maubourg; and of the 3rd brigade, which includes the 6th and 7th provisional regiments composed of the 8 squadrons belonging to Milhaud's division. That will make therefore 20 squadrons, able to furnish more than 5000 men present under arms. Of the 5 dragoon brigades there remain 2 to dispose of—the 2nd and the 4th. You will order the 2nd and 4th brigades, as soon as they reach Bayonne, to continue their march, and both to proceed to Burgos.

Sundry orders.—Desire the battalion of Neufchâtel, and all the troops at Bayonne belonging to head-quarters and to the first battalion of drivers, to leave Bayonne for Vittoria, where they will wait for further orders, taking with them 180,000 pairs of shoes.

The company of guides, the horses of the staff, and half of mine,* will leave Bayonne under the escort of the battalion of Neufchâtel. Order all the lancers to be sent from Bayonne. Repeat the order to Generals Loison, Reynier, and Suchet, to forward to Madrid all the Polish lancers whom they have under their orders. Desire the 11th baggage battalion to start for Bayonne as soon as possible. Immediately on the arrival at Bayonne of the infantry belonging to the gendarmerie of the army of Spain, make it cross the frontier and proceed toward Vittoria. The Duke of Abrantès' 3rd division, composed of 4 marching regiments and 12 auxiliary battalions, is not to move without further orders from you.

Let me know what will be the situation of these corps on the 1st of February, as well as that of the 20 squadrons of gendarmes and the rear-guard division which I ordered to be assembled at Orleans. Will it be brought together at Orleans by the 1st February? Besides the 4 marching regiments of infantry, the 12 auxiliary battalions, the 20 squadrons of gendarmes, the 3 divisions of the guard, and the rear-guard which is preparing at Orleans, I have ordered the formation of several marching regiments of cavalry. Send me a return of these corps, mentioning their strength and their position. Write to the chief of the staff in Spain to repeat all the orders he has already given for assembling the corps and collecting the detachments of infantry and cavalry, as well as artillery, and even the baggage and train battalions; for dispersion produces nothing but disorder.

[577.] NAPOLEON TO BERTHIER.

Paris, Jan. 20, 1810.

My Cousin,—Tell General Buquet that as soon as the 16 first squadrons of gendarmes, which are placed between Bourdeaux and St. Benoit, have each more than 150 men present under arms, I propose that he should distribute them in the following manner:—The 1st at Irun, the 2nd at Ernani, the 3rd at Tolosa,

* This order that one half of his own horses should be sent to Spain shows that Napoleon had resolved to go there himself.—TR.

the 4th between Tolosa and Vittoria, the 5th at Vittoria, the 6th at Miranda, the 7th at Briviesca, the 8th at Burgos, the 9th at Lerma, the 10th at Aranda, the 11th between Aranda and Somo Sierra, the 12th at Somo Sierra, the 13th at Buytrago, the 14th at Cabecillas, the 15th at Alcorendas, and the 16th at Madrid. The other 4 squadrons of gendarmes will be formed into a reserve to reinforce the line wherever they may be wanted, or to remain at Madrid, where I wish to have 6 available squadrons. As soon as the first 6 squadrons are ready to start, you will desire General Buquet to distribute them between Bayonne and Miranda, and to push them on in succession towards Madrid as fast as the others are ready to replace them.

You will inform the Duke of Dalmatia of these dispositions, and of the strength of these squadrons, which, as they will amount to 4000 men and 1600 horses, will be able to maintain perfect security all along the line from France to Madrid. You will also let him know that I wish the line of communication between Bayonne and Madrid to pass through Somo Sierra, as it is the shortest road, and the least exposed to attack from Portugal. You will order 300 infantry, with 3 or 4 pieces of cannon, to be always placed at Somo Sierra, and carry on the works of the redoubt which I ordered to be raised there, in order to prevent this communication with Madrid from ever being intercepted, so that, even if the enemy should penetrate as far as Salamanca, Valladolid, and the Guadarrama, he may yet be far from cutting off our passage by Somo Sierra.

You will ask the Duke of Dalmatia to give you a plan enabling the captains of gendarmes to see to the safety of the road for 10 leagues on the right and on the left For this purpose it will be necessary to have considerable magazines and establishments at Aranda and Burgos. The troops must take their bread at Burgos, Aranda, and Buytrago. This will be in future the line of operations of the army of Spain, Aragon being subdued. That by Valladolid may be interrupted at any time from Portugal. Let General Hédouville know these arrangements, that he may inform you when the first companies of gendarmes under his command will be ready to move.

[578.] NAPOLEON TO BERTHIER.

Paris, Jan. 20, 1810.

My Cousin,—Put an extract into the 'Moniteur' from General Loison's despatch of the 1st of January, in which he relates the destruction of the insurgents. You will remark on the importance of the services thus rendered by General Loison. Write to the King of Spain that, out of the 1,500,000 francs which General Loison has levied by contribution, 400,000 should be assigned to the artillery, and 400,000 to the engineers. Let my minister of war in Paris know this.

You will insert in the 'Moniteur' an extract from General Solignac's letter of the 5th of January, announcing the defeat of Cubichas, and a narrative of the whole of Milhaud's expedition, when he destroyed the bands of Empecinado. Take care that in these insertions neither the word "Pole" nor the word "German" be used.

You will extract from General Suchet's correspondence a history of his late successes in Aragon, of the capture of Venasco, of the engagements of Alfara, and of his march upon Terruel and Mora, after General Musnier's actions with the garrison of Tortosa in the neighbourhood of Alcaniz and Balca.

[579.] NAPOLEON TO BERTHIER.

Paris, Jan. 20, 1810.

My Cousin,—Write to General Lagrange, who will reach Logroño on the 25th February with part of his division, that he ought to make incursions to the distance of five or six days' march from Logroño, to attack the banditti, destroy them, and keep the communications open for 40 miles round, in concert with the commandants of Navarre, the Biscays, Burgos, and Aragon; that he should form moveable columns, and make use of the time during which his division remains there to pacify and disarm the country.

Write the same thing to General Solignac. The dragoons who will reach Burgos on the . . . . . ,* added to the troops in

* Illegible.—Ed.

the provinces of Valladolid, Santander, and Bilbao, will enable him to pursue the banditti to a distance of five or six marches, rout them, and deliver the country from them.

[580.] NAPOLEON TO BERTHIER.

Paris, Jan. 20, 1810.

My Cousin,—Write to General Avril that I am much surprised at his not having marched with all his forces to destroy the enemy when he heard that they had re-appeared at Frias, and even in the neighbourhood of Orduna. At Orduna itself there were 515 men of the 26th of the line whom he ought to have put in motion.

Tell General Reynier to order his troops to march upon Frias, and to clear the whole country as soon as possible; to levy contributions, as General Loison has done, and to deposit them provisionally in the hands of a French paymaster.

[581.] NAPOLEON TO THE MINISTER OF WAR.

Jan. 20, 1810.

M. le Duc de Feltre,—Desire the Duke of Castiglione to express to General Souham my satisfaction with the manner in which he conducted the assault and capture of Olot. You will let me know the proposals which he makes for rewarding and promoting his officers.

Urge the Duke of Castiglione to put his troops in motion,* in order to raise the blockade of Barcelona and re-provision it, and to lay siege to Hostalrich, that in future there may be no obstacles in the way of his communications.

Put into the 'Moniteur' an account of General Souham's expedition to Olot, Campredon, Ribas, &c., and of the services

* The words of the original are, "pour faire le blocus de Barcelone, et pourvoir à son rétablissement." They are obviously corrupt. Barcelona was then in the hands of the French, and blockaded by the Spaniards. Probably the word "faire" ought to be read "lever," and the word "rétablissement" ought to be "ravitaillement," and the translation then will be, as I have made it, "in order to raise the blockade of Barcelona and re-provision it."—TR.

rendered by the Duke of Castiglione in directing this important operation.

[582.] NAPOLEON TO BERTHIER.

Jan. 22, 1810.

My Cousin,—My orders relating to the disposition of the gendarmes' squadrons are to be executed in the following manner:—The 1st squadron is not to be at Irun, the 2nd at Ernani, &c. &c. As soon as the first six squadrons are ready, they are to be placed thus:—The 1st at Miranda, the 2nd at Vittoria, the 3rd between Vittoria and Tolosa, the 4th at Tolosa, the 5th at Ernani, and the 6th at Irun. When the 7th is fit for service, it must proceed to Irun, and the 1st to Briviesca, and so on in succession as the other squadrons are ready to start. Order all these changes to be made.

[583.] NAPOLEON TO BERTHIER.

Paris, Jan. 27, 1810.

My Cousin,—Order General Digeon to repair to Madrid to take the command of the 1st brigade of the 4th division of dragoons, which is with the 2nd corps. Desire General Fouler to proceed likewise to Madrid, to take the command of the 4th brigade of the 3rd division of dragoons of the 4th corps. Write to General Solignac that General Loison did right in raising contributions to the amount of 1,500,000 reals,* but that this money must be paid into the military chest, to supply the wants of the army. Write to the same effect to Generals Loison and Reynier. I approve of all the French and foreigners, who were taken with General Dupont, returning to France. They must be distributed among the different depôts, clothing and arms given to them, and they will recover heart and French feelings.

* So in the original. But it appears from the letter of the 20th January that the contribution was 1,500,000 francs, which is more than four times as much.—TR.

[584.] NAPOLEON TO BERTHIER.

Paris, Jan. 27, 1810.

My Cousin,—Send back the King's aide-de-camp (Clermont Tonnerre) to Spain, with a letter which you will write to the King. Do not send him until you have received my orders.

[585.] NAPOLEON TO BERTHIER.

Paris, Jan. 28, 1810.

My Cousin.—Let the King of Spain know that my finances are getting into disorder; that I cannot meet the enormous cost of Spain; that it is become absolutely necessary that the funds required to keep up the artillery, the engineers, the administration, the hospitals, surgeons, and administrators of every description, should be furnished by Spain, as well as half the pay of the army; that no one is bound to do what is impossible; that the King ought to feed the army of Spain: that all I can do is to give two millions a month towards its pay; that, if all this cannot be done, there is but one course left, that is to administer the provinces for the benefit of France, seeing that the state of my finances will not allow me to continue to make such great sacrifices. You will acquaint the intendant-général and the commanding officer of engineers with this state of affairs.

[586.] NAPOLEON TO BERTHIER.

Jan. 31, 1810.

My Cousin,—Despatch the King of Spain's aide-de-camp, and let him carry the following instructions:—

1. When marching on Seville and Cadiz, care must be taken to be provided with all materials necessary for siege operations; for if the enemy is aware that the means for bombarding and mining are wanting, it will increase his resistance.

2. It must be foreseen that the English may make a diversion by marching upon Talavera. The 5th corps, which is composed of our best troops, should therefore be left to oppose them; and all the small bodies whose duty it is to keep up the communication with Madrid should be put under the orders of the com-

mander of the 5th corps, that he may be able to assemble them, and check the English. This corps might proceed to Alcantara, and even to the frontier of Portugal, to find out what the English are about, and to correspond with the Duke of Elchingen.

3. If the English should not make their diversion by a march upon Madrid, they may move on Salamanca; in this case the 6th corps should be reinforced by Loison's division, by the 8th corps, and by 1200 cavalry, which would make any serious operation in the plain impossible.

4. If the corps opposed to the English is not sufficiently strong; if the detachments between Sierra Morena and Madrid are not under the same command; if the English can hope to make an aggressive movement; Cadiz will be encouraged to resist. The least retrograde movement on the part of one of the corps belonging to the Andalusian expedition would be contrary to all military principles, give spirit to the insurgents, and discourage the French army. Only the necessary troops must therefore be sent to Andalusia, since a diversion on the part of the English must be foreseen.

5. His Majesty was not satisfied with the plans which I submitted to him; there is a want of strength in the arrangements. The English alone are to be feared in Spain, the rest are mere partisans, who can never keep the field.

The communication between Lisbon and Seville is rapid. If an insufficient corps is left upon the Tagus, the success of the operation will be endangered.*

[587.] NAPOLEON TO BERTHIER.

Paris, Feb. 8, 1810.

My Cousin,—Send an officer with the annexed decree to the King of Spain and to Marshal Soult, to whom he will

* This is the first time that the Emperor gives any advice on the Andalusian expedition, although the reports of his minister, to whom Marshal Soult had given every detail, had informed him of the dispositions made at Madrid for the approaching campaign.—ED.

deliver your letter.* All orders must be issued in accordance with this decree. I can no longer stand the enormous expense of my army of Spain. I intend the administration of the conquered provinces to be in future in the hands of the military commandants, in order that all their resources may be applied to the maintenance of the army. In future I shall be able to send only two millions a-month to pay the troops which surround Madrid, and which form the nucleus of the army. You will take care that possession is not taken of the new government of Navarre till General Dufour arrives there with his division.

[588.] NAPOLEON TO BERTHIER.

Paris, Feb. 8, 1810.

My Cousin,—Write to the general commanding in Aragon that he is to employ the revenue of the province, and, if necessary, even levy extraordinary contributions, for the pay and support of his army; that France can no longer supply all these demands. You will see in my decree that I intrust General Dufour with the government of Navarre. Give similar instructions to him. There are enough troops in Biscay. Write to Generals Thiébault, Bonnet, and Kellermann, and to the Duke of Elchingen, that the provinces which they occupy afford resources sufficient for the maintenance of their troops; that they must not trust to the French treasury, which is exhausted by the immense sums which it is constantly obliged to send out; that Spain swallows up a prodigious amount of specie, and thus

* By this decree, often referred to as "the Decree of the 8th of February," the provinces of—

1. Catalonia,
2. Aragon,
3. Navarre,
4. Biscay,
5. Burgos,
6. Valladolid, Placencia, and Toros,

were erected into six governments under the absolute control, civil as well as military, of six French generals, who corresponded with Napoleon and were virtually independent of Joseph.—Tr.

impoverishes France. Let the Duke of Dalmatia's aide-de-camp take your letters. You will write at the same time to General Suchet to desire him to attack with one of his divisions, and press vigorously, Mequinenza; at the same time he is to continue to threaten Valencia, and to maintain the tranquillity of Aragon. Tell him that Dufour's division, 7000 or 8000 strong, will reach Navarre towards the end of February, and that Montmarie's brigade, which is composed of detachments belonging to these corps, is about to proceed to Saragossa.

[589.] NAPOLEON TO BERTHIER.

Paris, Feb. 8, 1810.

My Cousin,—Order the brigade of dragoons, composed of the 4th and 5th provisional regiments, under the command of General Gardanne, which has reached Burgos, to repair to Valladolid, where it is to be broken up, and the squadrons belonging to the 3rd, 6th, 10th, and 11th dragoons are to rejoin their corps, which will raise the numbers of General Kellermann's division to nearly 4000. Order the 11th provisional regiment of dragoons, which is at Vittoria, to proceed to Madrid, whence it will be sent to the 2nd corps and dissolved. Thus the 13th and 22nd dragoons will each have their four squadrons. As by this means the 11th, 12th, 4th, and 5th provisional regiments, will be broken up, there will remain only eight regiments, amounting to more than 6000 men, who will form part of the 8th corps. Desire the Duke of Abrantès to occupy the plain with this body of cavalry, to establish magazines, and to pursue the banditti. Ask him if it would be possible to raise a couple of millions from the province of Burgos to supply the wants of his army.

[590.] NAPOLEON TO BERTHIER.

Paris, Feb. 12, 1810.

My Cousin,—Order Valentin's brigade to be broken up as soon as it has been replaced at Bilbao; and all the detachments of this brigade belonging to the 32nd and 6th light troops, and to the 76th of the line, to join the 6th corps, to be incorporated in their respective regiments, and all belonging to the 118th, 119th, and 120th, to repair to Santander; General Valentin is himself to follow these three regiments, and to be under the command of General Bonnet. Montmarie's brigade:—As soon as this brigade has been replaced by General Dufour, you will order General Montmarie to assemble it at Tudela, and thence repair to Saragossa, where General Suchet will incorporate the detachments of which it is composed into their respective regiments in the 3rd corps. Lamartinière's brigade:—Order all the men in this brigade belonging to the 3d corps to proceed to Saragossa, and the remainder to Burgos, whence it will supply garrisons to keep order in the province; it should send strong detachments towards Frias to keep up the communication with Santander. Dufour's division:—Order this division to be composed of only the 1st and 2d marching regiments; the 4th marching regiment is to continue its progress to Salamanca, where it will be incorporated into the 6th corps (with the exception of the detachments of the 43rd and 55th, which are to garrison the citadel of Burgos till further orders), and the 3rd foot marching regiment of this division is to be broken up at Tolosa, and to be thus disposed of: The 700 men belonging to the 4th Swiss regiment, and the 30 men of the 3rd, will proceed to Valladolid, under the orders of General Kellermann, which will complete the numbers of the Swiss battalions in his division to 2000. All troops belonging to the Hanoverian legion are to join the 6th corps. All belonging to the Irish battalions are to join the 8th corps. All belonging to the legion of the Vistula and to the Polish regiments will repair to Saragossa to be embodied in the legion of the Vistula. 8th corps:—Order all the men in the 8th corps who belong to the 14th and 121st regiments to proceed to join these regiments at Saragossa; all those of the 122nd to join Bonnet's division; and all belonging to the 15th light infantry to join the 6th corps. In consequence of these dispositions, Lagrange's division will in future be divided into only two brigades; Bonnet's division will receive an addition of more than 2000 men; and the 3rd corps of more than 4000. Order the Duke of Abrantès to carry his head-quarters to Valladolid, to collect all his troops there, to occupy the kingdom of Leon, Benevento, and the frontier of Gallicia with small detached posts of cavalry, in order to enable Loison's division to fall back upon Salamanca; to keep up a constant communication with the 6th corps, and to subdue the whole plain. Kellermann's division:—Order Kellermann's division of dragoons, that is to say, the 3rd, 6th, 10th and 11th regiments, as soon as they are completed by the 4th and 5th provisional regiments, which will carry their numbers to 3400, to march towards Salamanca, where they will be under the orders of the Duke of Elchingen, who commands the 6th corps. When you inform the Duke of Abrantès that Kellermann's division forms part of the 6th corps, you will direct him to send his cavalry to occupy the posts which were held by General Kellermann. 6th corps:—You will write to the Duke of Elchingen that, in consequence of the arrival of the Duke of Abrantès at Madrid, and the occupation by him of the kingdom of Leon and the frontier of Gallicia, the Duke of Elchingen ought to desire Loison's division to join him; that with the additions which his corps has received in cavalry, and, lastly, by his junction with Kellermann's division, he must have at least between 6000 and 7000 cavalry; that Loison's division will increase his numbers to more than 36,000; that besides these, the Duke of Abrantès, with another corps of 30,000 men, is on his rear, ready to support him; that he must not lose a moment in filling the passes from Portugal with strong patrols of cavalry, in order to find out what is going on, alarm the English, and prevent them from coming south; that he may spread in Portugal the news of the Emperor's arrival with 80,000 men; that he should occupy the summit of the pass which separates the Portuguese frontier from Ciudad Rodrigo, and place strong detachments round the town. Confer with General Lariboissière as to the possibility of sending 1000 horses, laden with siege materials, from Burgos to Valladolid, and thence to Salamanca. Let a return of the 6th corps be drawn up for me, including the additions which I have ordered it to receive. Bonnet's division:—Let General Bonnet know that he is to take possession of the Asturias, and be under the command of the Duke of Abrantès, who occupies the kingdom of Leon and the frontiers of Gallicia; that his principal business is to threaten Gallicia perpetually through the Asturias, find employment for enemies' troops there, and prevent their marching elsewhere. Gendarmes:—Write to General Buquet that the four first squadrons of gendarmes which enter Spain are to be placed in the three Biscays; that the next four are to occupy Navarre; that he is to place them in such a manner as to keep perfect order in the Biscays and in Navarre; that he is to send in a report on this matter; that I wish the other squadrons to be posted in Aragon, on the left of the Ebro, to secure the communications between Jaca, Venasco, and the frontiers of France; lastly, that no squadron is to go beyond Miranda or the Ebro without my order, except it be to a distance of only two or three marches to pursue banditti or escort convoys. 3rd corps:—Tell General Suchet that, since the 1st of January, his corps has been increased by more than one half, and his cavalry has been more than doubled; that I expect him to send moveable columns all over Aragon, to endeavour to put himself into communication with the 7th corps, and before the 1st of March to invest Mequinenza and Lerida, and push on both sieges vigorously. Let him know that I intend to send gendarmes, both horse and foot, to bring into order all the portion of Aragon which is between the Ebro and the Pyrenees, and that I wish him to send me a proposal for the details.

SUMMARY.

In consequence of the dispositions contained in this letter, Reynier's division is broken up; Montmarie's brigade becomes part of the 3rd corps: Valentin's brigade is sent, half to the 6th corps, and half to Bonnet's division; and Lamartinière's brigade is to repair for the present to Burgos. I intend to send it farther as soon as the six auxiliary battalions arrive.

The six auxiliary battalions are to continue to march towards Vittoria. Communicate these dispositions to the King and to the Duke of Dalmatia. Send to them copies of all the orders issued since the 1st of January, in order that, if any of the expresses should have been lost, they may have the duplicates.

[591.] NAPOLEON TO BERTHIER.

Paris, Feb. 15, 1810.

My Cousin,—I do not approve of changes being made in the organization of the gendarme squadrons. They will set off as soon as they are complete or nearly so. The first four squadrons will proceed to Biscay, and the four next to Navarre. I wish them to enter Spain on the 1st of March. Desire the Duke of Abrantès to take with him the first provisional battalion of the field equipages. By this means the Duke of Abrantès will have 140 carriages belonging to the 10th battalion, and 140 belonging to the 2nd provisional battalion, altogether 280 carriages. Desire him to put them into a good condition, to establish a good system, and to keep them loaded with biscuit, which he will procure either from Bayonne or from Burgos. He will thus be ready for any undertaking. Hasten the departure of the 11th battalion of field equipages for Bayonne, and let me know when it arrives there. Write to General Hedouville to keep at Bayonne the 51,000 pairs of shoes which were left there by the 1st battalion of field equipages. They will supply the troops which pass through.

[592.] NAPOLEON TO BERTHIER.

Paris, Feb. 17, 1810.

My Cousin,—Let General Suchet know that I reiterate my order that he lay siege to Lerida and Mequinenza, and employ the rest of his troops on the frontier of the kingdom of Valencia; that I am especially anxious to finish with Catalonia. Tell him that the Duke of Castiglione has reached Barcelona, and that he is to try to put himself into communication with him. Give notice to General Suchet that, if he should receive from Madrid any orders contrary to mine, he is to consider that they have not reached him, particularly in administrative matters.

[593.] NAPOLEON TO BERTHIER.

Paris, Feb. 19, 1810.

My Cousin,—Desire the 1000 artillery horses which will reach Bayonne on the 28th, and the 370 which will arrive on the 24th—making nearly 1400 horses—to proceed to Saragossa, where they will be at the service of General Suchet for the siege of Lerida. They will draw the powder and every thing that is required for the siege, taking care to carry from Bayonne only such things as cannot be procured at Pampeluna or at Saragossa. Order all the detachments of the 3000 horses which are coming from Germany to be filled up with mules on passing through Poitiers. Desire General Lariboissière to send an artillery officer to superintend the operation. Write to inform General Suchet of this, and tell him that after the capture of Lerida he may make use of these horses for Tortosa and Valencia; that he must invest Lerida between the 1st and the 8th of March; that the Duke of Castiglione has received notice to put himself into communication with him.

[594.] BERTHIER TO GENERALS THOUVENOT AND DUFOUR.

Rambouillet, Feb. 22, 1810.

I have sent to you the Emperor's order, appointing you governor of the province of . . ., which has been placed in a state of siege. Placing this province in a state of siege gives you full power, both military and civil, and you will in future correspond directly only with me. Your relations with the staff of the army of Spain are concerned only with the movement of troops and other purely military arrangements. As I have already informed you, all the resources of the province must be devoted to the pay, the food, and the clothing of the troops, taking, of course, proper precautions that every thing be done regularly and economically

[595.] BERTHIER TO SUCHET.

Rambouillet, Feb. 22, 1810.

I repeat to you, M. le Comte, the order to take possession of Lerida and Mequinenza, and to put yourself in communication with the Duke of Castiglione. The Emperor wishes that Aragon, which is placed in a state of siege, should communicate as little as possible with Madrid. Placing this province in a state of siege gives to you absolute authority, and it is your duty to employ all its resources to the pay, the food, and the clothing of your army. If the King, as commander-in-chief of the armies of Spain, should give you any orders affecting your administration, then and then only you will declare that, as Aragon has been placed in a state of siege, your army receives its orders only from the Emperor. You must feel, M. le Comte, that this declaration is to be made only in a case of absolute necessity: his Majesty relies on your prudence, on your devotion to his person, and on your attachment to the French empire. You must be aware that some portions of Aragon may have to be included within the new frontier of France. This communication, M. le Comte, is between you and me alone.

[596.] JOSEPH TO QUEEN JULIE.

Cordova, April 12.

My dear Friend,—M. Deslandes will explain to you my position, and will tell you how necessary it is that it should end, and that I should know what are the real feelings of the Emperor towards me. As far as I can judge from the facts, they are unfavorable, and yet I cannot account for them. What does he want with Spain and with me? Let him once announce to me his will, and I should be no longer placed between what I appear to be and what I really am, in a country in which unresisting provinces are given up to the discretion of the generals, who tax them as they like, and are ordered not to attend to me. If the Emperor wishes to disgust me with Spain, I wish for nothing but to retire immediately. I am satisfied with having twice tried the experiment of being a king; I do not wish to continue it. I wish either to buy an estate in France, far from Paris, and to live there quietly, or to be treated as a king and a brother.

If the Emperor has been irritated against me by mischief-makers, by the persons who calumniated me to the Spanish people (and thus indeed did me good when I became known), and if you cannot make him see the truth, I repeat that I must retire.

I beg you, therefore, to prepare for me the means of living independently in retirement, and of being just to those who serve me well.

I embrace you and Zenaïde and Charlotte.

[597.] NAPOLEON TO BERTHIER.

Paris, Feb. 28, 1810.

My Cousin,—I return General Thouvenot's letters to you. Tell him in answer that it would be as yet premature to send for hostages; that he should govern the country with a steady hand, and make use of the resources which it affords for the maintenance of the troops; that four squadrons of gendarmes must have arrived; that he is to post them, and to make them do duty as in France; that six auxiliary battalions, amounting at least to 3000 men, ought to have arrived; that 3000 marines, armed with muskets, and commanded by Colonel Baste, will reach St. Sebastian in the beginning of March; that a division of my guard, 6000 strong, is at Logroño, and that, on an emergency, he may put them in requisition; that 6000 of the rear-guard, under the command of General Séras, are on their way; and that General Dufour has entered Navarre with a division of 6000 men; that, therefore, he cannot be in want of troops, and that he ought not to be uneasy; that he must be prepared to find that the measures which he has taken are not agreeable to the King's ministers, but that this must not prevent his carrying them out, and that he is to allege that he has orders from me. Let him know also that the American merchandise should be sent to Bayonne, where it will be sold more easily. Tell him likewise that the crews of the American ships ought not to be treated as prisoners.

[598.] NAPOLEON TO BERTHIER.

Paris, March 2, 1810.

My Cousin,—Order General Lamartinière's brigade, 5000 strong, to repair to Valladolid, where it will be under the orders of General Kellermann, who will unite it to the Swiss regiment, and to the other detachments under his command; he will thus have between 7000 and 8000 infantry. Desire him to support

General Bonnet, and to keep Castile quiet; the Duke of Abrantès will thus be free to proceed in any direction without uneasiness as to his rear. Order the six auxiliary battalions to continue their march from Vittoria to Burgos, and appoint a brigadier-general who is on the spot to command them. These battalions are to be drilled and exercised, and at the same time maintain order and security in the Castiles; they will communicate with Santander, and proceed whithersoever their presence may be required. General Séras with the vanguard will continue his march, and proceed to Biscay. By this means General Thouvenot will have at his disposal a good division of infantry, the 43rd and 44th battalions of the flotilla, and four squadrons of gendarmes—more than enough to make the country perfectly safe. You will inform the Duke of Abrantès of these movements, that he may dispose of the troops in case of emergency.

[599.] NAPOLEON TO BERTHIER.

March 5, 1810.

My Cousin,—Repeat the order that all colonial merchandise seized in American ships in the ports of St. Sebastian, Bilbao, Santander, and others, be sent to Bayonne for sale. The money thus obtained is to be paid into a special fund, and an account kept of it. I send you an answer to a question proposed by General Thouvenot. Tell him that the money must be paid into the custom-house fund at Bayonne, and that, until that has been done, the goods must not be delivered.

[600.] NAPOLEON TO CLARKE.

March 12, 1810.

M. le Duc de Feltre,—Send this despatch to the chief of the staff. He will answer to the Duke of Abrantès that the funds necessary for supplying all the wants of his army must be raised by the duke in the provinces of Valladolid and Burgos, and that they must be paid into his paymaster's chest.

[601.] NAPOLEON TO BERTHIER.

Paris, March 16, 1810.

My Cousin,—Write to the Duke of Abrantès that General Kellermann is to receive all his orders from him. General Gardanne is to join the corps of Marshal Ney, who will give him employment in his cavalry. General Marancin, who is at present at Valladolid, will be employed in the corps of the Duke of Abrantès.

[602.] NAPOLEON TO BERTHIER.

Paris, March 16, 1810.

My Cousin,—Express to General Bonnet my satisfaction at his conduct in the actions against the insurgents in the Asturias on the 14th and 15th of February. Desire the Minister of Marine Affairs to send from Bayonne some brigs or other small ships to carry off from Gijon the prisoners and any others who may be in General Bonnet's way. Write to the Duke of Abrantès that he must attack Astorga immediately, in order to support General Bonnet in the Asturias, establish a communication with him, and strike terror into Gallicia.

[603.] NAPOLEON TO BERTHIER.

Paris, March 16, 1810.

My Cousin,—Write to the Duke of Abrantès that he must levy contributions on the provinces of old Castile, Valladolid, and Leon, sufficient to pay his troops. Desire the Duke of Elchingen to do the same thing in the provinces which he occupies, and to arrange with the Duke of Abrantès the limits of the provinces from which they respectively are to raise contributions. Give the same order to General Bonnet, that there may be no arrears in the pay of his troops. Tell General Hédouville to let me know the state of his funds at Bayonne, and what sums he has sent to Spain up to the 1st of April; desire him to send no more to Navarre, Aragon, Biscay, Santander, Old Castile, or to the 6th corps. I wish, for my decisions, to know what money there is at Bayonne available for Spain. You must see the Minister of the Public Exchequer, and ask him what can be spared for Spain in the months of March and April, and do nothing till you have let me know the result.

[604.] Napoleon to Berthier.

Compiègne, April 9, 1810.

My Cousin,—Order General Buquet to distribute the twenty squadrons of gendarmes in the following manner:—Four in Biscay; four in Navarre; six in the portion of Aragon which is between France and the Ebro; so that all the valleys which lead into France may be watched, and that these gendarmes may be in communication with those of France; and six in the province of Santander, so that the communication between Vittoria, Bilbao, and Santander may be always open. Total twenty squadrons.

My object in establishing this service is, that the provinces of Biscay and Navarre, the portion of Aragon which lies between the Ebro and France, and the province of Santander, may be reduced to perfect order and under a regular police. The six squadrons in the province of Santander will keep order round Miranda, Briviesca, and as far as Burgos. Write to General Suchet that I do not wish him to keep a single gendarme squadron at Saragossa. Let him keep them in cantonments in all the Aragonese valleys between the Ebro and France.

[605.] Napoleon to Berthier.

Compiègne, April 9, 1810.

My Cousin,—Order General Abbé to repair to Saragossa, where he will be employed in the 6th corps. I approve of General Marancin's being employed in the 5th corps. Desire the horses which are wanted for the king's remounts to be sent to Spain. Order the 1st company of the 12th battalion of field-equipages, containing thirty-six ambulance carriages, to repair to Valladolid. Order the 2nd brigade of the rear-guard of the army of Spain, commanded by General Brenier, which will reach Bayonne on the 18th of this month, to continue its march towards Vittoria, where it will be at the disposal of General Séras. Desire the Duke of Elchingen to break up the first provisional regiment of chasseurs, and to despatch the different detachments out of which it was composed to their respective regiments. Write to the Duke of Elchingen that the province of Avila ought to be included in his command, and to supply provisions to his army. Order 250,000 rations of biscuit from Burgos, and an equal quantity from Valladolid, to be sent to Salamanca, and placed there at the disposal of the Duke of Elchingen.

[606.] IMPERIAL DECREES.

Compiègne, April 17, 1810.

Napoleon, Emperor of the French, King of Italy, and Protector of the Confederation of the Rhine,—

We have decreed and do decree as follows:—

Art. 1. An army is formed under the name of the Army of Portugal. It will be composed of the 2d, 6th, and 8th corps of the army of Spain; they will preserve their present organisation.

Art. 2. The accounts of this army will be separate from those of the army of Spain, dating from the 1st of May; it will have a chief of the staff, an *intendant général*, a general in command of the cavalry, another to command the artillery, and a third, commanding the engineers.

Art. 3. Our Ministers of War, of the Administration of War, of the Public Exchequer, and the Chief of our Staff, are intrusted with the execution of this decree, which will not be printed.

Marshal the Duke of Rivoli, Prince of Essling, is appointed commander-in-chief of the army of Portugal, created by our decree of the 17th of April, 1810.

[607.] NAPOLEON TO CLARKE.

Compiègne, April 17, 1810.

Monsieur le Duc de Feltre,—Write to the Duke of Castiglione that the plains between Lerida and Villa Franca are very fruitful, that General Suchet lost nothing in his retreat from Valencia, and that he has always beaten every thing before him. I presume that by this time the Duke of Castiglione has taken Tarragona, and that he is in communication with the army of Aragon.

[608.] Napoleon to Berthier.

Compiègne, April 17, 1810.

My Cousin,—I send you back M. Denniée's report. The King of Spain is to have no voice as to the confiscation and disposal of the British goods in Andalusia. He is only the commander of my army. All the English goods, all the money owing to the English on any grounds whatever, are to be paid into the treasury of the army. It is not with Spanish troops that the King is conquering Spain. I do not understand this constant refusal to use the means of paying the army.

[609.] Napoleon to Berthier.

Compiègne, April 17, 1810.

My Cousin,—Write to General Suchet that I am extremely displeased at his having marched upon Valencia, instead of marching, as I desired him, upon Lerida. You will also express to him my displeasure that he was not before Lerida in the beginning of March. Although his artillery was not to arrive till the 20th of April, he ought to have taken up his position in front of Lerida, and to have sent forward strong detachments to open a communication with the army of Catalonia. He ought to have left a strong division to watch Valencia, hold the country in check, and look out for the enemy's movements by sea. General Suchet went, in spite of my orders, to Valencia; he returned without sufficient cause, and risked his troops. Instead of performing his appointed task, he left inactive the fine army with which I intrusted him. His conduct has in no way answered my expectations. The Duke of Castiglione must have been much surprised, when he marched upon Villa Franca on the 20th of March, to find no troops to support his right flank. It is essential that General Suchet should repair his blunders.

[610.] NAPOLEON TO CLARKE.

Compiègne, April 22, 1810.

Monsieur le Duc de Feltre,—I wrote to you a few days ago to order the Polish light-horse to proceed to Spain. I wish you to give them counter-orders. It will be enough for the general in command of the guard to choose, from among the men most fit for active service, a sufficient number to complete the two squadrons of the regiments in Spain to four hundred men.

I told you to send the division of the Guard under General Dumoutier's command to Spain. Send immediately counter-orders to the brigade of fusileers, and stop it at Angers, or wherever it may be. Let General Dumoutier continue his march with the rest of his division. Order the brigade of conscripts which is at Paris to march from thence and replace the fusileers in the division of General Dumoutier. This division, reinforced by 6000 conscripts, will proceed to Spain. Give strict orders that these troops be marched carefully, without fatiguing them. The brigade of fusileers will remain at Angers, and the old guard at Paris.

The detachment of fusileers which is at Bayonne will remain there to garrison the castle of Marrac. Let me know what is the general depôt of cavalry which appears in your return as being in Paris.

[611.] NAPOLEON TO BERTHIER.

Compiègne, April 20, 1810.

My Cousin,—General Dorsenne is ordered to Burgos to take the command of my guard, composed of Roguet's division, consisting of two regiments of fusileers and tirailleurs, and of Dumoutier's division, consisting also of two regiments of fusileers and tirailleurs, which is under orders to march from Angers to Burgos. Each of these divisions is 6000 men strong, and has eight heavy guns.

Twelve pieces of light artillery will join Dumoutier's division as it passes through Bourdeaux, making altogether twenty-eight pieces. I have ordered to Bayonne the Berg lancers and the

Polish light-horse, which, joined to the two regiments of chasseurs, the dragoons, and the heavy horse, will make up the cavalry to 2500 men. I have ordered General Lepic to take the command of this cavalry. You will order General Dorsenne to correspond with you and to receive orders only from you. He will occupy Burgos and Aranda, and keep up the communication with Santander, Vittoria, and San Domingo. You will give him the chief command in the province of Burgos. I have added to my guard a corps of marines, commanded by General Baste, and a corps of marine-artificers, which will make this corps amount to 16,000 or 17,000 men. You will instruct General Dorsenne that, if the English march against the Duke of Rivoli, he is authorised to move to his assistance; but that, except in that case, his business is to keep quiet the country along the Douro, and as far as Santander, and to employ columns to protect the communications with Navarre and Valladolid. You will order him to be at Burgos on the 12th of May, to have always 500,000 rations of biscuit ready to move with the guard, to improve the fortifications of Burgos, to put the whole country in a state of defence, and to keep it quiet. You will join the battalion of Neufchâtel and the company of guides to my guard. I have ordered the 3rd, 4th, and 7th provisional demi-brigades and the infantry regiment of the Grand Duchy of Berg to proceed under the orders of a brigadier-general to Bayonne, and from thence to Vittoria. You will let me know the day of their arrival that I may give them further orders.

[612.] Napoleon to Berthier.

Compiègne, April 26, 1810.

My Cousin,—I send you back the whole correspondence with Spain; extract from it articles for the 'Moniteur,' which you will show to me to-morrow at St. Quentin before you send them to the press. Under the title "Siege of Cadiz" you may insert the journal of the siege from the beginning until now, suppressing any objectionable matter. Under the title of "Daily accounts of skirmishes and unimportant affairs which have occurred in different parts of Spain," you will insert a short narrative of the actions of Malaga and Ronda, of the smaller landings of the English, of the little affair of General Foy, of General St. Croix's reconnaissance in the North, of the affairs of General Bonnet; printing the notes which we have of them. The officers who have distinguished themselves should be named, for, although the actions were of little importance, they risked their lives in them. Besides, all this will throw light on the affairs of Spain.

[613.] NAPOLEON TO BERTHIER.

Berg-op-Zoom, May 9, 1810.

My Cousin,—Let the King of Spain and the Duke of Dalmatia know that, if the armies of La Romana and of the other insurgent generals obtain recruits, the reason is twofold: 1st, the creation of a Spanish army into which the peasants fear that they shall be pressed, and therefore leave their homes; and 2ndly, the errors committed in the treatment of the prisoners taken at Ocaña and elsewhere.

[614.] NAPOLEON TO BERTHIER.

Lille, May 23, 1810.

My Cousin,—Write to General Suchet that I approve highly of his exchanging Spaniards for French; that I give him carte-blanche, provided that he does not allow himself to be cheated, and that the exchanges take place simultaneously.

[615.] NAPOLEON TO BERTHIER.

May 27, 1810.

My Cousin,—Send a staff-officer to General Suchet with orders to destroy Lerida, employing the powder which he found there to blow up the fortifications in such a manner as to render it impossible for them to be rebuilt. He will keep only a citadel or fort commanding the town, in which 500 or 600 men may hold out for a long time. This citadel must be furnished with arms and provisions for six months. I shall wait till a report is sent to me before I decide on the preservation of the existing citadel or fort. All the rest of the stores will be sent to France by the shortest road. I conclude that General Suchet has commenced the siege of Mequinenza, and that I shall soon hear of its having been taken. After doing this he will march upon Tortosa, take the place, and write to Marshal Macdonald, who, at the same time, will march on Tarragona.

You will order General Suchet to levy a contribution of several millions on the town of Lerida, to enable him to pay his troops in full.

Lerida is capable of paying a war-tax of 12 million reals.*

[616.] NAPOLEON TO BERTHIER.

May 27, 1810.

My Cousin,—Write to the Duke of Dalmatia that Lerida and Hostalrich are taken; that by this time Mequinenza is no doubt also taken; and that I have ordered General Suchet to march upon Tortosa, and Marshal Macdonald to take Tarragona; that, when these two places are captured, General Suchet may, with a corps of 30,000 men and the necessary siege materials, march upon Valencia, and reduce it; that General Suchet's operation was premature, and could only occasion the loss of our men; that the siege of Ciudad Rodrigo may cause a battle; that therefore General Reynier with the 2nd corps should proceed towards Abrantès, under the orders of the Prince of Essling, to manœuvre on the right bank of the Tagus; that the 1st, 4th, and 5th corps and Dessolles' division are more than enough for the South; that the 5th corps should move towards Portugal on the side of Badajoz; that the Emperor cannot understand what is meant by arming all the towns in Spain, and how it is that experience has not shown the danger of putting arms into the hands of a people who have always made such a bad use of them; that such policy is madness; that it is equally inconceivable that no contributions should be raised in the country occupied by the army, in order to pay and to feed it.

* About 120,000*l.*—Tr.

[617.] NAPOLEON TO BERTHIER.

Dieppe, May 27, 1810.

My Cousin,—Write to the King of Spain that it grieves me to see him arming the Spaniards to such an extent; its only effect is to increase their resistance, and to spill the blood of the French soldiers. It is difficult to understand this obstinacy in a false system after having been so repeatedly deceived.

Write to the Prince of Essling that it appears from the English newspapers that the English army consists of only 23,000 English and Germans, and 22,000 Portuguese; that therefore, if the English attempt to interfere with the siege of Ciudad Rodrigo, he has more than enough troops to beat them; that he should march on that town with the 6th and 8th corps; that he should leave with General Kellermann 2000 dragoons and from 3000 to 4000 infantry belonging to the 8th corps, so that General Kellermann, with these troops, the auxiliary battalion, and his own, will have a body of about 10,000 men, infantry, cavalry, and artillery, which is enough to keep up the communication; that he, the Prince of Essling, with the 6th and the remainder of the 8th corps, making altogether more than 50,000 men, ought to take Ciudad Rodrigo, and to beat the English if they advance.

Order General Reynier to approach Alcantara with the 2nd corps to manœuvre on the right of the Tagus with the Prince of Essling, under whose orders he is.

Write to the King of Spain that, as the English alone are to be feared, he should put General Reynier, with the 2nd corps, under the orders of the Prince of Essling, to march upon Alcantara and manœuvre on the right of the Tagus; that the 1st, 4th, and 5th corps and Dessolles' division are more than enough for Andalusia; that this will assist the Prince of Essling to prevent the siege of Ciudad Rodrigo from being raised, to take the place, and to fulfil my intentions.

You will also write to the King of Spain that he is to give no orders to the army of Aragon; and that he ought to combine his operations with judgment, in order to finish this business once for all.

[618.] NAPOLEON TO BERTHIER.

Havre, May 29, 1810.

My Cousin,—Order General Reille, my aide-de-camp, to repair to Pampeluna, where he is to undertake the command of the whole of Navarre, with the title of Governor. You will give him instructions similar to those formerly given to General Dufour.

You will order General Dufour to proceed without delay to Seville, where the Duke of Dalmatia will employ him in a division on active service.

You will let General Reille know that, besides the troops already in Navarre, others are about to repair thither; that General Dorsenne may even furnish him with a few battalions of my guard, relying on his prudence to give them suitable employment, and not to compromise the honour of the corps.

[619.] NAPOLEON TO BERTHIER.

Havre, May 29, 1810.

My Cousin,—Send word to the Prince of Essling that, according to the English accounts, the army of General Wellington consists only of 24,000 men, English and Germans, and that the Portuguese have only 25,000; but that I do not choose to enter Lisbon at present, because I should not be able to feed the town, the immense population of which obtain their provisions by sea; that the summer must be spent in taking Ciudad Rodrigo, and afterwards Almeida; that the campaign must be managed, not by unconnected expeditions, but methodically; that the English general, as he has less than 3000 horse, may wait for the attack in a country where cavalry is useless, but will never offer battle in a plain.

The 3 infantry divisions of the 6th corps alone amount to 24,000 men. The 8th corps is to consist of two divisions, thus composed:—1st, Clausel's division as it stands, with the addition of the battalion of the 46th which is with Lagrange's division; this will bring it to 8500 men. 2ndly, Solignac's division with the 65th, which will raise it to 9000. Total of the 8th corps,

17,500 men. These 5 divisions will therefore amount to more than 40,000 men. The battalions of the 2nd, 4th, and 12th light troops, the 32nd and 58th of the line, under the orders of Brigadiers Corsin and Janin, will form part of the division of General Séras, who will thus have under his command these 5 battalions, 3000 men; the 4 auxiliary battalions, 3000; the 113th and the 4th battalion of the Vistula, 3000; in the whole 9000 men.

General Séras will also have under his command Brigadiers Corsin and Janin.

The cavalry is to be disposed in the following manner:—

The 3rd hussars and the 15th chasseurs, which ought to amount to 2000 men, will remain attached to the Duke of Elchingen.

The 15th, 25th, 3rd, 6th, 10th, and 11th dragoons, altogether 6 regiments and nearly 5000 cavalry, will compose the cavalry reserve which is to be commanded by General Montbrun. These alone will amount to 7000.

The 1st brigade of dragoons, 1500 strong, and composed of the 1st, 2nd, and 3rd provisional regiments, will remain attached to the Duke of Abrantès. The 2nd, composed of the 6th and 7th provisional regiments, will be attached to General Kellermann; and the 3d, composed of the 8th, 9th, and 10th, to General Séras.

The Prince of Essling will therefore have 40,000 infantry and between 9000 and 10,000 cavalry, without counting the artillery, sappers and miners, &c., which will constitute for him an army of 50,000 men. He will besiege with them first Ciudad Rodrigo, and afterwards Almeida, and will thus prepare himself to march systematically on Portugal, which ought not to be entered till September, when the heats are over, and, above all, after the harvest.

Lahoussaye's division will remain with the army of the south. [*written in the Emperor's own handwriting.*]

General Reynier will proceed towards Alcantara with two divisions of infantry, forming 14,000 men, with the 1st hussars, the 22nd chasseurs, the Hanoverian chasseurs, and the 8th dragoons, altogether 2000 cavalry, which will form a corps of between 16,000 and 17,000 men.

General Reynier will thus be placed to the left of Ciudad Rodrigo, occupying Alcantara, threatening Portugal from that side, and keeping up the communication with Madrid. The Prince of Essling is to maintain him in this position, and not allow him to be driven from it.

The Prince of Essling will thus have under his command seven infantry divisions, 54,000 strong, and 11,000 cavalry, which will make an army of from 65,000 to 70,000 men.

On his right will be General Séras, who, with 9000 foot and 1500 horse, will manœuvre between Astorga, the kingdom of Leon, and Zamora, so as to keep up his communication with General Bonnet, threaten Portugal on the side of Braganza, and cover the plain of Valladolid. General Séras will be under the orders of General Kellermann, who will have 1200 cavalry, counting the Swiss and the different depôts, to keep the plain quiet. In this way General Kellermann will have at his disposal between 12,000 and 13,000 men.

It is to be added that before the Prince of Essling enters Portugal a reserve of 20,000 men will have reached Valladolid. Give all the requisite orders to the Prince of Essling and to Generals Kellermann and Séras; let General Bonnet be informed; and, lastly, let the Duke of Dalmatia know of all these arrangements.

[620.] NAPOLEON TO BERTHIER.

Havre, May 29, 1810.

My Cousin,—Order General Séras, with the 113th of the line and the regiment belonging to the legion of the Vistula, to repair to Valladolid. He will take under his command the four auxiliary battalions, of which you will desire him to take particular care: his division will thus be composed of eight battalions. The Prince of Essling will give him 1200 horse and 3000 foot, that his corps may amount to 10,000 men. With these General Séras will hold the army of Gallicia in check.

[621.] NAPOLEON TO BERTHIER.

Havre, May 29, 1810.

My Cousin,—Answer to General Dorsenne that he has absolute command over the province of Burgos, over the military as well as over the police and the finances; that the troops of all kinds, artillery, engineers, French and Spanish, and of every nation, are under his orders. Fix clearly the boundary of General Dorsenne's command; tell him that I wish him to keep his troops in constant motion to repress the banditti; that he should even send columns to the frontiers of Navarre, to the defiles of Santander, and wherever they are required; that for this purpose he must form seven or eight moveable columns, consisting of Polish light horse and young soldiers; but desire him to keep my old soldiers together, so as to lose none by any accident. The 400 Polish light horse, the 800 lancers from the Grand Duchy of Berg, make together 1200 cavalry, which he may form into six columns, adding to them one or two companies of infantry, according to circumstances. These detachments may proceed in every direction, pursue the banditti without mercy, and drive them out of the borders of Navarre and the province of Santander. Besides these, he should always have in hand between 2000 and 3000 men, infantry and cavalry, to proceed whithersoever they may be wanted.

Send word to General Dorsenne that there are more troops on their way to him; that he must, therefore obtain from Soria, Aranda, and other parts of the province, provisions enough to supply him always with 500,000 rations of biscuit and several million rations of provisions stored in the country surrounding Burgos.

Write to the Prince of Essling to let him know the extent of General Dorsenne's command, and inform him that that command is independent, as General Dorsenne may at any time receive orders from me; but that General Dorsenne is to send columns in every direction, and not to refuse anything which may keep up and secure the communications.

[622.] NAPOLEON TO BERTHIER.

Havre, May 29, 1810.

My Cousin,—Write a circular to the different marshals commanding in Spain, and to the governors, to express my displeasure that, by their orders, sums of money have been taken out of the hands of the paymasters appointed by the Minister of the Treasury; that this step is illegal, and contrary to the rules of administration.

In the Emperor's hand:—They have no right to appoint receivers; those who receive contributions must be the men of the treasury.

[623.] NAPOLEON TO BERTHIER.

Havre, May 29, 1810.

My Cousin,—Write to General Dufour that I am extremely displeased at his want of activity; that, instead of remaining idle in the town, he ought to be at the head of his columns, and proceed in all directions to destroy the banditti.

[624.] DECREE OF NAPOLEON.

Havre, May 29, 1810.

Napoleon, Emperor of the French, King of Italy, Protector of the Confederation of the Rhine, Mediator of the Swiss Confederation, &c.,—We have decreed and do decree as follows:—

Art. 1. The province of Burgos is to form a separate government, under the name of the Fifth Government of Spain.

Art. 2. The provinces of Valladolid, Palencia, and Toro, are to form a separate government, under the name of the Sixth Government.

Art. 3. The Chief of our Staff, and our Ministers of War and of the Treasury, are charged with the execution of this decree.

[625.] DECREE OF NAPOLEON.

Havre, May 29, 1810.

Napoleon, Emperor of the French, King of Italy, Protector of the Confederation of the Rhine, Mediator of the Swiss Confederation, &c.,—We have decreed and do decree as follows:—

Art. 1. In each of the six governments of Spain are to be receivers, who will be appointed by our Minister of the Treasury, and who alone will receive the revenue arising from ordinary or extraordinary contributions.

Art. 2. In the other parts of Spain the ordinary and extraordinary contributions intended for the army shall be paid into the chests of the military paymasters.

Art. 3. The six receivers established in the six governments, and the paymasters acting as receivers in the other parts of Spain, will correspond with the receiver-general of the contributions of Spain, who will reside at Bayonne.

Art. 4. All our generals, intendants, and civil and military officers in our armies, are expressly ordered to have the contributions paid only into the receivers' chests for the six governments, and into the paymasters' chests for the other parts of Spain.

Art. 5. The receivers appointed by any other authority than that of our Minister of the Treasury will cease their functions as soon as this decree is made public, and will repair to Paris with the utmost diligence, and carry all the papers containing accounts of their receipts and expenditure to our Minister of the Treasury.

Art. 6. The Chief of our Staff, and our Ministers of the Treasury and of War, are charged with the execution of this decree as it concerns them respectively.

[626.] NAPOLEON TO BERTHIER.

Rambouillet, July 10, 1810.

My Cousin,—Order the 2nd division of the rear-guard of the army of Spain to continue its operations in Navarre, with the exception of the 1st provisional regiment, which is to remain at Tolosa, and to keep the whole province of St. Sebastian. This arrangement will allow the posts of my guard to collect together at Vittoria and Bilbao.

The 1st provisional regiment will stay in the province of St. Sebastian till fresh troops arrive to take its place. Desire General Reille to send back to their corps all the troops which do not belong to him. With his 6000 men, the gendarmes, and the two squadrons of the 9th hussars, he ought to re-establish order in Navarre.

[627.] NAPOLEON TO BERTHIER.

Rambouillet, July 10, 1810.

My Cousin,—Write to General Dorsenne that he is to scour the country, by keeping in constant motion six or seven columns, composed each of 200 cavalry, and from 600 to 700 infantry, and to combine their movements so that two or three may always be able to unite. Ask him why this has not been done already, and tell him to take advantage of the harvest to fill his magazines at Burgos.

[628.] NAPOLEON TO BERTHIER.

Rambouillet, July 14, 1810.

My Cousin,—Write to General Reynier that I am waiting to hear that he has raised contributions in the country which he occupies, in order to feed and pay his troops; that war is supported by war. Write the same thing to General Dorsenne; tell him that as yet I have not seen one letter from him giving an account of his administration, of the contributions which he levies, and of his resources. Send the annexed letter* to the King, to let him know that he must provide for the wants of the army.

[629.] INSTRUCTIONS FOR THE DUKE OF DALMATIA.

Rambouillet, July 14, 1810.

I enclose to you, M. le Duc, an Imperial decree, which M. le Duc de Feltre, the Minister of War, has sent to me. You will see by this decree that the Emperor has considered it expedient for the good of his service to appoint you commander-in-chief of his army of the South in Spain. His Majesty's object in this arrangement is, that your authority and your movements may be more direct and unembarrassed.

* The next letter but one.—TR.

In the Emperor's hand:—It must be added that I wished to throw the responsibility upon him.

The territory subject to your army extends to the left of the Sierra-Morena. His Majesty's desire is, that you should take the most effectual means of providing for the pay and the requirements of your army. You must act on the principle that war is supported by war. You must push forward the operations on Cadiz, and take measures for getting rid of the banditti. His Majesty supposes that you have occupied and entrenched the most important posts, to keep open your communications, and to prevent their being insulted by the banditti which infest the country.

If necessary, M. le Duc, the Emperor authorizes you to sell the English goods, and even to levy [*in the Emperor's hand*] extraordinary contributions, to supply the wants of your army. In case the ordinary contributions be not sufficient for the pay, you must raise large contributions, chiefly upon the countries which are yet unsubdued.

Your appointment as commander-in-chief of the army of the South makes no change in the actual state of things, since in fact you already command. A few words in your general orders will be enough. This new arrangement ought to excite as little sensation as possible.

I need not remind you of the respect which you owe to the King. You must act in concert with his ministers, although you have in reality the chief command. The Emperor did not choose to leave the movements of his army of the South any longer undecided. He thought that it was time to prove the confidence with which you have inspired him. Your talents prevented his having any doubt as to who should fill so important a command.

N.B. Write to the Dukes of Belluno and of Treviso, and to General Sebastiani, to give them notice that they form part of the army of the South, under the command of the Duke of Dalmatia.

[630.] BERTHIER TO JOSEPH.

Rambouillet, July 14, 1810.

Sire,—The Emperor commands me to have the honour of writing to your Majesty to inform you that, in consequence of your residence at Madrid, he considers the army of Andalusia as having no immediate chief, the Duke of Dalmatia having no legal authority; so that no one is responsible for what may happen to the three corps which combine their operations in the south of Spain, in the event of the slightest disturbance or insubordination on the part of one of the commanders of the three corps [*five illegible words in the Emperor's handwriting*], to form one army of the South, composed of the 1st, 4th, and 5th corps. Your Majesty sees that the appointment of a general directly responsible will enable the operations of this army to be more rapid. The Duke of Dalmatia, as he has been so fortunate as to deserve your Majesty's confidence, and also that of the Emperor, might be intrusted with this command.

The Emperor, Sire, is deeply grieved to hear that the army which is laying siege to Cadiz is in a state of complete destitution —that their pay is nine months in arrear. This state of things may be productive of serious misfortunes. His Majesty can send to Spain no more than the two millions a month which he has assigned to that employment, because the money of France is exhausted; because, in the present state of affairs in Spain, war must support war; because all the resources in the country must be employed to feed, pay, and clothe the troops which conquer it; because to discipline and pay Spanish troops is to discipline and pay one's enemies; because, lastly, soldiers must be paid before civilians, and above all the French troops, who alone support your Majesty in Spain. The Emperor thinks that Seville, Cordova, Malaga, and all those fine countries, ought to supply abundantly the wants of the army of the South, and furnish its pay.

[631.] BERTHIER TO SUCHET.

Rambouillet, July 14, 1810.

The Emperor, M. le Général Compte de Suchet, desires me to tell you that he wishes you, as soon as you have taken Tortosa, to put it into the hands of the Duke of Taranto, and to assemble your army in Aragon, to enable you to second the invasion of Portugal, which his Majesty proposes after the capture of Tortosa and Tarragona [*illegible words in the Emperor's writing*]. Divide your army into two bodies. With the first, consisting of about 15,000 men, you will march towards Valladolid, manœuvring so as to support our operations until the English have been beaten and driven into the sea. You will leave the other corps, consisting of 12,000 men, to hold Aragon; and as soon as the English are turned out of Portugal, you will return to Aragon with your first 15,000 men, and march upon Valencia with your whole army. At the same time the army of Catalonia will send a division by Tortosa, and the Duke of Dalmatia will assist your expedition with a corps of from 15,000 to 20,000 men.

While you are marching upon Valladolid, the horses belonging to your siege artillery will recover themselves, and your siege materials will be repaired ready for the attack upon Valencia.

[*In the Emperor's writing.*] In short, you must take Tortosa, and afterwards assemble your army and hold yourself ready to execute the Emperor's orders. You must, however, be somewhat governed by events; and after the capture of Tortosa you must not leave that part of the country without the Emperor's orders.

[632.] NAPOLEON TO BERTHIER.

St. Cloud, July 19, 1810.

My Cousin,—Order three millions to be sent in one convoy to the head-quarters of the army of the South, escorted by a corps of 1200 men, which is to be formed by General Quesnel at Bayonne, of all the available detachments from the 1st, 4th, and 5th corps, and of all that can be obtained from the Polish depôts. You will put this escort under the command of one of your aides-de-camp, or of an intelligent colonel, who will have orders to take this convoy untouched to its destination, and will be responsible that no money be subtracted from it, even at Madrid. He will carry an order from me to this effect. Governors Thouvenot and Dorsenne will make arrangements for adding to this escort of 1200 men, detachments of infantry and cavalry from every post in their governments. Write to the Dukes of Dalmatia, Belluno, and Treviso, and to General Sebastiani, that they also are to reinforce the escort in La Mancha and in the districts occupied by their armies. This convoy of three millions will go straight to

Seville. It is intended to bring up all arrears in the pay of the army of the South.

[633.] NAPOLEON TO CLARKE.

St. Cloud, July 27, 1810.

M. le Duc de Feltre,—Let the King of Naples know that all his troops in Spain desert, and are in a wretched state, and that I will have no more of them. Order Maréchal Perignon not to send any more, and General Miollis to let none pass. They are a gang of thieves, and poison the country through which they pass.

You do not say that Girona is destroyed, nor whether my orders have been fulfilled with respect to the destruction of Lerida.

[634.] BERTHIER TO MASSÉNA.

Paris, July 29, 1810.

The Emperor, M. le Prince d'Essling, desires me to express to you his satisfaction on the important capture of Ciudad Rodrigo. His Majesty sees with pleasure that according to your arrangements Almeida is now invested. It is essential to take Almeida as well as the fortress of the Concepcion; you will then be well supported when you march on Lisbon.

Ciudad Rodrigo ought to be put in good order, and to be the general depôt for the army of Portugal, both for provisions and ammunition. You have of course ordered the harvest to be brought in, and have collected in Ciudad Rodrigo all the provisions which can be obtained.

The Emperor is of opinion that Almeida may be taken towards the end of August, and that in the beginning of September you may be ready to march upon Lisbon. His Majesty leaves it to you to give battle or not to the English, as you think proper.

The Emperor considers that Badajoz ought not to be taken, as it would engage us in a long siege, and afterwards it would be necessary to lay siege to Elvas, which is stronger still; but when once the English have been well beaten, and have re-embarked, Badajoz and Elvas will fall of themselves.

General Drouet [in the Emperor's hand] *will reach Valladolid on the 1st of September with a corps of infantry and cavalry amounting to* 12,000 *men*, which, joined to the divisions of Séras and Bonnet, will form an army able to hold Gallicia in check, and to take possession of it as soon as you have marched on Lisbon [in the Emperor's handwriting], *or to keep up your communications.*

[635.] NAPOLEON TO BERTHIER.

St. Cloud, July 21, 1810.

My Cousin,—I send you back the Prince of Essling's proposals for granting rewards on account of the capture of Ciudad Rodrigo. Let me know the names of the individuals mentioned in the despatches relating to the capture or to the details of the siege, and tell me what rewards you propose. Let me also know what regiments were employed in the siege; they alone have a right to be rewarded.

[636.] NAPOLEON TO CLARKE.

St. Cloud, Aug. 3, 1810.

M. le Duc de Feltre,—The 9th corps of the army of Spain will be composed of two divisions, the 1st commanded by General Claparède, the 2nd by General Conroux, who is useless in Catalonia.

General Cottin will command the artillery, Colonel Dubreuille the engineers. Brigadier-General Fournier will command the whole of the cavalry. Brigadier-General Gérard will be employed in one of these divisions. General Dupellin, late colonel of the 85th, will be ordered to join Friant's division. Propose to me another brigadier to put in his place.

I do not approve of 12-pounders being replaced by 8-pounders. I choose to have 12-pounders: they are more useful in Spain than elsewhere, because they are wanted against convents and against the walls of the smaller towns. There are a great many 12-pounders at Burgos. General Drouet, having gunners, horses, and ammunition, may take 12-pounders from thence.

To take your artillery companies from Boulogne seems going too far. Have you none at Toulouse, or in the islands of Ré and Oleron?

I approve of your sending some Dutch artillery officers. I will not have any of the artillery belonging to my army of the North sent to Bayonne; the distance is too great. Keep back 300 horses from the train intended for Seville.

I think that the 5th company of the 2nd battalion, and the 5th company of the 1st battalion of sappers and miners at Alexandria, are too far off to be sent for; find some who are nearer.

It is necessary to have some waggons filled with engineering tools in the suite of the army. All these things will be found at Metz.

[637.] NAPOLEON TO BERTHIER.

Trianon, Aug. 8, 1810.

My Cousin,—Let the Prince of Essling know that the 44th battalion of the flotilla which is at Valladolid is at his disposal, and that it will be of use to him in crossing rivers, and above all when he crosses the Tagus before Lisbon.

If there are any shoes at Bayonne, order 6000 to be sent to Burgos.

Write to General Bonnet that he is authorised to send back to their depôts the invalided officers and soldiers who are unfit for active service. Tell him also that, if the regiments under his orders are reduced to less than 2000 present under arms, he had better send back to France the cadre of the 4th battalion, distributing the men among the other battalions, but not unless these regiments are reduced to less than 2000 men.

Write to General Drouet that on his arrival at Tolosa he is to obtain information with respect to Navarre, and that, if it is in so bad a state that his presence is absolutely indispensable, he may turn aside to re-establish order, and to pursue the banditti vigorously; but he is not to make this expedition if it be not absolutely necessary.

[638.] NAPOLEON TO CLARKE.

Aug. 6, 1810.

M. le Duc de Feltre,—I see in the 'Journal de l'Empire' that the 5th marching battalion, consisting of 1,000 men left Naples for Catalonia on the 25th of July. Order this battalion to be stopped as soon as it is met with, to be examined and kept back till further orders. I have no wish to crowd Catalonia with bad soldiers, or to increase the troops of banditti. If this battalion be composed of convicts or of banditti, or even ill clothed and armed, it must be sent back to Naples.

Write to the King, for his guidance in future, that I do not want any more Neapolitan troops in Spain, and that I will have no more.

[639.] JOSEPH TO NAPOLEON.

Madrid, Aug. 8, 1810.

Sire,—My position in this country, always difficult, often deplorable, is now such that it cannot continue under the arrangements which have been made and are threatened.

I shall endeavour to let the answer which I hope from your Majesty find me in Madrid, but I implore you not to make me wait long for it, for things are stronger than men; and on the day when I shall be completely abandoned by my guard, by my servants, and by all that constitutes a government, my only course will be to return to France to put myself at the disposition of your Majesty, requesting you to allow me to join my family, from which I have been separated for six years, and to find in obscurity and in domestic affections a peace of which the throne has robbed me, without giving me any thing in exchange. I find it a seat of punishment, from which I look passively on the devastation of a country which I had hoped to make happy.

I cannot now, as I did last year, take refuge in the army. When I was fighting the enemies of your Majesty and of Spain, my eyes were drawn aside from the sights which now afflict me, and my position was, at least, not dishonourable. If what is rumoured by the officers who come from Paris, and rendered probable by the Prince of Neufchâtel's letter of the 14th of July, turns out to be true; if your Majesty deprives me of the command of the army of Andalusia, and devotes the revenues of the province exclusively to the army, I have nothing to do but to throw up the game; in so doing I should be scarcely a free agent. In the present state of affairs in Spain the commander-in-chief in a province is its king. All its resources become inadequate, because what are called the wants of the army are indefinite, and the general increases them as he sees the means of supplying them. Thus the provinces commanded by generals who are not under my orders are nothing to me. In Andalusia alone I hoped to find a few resources, after having assigned to the army what was supposed to be sufficient, if your Majesty continues to send two millions every month. But to give the command of the troops to a general who does not recognise my authority, is to give him the administration and the government of the country. It is to take from me the only province in which I could hope to live: it is to confine me to Madrid, which gives me only 800,000 francs per month, while my indispensable expenses exceed four millions per month. I am here surrounded by the ruins of a great nation. I have a guard, I have depôts, I have hospitals, a garrison, a household, a ministry, a privy-council, refugees from all the other provinces, &c. &c. Even if my honour, if the sentiment of what is due to me allowed me to maintain so humiliating a position, this state of things could not last two months. For, in fact, if the army of Andalusia is taken from me, what shall I be? The porter of the hospitals of Madrid and of the depôts of the army, and the jailor of the prisoners.

Sire, I am your brother. You presented me to Spain as a second self. I feel the exaggeration of this praise as respects my talents, but I shall not fall below it as respects the truthfulness of my character, the magnanimity of my feelings, and the tenderness of my love for my brother.

I always hoped that your Majesty would come to Spain. With this expectation I bore up against every thing; but this hope recedes, and circumstances press on me. The step which I take is involuntary. I send to your Majesty M. Almenara, who has been my Minister of Finance since the death of M. de Cabarrus, and who knows the wretched details of his own office and of those of the other ministers, so as to enable your Majesty to act with full knowledge.

As for myself, Sire, who owe to you my full opinion, and give it to you, after having above expressed my unalterable decision, I think that if, in the first place, the French army is put under my orders; if, in the second place, I have a right to send back the officers who behave manifestly ill; if, thirdly, I am authorised to tranquillise the nation as to the changes of nationality and the partitions with which all who come from Paris threaten it; if, fourthly, your Majesty relies on me sufficiently to allow me to say and write to the Spaniards what appears to me suitable to their position and to mine, without being exposed to the poisonous interpretations of malignity and of sententious mediocrity; on these conditions I engage, 1st, that the French army shall not cost France one farthing beyond the two millions a-month which your Majesty has already dedicated to it (I hope, indeed, that in a few months I could release your Majesty from this burthen); 2ndly, that Spain will soon be made as quiet as Naples was; and, 3rdly, that Spain will soon be as useful to France as she is now mischievous.

If, on the contrary, I am forced to retire, and the provinces are divided into military governments, and ruled by generals, I fear that your Majesty will not witness the last of these terrible convulsions.

I implore your Majesty to see in this letter only what I have endeavoured to put into it—the simple truth, dictated by the fraternal friendship which attached me to you in your cradle, and, whatever may happen, will accompany me to my tomb. Can the emotion which I feel at this instant, and which interrupts my writing, be caused by personal feelings or by selfish regret? No, Sire, it is not so. I weep over the weakness of human nature; over the dispersion of a family once so united; over the change in the heart of my brother; over the gradual diminution of an immense glory, which would have been better preserved by generosity and heroism than by any extension of power.

Sire, if the conclusion of my letter does not recall to you the tender and valued friend of your infancy; if it does not tell you that I am to you what no other man can be, I have nothing to do but to retire.

P. S. During the two days which have elapsed since I wrote this letter, my position in Madrid has become still more dangerous, and I think of moving into Andalusia. It is possible that I may be there when your Majesty receives this letter.*

[640.] NAPOLEON TO BERTHIER.

St. Cloud, Aug. 14, 1810.

My Cousin,—Answer to the Prince of Essling that you have shown me his letter of the . . . of July, and that I have desired you to tell him that he is to repress severely all disorder and insubordination; that it is he who commands; that he ought to put an end to robbery, and to manage so that all the money which is raised for contributions may be employed for the benefit of the army; and that the slightest negligence in this respect is criminal.

[641.] NAPOLEON TO BERTHIER.

St. Cloud, Aug. 19, 1810.

My Cousin,—I am surprised that you have heard nothing of General Drouet. Let me know when his troops reached Bayonne. Write to General Drouet, as well as to General Dorsenne, that I think it advisable to reinforce Navarre with the whole of the Berg lancers, which, with the 9th hussars, will put 1500 cavalry under General Reille's orders. I also think that the brigade of the guard under General Dumoutier's command had better be sent to General Reille. He will therefore have his four marching regiments, the 5th, which he retains, two squadrons of the 9th hussars, and, lastly, the four regiments of the guard, with their horses, and the regiment of lancers. General Drouet may replace the regiments of the guard with some of the troops which

* This letter was not answered.—TR.

he brought from France. Write to him that I am too far off to give these orders positively; that I leave it to him either to execute them or to substitute others which he thinks more suitable; that what inclines me to send the regiments of the guard to General Reille is, that they are more accustomed to serve under him, and that, therefore, there will be less chance of insubordination; that besides, as the guard is intended for active service, it will be suitably employed in his hands. You will send General Dorsenne's orders open to General Drouet, who will send them on if he thinks proper. I wish you to choose for me four or five colonels, lieut.-colonels, or majors, all men of action, for General Reille to put at the head of his moveable columns; such men, for instance, as Colonel Ameil of the 24th chasseurs.

Order General Burke to proceed to Navarre, to serve under General Reille. Desire him to run no risks in the Spanish roads, and not to move without a strong escort.

[642.] BERTHIER TO THE GOVERNORS OF THE PROVINCES.

[CIRCULAR.]

Paris, Sept. 15, 1810.

I told you, M. le Général, in my letter of the 22nd of July, that I had been informed that there existed abuses in the collection of the contributions in some of the provinces of Spain, and I desired you to endeavour to put an end to them, and to prevent their occurring in your government. It appears from the information which I have lately received that the irregularity still continues in some parts of Spain. The complaints which ensue excite the displeasure of the Emperor. His Majesty's wish is that all the funds raised by contributions or by extraordinary taxes be paid into the hands of the officers of the treasury, to furnish the pay and requirements of the army, and that every individual guilty of peculation in collecting these funds be severely punished, as contributing towards keeping up the spirit of rebellion by exasperating the inhabitants against the French administration.

[643.] Napoleon to Berthier.

St. Cloud, Sept. 16, 1810.

My Cousin,—Write to General Suchet that, after the capture of Tortosa and Tarragona, Valencia will no doubt be his next object if circumstances allow it; and that our affairs with Portugal seem to be making so much progress that I probably shall decide on his marching upon Valencia when he has taken both those towns. Tell him that I have read the report of Colonel Haxo, of the engineers; that if it is possible to hold the citadel and fortifications of Lerida with 1000 men, I consent to preserving the walls of the town; but that the forts must be armed and provisioned, and only light artillery placed upon the walls, in order that, if necessary, it may be removed to the citadel, and that the heavy artillery and the real defence must be in the forts.

[644.] Napoleon to Berthier.

St. Cloud, Sept. 16, 1810.

My Cousin,—I am told that many Spaniards are sending their merinos to France, and that a flock of 10,000 is on its way. Order my generals and other authorities to protect the passage of these animals into France.

[645.] Napoleon to Berthier.

St. Cloud, Sept. 16, 1810.

My Cousin,—Write a letter to General Girard in my name to express my satisfaction at his good conduct in the affair of Villa Garcia; and insert in the order of the day that on this occasion I recognised the accustomed bravery of the troops of the 5th corps. Propose to me the rewards for which General Girard asks, both as regards the Legion of Honour and promotion.

[646.] Napoleon to Berthier.

Sept. 17, 1810.

My Cousin,—Let General Drouet know that serious complaints are lodged against the general in command of Santander; that I wish him to be superseded by another general, and a severe inquiry to be set on foot into the depredations which have been committed in the country, and that the same thing is to be done with regard to General Avril. You will write to him that great fault is found with General Drouet's nephew; that striking examples must be made; that the corruption is carried so far that the liberation of prisoners is made a matter of traffic; that I desire him to use the utmost zeal in hunting up these abuses. Tell him that similar depredations are committed in Biscay. Order him to seize all the depôts of colonial merchandise, cotton, sugar, coffee, &c., in the Biscays, in Navarre, and on the frontiers, which are intended to be smuggled into France. You will let him know that I do not wish my consuls on the coast to be displaced; that he is to allow them to correspond with the Minister for Foreign Affairs, and that I have not abolished the consulships. Write also to General Drouet that I desire him to obtain information on the contributions which have been levied in the provinces of Spain; that I require them to be all paid into the military treasury and employed for the benefit of the soldiers. Tell him that I pay the greatest attention to this subject, and that I shall require an account of all the contributions which are raised.

[647.] NAPOLEON TO BERTHIER.

Sept. 17, 1810.

My Cousin,—Heavy charges are brought to me on all sides against General X——. Send an officer to him with a letter, in which you will express to him my extreme displeasure at the abuses committed in his government; and ask him for a categorical statement of all the contributions which he has levied. In his government, at Valladolid, for instance, even the liberation of the prisoners of war is sold. Tell him that I consider him responsible for abuses which are so opposed to the well-being and the interests of the army. Let him know that I have asked for a report on these complaints; that the officer whom you send is desired to bring back an answer in which I expect you to be told that he has arrested the individuals guilty of these crimes, and tried them by a court-martial. Give him to understand that, if he does not deal severely with these horrible abuses and remedy them, I shall believe the general rumour that he connives at them. Tell him that, of all the governments in Spain, his is that in which most robbery is perpetrated.

[648.] NAPOLEON TO BERTHIER.

Sept. 17, 1810.

My Cousin,—Extortions of every kind are committed in Spain; even the freedom of the prisoners is made a subject of traffic. Send an officer with the letter which you are to write to General X——. Write at the same time to the Prince of Essling to arrest the individuals guilty of these crimes. Send officers to examine the garrison of Ciudad Rodrigo,* and especially the commanding officer of the artillery, from whom it is said that 200,000 reals were asked as a price for which the garrison would be allowed to go free. Desire General Buquet to inquire into this affair. It is time to put an end to this robbery. The Prince of Essling, in one of his letters of the 30th of August, says that he sent to you a return of the contributions levied by the Duke of ——, and not paid in. You did not show me this return. Let me have a report on the subject.

[649.] NAPOLEON TO BERTHIER.

Fontainebleau, Sept. 17, 1810.

My Cousin,—The rumour of a marriage between Prince Ferdinand and a Princess of Austria gains considerable credit. It is important that you should write to all the generals who have the command of corps in your army, to warn them that this report is a mere piece of gossip, the fruit of the idleness of Paris; that they ought to reject with indignation the bare idea of our making a retrograde step; and that nothing of the kind has ever been thought of.

* Apparently the Spanish prisoners belonging to that garrison.—TR.

[650.] NAPOLEON TO BERTHIER.

Fontainebleau, Sept. 18, 1810.

My Cousin,—I see that General Kellermann exhibits utter carelessness, and that, instead of placing his forces so as to support the army of Portugal, he allows them to be scattered in every direction. It seems to me that I included the province of Avila in the district of the army of the centre. Write again to General Drouet that I attach the greatest importance to receiving news from the army of Portugal; that the attempt to hold every post is impracticable; that he must content himself with holding only those in which there are depôts and hospitals, and must keep his troops in hand ready to act wherever they may be wanted, and, above all, on the rear of the army of Portugal.

[651.] NAPOLEON TO BERTHIER.

St. Cloud, Sept. 19, 1810.

My Cousin,—Send off to-morrow an officer with a letter for the Prince of Essling, in which you will let him know that it is my wish that he attack and destroy the English; * that Lord Wellington has not more than 18,000 men, of whom only 15,000 are infantry, and the rest cavalry and artillery; that General Hill has only 6000 infantry and cavalry; that it would be absurd for 25,000 English to hold in check 60,000 French: that if they are attacked boldly and without hesitation, they will experience great reverses. The troops to be left in the rear should be the provisional regiments of cavalry. The army has 12,000 horse; only 6000 are wanted in Portugal: there are, therefore, 6000 to leave between Ciudad Rodrigo, Alcantara, and Salamanca. The Prince of Essling should leave with them some guns, for artillery is the complement to cavalry. The Prince of Essling has four times as much artillery as is needed against the enemy's army. I am too far off, and the position of the enemy changes too often, for me to give advice as to the way in which the attack should

* The battle of Busaco was fought on the 28th of September, 1810. Masséna could scarcely have received this letter, but acted in its spirit.—TR.

be conducted; but it is certain that he is not in a state to resist it. According to the best intelligence, derived from secret sources in London, if to the British army in the Peninsula you add 4000 men who are at Cadiz, you will find that it consists of 28,000 men, and this is the entire strength of the English, though they have reinforced their army from Malta and Sicily.

[652.] NAPOLEON TO CLARKE.

Fontainebleau, Sept. 27, 1810.

M. le Duc de Feltre,—Order the officer of the depôt of the 28th dragoons, who was desired to furnish 100 men to the marching regiment of dragoons belonging to the army of Catalonia, and who presided over the formation of this detachment, to be placed under arrest for a month.

The detachment sent by this officer was in so bad a condition that Prince Borghese very properly sent it back; it was composed of men taken from the hospitals or on the point of being discharged; bad horses were substituted for good ones,—for instance, there was a lame waggon-horse, and two trumpeters'-horses, both lame and blind. The coats, trousers, boots, &c., belonging to the dragoons were taken away, and old rags given to them instead; their pistols were without cocks or pans. Their saddles, housings, cloaks, saddle-bags, all had been changed and replaced by worn-out articles.

Let me know the name of the officer who dared to take such a liberty, and order the depôt of the 28th to furnish immediately another 100 dragoons, well mounted and equipped, in good health, and able to take an active part.

[653.] NAPOLEON TO BERTHIER.

Fontainebleau, Sept. 28, 1810, at night.

My Cousin,—In my two letters of this evening I told you that I had altered the employment of General Drouet, and that I was most anxious that he should repair as soon as possible to Valladolid, in order to watch the rear of the army of Portugal. I told you that General Reille, who is in Navarre, had under his orders the division of the rear-guard, composed of four provisional regiments, more than 8000 strong, and Dumoutier's division of the guard, which amounts to more than 6000, making altogether 14,000 men; the two squadrons of the 9th hussars, 900 strong, and of the Grand Duchy of Berg, 800 strong. General Reille, therefore, has 15,000 men; order him to provide himself with a division of artillery with 6 pieces, which, added to General Dumoutier's artillery, will form a corps with which he may go all over Spain. The 5 regiments forming Claparède's division will receive orders to proceed to Valladolid. The two squadrons of the 20th, of the 7th, and of the 13th chasseurs, making 1500 men, will follow in the same direction. The battalion of Neufchâtel will join this division. General Dorsenne will contribute waggons for the infantry, 4 howitzers, and 2 guns, with 250 rounds of ammunition for each of General Drouet's guns. The addition of from 10,000 to 12,000 men, with Séras' division and 4000 or 5000 cavalry, will make General Drouet strong enough to beat all the Spanish armies that may fall in with him, to keep a strong hold upon Ciudad Rodrigo and Almeida, to march to the assistance of Astorga, and to keep up his communications with General Bonnet. Meanwhile, his 2nd division, of which two demi-brigades reached Bayonne long since, will repair to Vittoria as fast as they can; the other two demi-brigades will follow them. See that these four demi-brigades have their field-pieces.

Biscay will thus be held, but it must have a Commander-in-chief. Order my aide-de-camp, General Caffarelli, whom I intended to place at the head of the division of reserve in Catalonia, to start in the course of to-morrow, and to travel post to Vittoria, where he will take the command of the three provinces of Biscay and of Santander. You will instruct him to act in concert with Generals Reille, Dorsenne, and Bonnet, to keep all quiet in our rear, and to secure our communications. You will give him information as to all the troops which are in Biscay, and the demi-brigades which are on their way; and you will order Generals Thouvenot and Barthélemy to consider themselves under his orders. The Minister of War will order the 1st and

2d provisional regiments of light-horse, which are to reach Niort to-day, to go straight to Vittoria. By this means General Caffarelli will have under his command in Biscay two infantry regiments, consisting of six battalions, and four squadrons of horse. Notice must be given to General Drouet, that if, before the arrival of Claparède's division, and of General Fournier's cavalry, he is obliged to collect his detachments in order to march upon any troops threatening Ciudad Rodrigo or Almeida, he must call in his smaller outposts. In this case he must communicate with Madrid more slowly, and diminish the number of couriers and expresses, and, to ensure their arrival, send them once a week, or twice if possible, with large escorts. Tell General Drouet to take General Thiébault as chief of his staff. His acquaintance with Gallicia and Portugal will make him useful. Let General Thiébault know that I expect him to assist General Drouet by all the means in his power, and that the services which he will render on this occasion will give me great satisfaction. Write to General Drouet, that when he passes through Burgos he is to take one of the squadrons of gendarmes which are there. You had better repeat the order to send off General Conroux's two demi-brigades from Bayonne, and the two others as soon as they arrive. You must also reiterate the order to send off the 600 artillery horses from Bayonne to Burgos, if they have not already started.

[654.] NAPOLEON TO BERTHIER.

Fontainebleau, Sept. 28, 1810.

My Cousin,—Order General Thouvenot to confiscate all the English and colonial merchandise in his government. I am assured that he has let in English goods on paying a duty of 10 per cent. If this is true, he must pay back these sums and confiscate the goods which he has permitted to land. In so doing he committed a great fault.

[655.] NAPOLEON TO BERTHIER.

Fontainebleau, Sept. 28, 1810.

My Cousin,—Order General Drouet to go in person to Valladolid without delay, to take the command of the troops in Old Castile, with the title of Commandant of the 9th corps of the army of Spain, and to protect Almeida, Ciudad Rodrigo, Salamanca, and Astorga. Give orders to Generals Kellermann and Séras, to the Commandants of Ciudad Rodrigo and Almeida, and to all the Commandants of my forces in the rear of the army of Portugal, whatever their titles may be, to obey General Drouet's commands.

You will let General Drouet know that he will have under his orders, in the first place, General Séras' division, composed of the 113th of the line, the 4th regiment of the 1st legion of the Vistula, the 4th battalion of the 12th light infantry, the 32nd and 58th of the line, the 2nd, 4th, and 5th, and 7th auxiliary battalions, the 4th brigade of dragoons, consisting of the 9th and 10th provisional regiments; making in the whole from 6000 to 7000 infantry and 1500 cavalry; that he is also to have a battalion of the guard, 4 Swiss battalions, and 1200 dragoons of the 6th and 7th provisional regiments. He will, therefore, have more than 3000 horse. Besides these forces, he will have his own corps d'armée. With this cavalry General Drouet will be master of the field, and may bring together all his detachments to march to the assistance of Ciudad Rodrigo and Almeida, and afterwards return to the aid of Astorga. The hospitals and establishments which are at Benevento and elsewhere should be placed in fortresses or in Valladolid.

The above-mentioned troops are, no doubt, not enough to hold every post in Old Castile; but General Drouet, with a column of 8000 foot and 2000 horse, will be able without withdrawing troops from the most important posts, to prevent Ciudad Rodrigo and Almeida from being blockaded, or at any rate to raise the blockade. The Prince of Essling must have left several thousand horses in his rear, as he was ordered to leave behind him the provisional brigades of dragoons. I count on General

Drouet's reaching Valladolid the first week in October, to be ready to execute the necessary manœuvres.

You will desire General Drouet, when he leaves Vittoria, to order Claparède's division, composed of five provisional demi-brigades, to start for Valladolid, as well as the 20th and 7th chasseurs, and 13th chasseurs, which reached Bayonne on the 25th. These three regiments will give more than 1500 first-rate cavalry.

With regard to the 2nd division, the two demi-brigades which have reached Bayonne, and which have been ordered to repair to Vittoria, will be enough to keep the province quiet, and will await the arrival of the other two demi-brigades.

Dumoutier's brigade, with General Reille's division, reinforced by the 5th provisional regiment, which ought already to be incorporated into it, altogether 12,000 men, are more than sufficient to hold Navarre.

The other two demi-brigades, which are to reach Bayonne immediately, will join the two first at Vittoria and reinforce the 2nd division, which General Drouet may withdraw, as there is another division on its way to Biscay.

SUMMARY.

General Drouet will set off twenty-four hours after he receives your order, which you will send to him by an officer. He will immediately set in march for Valladolid the five demi-brigades forming his 1st division, and his six squadrons of horse.

As it passes through Burgos, the 1st division will be joined by the battalion of Neufchâtel with its two pieces of cannon.

Let these orders be given immediately.

[656.] NAPOLEON TO BERTHIER.

Fontainebleau, Sept. 29, 1810.

My Cousin,—Desire the Duke of Dalmatia to march directly with the 5th corps on La Romana, so as to hold him in check if he should attempt to cross the Tagus, or to attack the rear of the army of Portugal. Let the Duke know that the English have weakened themselves in Cadiz to reinforce their army in Portugal; that he has more troops than he wants; that his chief object should be to make a diversion; and that he is to support himself on the army of Portugal.

Write to the King that I am forming an army of the centre, which will consist of his guard, and of all the Spanish foot and horse; of the 26th regiment of chasseurs, of the Hanoverian Dutch, and Westphalian chasseurs; of General Lorge's division of dragoons, making nearly 4000 cavalry; and of two divisions of infantry, the first composed of the French regiments in Dessolles' division, or, instead of this division, of the battalions in the district of the army of the centre, amounting to 6000 men; and of the 2nd division of the troops of the Confederation of the Rhine, also amounting to 6000, which will make either way more than 15,000 men; that it is necessary to form a division of artillery to add to this army, that it may be in a condition to proceed whithersoever it may be wanted.

You will also tell the King that the Duke of Dalmatia has orders to press on the rear of La Romana, not to let him cross the Tagus, and to hold him in check.

Let the King and the Duke of Dalmatia know that General Drouet is on his way to Valladolid, with the 9th corps, to take the command of the country in the rear of the army of Portugal; that General Caffarelli is on his way to Vittoria to take the command of the provinces of Biscay and of Santander; that I am expecting to hear of the capture of Tortosa, which will be followed by that of Tarragona; and that we shall then be able to march upon Valencia with 25,000 men.

[657.] NAPOLEON TO BERTHIER.

Fontainebleau, Oct. 2, 1810.

My Cousin,—Send an officer from your Staff to order General Suchet to despatch, as best he can, three convoys to Barcelona, each of them consisting of 5000 quintals, either in flour or corn, to provision the town. The first convoy must arrive in the course of the month of November, the second in December, and the 3rd in January. You will also let him know that as soon as the first convoy has left Aragon, a sum equivalent to its value will be sent to him from Barcelona, towards the pay of his army. Tell him likewise that the army of Portugal under the command of the Prince of Essling, commenced on the 16th of September its march into the interior of Portugal. As soon as Tortosa is taken, it must be provisioned, and arrangements made for the siege of Tarragona, while, at the same time, detachments are to threaten Valencia. The glory of subduing this important province is reserved for General Suchet, after Catalonia has been reduced. But above all, it is of the greatest consequence to supply Barcelona well with provisions, that the new garrison which the Emperor intends to put into it may be able to subsist there, and to hold the country in subjection.

[658.] NAPOLEON TO BERTHIER.

Fontainebleau, Oct. 3, 1810.

My Cousin,—I send to you a decree which I have issued, to the effect that, in the six governments which I have established in Spain, English and colonial goods be seized and confiscated, and that all the goods which have been taken in prizes or sold by my agents, be subject to the duties mentioned in my decrees of the 5th of August and the 12th of September last. Send a courier to the Duke of Dalmatia and the Prince of Essling, and write to the King of Spain that all colonial and British goods are to be confiscated, and the others subjected to the tariff. This will give considerable funds.

[659.] NAPOLEON TO BERTHIER.

Fontainebleau, Oct. 4, 1810.

My Cousin,—I approve of the plan for the formation of the army of the centre under the comand of the King of Spain, with General Belliard as Chief of the Staff, and at the same time Governor of Madrid, and General Dessolles at the head of the French division. I think that you do not allow sufficient cavalry to this corps. You deprive them of the four regiments of Lahoussaye's division and the two regiments belonging to Marisy's brigade. I think that it will be enough if you withdraw the two regiments belonging to Digeon's brigade, which form part of Lahoussaye's division, and are on the other side of the Sierra Morena; and that they must be replaced by the two regiments belonging to Marisy's brigade, which you will put under the orders of General Lahoussaye. By this means the King will have a cavalry division consisting of four French regiments. This army will, therefore, have 4000 horse, including the royal guard; this number it requires.

I send you back your plan, that you may return it to me with these corrections. You must also divide into districts the provinces of Segovia, Avila, Soria, Guadalaxara, part of Estremadura, and the little provinces on towards Aragon. Add likewise Cuença. You must also specify in this plan that the marching squadrons, composed of detachments belonging to the regiments in Lahoussaye's division, which form part of the army of the centre, are to proceed to Madrid; which will bring up this division to 2400 men. The King has 600 men in his guard; with the 1900 light-horse his cavalry will amount to 5000.

[660.] NAPOLEON TO BERTHIER.

Fontainebleau, Oct. 12, 1810.

My Cousin,—Write to General Caffarelli that the first brigade of his division, called the division of reserve, will arrive on the first of November; that the 2nd and 3rd will arrive in succession between the 1st and the 10th; that, as General Drouet cannot have too many troops, I wish him to send on to Valladolid the two first demi-brigades which are at present under his orders: he is to keep the two last, which will arrive towards the middle of October, to hold the country till his division reaches him; but he will send them also to Valladolid as soon as he is joined by his first brigade. Send him word that I leave it to him to hasten or to defer the departure of these corps by a few days, according to the turn of events in Portugal; that the three brigades of his division, with General Vattier's brigade of cavalry, make altogether 10,000 men. Tell him that I expect great firmness on his part in putting down depredation, of which there has been much. You will desire him to set on foot an inquiry into the conduct of General Avril at Bilbao, and of General Barthélemy at Santander. He is even to tell me his opinion of General Thouvenot. He must take means of suppressing instantly every kind of abuse. Let him know confidentially that I intend to annex Biscay to France; that it is not to be mentioned, but that it must influence his conduct. Impart the same secret to General Reille with respect to Navarre. Desire these two Generals to arrest all the military commandants who are guilty of peculation, to inquire into past abuses, and to have the funds which were collected for the benefit of private individuals restored.

[661.] NAPOLEON TO BERTHIER.

Fontainebleau, Oct 25, 1810.

My Cousin,—The officer whom you send to General Drouet must go on to Madrid and Seville. He is to take to the Duke of Dalmatia news of the army in Portugal, extracted from the English newspapers, and orders to attack La Romana, if it be true that he has marched upon Portugal.

[662.] NAPOLEON TO BERTHIER.

Fontainebleau, Oct. 25, 1810.

My Cousin,—Repeat the order to General Reille that he is to send back to Madrid the 1st and 2nd marching regiments of infantry, which were formed some time ago. Order the 1st marching regiment, which was to reach Madrid on the 20th, to proceed towards Andalusia. The Duke of Dalmatia is to incorporate this regiment, and may employ the colonel and the officers in his corps.

[663.] NAPOLEON TO BERTHIER.

Fontainebleau, Oct. 27, 1810.

My Cousin,—Ask the Spanish Ministers in Paris to give you a precise statement of the abuses of which they accuse General X——. Send word to him that I am surprised at his having taken money which was not due to him; that he has taken 16,000 francs a-month, which is more than the pay of a marshal commanding an army; and that the Treasury will probably consider this sum as not having been legally received.

[664.] NAPOLEON TO BERTHIER.

Oct. 30, 1810.

My Cousin,—I send to you a letter from the Spanish Minister. Let me know what right had General X—— to change the forms of civil government, and why he stops the post.

[665.] NAPOLEON TO BERTHIER.

Fontainebleau, Nov. 2, 1810.

My Cousin,—I am surprised that General Drouet was still at Valladolid on the 23d. You must tell him that I am anxious that he should make a diversion to endeavour to re-open communications with the Prince of Essling.

Convey to him the news which we have from Portugal, that Lord Wellington was on the 17th of October with his army at a distance of four leagues from Lisbon, and that the Prince of Essling was in front of him; and that on the 18th no battle had taken place.

Express to General Dorsenne my displeasure at his having kept back a detachment of the 27th light infantry, forming part of the marching regiment. Desire him to send this detachment as soon as possible to Madrid.

[666.] NAPOLEON TO BERTHIER.

Fontainebleau, Nov. 3, 1810.

My Cousin,—I have received General Drouet's letter of the 22nd of October. His arrangements for re-opening the communication with Portugal do not appear to me to be sufficient. Repeat to him the order to go to Almeida, and to collect a considerable force to be of use to the Prince of Essling, and to communicate with him. He must give a detachment of 6000 men, with six pieces of cannon, to General Gardanne, or to some other general, to re-open the communications; and he must place an equal force at Almeida to correspond with General Gardanne. The power of communicating with the army of Portugal is of great consequence, in order that our rear may be protected till the English have re-embarked.

Send the 'Moniteur' of to-day to General Drouet. It contains news from Portugal extracted from the English newspapers.

As soon as the English have re-embarked, General Drouet will carry his head-quarters to Ciudad Rodrigo. I do not intend the 9th corps to be engaged in Portugal unless the English maintain themselves there; and even if this should happen, the 9th corps must not allow itself to be cut off from Almeida; it must manœuvre between that town and Coimbra. Make General Drouet understand that I am most anxious for news of the army of Portugal; that it is important in every point of view; and that the communications must be re-established, so that we may receive intelligence, if not every day, at least every week.

Ask General Drouet for a return of all the troops which are left in the rear of Séras' division, and those left by the Prince of Essling, cavalry, artillery, and infantry; in short, of all the troops in the 6th government. He may withdraw those that he has at Avila, and occupy the town with detachments from the army of the centre. There are many unembodied men who would do for this purpose. Let me have a report on all the country contained in the 6th government. Do not Leon and the country between Ciudad Rodrigo and Salamanca form part of it?

[667.] NAPOLEON TO BERTHIER.

Fontainebleau, Nov. 8, 1810.

My Cousin,—Express my satisfaction to General Dorsenne, and desire him to take severe measures against the officers who have permitted the powder to be stolen. This carelessness must be repressed by severe punishment.

[668.] NAPOLEON TO BERTHIER.

Fontainebleau, Nov. 9, 1810.

My Cousin,—Repeat the order to Navarre that General Dumoutier is to repair with his brigade to Burgos, and to take with him the regiment of the Grand Duchy of Berg.

Reiterate the order to General Dorsenne to keep a strong division of at least 8000 men, with artillery and cavalry, between Burgos and Valladolid, ready to set off, if necessary, to the assistance of the army of Portugal.

Order General Caffarelli to hasten the departure of Conroux's division, and of all belonging to General Drouet's corps, and to keep columns of infantry and cavalry in continual motion, to act in concert with those of General Reille and of General Dorsenne, and drive the banditti far away.

Repeat the order to General Drouet to proceed to Almeida with the brigade of light cavalry belonging to General Fournier, Claparède's and Conroux's divisions, General Gardanne's brigade of horse, and all other available troops.

The advanced guard will consist of General Gardanne, with his brigade, sustained by General Drouet and his corps. They will pursue the banditti, re-open the communication, and obtain at any price news of the Prince of Essling, but with a general direction not to allow themselves to be cut off from us. You will let General Drouet know that a division of from 7000 to 8000 of the guard are to be placed between Burgos and Valladolid, and will support him in case of an emergency; that it is absolutely necessary to obtain news of the army of Portugal, and to afford assistance to it.

Write to General Drouet that, if the squadrons of horse which have been ordered to join the army of the centre are still near Valladolid, he is to keep them till news is obtained from Portugal. They will be of great use in keeping order in the environs of Valladolid. They will continue their march towards Madrid, as soon as the state of the army of Portugal is ascertained.

[*In the Emperor's hand.*] Send one of your officers from Paris, with orders not to return without news from Portugal.

[669.] NAPOLEON TO BERTHIER.

Fontainebleau, Nov. 14, 1810.

My Cousin,—Express fully to the Duke of Dalmatia my displeasure that there is little energy in his operations; that the 5th corps, instead of following up La Romana (who, it appears, has sent a detachment to Lisbon), and thus threatening the left bank of the Tagus, opposite to Lisbon, and preventing the English from assembling their forces on the right bank, has fallen back upon Seville; that the French army is kept in check by rumours that ought to be despised, and that 10,000 wretched Spaniards, without steadiness, are defending alone the island of Leon. Tell him that there have never been more than three English regiments at Cadiz, and that they are gone to Lisbon; that, therefore, the whole island of Leon and the fortress are defended only by a Spanish garrison; that I am the more surprised at the return of the 5th corps to Seville, as I had given orders to them to press close upon the rear of La Romana, and to prevent his advancing towards Lisbon; that no progress is made against Cadiz; that nothing is attempted against the island of Leon, which cannot fail of being ill defended, as it is occupied only by Spaniards. I am sorry to see that there is no vigour whatever in the military operations in that quarter.

[670.] NAPOLEON TO BERTHIER.

Fontainebleau, Nov. 15, 1810.

My Cousin,—I wrote to you on the changes to be made in the squadrons of the gendarmerie in Spain. On thinking over the matter, I prefer making these changes myself.

The Minister of War will send to you the decree which I have issued. I, however, annex a copy, in order that you may gain two days. Despatch this decree to General Buquet, and order him to proceed in this organisation without delay. Prescribe the number of men which each governor is to furnish. Propose to me a safe man to command this legion, either a colonel taken from the gendarmerie d'élite, or one of the excellent soldiers whom we knew when we were with the army. Some of the gendermarie d'élite in Spain may be made quartermasters by way of promotion. Consult General Durosnel; he will point out the men whom General Buquet may take, if he requires them.

[671.] NAPOLEON TO BERTHIER.

Paris, Nov. 20, 1810.

My Cousin,—You will find annexed an extract from the last English newspapers. You will feel the importance of despatching a staff officer to General Drouet to tell him that on the 1st of November no battle had taken place; that the left of the French army was at Villa Franca, and the right at Torres Vedras, and that the British army is in position at four leagues from Lisbon; that 10,000 militia occupy Coimbra, and intercept the road; that cavalry is of scarcely any use; that he must, therefore, beware of sending small detachments, but that he must employ a larger corps in re-opening the communication with the Prince of Essling; that for the rest I depend upon his prudence not to allow himself to be cut off from Almeida.

It seems from the English newspapers that between the 10th and 15th of October the garrison in Coimbra allowed itself to be surprised, and 1500 sick and wounded to be taken prisoners.

Repeat the orders which I gave lately to Generals Caffarelli, Dorsenne, and Reille, to assemble the guard at Burgos, and to send to General Drouet all the troops which belong to him. Desire General Kellermann not to keep back Conroux's division, but to allow it to proceed towards Salamanca.

Let me know on what day the fusiliers of my guard reach Bayonne. I wish them to have a day's rest there.

The detachments which are at the camp of Marrac are to join their companies. Write to the Duke of Dalmatia to let him know what the English say of the army of Portugal, and to impress upon him the importance of making a diversion in its favour.

[672.] NAPOLEON TO BERTHIER.

Paris, Nov. 22, 1810.

My Cousin,—I send you some extracts from the English newspapers. Send a memorandum of them to the Duke of Dalmatia, and express to him my displeasure at his inactivity, and at the amount of the Spanish divisions at Lisbon.

[673.] NAPOLEON TO BERTHIER.

Paris, Nov. 28, 1810.

My Cousin,—Order all the goods of English manufacture, seized in any of the towns in Spain occupied by my troops, to be burnt without delay.

[673.*] NAPOLEON TO BERTHIER.

Paris, Dec. 2, 1810.

My Cousin,—Write to General Reille that I have ordered 6 chefs-de-bataillon, 10 captains, 15 lieutenants, and 15 ensigns to be sent to him. Let him know that I regret the loss of a convoy of powder; that these things ought not to occur; that convoys should be sent only twice a-week, or once if need be, and should be composed always of men joining their regiments, couriers, &c., with the addition of troops enough to carry the numbers of the escorts to 500; that I desire that this rule be adhered to, that I may never again hear of a convoy being intercepted. Write the same thing to General Caffarelli, and say that he is to despatch his couriers regularly thrice a-week, from Tolosa to Navarre, from Irun to Burgos, and from Vittoria to Bilbao, so escorted as to be safe. Powder, money, unembodied men leaving the hospitals, are all to wait for the departure of the convoys. We shall then hear no more of these accidents, now so frequent. Write in the same sense to Generals Buquet, Dorsenne, and Kellermann.

[674.] NAPOLEON TO BERTHIER.

Paris, Dec. 15, 1810.

My Cousin,—Let me know if it be true that merinos are exported from San Sebastian for America. Order General Thouvenot to forbid this, and to send them to France. Order the commandant of Burgos to allow the Bishop of Calahorra to pass and to receive him as bishop.

[675.] NAPOLEON TO BERTHIER.

Paris, Dec. 15, 1810.

My Cousin,—How is it that the gendarmes in Santander, Biscay, and Aragon are not paid? Write to General Caffarelli respecting Biscay and Santander, and to General Suchet respecting Aragon, to take measures for paying them immediately. Gendarmes must be paid before any others.

[676.] NAPOLEON TO BERTHIER.

Paris, Dec. 26, 1810.

My Cousin,—Send off to-night an express to Bayonne, and let General Foy know that we have news from London of the 22nd, from which it appears that up to the 3rd of December the Prince of Essling continued to occupy Santarem; that there have been some skirmishes with the advanced guard, in which the English were repulsed; that Lord Wellington has resumed his position near Lisbon; that Silveyra boasts of having succeeded in an attack upon General Gardanne's advanced guard; that it seems from the details given by Silveyra that his force was inconsiderable; and that, if General Gardanne had continued to march upon him, large magazines of corn and biscuit would have been exposed to us.

Send three copies of the 'Moniteur' of to-day to General Foy; it contains the news received from London yesterday: and tell him that the 'Moniteur' of to-morrow will be sent to him, with some articles in it bearing reference to these details, and also to the Regency in London, which is not without some influence on the affairs of our army.

CHAPTER XVII.

THE letters contained in this chapter extend from the 16th of January to the 31st of December, 1811.

Napoleon passed this year, as he had passed the previous one, within the French empire.

The annexation of the Hanse Towns and of Oldenburg to France, and the increasing disputes with Russia, were the principal events connected with the North of Europe.

In Spain, Napoleon was preparing to annex to France the provinces to the north of the Ebro, and was striving to seize and to apply to the use of his own army the whole resources of the remainder of the country.

The sufferings and the terror inspired by these measures, the constantly increasing influence of Lord Wellington and his army, and the jealousies and insubordination of the French generals, convinced Joseph that his cause was hopeless. He spent the year in fruitless attempts to escape from his uneasy throne.

[677.] NAPOLEON TO BERTHIER.

Paris, Jan. 16, 1811.

My Cousin,—I approve of your draft of the instructions for the Duke of Istria. Send them on to him, as well as my decree, which you are to consider as having been signed, and which you are to transmit to the Minister of War. Let General Lecamus join the Duke of Istria without delay. The Duke of Istria may act exactly as he thinks best; he may concentrate his hospitals and magazines; in short, whatever the good of my service requires. You will authorise him to correspond with the King of Spain, the Duke of Dalmatia, Generals Suchet and Drouet, and the Prince of Essling, that he may know what they are about. Tell him that, if General Drouet's corps returns to Spain, he is to command it, and that in unforeseen events he is to support the army of Portugal.

[678.] NAPOLEON TO BERTHIER.

Paris, Jan. 17, 1811.

My Cousin,—Let the King of Spain know that, having given the government of Madrid to General Belliard,* who has continued to serve me well, I do not choose that it should be taken from him, nor, above all, that it should be given to an officer who is not in the service of France; that, if it be true that the King has deprived General Belliard of the government of Madrid, he must restore it to him without delay; that this is my formal order; that generally speaking I do not intend any French troops to be under the command of officers in the Spanish service.

[679.] NAPOLEON TO BERTHIER.

Paris, Feb. 6, 1811.

My Cousin,—I think that you ought to send the 'Moniteur' of to-day to the Duke of Dalmatia, to the Duke of Treviso, to General Belliard, to the Duke of Istria, and to the commandant of Ciudad Rodrigo and Almeida. When you send the 'Moniteur' to the Duke of Istria, tell him that he will find in it the latest news from Portugal, apparently of the 13th; that things seem to be turning out well; that, if Badajoz was taken in the course of the month of January, the Duke of Dalmatia may have marched upon the Tagus, and assisted the Prince of Essling in establishing a bridge; that it is therefore of great consequence to make all the arrangements which I ordered, so that General

* Napoleon had appointed General Belliard chief of the staff of the army of the centre. Joseph thereupon deprived him of the government of Madrid and gave it to General Blaniac.—TR.

Drouet with his two divisions may be at the disposal of the Prince of Essling. Write at the same time to inform the Duke of Dalmatia of the position of the Duke of Istria, and to reiterate to him the order to assist the Prince of Essling in crossing the Tagus; tell him that I hope that Badajoz was taken in the course of the month of January, and that he joined the Prince of Essling on the Tagus towards the 20th of January; that, if necessary, he may withdraw troops from the 4th corps; that, in short, everything turns upon the Tagus.

[680.] NAPOLEON TO BERTHIER.

Paris, March 8, 1811.

My Cousin,—There are three millions at Burgos and two millions at Valladolid; the two millions which are at Valladolid are intended for the army of Portugal, as well as one of the three millions which are at Burgos. Order the Duke of Istria to collect the three millions intended for the army of Portugal, and to send them as soon as that army appears to have decided either to proceed towards the Alentejo or to return upon Coimbra. Everything inclines me to think that by this time the decision has been made. One of the other two millions at Burgos is intended for the army of Madrid; order the Duke of Istria to send it thither. The other million was intended for the army of the South, but it is less needed there. I authorise the Duke of Istria to dispose of 500,000 fr. in paying the detachments from the army of Portugal which are in the provinces of Salamanca, and to send the other 500,000 to Madrid for the use of the army of the Centre.

[681.] NAPOLEON TO BERTHIER.

Paris, March 8, 1811.

My Cousin,—Order three millions to be sent from Bayonne to Burgos. 500,000 fr. are to be distributed among the regiments in the province of Santander, and the other districts belonging to the army of the North which are most in want of money, particularly paying in full the gendarmes. You will set apart 1,500,000 fr. for the army of Portugal, which, with the

3,500,000 fr. which I have already ordered you to send thither, will make in the whole five millions. Send one million to the army of the Centre, and take this money from the funds of the armies of Spain and Portugal of 1810.

Let me know what is owing by the Treasury for the year 1810 and for the present year.

[682.] NAPOLEON TO BERTHIER.

Paris, March 9, 1811.

My Cousin,—I beg of you to write a private letter to General Suchet to express to him my satisfaction at his good conduct in the last campaign; tell him that I expect great things from his zeal in pushing forward the siege of Tarragona. This town taken, he will have conquered Catalonia. The officer whom you send must tell him verbally that in Tarragona he will find his marshal's baton. Write to him that he will have 40,000 men under his command; that with so large an army he may leave behind him troops enough to hold Aragon and threaten Valencia, while he lays siege to Tarragona. I agree with him that Valencia will fall of itself. It is there that the armies of Aragon and of Catalonia will find the rewards of their labours.

[683.] NAPOLEON TO BERTHIER.

Paris, March 9, 1811.

My Cousin,—Write to the King of Spain that his aide-de-camp, Clermont Tonnerre, brought me favourable news as to Valencia, but that unhappily it is not confirmed; that it seems however from the last reports, that there is much disturbance in the town; that General Suchet asks for 30,000 men and 40 pieces of artillery to subdue it; but that at present Tarragona is the chief object, and must be taken first of all.

[684.] NAPOLEON TO BERTHIER.

Paris, March 9, 1811.

My Cousin,—Write to the King of Spain that General Lahoussaye was very wrong to put himself into communication with the Duke of Dalmatia; that we have no news of the army of the South; that we know only from the English newspapers that on the 25th of January Ballesteros was entirely defeated by General Gazan; that the troops ought not to have been sent towards Cuença, but towards Portugal, where the most important events are being decided.

[685.] NAPOLEON TO BERTHIER.

Paris, March 9, 1811.

My Cousin,—The government of Aragon will be increased by the provinces of Tortosa, Lerida, and Tarragona, and by the country which lies to the west of a line drawn from the tower of Garraf, on the sea-coast, crossing the pass of Ordal, following the course of the Noya as far as Horra, that of the Llobregat to the Segra, and from thence along the frontiers of the provinces of Lerida to the Noguera, which will separate, as it formerly did, the two governments as far as the Pyrenees. You will inform General Suchet of this arrangement, and tell him that all the troops belonging to the army in service in Catalonia are immediately to pass under his orders,—that is to say—the 7th of the line, the 42nd of the line, the 1st light infantry, and the 10th of the line, the Italian and Neapolitan divisions, the 24th dragoons, the dragoons of Napoleon, and the Royal chasseurs. He will leave under the command of the Duke of Taranto the 29th chasseurs, the battalion of the 93rd of the line, the battalion of the Grand Duchy of Berg, and a company of artillery; this detachment will proceed to Barcelona to reinforce the garrison, and to form part of the army of Catalonia, of which the head-quarters will be at Barcelona.

The squadron of the 24th dragoons, and the Italian and Neapolitan detachments of the corps belonging to the army of Aragon which are in Upper Catalonia or Barcelona, will rejoin their corps as soon as they can do so with safety. The army of Catalonia is to occupy Montserrat, and to besiege Cardona, Berga, and Urgel; it is the business of the army of Aragon to lay siege to Tarragona. General Suchet and the Duke of Taranto will consult together respecting the march of the Duke and his detachment towards Barcelona. They will see whether it be better for all the division of the army of Catalonia, which is on active service, or a part of it, to move, either to take final possession of Montserrat and drive the enemy back upon Tarragona, or, if this is not considered to be absolutely necessary, to protect the re-entrance of the Duke of Taranto's detachment into Barcelona. In the latter alternative the Duke of Taranto will threaten Montserrat with an attack, to keep in the enemy and prevent his disturbing the siege of Tarragona. You will consult with the Minister of War as to the means of your each sending an officer carrying a duplicate order; one by way of Pampeluna, and the other by way of Jaca.

The officer sent by the Minister of War will carry both your orders and his; he will go first to General Suchet, whose orders he will deliver; he will not proceed to deliver those of the Duke of Taranto until he is directed to do so by General Suchet. The officer whom you send by the other road with duplicates of your orders and those of the minister, will likewise proceed first to General Suchet, who will give him directions as to the day and hour he is to reach Lerida.

I wish General Suchet to join the army soon after the arrival of this officer. You must choose intelligent officers who understand their duty, so that, in case of General Suchet's absence, or even death, they may deliver no order to the Duke of Taranto, if they have not seen General Suchet. You are aware of the importance of not leaving the army of Catalonia without a general, and of giving General Suchet such instructions that he may be able to direct the whole operation.

Desire General Suchet to set about the siege of Tarragona immediately; he will choose his line of occupation either by Lerida or by Mora, and fortify the intermediate posts. It seems to me to be of great importance to intrench that of Mont Blanc thoroughly. He will provision largely the Col Balaguer, and consider whether he had better provide himself with some boats on the sea. I leave it to him to compose his divisions as he pleases, mixing the troops of the army of Catalonia with those of the army of Aragon.

The capture of Tarragona will crown the glory obtained by General Suchet in this campaign, and will give him new claims upon me.

[686.] NAPOLEON TO CLARKE.

Paris, March 9, 1811.

M. le Duc de Feltre,—I send to you the Duke of Taranto's report upon the state of affairs in Catalonia.

He has not advanced the war in that province by a single step. He does not appear to be acquainted with the system to be observed among mountains. The marches which he has forced his army to make across a difficult country, and without a well-concerted plan of operations, must have fatigued his troops without a hope of advantage.

If latterly he had marched without hurry from Lerida to Tarragona, and establishing fortified posts all along the Mont Blanc road, he would have reached Reuss, and been safe against the efforts of the insurgents.

I approve, however, of the principal measures which he proposes.

[The beginning of the last letter to Berthier is here repeated, with the exception of the following two passages.]

The 102nd of the line, and all the detachments belonging to the 93rd and to the other regiments at Barcelona, will be added to the garrison, which will then amount to 8000 men.

When Montserrat is taken, a garrison of from 1000 to 1200 men must be properly entrenched and established there.

[687.] NAPOLEON TO BERTHIER.

Paris, March 10, 1811.

My Cousin,—Despatch orders to the army of the Centre to send its detachments to establish a communication with the Duke of Dalmatia by way of Merida, and to obtain news of his operations. Write at the same time to the Duke of Istria to send a circular to all the generals in the district of the army of the

North to put them on their guard against the news and the ridiculous reports which are brought to them; they ought to know that they are victims of the impostures of the English, Portuguese, and Spaniards.

[688.] NAPOLEON TO CLARKE.

Paris, March 10, 1811.

M. le Duc de Feltre,—I return to you General Baraguay d'Hilliers' letters. Send an officer to him. It is not yet time to let him know of the changes which I have made in Catalonia, as it would not be proper for the Duke of Taranto to hear of them indirectly; but you must send word to him that, as soon as General Quesnel reaches Puycerda and attacks the fortress of Urgel, the enemy's attention will be drawn in that direction; that he must occupy the positions of Olot and Vico, reconnoitre the other positions which should be occupied in order to keep up effectually the communication with Barcelona; that the enemy is about to be hard pressed at Tarragona, and threatened at Urgel; that he must prevent the enemy from establishing himself between Puycerda and the valleys of the Segra and Girona; that for this purpose Olot, Ripoll, and Vico must be occupied, and one or two posts between Barcelona and the castle of Hostalrich fortified and loopholed; these forts should be placed towards Granoller, where the two roads of Vico and Hostalrich meet; that if General Baraguay d'Hilliers is able to occupy Granoller and Vico, he will be in communication with Barcelona, and he may execute a combined movement with the garrison: in this case it will be useless to send the 102nd to Barcelona, as the same effect will be produced; but that for this purpose, as soon as he reaches Vico and Granoller, he must begin to turn up the ground and to loophole the houses, in which he should place a few pieces of cannon, and in short take every precaution to protect himself against the banditti and other enemies. Tell him that it is the duty of the officer whom you send to him to bring back his opinion on this plan, and on the means of accomplishing it and of preventing the enemy's establishment between the Cerdagna and Girona; also his opinion whether it be advisable to occupy Olot and Ripoll with our forces, and to place them at Vico and Granoller, so as to send detachments of between 200 and 300 men to communicate with Barcelona; it being always understood that the columns of Vico and Granoller will make sorties in concert with the garrison of Barcelona whenever the enemy presents himself.

Tell him that these operations will become easy when Quesnel's division reaches Puycerda, Tarragona is invested, and the army re-enters Catalonia (for I do not consider it as in Catalonia when it is at Lerida on the other side of the mountains); that all these dispositions will contribute greatly to the subjection of the country; but that in order to obtain this result he must fortify himself so strongly that detachments of 50 or 60 men, if they have guns, will be exposed to no attack; that this is done in the interior of Spain, and succeeds everywhere; that he has sappers and miners and artillery, and that he may immediately fortify Vico and the other posts which he thinks fit to occupy.

That this plan presents more advantages than that of reinforcing Barcelona, especially as the troops which he sends thither may occupy posts on the road and in advance of the town.

[689.] NAPOLEON TO CLARKE.

St. Cloud, March 12, 1811.

M. le Duc de Feltre,—Send word to Marshal Macdonald that it would be of great use if, without endangering the blockade of Figuèras, he could march towards Barcelona to scour the country, advance upon Vico, and disperse the bands which are collecting there, and endeavour to take Montserrat, or, if he considers it imprudent to attack, at any rate to threaten it, and make a diversion in favour of Tarragona. He should be accompanied by a corps of from 5000 to 6000 men, to which, if he pleases, he may add the squadron of the 20th which is at Mont Louis. But that the chief thing is to keep up the blockade of Figuèras; that I intrust it to his care, and that I conclude that he has forced the English, who had effected a partial landing, to re-embark.

[690.] NAPOLEON TO BERTHIER.

Paris, March 16, 1811.

My Cousin,—Impress upon the King of Spain the necessity of sending to Seville all the detachments of the 4th, 5th, and 1st corps which are in the district of his army; let him know that this is indispensable, and that General Lahoussaye must rest his army on the left bank of the Tagus, to put himself in communication with the Duke of Dalmatia.

[691.] NAPOLEON TO JOSEPH.

Paris, March 20, 1811.

Monsieur mon Frère,—I hasten to announce to your Majesty that the Empress, my dear wife, has just been safely delivered of a prince, who at his birth received the title of King of Rome. Your Majesty's constant affection towards me convinces me that you will share in the satisfaction which I feel at an event of such importance to my family and to the welfare of my subjects.

This conviction is very agreeable to me. Your Majesty is aware of my attachments, and cannot doubt the pleasure with which I seize this opportunity of repeating the assurances of the sincere esteem and friendship with which I am, &c. &c.

[692.] NAPOLEON TO JOSEPH.

Paris, March 20, 1811.*

. . . . . This evening at eight o'clock the child is to be privately baptized. As I do not intend the public christening to take place for the next six weeks, I shall intrust General Defrance, my equerry, who will be the bearer of this letter, with another in which I shall ask you to stand godfather to your nephew.

[693.] NAPOLEON TO BERTHIER.

March 30, 1811.

The chief of the staff will take 200 copies of to-morrow's 'Moniteur,' and send them off before 10 P.M. by an extraordinary

* This letter begins by some surgical details as to the birth of the child, which I have not thought worth translation.—TR.

express, with orders that they may be despatched from Bayonne to Spain, likewise by a special courier.

The Prince of Neufchâtel will transmit 50 copies of the 'Moniteur' to the commandant of Bayonne, who will give 25 to Casabianca as he passes through, and will send some to General Reille in Navarre.

The Prince of Neufchâtel will send the remaining 150 copies to the Duke of Istria, who will pass some on to Madrid and to the army of Portugal, and will distribute them all over Spain.

[694.] NAPOLEON TO BERTHIER.

[Undated.]

DESPATCHES AND INSTRUCTIONS TO BE SENT TO THE DUKE OF DALMATIA.

The Prince of Neufchâtel will write by this express, and will send a duplicate by the officer whom he is to despatch to-morrow, to explain to the Duke of Dalmatia the state of affairs since the capture of Badajoz; and he will also tell him that I was sorry to see the disasters which happened to the 1st corps before Cadiz; * that I cannot approve of the dispositions which he made in that quarter; that these misfortunes would not have occurred, and that the siege of Cadiz would not have run such risks, if, on leaving Estremadura, the Duke of Dalmatia had placed Godinot's division and General Sebastiani's corps under the command of the Duke of Belluno; that by this means he would have had six French and three Polish regiments, that is to say an extra force of nearly 20,000 men; that when he found himself threatened by the landing at Algesiras, by ordering 8000 men from General Sebastiani's corps and a brigade of General Godinot's to join him he would have had three times as many troops as he wanted; that the only two posts worth holding during the expedition to Estremadura were Seville and Cadiz; that all the hospitals should have been collected within Seville; that, besides, a third part of the 4th corps would have been more than enough to keep at a

* The battle of Barrosa, fought on the 5th of March, 1811.—TR.

distance such troops as those in Murcia, and generally to hold the whole of that country.

The Duke of Dalmatia has 60,000 men under his orders; he might have given up 30,000 to the Duke of Belluno, and yet have had more troops than he wanted before Badajoz. The mania of attempting, in a moment of difficulty, to hold every point may be productive of great misfortunes. The Emperor is displeased that, whilst the siege of Cadiz ran great risks of being raised, the 12th, 32nd, 58th, and 43rd, altogether a division of more than 8000 men, were scattered about in posts of trifling importance.

The six Polish battalions and General Sénarmont's light horse were more than enough to watch that side; and thus the four French regiments and Count Milhaud's division of cavalry would have been available for sustaining the siege of Cadiz. On the other hand, General Godinot's two regiments, consisting of six battalions, were perfectly idle and useless in their cantonments.

The chief merit of a general lies in the proper disposition of his troops. His Majesty sees with regret that on this occasion the proper dispositions were not made. His Majesty desires that all the hospitals may be collected within the walls of Seville, in order that, although the country may be generally occupied for the purpose of obtaining food and other resources, it still may be possible, in an emergency, to assemble the troops and hold only a few citadels.

Neither does His Majesty approve of the decision which has been taken of holding Olivenza; it should be blown up and the fortifications destroyed. As to Badajoz, everything depends upon the possibility of victualling it: if it can be done quickly, and for six months, the town should be kept; if not, only the citadel must be preserved, and the fortifications of the town must be blown up.

The Emperor has ordered all the men belonging to the 51st and 55th regiments which are at present with the army of the Centre to march immediately towards Andalusia. The Emperor has given similar orders with respect to the 5000 men, both foot and horse, belonging to the army of the South, which are at present with the army of the Centre. I transmit His Majesty's orders positively, in order that they may be executed without delay. At the same time I order the Duke of Istria to send to you 8000 infantry and 2000 cavalry, also belonging to the army of the South, which are at present under his command.

These reinforcements will repair all losses, and reinstate the army of the South in a suitable position. Besides these, in the course of the next fortnight another corps of 6000 men, belonging to the army of the South, will join it. As soon as these dispositions are made, the Duke of Dalmatia must prepare himself for resisting an attack from the British army; and, when the time comes, for marching upon Lisbon with 30,000 men, whilst the army of Portugal advances upon the town in another direction with 60,000. But this aggresive movement is adjourned till the North of Portugal is brought into order.* . . . . Coimbra will continue to be the head-quarters of the army of Portugal; Oporto will be occupied by a detachment. The strength of this army amounts to 60,000 men under arms; its orders are to fight Lord Wellington if he advances on Coimbra; to harass and to threaten him incessantly towards Lisbon, in order to prevent his sending large detachments against Andalusia. Lord Wellington has only 32,000 English under his command; he can therefore send detachments of only 8000 or 9000 men with between 5000 and 6000 Portuguese. A body of 15,000 men, consisting of cavalry, infantry, and artillery, in good condition, and belonging to the best regiments, must be always kept at Badajoz, so that, if the English should make the slightest movement in that direction, the Duke of Dalmatia may march thither with 8000 or 10,000 men, and assemble between 25,000 and 30,000 in Estremadura. In this emergency only a corps of observation should be left at Granada, which should be under the orders of the Duke of Belluno.

The Duke of Dalmatia should correspond with the Prince of Essling and the army of the Centre by way of Madrid. The King should always keep a body of 6000 men (cavalry, and

* Illegible.—ED.

artillery) between the Tagus and Badajoz, ready to join the Duke of Dalmatia's corps if the English move on Andalusia. But, for this purpose, the country must be entirely cleared, the hospitals collected in Seville, and Cadiz, Seville, and Badajoz the only posts held, keeping at the same time a corps of observation at Granada. In this case the Duke of Belluno would have the command of the troops remaining at Seville, of those before Cadiz, and of the corps of observation towards Granada, whilst the Duke of Dalmatia commands the corps which is to oppose the English. He will likewise have under his orders the division of the army of the Centre, and will thus be able to assemble 30,000 or 36,000 men. The siege of Cadiz ought to be pushed on with the utmost vigour; the requisite number of men may be placed there, with a better distribution. The 51st and 55th should be replaced by the regiments which have suffered most at Cadiz; some French regiments belonging to Sebastiani's division should be changed. In short, the Duke of Dalmatia, having with him the division of the army of the Centre, would have 35,000 men to resist 30,000 English, supposing Lord Wellington to march upon him with the whole of his army; but this supposition is impossible, as the Prince of Essling would then march upon Lisbon, and the English would be placed between two fires, and cut off from their base of operations. The Prince of Essling will remain at Coimbra, and threaten Lisbon, which will be attacked after the harvest by 70,000 men belonging to the army of Portugal, and by all the troops which can be procured from Andalusia to manœuvre, according to circumstances, upon Badajoz, and the Tagus. These 100,000 men, resting on Coimbra and Badajoz, will accomplish the conquest of Portugal, an event which will have serious consequences for the English.

The Prince of Neufchâtel wiil annex to this despatch a return of the detachments which are ordered to join the army of the South. In two days the duplicate of this order will be taken by one of the Prince of Neufchâtel's officers.

MISSION OF GENERAL MONTHION TO BAYONNE.

The Prince of Neufchâtel is to send General Monthion to establish a staff-office at Bayonne. General Monthion will command the dapartment and the different depôts. General Boivin will return to Bourdeaux. General Monthion will appoint agents to ascertain what officers pass through, and will send on the news which they bring, if it be interesting, by an extraordinary express, so as if possible to precede their arrival in Paris by 24 hours.

General Monthion will manage all the details relating to the departure of money and of convoys; he will send off as many extraordinary couriers as he pleases. The Prince of Neufchâtel will give notice of this to Count Lavalette.* I wished to diminish the number of expresses traversing Spain, because their frequency fatigued the escorts, but between Bayonne and Paris there are not the same objections. General Monthion will correspond regularly with Generals Caffarelli, Thouvenot, and Reille, and with the Duke of Istria.

DESPATCH FOR THE KING OF SPAIN.

The chief of the staff will send a despatch to the King of Spain, to acquaint him with the existing position of the armies of the South and of Portugal, and with that which I have ordered them to assume; he will inform the King that, if the English advance upon Badajoz, the army of the Centre must send a division thither, or even as far as Cordova, to support the army of the South if it should be attackd by Lord Wellington. The Prince of Neufchâtel will let the King know how much money has been sent to the army of the Centre, and the amount which is to follow.

* The Postmaster-General.—Tr.

DESPATCH FOR GENERAL SEBASTIANI.

The Prince of Neufchâtel will write to General Sebastiani that I am displeased at his keeping 16,000 of my best troops doing nothing; that what has happened at Cadiz is his fault; that he commanded the army of observation, and that it was his duty to protect the besieging army.

SUPPLEMENT TO THE DUKE OF DALMATIA'S DESPATCH.

The Prince of Neufchâtel will, as soon as possible, let me have a memorandum of all the rewards for which the Duke of Dalmatia asks, and which appear to be just, that they may be sent off in a few days; and, in the mean while, he will write word to the duke that he will soon receive them. The Prince of Neufchâtel will also announce to the Duke of Dalmatia the arrival of several marching regiments, commanded by lieutenant-colonels, to whom he may give vacant regiments.

The Prince of Neufchâtel will tell the Duke of Dalmatia that a company of 80 men belonging to the 1st regiment of foot-artillery is at Cordova, and that several other artillery companies are scattered in the same way; that they must be assembled to be sent to Cadiz.

FRESH REINFORCEMENTS FOR THE ARMY OF THE SOUTH.

The Prince of Neufchâtel will order the whole of the 29th chasseurs to join the army of the South; this order must be peremptory, and the Duke of Dalmatia will be advised to despatch this regiment towards Badajoz to strengthen his cavalry against the English. The Prince of Neufchâtel will order the 8th company of the 7th artillery, which is at Guadalaxara, the 7th company of the 3rd artillery at Segovia, the company of the 6th regiment which is at Madrid, the 2nd company of the 2nd battalion of sappers and miners at Madrid, and the 3rd company of the train of engineers, composed of 70 soldiers and 63 horses, also at

Madrid, to proceed to Andalusia to reinforce the army of the South. The Prince of Neufchâtel will let me know whether there are at Bayonne any companies of artillery, which may likewise be sent to Andalusia.

[695.] NAPOLEON TO BERTHIER.

Paris, April 9, 1811.

My Cousin,—I wish you to send off this evening Senator Lecoulteux's son, aide-de-camp to the Prince of Essling; he will take with him several copies of the 'Moniteur' of to-day addressed to the Prince of Essling, to the Duke of Istria, and to General Caffarelli. Tell the Prince of Essling that an express has been intercepted, and it is to be feared that it contained despatches from him, since between those which Colonel Pelet brought, and the one written from Guarda, none have been received from him.

You will send the Prince of Essling by his aide-de-camp a duplicate of yesterday's despatch; you will let him know that I have given the command of the 1st division of the 6th corps to General Foy; that therefore there is no occasion to appoint General Maucune general of division; that he should arm Almeida as soon as possible, since it appears that it would take a long time to destroy the place and to remove the artillery.

Desire him to hasten the departure of General Drouet and his corps for Andalusia, and let them take the shortest road: this is important, for it is to be feared that the English will use their utmost endeavours to raise the siege of Cadiz. He must take measures to protect Almeida and Ciudad Rodrigo, and, on the other side, communicate with Madrid and Seville, in order to combine operations with the army of Andalusia, and to afford it assistance.

Send word by the same officer to the Duke of Istria to hasten the departure of all the provisional regiments which are intended for Andalusia, as it seems that the enemy is turning all his efforts in that direction. Reiterate my orders with respect to the expresses. You will send 'Moniteurs' to Madrid and to the Duke of Dalmatia. You will let it be known at Madrid that it is necessary to communicate with the Prince of Essling; that he was at Guarda on the 27th, extending his left flank towards Alcantara; that he is in want of powder, ammunition, and provisions, which must be sent to him, if possible, by way of Alcantara and Placencia.

You will let General Belliard know that we are waiting impatiently for news from Andalusia; that the 3rd corps, under the orders of General Suchet, has received a reinforcement of 16,000 men; that in the course of the month of May, General Suchet intends to commence the siege of Tarragona, an undertaking which will be difficult on account of the want of provisions, but which will decide the submission of those provinces; that General Quesnel has entered Puycerda, and is proceeding to lay siege to Urgel; that Campoverde has been decoyed even into the ditch of the fortress of Montjouy, and has lost 3000 men.

Tell General Belliard that he must send patrols as far as Cordova to obtain news of the army of Andalusia. Write to the Duke of Dalmatia, when you send the 'Moniteurs' to him, to inform him that General Suchet, whose corps has received a reinforcement of 16,000 men, is about to lay siege to Tarragona, and that, as soon as the town is taken, this fine army will be available. Let him know the situation of the Prince of Essling, and the necessity of putting himself into communication with that army, whose chief object is to hold Lord Wellington in check, and to combine operations with the army of the South. You will send him a duplicate to inform him of General Drouet's march towards Andalusia.

Write to him in cipher, if you have one, that two French frigates and a transport of 800 tons, laden with ammunition and 600 conscripts, are on their way from Toulon to Malaga; that this expedition takes the shells and ammunition which are wanted for the siege of Cadiz: that it sailed from Toulon on the 4th of April, and took in troops at Porto Ferrajo. If you have no cipher, it will be enough if you give this information *vivâ voce* to the officer, who will repeat it to the Duke of Istria, who again will transmit it through an officer to the Duke of Dalmatia. It will be sufficient to write in a memorandum-book:—"Two frigates and a transport of 800 tons, shells and shot; 600 conscripts.

Porto Ferrajo Malaga, April the 4th." These indications will be enough.

You will let the Duke of Ragusa know that I have appointed General Foy to command the 1st division of the 6th corps; you will order him to hold himself in readiness to start. Send off all these despatches. When they are gone, you will come to the Tuileries at 6 o'clock, or at half-past 6 o'clock, with the general orders which you will despatch to-morrow by another officer to the Prince of Essling. Bring me at the same time the proposals for rewards and promotions.

[696.] NAPOLEON TO BERTHIER.

Paris, April 15, 1811.

My Cousin,—I return to you General Suchet's letter of the 6th of March. Order the supplies of corn for which he asks to be sent to him from Navarre; write also to General Suchet that he must absolutely present himself before Tarragona by the 1st of May at latest. It is the only means of preventing the insurgents from invading Upper Catalonia.

[697.] NAPOLEON TO BERTHIER.

Paris, April 24, 1811.

My Cousin,—You must send an officer to General Suchet to inform him that, in consequence of the treachery of two magazine-keepers, who were Catalonians, a door of one of the magazines of Figuèras, which looked towards the ditch, was opened at 2 o'clock in the morning, and that 800 Miquelets thus got into the fortress and took in their beds 500 Neapolitans and Italians and 150 French; that this unpleasant event has forced General Baraguay d'Hilliers to concentrate his forces round Figuèras; that it is therefore indispensable for General Suchet to advance upon Tarragona, to hold in check Campoverde, and prevent his making a diversion; that the season is favourable, and that it would be a great pity if his fine army were to remain inactive.

[698.] NAPOLEON TO BERTHIER.

St. Cloud, April 27, 1811.

My Cousin,—Desire General Thouvenot to take particular care of St. Sebastian, and to watch the service of that place, so as to prevent the possibility of a surprise.

[699.] NAPOLEON TO BERTHIER.

St. Cloud, April 27, 1811.

My Cousin,—Write to the Duke of Ragusa, under cover to the Duke of Istria, to inform him that he must take all the measures which are requisite for the organisation of his army; that I permit him to form it into six battalions, without making a corps-d'armée; that he may send back to France the generals and officers who do not suit him. He will desire them to march first towards Valladolid, where they will await further orders. Send word to him that as soon as General Brenier, who is commandant of Almeida, enters the line, attention must be paid to him, and he should be employed as general of division; that it is useless to promote him as long as he remains at Almeida; that he is an excellent officer, and may be usefully employed.

[700.] NAPOLEON TO BERTHIER.

Fontainebleau, May 7, 1811.

My Cousin,—I send to you a translation from the English newspapers. You will see that on the 18th of April Wellington had crossed the Tagus. I beg you to have copies made of these despatches, and to send them this evening to the Dukes of Istria and of Ragusa, and even to General Belliard. It seems that, at that time, only half the British army was in Castile. What has occurred near Almeida must have already made these facts known to the generals, and have taught them how to support their troops upon the Tagus. You see that what I foresaw has come to pass; some troops were foolishly left at Olivenza, and 300 prisoners have been taken.

Olivenza was captured on the 14th. It seems to me strange that, although the Duke of Dalmatia heard that Lord Beresford had crossed on the 4th, he should have taken no measures up to the 25th of April for relieving Badajoz before Lord Wellington's arrival. Return these newspapers to me as soon as you have had them copied.

[701.] NAPOLEON TO BERTHIER.

St. Cloud, May 20, 1811.

My Cousin,—Send back General Suchet's aide-de-camp, Ricard, with orders to General Suchet to march upon Tarragona. Impress upon him the necessity of leaving Klopiski's brigade to defend the country on the side of Navarre. Tell him of General Baraguay d'Hilliers' victory, on the 3rd of this month, over Campoverde, who, at the head of 12,000 of his best troops, endeavoured to introduce a convoy into Figuèras; 1200 mules, which composed the convoy were seized, 100 officers and 2000 men taken prisoners, and the rest killed and dispersed in every direction. Say to General Suchet that it is mortifying, that, while he has such a force in his hand, he allows them to go to sleep instead of taking advantage of these events to invest Tarragona.

[702.] NAPOLEON TO BERTHIER.

Caen, May 25, 1811.

My Cousin,—There are many fathers of families in the gendarme squadrons which are in Spain; I am told that a return of them has been sent to you; let me have it, that I may see whether I can permit some of them to return.

[703.] NAPOLEON TO BERTHIER.

Caen, May 26, 1811.

My Cousin,—I have received your letter. I have not yet seen Lecoulteux, so I can tell you nothing of what is going on in Portugal. I do not lose a minute in desiring you to write every day to General Marmont, and to send the 'Moniteurs' to him; several of them contain news from Spain. Let General Marmont know that he has full powers to reorganise his army, to form it into six or seven divisions, and to send back the generals who do not suit him; that he may take lieutenant-colonels from General Drouet's corps to put at the head of the vacant regiments, choosing for this purpose men of action: that he should send back the commissaries who are of no use to him, and collect his troops so as to be in hand; that he must seize all the mules in the province of Salamanca, and in his rear; that there are many in those provinces; that the Duke of Istria has orders to assist him with all the means in his power, and even to give him as many of my guard as he can spare; that I have contracted for the purchase of 4000 pack, saddle, and draft mules at Bayonne; but that, of course, it will take some time.

Write to the Duke of Istria that he must contribute 500 horses or mules, and even the necessary materials, horses and harness; in short, everything that is required to put the Duke of Ragusa's artillery into perfect order, for it is essential that it should have the proper means of transport and be in a good condition; that he may take mules to supply the place of his horses till fresh ones arrive; that 4000 artillery and baggage horses are at this moment on their way to Bayonne; that he must keep no useless stores at Salamanca, but despatch them all to Burgos; that he is to provide for the wants of the army of Portugal with the utmost activity; that if the English advance upon Ciudad Rodrigo, he must assemble all his forces, proceed to the assistance of the Duke of Ragusa, and, finally, engage the English in a decisive battle.

Remark to him that his letters are not sufficiently frequent; that instead of writing every day he scarcely writes at all, and gives no intelligence of what is going on. Desire the Duke of Ragusa to put his army into proper order, and fight the English if they march upon Ciudad Rodrigo; that in this case he may be reinforced by the Duke of Istria with a division of infantry composed of 10,000 of my guard; that he should announce my approaching arrival and his own march upon Lisbon as soon as the harvest is over.

Desire the Ministers of War and of the Administration of the War, to hasten the purchases which I have ordered for remounting the detachments of the artillery train and the horse artillery, which are in the depots at Auch, Pau, and Toulouse.

I think that an officer should be sent to inform the Duke of Istria that I expect him to take every means of giving decisive assistance to the army of Portugal.

[704.] NAPOLEON TO BERTHIER.

Cherbourg, May 29, 1811.

My Cousin,—I send to you your Portuguese correspondence. Let the Duke of Ragusa know that I have appointed General Maucune to be a general of division. Repeat to him that he may send back to France all the generals who do not suit him, and that he is to organise his army in the way which he thinks best.

[705.] NAPOLEON TO BERTHIER.

Havre, May 29, 1811.

My Cousin,—Let there be long details put into the 'Moniteur' on all that has taken place at Lerida. Send the plan of attack to the War-office to have an engraving made of the siege of Lerida, as well as of that of Girona. Express my perfect satisfaction to General Suchet, and let him know that I have granted all the promotions for which he asked.

Reiterate to him the order to levy a contribution of several millions upon Lerida, in order to obtain food, pay, and clothing for his army. Tell him that the war in Spain makes such an increase of forces necessary, that I am no longer able to send money thither; that war must support war. Order him to have no Spanish officers in Spain, but to send them all to France; I should have censured the whole capitulation if he had approved of that article.

Write to him that he ought to suffer no other than the French flag to be planted on the castle of Lerida. Repeat the order for him to blow up the fortifications of the town. Write to him that I suppose him to be master of Mequienza; that he should take measures for the capture of Tortosa; that Marshal Macdonald is to march at the same time on Tarragona; that he is to collect all the artillery and materials which are required to march on Valencia and force his way through its walls; but that, before this is attempted, Tortosa and Tarragona must be taken.

[706.] NAPOLEON TO BERTHIER.

Alençon, June 1, 1811.

My Cousin,—I return to you your Portuguese and Spanish correspondence, in order that you may present to me the decrees for the appointment of the different lieutenant-colonels, and for their employment in the regiments of the army of Andalusia, which are without commanding officers. You may show most of my letters to the King of Spain;* they will prove to him how insane it is for him and the Spaniards to assert that they can do without French troops.

[707.] NAPOLEON TO BERTHIER.

Chartres, June 8, 1811.

My Cousin,—I send to you the English account of the action at Fuente de Onoro. Send a copy to the Dukes of Ragusa and of Istria. You may have copied even what is scratched out, that they may know the whole. You may bring this account back to me to-morrow, on my arrival at St. Cloud.

[708.] NAPOLEON TO BERTHIER.

St. Cloud, June 8, 1811.

My Cousin,—Write to the Duke of Istria that he is to think twice before he orders General Bonnet to evacuate the Asturias; that I consider this measure as in itself very bad; that General Bonnet, by occupying Oviedo with 6000 men, covers the whole plain of Valladolid and Leon, and threatens Gallicia; that his position is defensive with respect to Valladolid, the mountains of Santander, and Biscay, and offensive as

* Joseph was now in Paris. He arrived there on the 15th of May.—TR.

regards Gallicia; that I attribute to it the inactivity of the Gallicians, as they are in constant fear of being attacked by him by their rear; that, if General Bonnet were to evacuate the Asturias, the Duke of Istria would be obliged to place him at Santander, the only effect of which would be, that Leon and Valladolid would be unprotected, and the insurgents would have full liberty to disturb the plain, and even to march upon Astorga and Benevento; that this would be a retrograde step; that the Junta of Oviedo would be formed again, and would infest all those mountains; that it would be a detestable operation.

General Bonnet should not evacuate Oviedo, unless it were necessary at some particular time to assemble the whole army to give battle to the English. It would be a fortnight's absence, after which he ought to return; but this emergency is not probable, as at present the South is the field of action.

As to the frontiers of Portugal, all the stationary artillery, powder, ammunition, and everything which is not wanted for the defence of Ciudad Rodrigo, should be sent to Burgos. There are some waggons without horses, and some ordnance at Salamanca, which ought to be sent to Burgos; and if some unexpected event were to force the Duke of Istria to evacuate Valladolid, he should leave nothing of the kind in the town. I am told that there are waggons at Placencia and in other places. Desire them to be sent to Burgos.

[709.] Napoleon to Berthier.

St. Cloud, June 10, 1811.

My Cousin,—Order General Caffarelli to trace out and begin to construct a tête-de-pont at Miranda, in order that, whatever happens, the passage of the Ebro may be secured. The position of this tête-de-pont requires that it should be of some extent; a square tower of the second size must be built in masonry, to serve as a guard-house, magazine, and redoubt for the tête-de-pont. The Minister of War will send to you a plan of this tower.

The tête-de-pont ought to be so constructed as to enable the army to cross the Ebro at any time without molestation. Send word to General Caffarelli that it would be advisable to build some towers on the heights in the defiles between Vittoria and Irun. Ten of these towers, placed upon the highest points, affording a retreat to twenty men, would be of great use. They would serve as outposts to reconnoitre the heights, and to keep us always masters of them. These towers would not cost more than 10,000 francs a-piece, and it would be money and labour well employed.

[710.] NAPOLEON TO BERTHIER.

St. Cloud, June 14, 1811.

My Cousin,—I see that at Mequinenza, in Aragon, there are 6000 tools; why are they not sent to Madrid? Order this to be done.

[711.] NAPOLEON TO CLARKE.

St. Cloud, June 23, 1811.

M. le Duc de Feltre,—I am told that some generals, staff, and commissariat officers, are in the habit of taking as servants men from the army, and thus weakening the regiments. This abuse is particularly frequent in Spain. Order the soldiers to be arrested and sent back to their corps.

[712.] NAPOLEON TO BERTHIER.

St. Cloud, June 25, 1811.

My Cousin,—Order the Duke of Istria and the general in command of the army of the centre to give proper escorts to 20,000 merinos belonging to me, which are at Madrid, and are to be brought to France.

[713.] NAPOLEON TO BERTHIER.

Trianon, July 11, 1811.

My Cousin,—Order 10,000 pairs of shoes out of the 20,000 which are at Valladolid, and 6000 out of the 12,000 pairs which are at Madrid, to be sent to the army of Portugal: which will make altogether 16,000 pairs of shoes for that army. The Duke of Ragusa will distribute them to the different regiments.

[714.] NAPOLEON TO BERTHIER.

Trianon, July 17, 1811.

My Cousin,—Let Marshal Jourdan have the necessary sum to equip himself and proceed without delay to Spain, where he may be of use. Arrange everything so as to enable him to start as soon as possible.

[715.] NAPOLEON TO BERTHIER.

St. Cloud, July 31, 1811.

My Cousin,—The tower of the Bidassoa is to be constructed at Bayonne. The minister of war should have given orders to this effect. It does not in the least concern Biscay. The towers should be built only on the tops of the heights. They are all to be of the third size; there are to be none of either the first or second.

The first tower must be placed on the height of Salinas, situated so that signals made from it may give information as to what is going on in the mountains. The officer who examined the country did not quite understand what was intended: three towers were to be constructed; one at Salinas, and the others on the watersheds of the mountains.

It must be seen how many such there are from the Bidassoa to Miranda, and the three principal positions chosen for the construction of three towers. As soon as these are finished, three more positions must be determined on, and the towers must be placed so as to overlook the road and the defiles which join it, to correspond easily with each other by means of signals, to give notice of what is going on in the mountains, and in short to serve as a refuge for my troops. Towers of the third size will cost 15,000 fr. apiece, that is to say, 45,000 fr. for the three. Too much haste cannot be made in establishing one of these towers on the heights of Salinas. The plans sent by General

Thouvenot do not carry out my intentions; they must be begun all over again.

[716.] NAPOLEON TO BERTHIER.

St. Cloud, Aug. 6, 1811.

My Cousin,—Write to General Souham that, as his regimental artillery, his waggons, and the artillery belonging to his division cannot yet be ready, I wish him in the mean while to second General Reille in Navarre; that one of his regiments should guard the valley of Bastan; that, with the other three, he should pursue Mina, and do all he can to destroy the banditti and pacify Navarre; that while this is taking place the great heats will pass off, the artillery will be brought into order, and he will then be directed to proceed whithersoever he may be wanted. He should fix his head-quarters at Logroño.

Write to this effect to General Reille; tell him that I also intend to send the Italian division to Navarre; but that he must at length make an end of the banditti, terrify them, shoot them by hundreds, disarm the country, and keep safe the ammunition and horses.

[717.] NAPOLEON TO BERTHIER.

St. Cloud, Aug. 24, 1811.

My Cousin,—It will be easy for you to make the King of Spain* understand that, as the whole of his left is safe, now that the army of Portugal is at Almaraz, he must have a sufficient number of troops, and that he should send to the army of the South all that belong to it; that the 26th chasseurs is most useful to the army of Portugal, the cavalry of which has been ruined. Repeat the order to General Dorsenne to assemble all the men belonging to the 75th and 28th, as well as to the dragoons of the army of the centre. Reiterate the same orders to the Duke of Dalmatia, and include the Germans, who ought not to form part of his corps. Tell the King of Spain to send

* Joseph was now at Madrid. He returned on the 15th of July.—TR.

back all the dismounted men belonging to the army of the South who are in any of the depôts within the district of his army.

[718.] NAPOLEON TO JOSEPH.

Trianon, Aug. 25, 1811.

My Brother,—I thank you for your letter on my birthday. I entreat you not to doubt my friendship or the interest which I take in you. My affection for you will always remain unchanged.

[719.] NAPOLEON TO BERTHIER.

Trianon, Aug. 25, 1811.

My Cousin,—Answer to General Dorsenne that Baron Dudon, intendant of the provinces under the jurisdiction of the army of the North, is not to follow the army, but to stay at Valladolid; that he is invested with the government of the province, under the immediate orders of the general commanding in chief, who is to let every administrative measure pass through General Dudon's hands, and to pay every contribution to the agents of the treasury; that the commissary-general is always to follow the army and to provide for its wants; that the Intendant Dudon represents the administration of the country, and is to be considered in the same light as a prefect in France; that the commissary-general is to have the management only of the administration of the army; that Spaniards must not be employed under the intendant; first because no reliance can be placed on their fidelity or attachment, and secondly because they would have no influence over the French governors and military authorities, and could not prevent the irregularities which are so frequent in Spain, and which have been the chief cause of the crimes which have been committed there. On the other hand, French auditors, who keep up a correspondence with France, know the limit to the authority of each, and will not allow themselves to be imposed upon, may be consulted as witnesses whenever a point is in dispute; that therefore auditors must be placed everywhere; that the commander-in-chief must give no administrative orders except through the medium of the Intendant Dudon, and that the revenues are on no account to be paid except into the hands of the French cashiers, and the expenses are to be defrayed only by the paymasters of the treasury; that in this case all intervention of the Spanish authorities would be suspicious; that I wish General Dorsenne to make use of the talents of Baron Dudon, and of the zeal of the auditors: that it is the only way of placing everything under supervision, and of putting an end to irregularities.

That I have no objection to the creation of superior intendants, each with the command over a whole province; that I established one lately in Navarre; that similar officers may be placed in all the provinces; that, with respect to the King, my general orders must have shown clearly enough that he is to make no appointment in the district of the army of the North except to ecclesiastical or judicial functions; but that no military or administrative agent is to be appointed by the King; that in short I wish General Dorsenne to act in accordance with the administration, and, instead of causing annoyance to the intendant and to the auditors, he is to encourage and support them.

[720.] NAPOLEON TO CLARKE.

Trianon, Aug. 25, 1811.

M. le Duc de Feltre,—I am delighted to hear of the capture of Figuèras. Send an extraordinary courier to the Duke of Taranto to express to him my satisfaction, and tell him that I have asked you to send me a report on the promotions and rewards to be given to the army. You will tell him that I have issued a decree for uniting Catalonia to France (you will receive it in a few days); that Marshal Suchet occupies at present Montserrat; that I have ordered him to place a French division, composed of 4 regiments and 10 pieces of artillery, between Barcelona, Montserrat, Tarragona, and Lerida; likewise to garrison Mequinenza and Tortosa with his troops; that both these places will continue under the command of Marshal Suchet, who is ordered to march with the remainder of his army upon

Valencia; that I wish the Duke of Taranto to repair to Barcelona and inspect Montserrat, to see what use can be made of that important position; that he is to add 6000 of his troops to the division which Marshal Suchet gives up to him; that he is to take as many men as possible from Barcelona, and to form an effected corps of from 12,000 to 14,000 men to manœuvre between Tortosa, Lerida, Barcelona, and Montserrat; to take Cordova and Urgel, disperse the assemblages in Catalonia, and subdue the country. An aggressive movement on Valencia will concentrate there all the efforts of the enemy, which will be a real deliverance for Catalonia. The Duke of Taranto should establish a good commandant at Figuèras, and supply it with provisions for several months. It would be a good thing to publish an order prohibiting any stranger, not belonging to the garrison, from entering the fortress on pain of death. I suppose that he has inflicted severe punishment upon the traitors who gave it up.

[721.] Napoleon to Berthier.

Compiègne, Sept. 11, 1811.

My Cousin,—I return to you the Duke of Dalmatia's and General Dorsenne's letters; give orders yourself as to these trifles. The notion of paying duty on the clothing of the officers and men is absurd; write to put an end to it. Answer to General Dorsenne that he ought not to place the intendant-general on the same footing with the receiver of taxes; that the way to obtain assistance from the intendant is to treat him with proper respect; that Baron Dudon may be of great use to him, if it be only in repressing abuses and depredations; that to offend him therefore shows a want of regard to his own interests. Write to M. Dudon that a functionary does not resign; that if he has any complaints he should make them, but not talk about quitting the service; that this proceeding does him no honour, and shows a want of knowledge of his duty.

[722.] NAPOLEON TO CLARKE.

Antwerp, Oct. 8, 1811.

M. le Duc de Feltre,—I enclose to you the Duke of Taranto's letters. Give the command of the army of Catalonia to General Decaen.

Answer to the Duke of Taranto that he ought not to correspond with the King of Spain upon any subject, nor to answer any letters from his ministers.

Give the same instructions to General Decaen.

[723.] NAPOLEON TO BERTHIER.

Utrecht, Oct. 9, 1811.

My Cousin,—Write to the King of Spain that, till further orders, he may keep everything that reaches Madrid from France, intended for the army of the south, as that army is in want of nothing. Repeat at the same time the order that everything belonging to the army of the centre, which is now in the possession of the army of the south, may be returned without delay to the army of the centre. Write also to the King to tell him that I have ordered the money which he requires to be sent to him.

I approve of the Duke of Dalmatia's measure for raising independent companies composed of the French who are in Andalusia.

[724.] NAPOLEON TO BERTHIER.

St. Cloud, Nov. 19, 1811.

My Cousin,—The last letters which you sent to me from General Monthion were dated the 29th of October. That is now three weeks ago: I am surprised at his not sending his reports more frequently. Nor have I heard anything for the last three weeks from Generals Caffarelli and Reille: such negligence is intolerable. Generals Monthion, Thouvenot, Caffareli, and Dorsenne must be desired to write to you every day, and your correspondence must contain more information. Let me have the last returns from the army of the north, that I may know how many sick there are in Biscay. Let me also have a report of the orders which you have given to the marching battalions, and of those which you have sent to General Monthion as to the disposition of these battalions.

[725.] NAPOLEON TO BERTHIER.

St. Cloud, Nov. 19, 1811.

My Cousin,—Despatch immediately an officer to Marshal Suchet to inform him that General Reille is about to march towards Aragon in order to support him. Tell him that on the very day when he thought that Mina had joined Empecinado to assist Genral Blake, Mina was near Mondragona, fiercely pursued by General Burck; tell him that we have news from Gibraltar of the 25th of October; that the army of the south has carried the camp of St. Roch and Algeciras; that Ballasteros is hemmed in under Gibraltar; that General Decaen has gone to succour Barcelona, and will do all that he can; that the King writes word that since the 1st of November he has occupied Cuença in force in order to support him, and that the Duke of Ragusa has orders to send thither a division. Inform him that the English have 18,000 sick in Portugal, and are unable to undertake anything; that the Duke of Dalmatia is ordered to send a column to make a diversion in Murcia; that, therefore, Valencia must be vigorously attacked and taken.

Send back the Duke of Ragusa's aide-de-camp to him; let him know that the great object at present is the capture of Valencia; tell him of the successes lately obtained by Marshal Suchet: send the 'Moniteur' of the last month to him; he will see that the English have 18,000 sick, and appear to be determined to remain on the defensive.

If Valencia has not yet fallen, he must send a detachment of 6000 men to join all the available troops belonging to the army of the centre, and to march to Marshal Suchet's assistance. As soon as Valencia is taken, a great many troops will be set at liberty, and he will be largely reinforced; his army will then commence its great operations. At this period, that is to say, towards the end of January, after the rains, he should march with the army of Portugal and part of the army of the south upon Elvos, and overrun the Alentejo, whilst the army of the north, reinforced by part of the army of reserve, advances on Coa and Alfayates. But the important point now is to take Valencia; he must therefore put a division in motion without delay.

Write to the King to this effect. I conclude that he has sent all his available troops to communicate with Marshal Suchet and to support him. Tell him that, if Valencia is not yet taken, I have ordered the Duke of Ragusa to send a division to join him, so as to form altogether a corps of from 10,000 to 12,000 men, who will march to General Suchet's assistance.

Send the 'Moniteur' for the last month to the King, to Marshal Suchet, and to Generals Reille, Caffarelli, and Dorsenne. Write to General Reille that I hope that he received news of the 6th from Marshal Suchet, whom he must support by sending without delay to him Severoli's division, and by marching himself with his whole division towards Aragon: tell him that General Decaen is advancing on Barcelona.

Order General Caffarelli to proceed with his division against Mina; to pursue him in every direction till he is utterly routed; to assume the command of Navarre, and to support General Reille in Aragon. General Dorsenne is sufficiently strong; write to him that the great object is to take Valencia.

[726.] NAPOLEON TO BERTHIER.

St. Cloud, Nov. 20, 1811.

My Cousin,—Write to Generals Dorsenne, Caffarelli, and Thouvenot, that a detestable system is followed in the countries where they are; that immense forces are stationed in the villages to resist troops of banditti that are in motion; that this produces continual misfortunes; that the opposite course should be adopted, only the principal posts should be occupied, and moveable columns sent from them in pursuit of the banditti; that if things were managed in this way, many accidents would be prevented; that this plan must be immediately adopted and the banditti actively attacked; that experience in La Vendée has taught us that the best way is to have moveable columns scattered and multiplied in every direction, and not stationary bodies.

[727.] NAPOLEON TO BERTHIER.

St. Cloud, Nov. 20, 1811.

My Cousin,—Express my displeasure to General Dorsenne at his not having relieved the troops belonging to General Wandermaesen's division at Soria and Aranda, so that they have not yet been able to rejoin the army of Portugal. To act in this manner is to try to destroy the army.

[728.] NAPOLEON TO CLARKE.

Paris, Dec. 6, 1811.

M. le Duc de Feltre,—I return to you the papers belonging to the Catalonian correspondence.

I can determine nothing about the army until I have more recent returns; send me those of the 1st of December, or at least of the 15th of November.

The losses in the army of Catalonia are produced by its obstinacy in remaining at Figuèras. I have advised them perpetually to leave Lampourdan, a country which is said to be as unwholesome as Walcheren. This obstinacy will destroy the whole army.

When the siege of Figuèras rendered it necessary to assemble a great many troops there, the presence of the army may have been required; but as soon as the fortress was taken they should have passed on and quitted Lampourdan, which has always been fatal to the French.

A million francs has been sent to bring up the arrears in the pay. I am expecting to hear of the arrival at Barcelona of the convoy under General Decaen's escort.

[729.] NAPOLEON TO BERTHIER.

Paris, Dec. 6, 1811.

My Cousin,—I return to you the Spanish correspondence. Make a list of the promotions and rewards which are demanded, as I propose to grant them. Write to the Duke of Ragusa that, if the enemy's movements force him to march towards the north, General Dorsenne will be under his orders; but the great thing at this juncture is to take Valencia. Express to the Duke of Dalmatia my disapprobation of the flank movement performed by General Girard in the presence of the enemy, a march which lasted for three days, and was so ill managed that the enemy might have cut him off at any time: he should have been supported by a strong detachment. It is unfortunate that, with an army of 80,000 men, they could not make the dispositions which prudence demanded to avoid being beaten by a troop of 6000 English.* Remind him that, when one has to fight, particularly against the English, one must not divide one's forces, but collect them and present imposing numbers: all the troops which are left behind run the risk of being beaten in detail or forced to abandon their positions. Repeat to him the order to provision Badajoz for a twelvemonth. If the capture of the island of Leon is considered impossible, Murcia must be vigorously attacked, in order to relieve the army of Valencia. Tell him that I have issued a decree with respect to the expedition. I do not intend it to be made at my expense; it would cost me enormous and absurd sums. Write to him that he may organise his army as he thinks proper, in six or seven divisions, retaining always the generals according to their rank and seniority. I grant permission to the Duke of Belluno to return to France; but as he may be engaged in some operation requiring his presence, you will enclose this permission to the Duke of Dalmatia, who will deliver it at the right time to the Duke of Belluno. The Duke of Dalmatia has the finest army in the world, and yet he holds in check neither General Hill nor the army of Murcia, the whole of which has marched to the assistance of Valencia.

You will render an account to the ministers of the treasury of the 500,000 francs which were missing in the convoy escorted by General Avy to the army of the south.

NB

* At Arrozo del Morino, where General Girard was surprised and defeated by General Hill on the 28th of October.—TR.

[730.] NAPOLEON TO BERTHIER.

Paris, Dec. 6, 1811.

My Cousin,—Suspend Colonel X—— of the 12th dragoons, employed in the army of the south, whose incapacity has occasioned the loss of a detachment in the Alpujarès: give notice of this to the minister of war, that he may be sent for to give an account of his conduct. Express my displeasure to Major Pillay at his not attacking the army of Mina in Biscay; let him repair to Bayonne, where his conduct will be examined into. Obtain the necessary information from Generals Thouvenot and Buquet. Order the Italian soldiers who were taken prisoners by Mina, but thrown upon the coast of Bilbao and set free, to be clothed immediately and kept at Bayonne: let General Monthion take the greatest care of them. Order General Thouvenot to pay the marching regiments which are placed in Biscay out of the revenue of the province. Wine should be distributed to the troops which are there; there is plenty to be had in Spain. The soldiers fall into bad health for want of proper food.

Tell General Dorsenne that I am surprised to see that the magazines are empty; they have never been so low. General Dorsenne spoils everything by his attempt at centralisation. This system acts as a perpetual clog in Biscay and Navarre. Convoys must start from Bayonne without delay.

Let me have a report upon Santona, and of all that it has cost me up to this time: propose to me to grant large sums this winter in order to finish the fortifications. Measures must also be taken for sending thither all the requisite ammunition and provisions by sea from Bayonne and San Sebastian, under an escort of fishing-boats. I allow 100,000 francs out of the funds which I have at Burgos to the engineers for the works of that fortress. Write to General Dorsenne that I am sorry to see that he has not yet marched regularly upon Potès, and destroyed Mendizabal and the Marquisito; this was the first thing to be done after reconquering the Asturias.

General Bonnet should employ all the contributions which he levies on the Asturias in paying his troops and improving their condition; he has made frequent levies; his accounts must in future be kept with regularity. Write to the King that the Dutch hussars are free to enter his service; he must incorporate them in his guard.

[731.] NAPOLEON TO BERTHIER.

Paris, Dec. 9, 1811.

My Cousin,—I have three divisions to add to the army of observation on the Ebro, the 6th, 8th, and 9th. The 6th and 9th should be composed of troops who speak German; the 8th of French troops. Let me know whom to appoint to these commands. The 9th division will consist of eight Swiss battalions and of the Illyrian regiment: the command of this division may, I think, be given to General Legrand: can he speak German? The 6th division may be given to General Daëndels, and the 8th to General Verdière. The Duke of Padua and General Sebastiani and Belliard have no command; ask them what they wish for; would they like to serve in the infantry or in the cavalry? You must also find me out some brigadier-generals among those who are now in Paris, and who want employment.

General Compère is in the King of Naples' service; he is an excellent general, and might be employed in the army. He has nothing to do in the Neapolitan service.

[732.] NAPOLEON TO BERTHIER.

Paris, Dec. 15, 1811.

My Cousin,—I wish to recall General Montbrun to France. Let me know to whom I can give the command of the cavalry belonging to the army of Portugal, and who are the cavalry generals still remaining in that army. If I recall the guard, General Chastel will come back. Tell me what generals would remain, capable of commanding the cavalry of the army of the North. Before I consent to the return of the General of Division Latour Maubourg to France, let me know what other generals of cavalry there are belonging to the army of the South. I have already asked you when the reserve at Bayonne will be able to send off the men who are wanted to complete the battalions which are with the different marching regiments. Tell the Duke of Ragusa that 300 men of the 14th chasseurs, among whom is the company of picked men, are on their way to join him, and will complete that regiment to at least 800 men; that he is not to consider it as belonging exclusively to Souham's division, but has perfect liberty to place it wherever he pleases; that I am most anxious to hear that his artillery is at length organised, and that his army has 100 pieces of cannon.

[733.] NAPOLEON TO BERTHIER.

Paris, Dec. 15, 1811.

My Cousin,—I wish you to draw up a report on the army of the North. I believe that I have already ordered my grenadiers, a company of foot artillery, my gendarmerie d'élite, and the guides, to return to France: if this order respecting the gendarmerie d'élite has not yet been delivered, let it go without delay, and let all my gendarmes belonging to the guard proceed to Bayonne. I think that I ordered the Duke of Ragusa to give a company of light artillery to General Dorsenne: repeat this order. Let me know what companies or detachments of artillery and of the train are under General Dorsenne, for I wish to recall to France, first, my two companies of horse artillery, and, secondly, all the drivers belonging to my horse artillery. I have no objection to leave the horses and harness there, but I want the men to return to France. There would remain then only the companies of conscript gunners and the teams which are required for the guns belonging to the infantry. Let me know if I could not obtain from Auch, Carcassonne, and Bayonne artillery officers and men, teams, and drivers to relieve those belonging to my guard. Let me also have a detailed report on the artillery of the army of the North. I should like to recall immediately to France my chasseurs, Poles, and dragoons, but I must first have a report on the cavalry of the army of the North. The Grand Duke of Berg's lancers, the legion of gendarmes, the 1st hussars, and the 31st chasseurs will remain there; altogether four regiments, including the men engaged in Spain, those in the marching regiments, and even those in the depôts, that I may endeavour to make their numbers as large as possible. As there is more cavalry in the army of the South than is wanted, tell me whether from the marching regiments belonging to that army which have not yet got beyond Burgos, a sufficient number might not be taken to increase General Dorsenne's cavalry to 3000 men. I consider all questions respecting the cavalry of the army of the North to be connected with those respecting the cavalry of the army of Portugal; for my reason for wishing General Dorsenne to have more than 3000 men is clearly that I foresee the possibility of his having to repulse the British army, and, in that case, I should like the armies of Portugal and of the North to be able to assemble 9000 horse on the field of battle, which would prevent any movement on the part of the English; I say on the field of battle, not 9000 effectives, and you know what an immense difference that makes.

Let me therefore have a return of the cavalry belonging to the armies of Spain, including all the marching regiments on their way to it. I shall wait till I have received this return before I give final orders to the cavalry of my guard. As to the infantry of my guard, I certainly wish it to return, but I am waiting till Valencia is taken; besides infantry have the advantage of being able to travel by post. I wish you also to give me an accurate account of the army of Portugal, including all the provisional regiments in the rear, as well as those which are at Bayonne.

[734.] NAPOLEON TO CLARKE.

Paris, Dec. 26, 1811.

M. le Duc de Feltre,—I return to you General Decaen's despatches. Write an account of what has taken place; make it of sufficient importance to satisfy the generals, without, however, magnifying too much operations which were merely against peasants.

Write to General Decaen that I am sorry to see that he has broken up Freyre's division, as, in consequence, there is no longer an efficient force in the south of Catalonia, between Lerida,

Tortosa, and Barcelona; that he must disperse the rebels who are collecting about Vico, and that he must prepare to send a convoy, by land, to Barcelona. Let me know the number of coasters which have sailed from Agde since last October, how many have reached Barcelona, and how many have been taken. Write to General Decaen and to Adjutant Carrion-Nisas that up to this time the contracts made with the coasting-trade have not answered. A contract must be made for the transport of provisions by land; I have on this subject some new ideas, which I will explain. I suppose the garrison of Barcelona to require 8000 rations, which makes 3000 quintals a month. All the contracts which have hitherto been made with the coasting-trade must be considered as intended for the supply of a place besieged. A regular contract should now be made with a company for the transport of 4000 quintals a month, conveyed in great waggons, capable of holding from forty to fifty quintals. The army of Catalonia must provide an escort for this convoy every month. I shall bestow a great privilege upon this company—that of bringing back foreign goods and merchandise on its own account. At present the important thing is to insure the arrival of a convoy at Barcelona in the month of January, and another in February, that there may be no anxiety about the daily supply of the place. I have ordered the Minister of the Treasury to send to Barcelona one million francs, half of which is for the troops, and the other half to be given to the commissary-general, for the purchase of corn, meat, vegetables, and other provisions. There will be 400,000 francs in money and 600,000 in a draft. I conclude that Marshal Suchet has blown up the fortifications of Tarragona, at least all that constituted it a fortress, and that he has preserved only a redoubt.

Inform General Decaen that Marshal Soult was to invest Valencia on the 25th, and open the trenches on the 26th; he hopes to carry the entrenched camp on that day, which will give him such facilities for attacking the town, that he may become master of it in the course of January.

Propose to me some rewards and promotions for the army of Catalonia.

[735.] NAPOLEON TO BERTHIER.

Paris, Dec. 30, 1811.

My Cousin,—I beg of you to make an extract of the different corps belonging to the army of the South, so that I may see at once the state of every infantry regiment, how many they have under arms, detached no matter whither, sick, &c., including only those belonging to the army of the South; you will afterwards make a similar abstract of all that are to be found belonging to the army of the South in the districts of the armies of the Centre and of the North.

You will have a similar account drawn up of the foot-artillery, including all the companies of the same regiment which are with the army of the South, without distinguishing the different corps: the same thing with respect to the train, the baggage-train, the engineers, and sappers and miners. I require these abstracts to be made in order to see how to curtail the cadres, particularly those of the artillery and engineers, and to recall some of the officers to France.

Express my displeasure to the Duke of Ragusa at his having sent no return of the army of Portugal to me since the 1st of October. Similar abstracts must be made of his army.

[736.] NAPOLEON TO BERTHIER.

Paris, Dec. 31, 1811.

My Cousin,—Order the Duke of Dalmatia to send Generals Girard and Britche back to France

CHAPTER XVIII.

THE letters in this chapter extend from the 2nd January to the 24th of December, 1812.

Napoleon's power, which at the beginning of this year appeared to have acquired its greatest strength, before its end was irrecoverably broken.

His reverses began in Spain, where Lord Wellington took Ciudad Rodrigo, Badajoz, and the forts of Salamanca, defeated Marmont at Salamanca, drove Joseph from Madrid, and forced Soult to raise the siege of Cadiz. Napoleon left Paris on the 9th of May, reached Dresden on the 16th, and held there his celebrated receptions, in which kings were the courtiers; crossed the Niemen on the 24th of June; fought the battle of Borodino on the 7th of September, entered Moscow on the 14th of Sept., left it on the 19th of October; crossed the Berezina on the 26th of November; left the remains of the Grand Army on the 5th of December, and reached Paris on the 18th.

[737.] NAPOLEON TO BERTHIER.

Paris, Jan. 2, 1812.

My Cousin,—I wish you to write for me a report, which will be printed, on the correspondence respecting General Girard's affair. It seems that General Britche was posted on the side by which the enemy attacked; that he was completely surprised, not in his bivouac, but in bed in a comfortable house, while the horses of his hussars were unsaddled. I will dictate this report to you. My object is to impress on the colonels and generals of light troops the general principle that a colonel of chasseurs or hussars who goes to bed, instead of spending the nights in bivouac and in constant communication with his main-guard, deserves death. I think that Marshal Mortier has some information on the subject. As my object is not merely to punish General Britche, but to excite the zeal of the whole light cavalry, this report must be vigorously drawn up.

[738.] NAPOLEON TO BERTHIER.

Paris, Jan. 6, 1812.

My Cousin,—Among the Rêveries of Marshal Saxe, mixed up with much that is extremely commonplace, are some hints on the means of levying contributions on foreign countries without fatiguing the army, which seem to be useful. Read them, and put the contents into the form of instructions for my generals in Spain.

[739.] NAPOLEON TO BERTHIER.

Paris, Jan. 14, 1812.

My Cousin,—Prepare the following instructions, which I wish to have sent to Marshal Suchet, as soon as I have approved of the draft.

You will tell him that, immediately after the capture of Valencia, I intend the Polish generals and staff officers, as well as the 1st, 2nd, and 3rd regiments of the Vistula to return to France. You will point out the shortest road for their return. Marshal Suchet will retain the government of Valencia, together with the command of the 3rd corps of the army of Spain, which he will organise in the following manner:—He has the 114th, 121st, 7th, 116th, 44th, 16th, 117th, and 5th light infantry; total 8 regiments. As soon as I hear of the fall of Valencia, I shall order the provisional regiment of Aragon, which is at Pampeluna, to repair to Valencia to complete the numbers of those eight regiments. Let me know the effective, the number of sick, and the present under arms of the eight regiments, supposing the provisional regiment to have been already incorporated in them.

These eight regiments will be formed into three divisions in the manner which he thinks best. They will be joined by all the detachments in Aragon. The cavalry will consist of the 4th hussars and the 13th cuirassiers. You will desire him to send to me all the companies of the artillery-train, all those of the baggage-train, and all the companies of sappers, miners, and artillerymen whom he does not want. For this purpose you will send me a return of them in the greatest detail, and you will propose to me to incorporate the men who are required to complete the companies which will remain with the army of Valencia. The skeletons of the artillery-train will be composed of all the men who have no horses; the skeletons of the sappers, miners, and pontoneers will consist of the non-commissioned officers and corporals, and of 20 soldiers chosen by the captain, so that each company which is sent to me may amount at least to 30 men, who will animate and encourage the conscripts placed in their regiments. I suppose that the necessity of occupying several strong posts and of defending the coast will make it requisite to keep some of the officers and men attached to the siege-train. Marshal Suchet's corps will consist, therefore, of between 20,000 and 22,000 men; he will retain the Neapolitan division, which is 1200 strong.

Palombini's division, consisting of from 5000 to 6000 infantry and 400 cavalry; Severoli's division of 5000 infantry and 400 cavalry (altogether 11,000 Italian foot and 800 horse, with the artillery which belongs to them), with Reille's division of 9000 infantry and 600 cavalry, will form a corps of from 20,000 to 21,000 foot and 1500 horse. This division will proceed to Tortosa, and Reille will take the command of Lower Catalonia.

You will afterwards organise the artillery of these three divisions; it will be necessary to take some companies from the army of Aragon in order to form the park.

You will divide the territory of Catalonia into two parts; one will include Tortosa, Mequinenza, Lerida, Tarragona, Montserrat, and Barcelona, near which place it will end. You will consult on this subject General Guilleminot, who has been on the spot.

General Reille may carry his head-quarters to Tarragona, Lerida, or Barcelona; his corps will be increased by the garrison of each place, with the exception of the detachments forming part either of the garrison of Girona or of the army of Valencia, composed as I have already described.

You must see the Minister of War in order to obtain from him all the details respecting the army of Catalonia and the different fortresses, to enable you to propose to me the organisation of the army of Catalonia, which will receive all the detachments belonging to it in the garrison of Barcelona, and will send back all that ought to belong to the army of Valencia.

Caffarelli's division will also be added to General Reille's corps, which will thus amount to 30,000 infantry and more than 2000 cavalry. Its duty will be to defend the whole of Aragon. General Labbé will take the command of Caffarelli's division.

General Reille's division will be called the corps of the Ebro. You will submit for my approbation a scheme for the final organisation of the whole of Catalonia, both Upper and Lower, dividing it into departments.* General Reille's chief duties will be to keep the country quiet, and to supply Barcelona amply with provisions; he will keep open the communication with the army of Valencia, with the army of Portugal at Valladolid, and with the army of the centre at Madrid, and he will protect Aragon; his general orders will be to have always one or two of his divisions placed so as to afford a strong support to the army of Portugal, if the English should move against Valladolid.

General Dorsenne, with the whole of my guard, is to return to France. General Caffarelli will take the command of the army of the north at Burgos, and will have under his orders the 130th, 34th, and 113th regiments (as the 4th regiment of the Vistula is Polish, it must return to France). Let me have a detailed ac-

* This order shows that Napoleon had decided on the annexation of Catalonia to France.—TR.

count of the strength of this army: Palombini's Italian division ought perhaps to be added to it.

I also wish to make an exchange: to return to the army of Portugal the four marching regiments, and to send a division from the army of Portugal to Burgos, consisting of an equal number of men. The army of the north will thus be sufficiently strong, and composed of good troops. Write to the Duke of Dalmatia to despatch immediately the three regiments of the Vistula, the regiment of lancers of the Vistula, and all the Polish staff. This diminution in strength of the army of the south is of no consequence, and you will desire the order to be executed in 24 hours after the receipt of your letter. You will send to me a plan for recruiting the cadres which are to be withdrawn from the different armies, and also the skeletons of the companies of artillery, and the battalions of the train, as well as of the sappers and miners who are to be recalled.

The three companies of baggage-mules which are with the 3rd, 4th, and 13th battalions at Pau are to be sent to the corps of the Ebro; they will therefore leave Pau with a strong escort, taking advantage of that which will convey the prisoners from Valencia to Saragossa. General Reille will thus obtain 600 baggage-mules, which will be of great use to him. As these three companies belong to three different battalions, you will desire the general of the army of Portugal to settle about the exchange with General Reille, in order that the army of Portugal may have one complete battalion, and the corps of the Ebro another. Lastly, propose to me to add to the grand army the company of engineers which was at Bayonne, intended for the army of observation, a company of pontoneers, another of sappers and miners, and, I think, two companies of artillery, which were intended for the same corps. There will still be left a considerable number both of men and materials. I intend to make use of the teams, as soon as I understand the nature of those belonging to the army of Portugal. As this army is in the presence of the English, it should be well provided in this respect. If you have no return, the Duke of Ragusa's aide-de-camp, who is an artillery officer, may be able to supply you.

I consider it as of the utmost importance that the army of Portugal should have at least 100 mounted guns, with proper ammunition. Souham's division ought to have 22, the army of Portugal 80, Bonnet's division 4 or 5, making in the whole 110. It requires quite as much, and the artillery must be well horsed and of large calibre. As soon as I know the organisation of the artillery of the army of Portugal, of the corps of the Ebro, of the army of Valencia, and of the corps of the army of observation, I will give a destination to the 1000 artillery horses which I have left at Toulouse. The army of reserve being thus broken up, let me know the respective destination of each of its parts, whether to be joined to the corps of the Ebro or to some other corps. Let me have a detailed report on the subject, supported by the returns. The result of these measures will be to deprive the armies of Spain of the four regiments of the Vistula, consisting of eight battalions; of three Polish regiments, composed of six battalions: in the whole seven regiments or 14 battalions, which will make a splendid division for the Grand Army.

I have desired the 40th and the 34th to return to France; you will repeat these orders. I shall likewise have deprived the armies of Spain of the regiment of Polish lancers, of a few Polish generals and staff officers, and of 22 battalions of the guard, altogether 36 battalions. But a short time ago I sent thither Souham's division, which consists of 14 battalions, and Reille's division, and Caffarelli's, which are both equally strong; in the whole 42 battalions. Therefore, instead of having lost, the armies of Spain will find that they have gained.

It is essential that you should let the Duke of Dalmatia know that, as soon as he has parted with the 34th and 40th, as well as the three Polish regiments, the nine marching battalions which are in the 5th government, and which belong to his corps, will set off to join him.

When the Minister of War has shown to you the return of the troops in Catalonia, I wish you to propose to me to diminish the number of their cadres, and to recall those which are fit to receive conscripts.

[740.] NAPOLEON TO BERTHIER.

Paris, Jan. 25, 1812.

My Cousin,—I have not yet decided upon giving the command of the army of the North to General Caffarelli; let this decree be kept back. If Marshal Suchet persists in returning, and his health renders it necessary that he should, I shall send General Caffarelli to take the command before Valencia.

[741.] NAPOLEON TO BERTHIER.

Paris, Jan. 25, 1812.

My Cousin,—Write to General Reille that I bestow upon him the command of the army of the Ebro; it will be composed of 4 divisions in the field; 1st, his own division; 2ndly, Palombini's; 3rdly, Severoli's; and 4thly, Ferino's division; to which he will add the 1st light infantry, and the 14th, 115th, and 5th of the line.

As soon as he occupies the country round Barcelona with the part of his army which is in the field, the depôts of the regiments from Nassau, the 2d battalion of the 23d of the line, the 2d battalion of the 18th light troops, 4 companies of artillery, and the sappers and miners, will make the garrison of the town sufficiently strong.

With these 4 divisions he ought finally to subdue the whole of Lower Catalonia, to keep Aragon quiet, and be able to bring the administration of the country into order.

You will find annexed the decree by which Catalonia is divided into 4 departments; you will send a copy to General Reille.

His cavalry will be composed of the 9th hussars, the regiment of royal Italian chasseurs, a regiment of Neapolitan dragoons, and the 24th dragoons.

General Caffarelli will not have the command of the army of the North. If Marshal Suchet cannot remain at Valencia, General Caffarelli will be sent thither.

General Caffarelli will despatch the 2 battalions of the 5th light troops to reinforce the army of Valencia.

Add to General Reille's orders that he may take a company from the legion of gendarmerie which is at Burgos, and send it to Barcelona; it will be useful in a large town.

Order General Dorsenne to forward to the army of Portugal the marching cavalry regiments belonging to it; and to send those which belong to the armies of the Centre and of the South to Madrid. The King may keep them if he thinks proper.

To the Minister of War:—Desire General Decaen to forward to Barcelona all the troops belonging to the 18th light infantry and the 23d of the line.

To Marshal Suchet:—If General Musnier is not wanted, the Emperor would like him to proceed to the army of observation of the Ebro, to receive from General Reille the command of Aragon and Saragossa. Write to General Reille.

Order the King to forward to Valencia one of the 4 regiments of dragoons which are with the army of the Centre. This regiment will form part of the army of Valencia, where it is required by the difficulty of the country.

Order the King to occupy Cuença, and to keep up his communications with Marshal Suchet.

[742.] NAPOLEON TO BERTHIER.

Paris, Jan. 27, 1812.

My Cousin,—Write by to-night's express to General Dorsenne that I have received intelligence of the advance of the English upon Ciudad Rodrigo;* that this being the case, I approve highly of his putting off the departure of the guard, in order that he may support the Duke of Ragusa with his whole force; that General Montbrun must shortly arrive, since Marshal Suchet sent a messenger to desire him to return; and that on the 11th he ought to have commenced his retreat on Madrid, where, according to my calculation, he may have arrived on the 18th, and have joined the army towards the end of the month; that on his arrival the army of Portugal was to take up its final position.

* Lord Wellington took Ciudad Rodrigo on the 19th of January, 1812. —TR.

The English appear to have marched in order to effect a diversion from the siege of Valencia, and because they heard of the strong detachment sent from the army of Portugal. Say that I am not so anxious for the return of my guard as to wish it to be sent before affairs assume a different aspect in the north.

[743.] BERTHIER TO MARMONT.

Paris, Feb. 11, 1812.

The Emperor regrets, M. le Duc, that, having with you Souham's division and the other three divisions which you had assembled, you did not return to Salamanca to see what was going on. This would have embarrassed the English, and might perhaps have been of use to Ciudad Rodrigo. In your present position you should fix your head-quarters at Salamanca, and concentrate your forces there, despatch one division towards the Tagus, re-occupy the Asturias, and force the enemy to stay at Almeida and in the north, for fear of an attack. You may even march upon Ciudad Rodrigo, if you have enough siege artillery, and retake the place (your honour requires this); or if a deficiency of provisions or artillery force you to adjourn this operation, you may at least invade Portugal, and advance upon the Douro and Almeida. This threat would hold the enemy in check.

The army of the South is powerful; its right is protected by the army of Valencia, which extends its outposts towards Alicante.

Your position, therefore, at Salamanca should be offensive as respects Almeida. As long as the English know that your forces are assembled at Salamanca they will attempt nothing; but if you proceed in person to Valladolid; if your troops are sent to be wasted in your rear;* if, above all, your cavalry is not prepared for action after the rains, you will expose the whole of the north of Spain to disasters.

It is absolutely necessary to re-occupy the Asturias, because more troops are required to keep the borders of the plain as far

* Si vos troupes sont envoyées se perdre sur les derrières." I am not quite sure of the meaning of this sentence.—TR.

as Biscay, than to hold the Asturias. Since the English have divided their army in two, one part towards the south and the other against you, their numbers cannot be very considerable; yours are much greater. My letter which you received on the 13th told you what to do,—to threaten the English; and if you think it impossible at present to retake Ciudad Rodrigo, you should repair the roads leading towards Almeida, fortify Salamanca, collect your siege-artillery, and send large detachments upon Ciudad Rodrigo. This plan will hold the English in check without fatiguing your troops, and is open to far fewer objections than that of again scattering your forces, as you propose.

I conclude that Montbrun has arrived, and that you have at length collected together your army.

The capture of Valencia has considerably strengthened the army of the South, and you must think the English mad if you imagine that they are capable of marching upon Badajoz while you are at Salamanca, that is to say, of allowing you to reach Lisbon before they do. They will go south. If you should unadvisedly despatch two or three divisions towards the Tagus, the English will be re-assured, for it will tell them that you intend to attempt nothing against them.

I repeat, therefore, that the Emperor desires you not to quit Salamanca, to re-occupy the Asturias, to rest your army on Salamanca, and to threaten the English from thence.

[744.] NAPOLEON TO CLARKE.

Paris, Feb. 17, 1812.

M. le Duc de Feltre,—Order the intendants, prefects, and sub-prefects whom I have appointed for Catalonia to start before next Sunday for their destination. Give notice of their arrival to the generals in command of those provinces. These functionaries must have no absurd pretensions; their duty is to bring the administration of the provinces into order, and to assist the governors instead of thwarting them.

[745.] Napoleon to Berthier.

Paris, Feb. 18, 1812.

My Cousin,—Write to Baron Dudon that he does wrong when he interferes with the operations of war; that I was sorry to see his reports on the subject; that it is no business of his; that all he had to do was to send the Spanish newspapers to General Dorsenne, without observations of his own; that he has too little experience of the profession of arms either to blame or to praise the generals.

[746.] Orders of Napoleon.

Feb. 20, 1812.

The chief of the staff will write to the Duke of Ragusa that I read his letter of the 6th of February; that I lament his having sent Bonnet's division to the army of the North; that this division is the only one which could have occupied the Asturias with advantage, because the troops are acquainted with the country and with the inhabitants; that it would have been better to send nothing to the army of the North, and to order General Bonnet's division back to the Asturias; that I require, be it where it may, that it return thither; that, even as respects the north, Bonnet's division is better in the Asturias than at Burgos; that the army of Portugal is unsupported; that communication between * . . . . and Irun cannot be kept up if the Asturias are not held; that the Asturias must be occupied when the army has reached as far as Salamanca, and the lines of posts and of Reynosa when it has reached as far as Valladolid or Burgos; but that to allow the peasants to be masters of the mountains which communicate with the sea is the greatest misfortune which can happen to us in Spain; that the population of Gallicia will flow into the provinces occupied by the army; that this theory has been proved by experience; that when the Duke of Istria evacuated the Asturias, the whole country was in commotion; that more than 6000 men are required to hold the mountains; that whether they are placed in the Asturias or in

* Illegible—Ed.

Santander does not signify, except that from Santander they will not cover the kingdom of Leon, nor occupy that province, which is the most important to the insurgents.

Tell him that I put Bonnet's division at his disposal for this purpose; that he is to order it to proceed towards the Asturias, taking the route which General Bonnet thinks the best; that I disapprove of his armies being scattered, and see nothing but indecision in his conduct. How can he expect at Valladolid to be informed in time of the enemy's movements? It would be impossible in any state of things, but especially if the country be in a state of rebellion. How, from Valladolid, can he foresee what the enemy will do? Say that you can do nothing but blame him; that, in the Emperor's opinion, the only operation honourable to his arms is to occupy Salamanca, to have advanced posts of light troops exchanging shots on the frontiers of Portugal and with Ciudad Rodrigo, and to have his army collected around him, so that it can be united in four or five marches; that until the army of the Centre is able to place troops at Almaraz, till the army of Portugal occupies Salamanca, and the Duke of Dalmatia's movement upon Merida and Badajoz produces some effect upon the enemy, he may occupy Almaraz with a light division, which may rejoin him at Talavera; that, when he has occupied Salamanca, and placed his outposts, as I have ordered, in that direction, and this military blister has had its effect on the enemy, he may order the division which he left upon the Tagus to rejoin him, and the army of the Centre may send troops to hold the valley; that he attends too much to things which do not concern him, and not enough to his own business; that his duty was to defend Almeida and Ciudad Rodrigo, and that he allowed them both to be taken; that he has to keep down and to govern the North, and yet he gives up the Asturias, that is to say, the only means by which the North can be kept in subjection and managed; that he gives himself trouble because Lord Wellington sends one or two divisions towards Badajoz, although Badajoz is extremely strong, and the Duke of Dalmatia's army amounts to 80,000 men, and can be reinforced by Marshal Suchet; when, in short, if Lord Wellington were to march upon

Badajoz, there would be a certain, prompt, and decisive method of recalling him, by advancing upon Ciudad Rodrigo and Almeida.

That his army is composed of eight divisions, one of which should remain in the Asturias, and be employed only in marching upon Gallicia; that, if even he were beaten by the English, he should not allow this division to abandon the Asturias, but make it retire into the mountains on the right; that in a few days there will be fighting at Mondragona, unless the mountains are occupied; that in case of the evacuation of Salamanca or Valladolid the division of the Asturias should move towards the mountains, as otherwise Burgos would not be tenable, nor even Vittoria; that, I repeat again, he has to oppose not only the English army but the whole of Gallicia; that these 6000 men would advance by the defiles into Gallicia and hold the province; that 6000 men in the Asturias stand in lieu of 18,000 at Astorga or on the coast; that after the fall of Valencia the rebels, as their communications were cut off, were in despair; that the arrival of bands at Potu and Oviedo and the re-establishment of their communication with the coast* restored their courage: and that all this was caused by the want of reflection and of local knowledge.

To sum up—one of his eight divisions should be placed in the Asturias and not suffered to move from thence; the remaining seven should be collected round Salamanca. He will thus have an army of 50,000 French and 100 pieces of cannon, which, in a country with which they are acquainted, protected by field-works, sure of their provisions, and supported by Salamanca, would not be beaten by 80,000. But add that he must take care not to make an intrenched camp round Salamanca; that the English would conclude that he had taken up the defensive and would no longer fear him, and that what is wanted at Salamanca is merely a fortress.

* In the original "avec la cour," which must be corrupt: probably the word is "côte."—TR.

[747.] NAPOLEON TO BERTHIER.

Paris, Feb. 22, 1812.

The chief of the staff will write to the Duke of Ragusa that he has mistaken my intentions with regard to Valencia; that I ordered 12,000 men to be sent to Valencia, including the troops belonging to the army of the Centre; that I expected their route to lie through Cuença, where there were already 4000 men; that the King would have contributed 3000 more, and that therefore only between 3000 and 4000 men should have been sent by the army of Portugal to Cuença; that his complaints are unfounded, that it would have been madness in the King to have proceeded from Cuença to Albacete; that this manœuvre would have allowed the enemy, who was at Requena, to march on Madrid; that it was plain that this manœuvre could not have been effected without an immense force, as it required an extensive line of operations; and that it would have been of no assistance towards subduing Valencia, since it would have been useless if Marshal Suchet had been foiled in breaking through the Spanish lines; that the art of war consists in keeping one's forces undivided; that the march from Cuença to Requena, so as to be in communication with the left of Marshal Suchet before he attacked Valencia, would have been an operation according to the rules of war; that detaching 3000 men under General Darmagnac would not have weakened the army of Portugal in the least; that the English would not have found it out; that this operation might have been effected by sending troops from the army of the Centre to Cuença, and replacing them by troops from the army of Portugal; that the road by Cuença is no doubt ill-suited for artillery, but that none was wanted against the rebels, and that at any rate Marshal Suchet had some; that the Duke of Ragusa's fault cannot be justified, as he was in front of the enemy, and evidently exposed the whole of the north of Spain; that, if a grand military operation had been intended, the Duke of Dalmatia would have been chosen for the purpose; and that the chance of the English advancing upon Madrid or Salamanca would have been provided against.

[748.] NAPOLEON TO BERTHIER.

Paris, Feb. 29, 1812.

My Cousin,—Write to General Reille that I have ordered General Decaen to join him in investing Urgel and occupying the valleys of Puycerda. Tell him of the incursions of the rebels into our territory, and that it is necessary to obtain possession of Urgel in order to put an end to these insults. Send him word that for this purpose he must direct a strong column either upon Berga or upon Urgel; that he must harass the enemy, and finally act in concert with General Decaen.

[749.] NAPOLEON TO BERTHIER.

Paris, March 8, 1812.

My Cousin,—Repeat the order to General Reille to advance upon Berga and the French part of Cerdagna, in order to drive out the rebels. It is but too true that they obtain their provisions from France, and that they are cantoned at Puycerda, and do not stir from thence. Order him again to send one Italian division to Navarre; he will leave the other in Aragon and will keep with him the French division.

[750.] NAPOLEON TO BERTHIER.

Paris, March 11, 1812.

My Cousin,—Despatch the Duke of Ragusa's aide-de-camp to-day. Tell the Duke that you showed me his last letter; that uniting his forces at Salamanca is not sufficient for the object which he has to accomplish; that he must throw a bridge across the Agueda, and construct a tête-de-pont there, so that, if the enemy leaves less than five divisions on the right bank of the Tagus, he may be able to advance upon the river Coa and Almeida, and lay waste all the north of Portugal; that the rainy season must come to an end; that if Badajoz should be taken by no more than two English divisions, while the Duke of Ragusa keeps the other five engaged on the right bank, he will not be answerable for its capture, which will be entirely laid to the charge of the army of the South; that if, on the other hand, the enemy leaves only two, or even three or four divisons on the right bank, the army of Portugal will be in fault, unless it marches on the enemy's main body, invests Almeida, lays the north of Portugal waste, and sends out detachments as far as the Mondego. That, in short, the duty of the army of Portugal reduces itself to this: to hold in check six or at least five divisions of the British army; take up the offensive in the north, or, if the enemy should begin the attack, or if any other circumstance should render it necessary, in order to raise the siege of Badajoz, to send across the Tagus by Almaraz as many divisions as Lord Wellington has despatched.

When you have finished this letter, you will desire the aide-de-camp to come to the Elysée at 8 o'clock; I have something to say to him.

[751.] NAPOLEON TO CLARKE.

Paris, March 14, 1812.

Monsieur le Duc de Feltre,—I have seen General Plauzonne to-day, and I return to you General Decaen's despatches to acquaint him in a few words with General Plauzonne's mission.

He is ordered to proceed to Girona and to return within eight or ten days, bringing me a detailed plan of operations and administration for Catalonia. Tell General Decaen especially that I give him carte blanche as to the military manœuvres, which, as they are directed against rebels without artillery or line of operations, can be conducted only by the commander-in-chief on the spot. Desire him, however, to keep an eye continually on my frontiers and to observe them with particular care. Whenever more than 3000 of the enemy approach the frontier he should attack their rear and drive them into France. Let him know that I wish General Quesnel to occupy Puycerda, in order to begin the organisation of that department; that I suppose that he must enter it with 5000 men; but that, when once he is established there, 1500 good French troops, formed into two or three battalions, will be sufficient, as he will be immediately joined by General Gareau from Mont Louis, who will bring with him 1200 men, at present under his orders, as well as the provisional regiment which has been taken from Bayonne, consisting of 1500 men, with the Berg battalion 700 strong, which might be completed by the addition of 4000 National Guards. These forces and the 1500 good troops, contributed by General Decaen, would form a column of 5000 men, enough to keep Puycerda. General Travot should send thither a company of artillery: this division should live in the valley or perhaps be fed from France; it should construct works or a fort in the pass between Puycerda and Urgel, place in it artillery from Mont Louis, which with a little labour would protect it from the rebels, who have no cannon. General Travot would furnish 200 cavalry from the provisional regiments which General Avyce is forming. Thus at the sacrifice of only two or three battalions, the army of Catalonia would gain the important advantage of an active force of 6000 men, who would protect our frontiers and threaten Urgel.

Say to General Decaen that this operation ought not to be performed till General Travot is able to furnish the 4000 men, nor until the other movements of the army render it advisable in General Decaen's opinion; that this column might even be increased progressively, as the country behind it is brought into order; that I wish the four departments of Catalonia to be placed under the orders of General Decaen; that Upper Catalonia may be under the command of General Lamarque, who may have at his disposal two columns, each consisting of 4000 men; that a reserve of 3000 men may be attached to General Decaen, who thus would have 11,000 men under him; that 1500 should be placed at Puycerda; there would therefore be from 6000 to 7000 inactive remaining in the garrisons to support General Lamarque, if he should require them; that General Maurice Mathieu should also have two brigades, consisting each of 4000 or 5000 men, in Lower Catalonia, between Lerida and Barcelona, and between Barcelona and Tarragona, and, besides these, 6000 men garrisoning Barcelona, Lerida, and Tarragona; that a good commandant must be placed in Barcelona; that General Decaen would have in hand five divisions in the field, consisting of from 20,000 to 24,000 men; that he should combine his movements so as to be constantly pressing on the rebels; that he should correspond every week with Barcelona; and that General Maurice Mathieu should correspond every week with Lerida and Tarragona.

Say that, as a part of this plan, it would perhaps be advisable to have an intrenched position at Monblanc, and another between Tarragona and Barcelona; that when General Decaen wishes to proceed in person to Lower Catalonia he should take with him his own 4000 men, and be escorted half way by a portion of General Lamarque's troops, which he should immediately send back to protect Upper Catalonia; that he would find in Lower Catalonia 12,000 men in the field, to whom he would add his own 3000; that with this force of 15,000 he should pursue the rebels in whatever direction they take, even towards the Ebro, Tortosa, or the frontiers of Aragon; that small garrisons are sufficient when the communications are occupied by divisions in the field, who hold the country in check, and prevent the enemy from collecting in numbers.

Say that, in order to carry out this plan, which, if well executed, ought to subdue Catalonia, from 33,000 to 34,000 men are requisite; that there are already 30,000 under General Decaen, including those in Barcelona, Lerida, and Tarragona; that I will withdraw 6000 men from General Reille to add to this army; that in this manner both Puycerda and Upper Catalonia would be well defended.

The general commanding in chief should hear every week from the different divisions of his army, and with his characteristic activity should march sometimes on Upper, and at other times on Lower Catalonia, become master of the province, raise his own reputation, and beat the insurgents until the country becomes quiet. Moveable columns and small garrisons are better than large garrisons and stationary armies; the towns are safer and the cantonments are better protected; besides that this aggressive attitude would be productive of events which would secure the tranquillity of the province. The harvests of the plains of Vich, Urgel, and others in Catalonia, may be gathered in to supply the army, and the enemy's magazines seized.

This state of things being established at the end of March,

General Quesnel (who would have had time enough to make frequent reconnaissances on Urgel, and to prepare his siege-train at Mont Louis) might in the course of the month of April at length take this last refuge of the insurgents. General Decaen, in arranging his marches, would take care to advance upon Cardana, Berga, and every other post where the rebels have formed magazines, and perhaps the time is not far distant when, after a few successful rencounters, he may fix his head-quarters at Barcelona, which is the centre of public opinion and of the administration of the province, and, by assembling the notables and the other usual means, gain influence, and reorganise Catalonia, which the existence of two separate commands renders difficult at present.

Summary of the arrangements relating to Catalonia communicated by the Emperor to General Plauzonne :—

Catalonia is no longer to be divided between two commanders-in-chief. General Reille's division is to pass under the orders of General Decaen, who will have at his disposal about 8000 men between Barcelona and Lerida, exclusive of the garrisons of those towns. General Mathieu will command this division in the field, having under his orders the governor of Barcelona, who is to be proposed to his Majesty by General Decaen. Thus, while General Lamarque will manœuvre with his division in Upper, and General Mathieu in Lower Catalonia, General Decaen will repair in turn to the point from which he wishes to act, reducing or increasing one or the other corps, according to circumstances and to the scheme of his operations. The principal aim of General Decaen ought to be the protection of the frontier of France, without losing sight of the objects for which he proposed to occupy the coast. His Majesty does not insist upon forming a corps of 5000 men in Cerdagna if the frontier can be otherwise protected. The corps may consist of only 3000 men, if 3000 be enough. In short, the integrity of the territory of France ought to be the chief care and the great object of the movements of General Decaen : the arrangement of their detail will belong to him ; and for this purpose his Majesty places in him entire confidence. He will propose, on the above principles, the measures which he thinks expedient. He will propose a chief of the staff in place of General Plauzonne. He will propose as governor of Barcelona an energetic officer, capable of commanding, under the orders of General Mathieu. General Garnier, the present commandant of Barcelona, will be recalled. From these arrangements it follows that the garrison of Barcelona will continue to receive its supplies by the old line of communication.

[752.] NAPOLEON TO BERTHIER.

Paris, March 15, 1812.

My Cousin,—Give strict orders to General Dorsenne to despatch the three marching regiments belonging to the army of Portugal to their destination. This order must not be delayed; these three regiments must join their corps.

Order him to send some officers to hasten the march of Palombini's division. The marching regiments of infantry belonging to the army of the south, forming one column, with the marching regiments of cavalry, will proceed to Madrid, and from thence to Seville, to reinforce their regiments. All the marching regiments of the army of Portugal are to repair thither, be broken up, and the cadres to rejoin their depôts.

The army of the north will be composed in the following manner: of Caffarelli's division, Palombini's division, the division of the guard, the 2nd and 3rd regiments of voltigeurs and tirailleurs, the 2nd and 3rd of the Vistula, and a division formed of the 40th and 34th of the line, and the remainder of the 34th light troops, of the 113th of the line, and the Swiss detachments.

Repeat the order that all troops belonging to the Parisian guard are to return to France without delay.

Let General Dorsenne know that marching regiments are to be sent to St. Sebastian, Vittoria, and Bayonne; but that it is essential that, when troops are leaving Spain, the Spaniards should at the same time see others entering.

Order all troops belonging to the army of Valencia to leave the army of the north and repair to their own corps. All these orders must be executed immediately.

[753.] NAPOLEON TO BERTHIER.

Paris, March 16, 1812.

My Cousin,—Order General Dorsenne to keep at Vittoria the 40th, as well as the 34th of the line. Into the 40th, he will incorporate the 250 men of the marching battalion which are intended for the army of the south, and into the 34th the 63 men in the same battalion which are intended for the army of Portugal. He will incorporate into the Polish regiment the 73 men of the 6th battalion of the marching regiment belonging to the army of the south. Tell him to form into a single column and send off to Madrid the seven marching battalions of the army of the south; he will also send off the 386 men of the 1st marching regiment of light cavalry to that army, and the 145 men of the light cavalry and dragoons belonging to the armies of the south and of the centre. He will order the 200 men of the 7th Polish light horse who are at Haro, to return to Bayonne. These measures will deprive his army of seven marching battalions, but instead of them he will have six battalions of good troops of the 4th and 34th of the line, and he will lose a weak cavalry which is of little use. He must therefore despatch these troops immediately, by way of Aranda, if he thinks proper.

The Belle-Isle battalion must be broken up and incorporated into the 130th. Order all the troops which are at Bayonne or in the valley of the Bastan belonging to the 40th and the 34th to join their regiments at Vittoria. Announce to the Duke of Dalmatia the arrival of this reinforcement of 6000 infantry and 500 cavalry, and repeat to the King of Spain the order to send to the south all the detachments of infantry and cavalry which belong to the army of the south. Reiterate the order to Palombini's division to proceed to Navarre, to be at General Dorsenne's disposal, and to form part of the army of the north. Let me know what there is at Bayonne or elsewhere belonging to the 34th and 113th of the line, as well as what they have at Ciudad Rodrigo, that I may see how many battalions can be organised.

If you do not possess the requisite information, obtain it from General Dorsenne; make him draw up a report. Repeat to the

Duke of Albufera the order that, if the English advance on Badajoz, he is not to remain idle with an army of 20,000 men; he should send a detachment to occupy Murcia and enable the Duke of Dalmatia to assemble a large force to disengage his right; he ought even, if necessary, to send a strong division towards Madrid, to relieve the troops at Almaraz.

[754.] NAPOLEON TO BERTHIER.

Paris, March 16, 1812.

My Cousin,—Send an extraordinary express this evening to inform the King of Spain that I intrust to him the command of all my armies in Spain, and that Marshal Jourdan will perform the duties of chief of the staff. You will send this order at the same time to Marshal Jourdan. Inform the King that I shall let him know my wishes on political matters through my ambassador.

You will write to Marshal Suchet and to the Dukes of Dalmatia and of Ragusa that I have bestowed the command of all my armies in Spain upon the King; that I have appointed Marshal Jourdan to be chief of the staff; and that they are to obey all the King's orders, so as to prevent discordant action.

You will also write separately to the Duke of Ragusa that the necessity of obtaining concurrent action in the armies of the south, of Valencia, and of Portugal, has determined me to give the command of these armies to the King of Spain, by whose orders he is to regulate his movements.

In the course of to-morrow you will write to the King more in detail; but it is necessary to despatch this evening an express to Bayonne. You will desire General l'Huillier to send an officer by post to take your letter to the King.

[755.] NAPOLEON TO BERTHIER.

Paris, March 30, 1812.

My Cousin,—I beg you to send me a return of what there is belonging to the 34th and 40th regiments in the seven marching battalions belonging to the army of the south, and in the reserve at Bayonne, and of the troops belonging to the 20th dragoons and 10th hussars which are in the different marching companies.

Repeat the order to General Dorsenne to complete the 34th and 40th by calling in all the detachments in the different marching regiments, and to fill up in the same manner the 10th hussars and 20th dragoons, and hasten the arrival of Palombini's division in Navarre; and to take advantage of this union of forces to march on Mendizabal, clear the mountain, and carry Potès.

Write to General Dorsenne that the presence of General Caffarelli is enough to keep down Navarre, and that he ought to proceed in person to Vittoria, to check the disturbance in Santander.

Reiterate the order for the three Polish regiments to continue their route. Ask again for a return of the 113th and 34th.

Despatch an officer to carry these orders to General Dorsenne.

[756.] NAPOLEON TO BERTHIER.

Paris, April 3, 1812.

My Cousin,—Write to Marshal Suchet that I think it necessary that General Reille should proceed to Aragon, to take the command of that important province.

I wish General Reille to leave under the orders of General Maurice Mathieu 6,000 men, that is to say, one French and one Italian brigade, and at least 300 horses. He is to take with him to Aragon a French and an Italian brigade. General Reille should also leave in Catalonia all that belong to the corps in garrison at Tarragona, Lerida, and Barcelona. The whole of Catalonia, except Tortosa and Mequinenza, will be under the command of General Decaen, for the sake of concurrent action. General Reille, when placed at Saragossa, will be able to prevent the spread of mischief in Aragon, and he may pursue the banditti in concert with Generals Maurice Mathieu and Caffarelli.

Tell the Duke of Ragusa that his aide-de-camp will inform him that I leave him *carte blanche*; that, seeing the importance of combined operations, I have given to the King of Spain the command of the armies of Portugal, of the South, and of Valencia, in order that they may be all directed towards one and the same end; that occupying the Asturias is the greatest possible economy of troops, as otherwise the rebels will advance upon St. Sebastian and the rear, and will require six times as many troops to put them down as would suffice to occupy the Asturias.

Write in cipher to the King of Spain that I have intrusted him with the political and military direction of all the affairs in Spain; that the army of Portugal, consisting of eight divisions of infantry, is ordered to keep one division in the Asturias, and is forced by the present state of things to place two divisions in the North, to hold Gallicia and the north of Portugal; that there will remain therefore only five, or at most six divisions available to succour Badajoz; but that in this case he may dispose of the division of his guard and of the division of dragoons, which, joined to the Duke of Dalmatia's forces, will be enough to baffle the attempts of the English; that perhaps the Duke of Albufera might threaten Alicante and occupy Murcia; that, if the Duke of Ragusa has marched on Almeida, which is not yet protected against a surprise, and has sent out detachments in every direction, I think it improbable that Lord Wellington would risk seeing the French enter Lisbon in seven or eight marches; but if, on the other hand, the Duke of Ragusa has remained at Salamanca without making preparations for the war in the Agueda, and has allowed General Wellington to take up the initiative, or if, either for want of provisions, or on account of some other local difficulty, he should be obliged to follow the enemy's lead, he may, as soon as the siege of Badajoz is begun,* collect together five or six divisions of the army of Portugal, the available troops of the army of the Centre, which, joined to the army of the South, will bring his numbers to double those of the English, for at most they have not more than from 25,000 to 30,000 men, and, counting the Portuguese, 50,000.

Either we must take the initiative by providing for the defence of Salamanca, constructing a *tête-de-pont* on the Agueda,

* At the date of this letter the siege of Badajoz was nearly terminated. The place was taken on the 6th of April, 1812.—TR.

keeping up the war in the north of Portugal and pursuing the enemy, which is taking the initiative, or, if this is not done, we must follow the enemy's lead, and go wherever he goes. In this case, several divisions of the army of Portugal must undoubtedly proceed towards the Tagus, leaving at Salamanca sufficient forces to fortify that important post and to hold the north. It appears that the English have 1500 men in Carthagena, as many in Alicante, 3000 or 4000 at Cadiz, and 30,000 in Portugal, and besides these from 20,000 to 25,000 Portuguese disciplined and under arms.

[757.] BERTHIER TO MARMONT.

April 16, 1812.

M. le Maréchal,—I have laid before the Emperor your letters of the 22nd and 25th of March.* In my despatches of the 18th and 20th of February I prescribed to you the measures necessary for taking the initiative, and giving the war a character suited to the glory of the French arms, by getting rid of the irresolution and change of plans which at present belong to it, and which foretell a conquered army; but instead of studying and trying to act up to the spirit of these instructions, you have chosen to misunderstand the letter of my orders, and to act in absolute contradiction to their spirit. These instructions were carefully reasoned out, and their motives developed, as the orders of a Government ought to be; they were given at 300 leagues of distance, and six weeks of time; they supposed you to be in front of the enemy, and they enjoined you to hold him in check, and to oblige the greater part of his army to remain in the north by fixing your head-quarters at Salamanca, and exchanging shots perpetually with Ciudad Rodrigo and Almeida. In these instructions you were told, "If, under these circumstances, the enemy remains before you with less than five divisions, march towards him, keep him in view. As his hospitals and magazines are between Lisbon and the Coa, he will not be able to empty them so rapidly as to prevent your com-

* These letters do not appear.—TR.

ing up with him." I added that, in these circumstances, it was absurd to think that the English General would abandon the whole of the north to attack a place which threatened . . . . . .*

You are recommended to second the King, and, for the sake of your attachment to his person and the glory of his arms, to do all that is in your power to prevent 40,000 English from spoiling all the affairs in Spain, which will infallibly be the case if the generals of the different corps are not animated by the desire of glory, and by the patriotism which alone can overcome obstacles, and prevent the sacrifice of the public good to personal ambition and private passions.

When His Majesty returns from Poland he will proceed to Spain: he hopes that your conduct will in future deserve nothing but praise, and that you will acquire fresh claims to his esteem.

[758.] BERTHIER TO JOSEPH.

Paris, April 16, 1812.

Sire,—I had the honour of acquainting your Majesty with the letter which I wrote to the Duke of Ragusa on the 18th of February last. As the dispositions contained in it were misunderstood by the Marshal, I sent to him on the 12th March, by his aide-de-camp, Colonel Jardet, the annexed letter,† which reached him on the 25th. Acknowledging the receipt of this despatch, in a letter dated the 27th, the Duke of Ragusa informs me that on the 1st of April he will be, with three of his divisions, before Ciudad Rodrigo; but from the same letter it appears that he proposed to direct upon Placencia General Foy's division, which was at Almaraz. The Emperor trusts that better information as to the English position prevented his committing this error. In another letter, dated the 30th, the Duke of Ragusa says that he has received the letter by which I announced to him that your Majesty had the command of the armies in Spain; I have no doubt but that he has hastened to take your orders. I send to you, Sire, my answer to his letter of the 27th of March. Just

* Illegible.—ED.

† See this letter p. 180.—TR.

now, when the English have assembled their forces to lay siege to Badajoz, the movements and the direction of the armies of the Centre, of the South, and of Portugal are so important, that the Emperor is persuaded that your Majesty bestows serious attention upon them, and that you have taken Marshal Jourdan and General Daultanne into your councils.

Reinforcements are on their way to Spain, and convoys of money are despatched regularly every month. The Duke of Albufera sends word that nearly half of the contribution imposed on Valencia has been paid.

The French troops in Spain are very numerous, and your Majesty is empowered to direct them. You have doubtless given the requisite orders to the Duke of Ragusa's army, that it may hold the English in check, and act in concert with the army of the south.

The Emperor expects your Majesty to act with vigour, and to enforce obedience.

[759.] BERTHIER TO SUCHET.

Paris, April 24, 1812.

M. le Maréchal,—In the present state of affairs the Emperor may at any time set off to join the Grand Army. Before removing further from Spain, His Majesty thinks fit to place under the same command Upper and Lower Catalonia, Aragon, and the kingdom of Valencia, and this command the Emperor bestows upon you. The army of Catalonia, which is under General Decaen's orders, is at your disposal. You will therefore, M. le Duc, immediately furnish all the places in Upper and Lower Catalonia with provisions, and pay particular attention to Barcelona. You are to employ all the forces under your orders for the general good of the country which you command, including in your plans the garrison of Barcelona and the troops under General Decaen.

The Emperor desires that from the day on which you receive this letter you correspond with the Minister of War instead of with me: you will continue nevertheless to correspond with the King, who is commander-in-chief of all the armies in Spain.

You are to make no change in General Decaen's command, except that he is under you, as your command will in future extend over Upper and Lower Catalonia, Aragon, and Valencia.

You are aware of the importance of supplying the places in Catalonia with sufficient provisions, and of keeping the country quiet.

I will inform General Decaen and General Maurice Mathieu that they are under your orders. General Reille and the troops under his command continue to form part of your army.

I will send a copy of your cipher to the Minister of War..

[760.] NAPOLEON TO CLARKE.

St. Cloud, April 28, 1812.

M. le Duc de Feltre,—I see no change to be made in the army of Catalonia. General Decaen may take the title of Governor of Catalonia. You must make him understand that the superior command of Marshal Suchet is not to prevent his corresponding with you and doing whatever is necessary. My motive for this measure was that all the troops in that part of the country might, in case of an emergency, be united for the same object.

[761.] NAPOLEON TO CLARKE.

Dresden, May 28, 1812.

M. le Duc de Feltre,—I return to you the Spanish correspondence. Write to the Duke of Ragusa that he is to take his orders from the King; that I suppose that he conducted his retreat according to the rules of war, not retiring before Lord Wellington's light cavalry, but obliging him to bring up his forces in large bodies; that he has preserved his têtes-de-pont upon the Agueda, which alone will enable him to obtain every day news of the enemy, and to hold him in check; that if, on the other hand, he has placed 30 leagues between himself and the enemy, as he has done twice before, against all military principles, he permits the English general to proceed whithersoever he pleases, he perpetually loses the initiative, and is no longer of any weight in the affairs of Spain.

That Biscay and the north are in a dangerous position in consequence of General Bonnet's division having evacuated the Asturias, which have not yet been re-occupied; that the north is exposed to disasters; that Santona and St. Sebastian are in danger; that the free communication of the guerillas with Gallicia and the Asturias by sea renders them formidable; that unless the Asturias are speedily re-occupied, his position cannot improve.

Desire General Caffarelli to keep his troops more together and to have always a column in hand.

Write to General l'Huillier to keep an eye on St. Sebastian, and always to hold 3000 men ready to send thither, if it should require assistance.

In order to guard against the ill-concerted movements and the unfortunate direction given to our affairs by the Duke of Ragusa, it is necessary to have generally many troops at Bayonne. Hasten the march of the 3rd, of the 105th, and of the 5th provisional demi-brigade to Bayonne, and keep two brigadier-generals there; that there may always be sufficient forces at the disposal of General l'Huillier to enable him to act according to circumstances.

Collect 1000 cavalry from the depôts of the armies of Spain, form them into a marching regiment, and send them to Bayonne.

Write to General l'Huillier to keep his troops in the valley of the Bastan, at Bayonne, at St. Jean de Luz, and at Irun; to feed them well, hut them, drill and exercise them. If the Duke of Ragusa continues to commit blunders, this reserve will prevent their becoming irremediable.

[762.] MARMONT TO JOSEPH.

Arevalo, July 25, 1812.*

I have the honour of giving an account to your Majesty of the events which took place before my arrival on the Douro, and of the motives which led me thither. Having increased my

* This letter of Marmont's is inserted in consequence partly of its intrinsic interest, and partly to render intelligible Napoleon's criticisms on it in the next letter.—TR.

artillery and cavalry, and joined by General Bonnet's division, I set about to resume the offensive. On the 17th of this month, after having, in order to deceive the enemy, manœuvred for four or five days to my right in the direction of Toro, I crossed the bridge of Tordesillas and arrived without difficulty upon the table-land of Rueda: the same night the army halted at Nava del Rey. On the 18th, having surprised the advanced guard of the enemy at Tordesillas, I pressed it with vigour, and forced it to make a retreat of more than three leagues with much precipitation and great danger, and constantly under the fire of my artillery. That day I reached the banks of the Zuarena, where the enemy took up a position. The strength of that position having prevented me from attacking, I manœuvred to effect the passage of the river, which took place on the 20th. The enemy, who had followed me in my movement, sought to gain possession of the table-lands, on which depended the security of my operation, but he failed, and we manœuvred under a constant cannonade from each other's artillery. This sort of operation is the only one which is good against the English, who have a peculiar talent for taking up positions, and whom therefore it is advisable to thwart by preventing them as much as possible (before entering into action) from establishing themselves as they wish to do. On the 20th the enemy moved to the strong position of St. Cristobal. On the 21st I effected the passage of the Tormès, after having taken possession of the bridge of Alba; the army placed itself between Alba de Tormès and Salamanca, at the entrance of the woods. On the night of the 21st the English army passed the Tormès, and placed itself in position opposite to me at a distance of three-quarters of a league.

I made a reconnaissance at daybreak, and I passed the morning in making my dispositions, first with a view of preparing a good defence, and secondly with that of attacking, if circumstances should appear favourable. Everything promised well. I thought it necessary to occupy a table-land which completed our system of defence, and, at the same time, would be very useful in case we should act upon the offensive, on which I had almost determined. I caused it to be occupied by the 5th division and the reserve of the horse-artillery, with strict orders to confine themselves to taking possession of the table-land. As it was possible that the enemy, when he saw that we were masters of it, would attack it before I had time to collect all my forces, I directed two divisions to draw near as a support. General Maucune broke and drove off the English detachment which occupied the heights.

Up to that time we had had nothing but success, and everything promised that it would be complete. I thought it necessary to bring up fresh troops to act with vigour in support of General Maucune, and to crush the enemy, who was assembling his forces. I immediately collected together all the troops at my disposal, and I was proceeding to lead them and to take the immediate command of this part of the battle, when, by a cruel accident, at the moment when my presence was most required, a round of grape-shot threw me over, shattering my right arm, and inflicting two severe wounds in my side, thus rendering me incapable of taking any part in the command. The anarchy consequent upon this accident and on the wound of General Bonnet, my next in command as the senior general of division, who was struck a few instants afterwards, prevented the execution of my orders; so that General Maucune, notwithstanding the brilliant success which he had obtained, was forced by superior numbers to retire. The troops which came to his assistance, performing prodigies of valour, but acting without concert, were also forced to retreat. At length, Sire, the army, having maintained the combat for three hours, quitted the field of battle.

General Clausel, who is in command, has judged it necessary to recross the Tormès, and will take a position on the right bank of the Lesma and the Douro.

The condition in which I am, obliges me to offer to your Majesty a very brief report. As soon as I can, I shall have the honour of entering into fuller details upon this event, which illustrates but too forcibly the caprices of fortune and the dissipation of the most flattering hopes by sad realities. The army has to regret the loss of a considerable number of officers of every rank. The Generals Ferez-Thomière and Desgravier have fallen; General . . . . . has received a ball through the thigh; General Menne is wounded, as is also General Clausel, but slightly. We estimate our loss at nearly 5000 men: that of the English must be much greater. I can hardly describe the mischief which was done to them by our artillery.

[763.] NAPOLEON TO CLARKE.

Ghiast, Sept. 2, 1812.*

Monsieur le Duc de Feltre,—I have received the Duke of Ragusa's report on the battle of the 22nd. It is impossible to read anything with less meaning; it is fuller of intricacies and wheelworks than a clock, and it contains not one word of information as to the real state of things.

Here is the view which I take of the affair and of the conduct to be held by you:—

You will wait till the Duke of Ragusa has arrived, till his wounds are cured and his recovery is nearly complete. You will then ask him for a categorical answer to the following questions:—

Why did he offer battle without the orders of his commander-in-chief?

Placed, as he was, by the general dispositions of the army, at Salamanca, it was natural that he should defend himself if attacked; but since he had evacuated Salamanca, and left it several marches behind him, why did he not inform his commander-in-chief? Why did he not ask for orders as to his conduct, dependent as that ought to have been on the general system of my armies of Spain?

His insubordination has caused all these disasters. And even supposing that he was not obliged to put himself into communica-

* Ghiast, or Gjatz, is a town about 95 miles from Moscow and about 30 from Borodino. Napoleon remained there from the 1st to the 4th of September preparing for the battle of Borodino. This letter, calm, considerate, full, and precise, written at a moment of such anxiety, and almost on the eve of so tremendous a struggle, is a striking example of Napoleon's moral and intellectual strength.—TR.

tion with his commander-in-chief and to obey his orders, what could have induced him to abandon his defensive position on the Douro, when, without overstraining his imagination, he might have supposed it possible that he might be reinforced by the arrival of the division of dragoons, of 30 pieces of cannon, and by more than 15,000 French troops whom the King had in hand?

How could he exchange his defensive for an offensive position, without waiting for the junction and assistance of a corps consisting of from 15,000 to 17,000 men?

The King had ordered the army of the North to despatch its cavalry to his assistance; they were on their way; the Duke of Ragusa must have been aware of it, as the cavalry arrived on the evening after the battle.

There are several marches between Salamanca and Burgos; why did he not make a delay of two days in order to obtain this reinforcement of cavalry, which was of so much consequence to him?

You must demand an explanation of the reasons which induced the Duke of Ragusa to offer battle without the orders of his commander-in-chief, and without waiting for the reinforcements which the King, as commander-in-chief of my armies of Spain, might have collected from the armies of the Centre, of Valencia, and of Andalusia?

The army of the Centre alone furnished 15,000 men and 2500 horse, which might have arrived at the very time when the Duke of Ragusa was occasioning the defeat of the French army; indeed, from his two armies the King might have brought to him 40,000 men.

Again, when the Duke of Ragusa knew that 1500 horse were on their way to him from Burgos, why did he not await their arrival?

Putting these two circumstances together—his taking up the offensive without the orders of his commander-in-chief, and his not postponing the battle for two days in order to receive the 15,000 infantry which the King was bringing to him, and the 1500 cavalry which were coming to him from the army of the North—one is inclined to think that the Duke of Ragusa was afraid of the King's sharing in his success, and that he sacrificed to personal vanity the glory of his country and the good of my service.

Order the generals of divisions to send returns of their losses. It is intolerable that false accounts should be sent and the truth disguised.

Order General Clausel, who is in command of the army, to send a return of the troops before as well as after the battle.

Ask the generals of the different corps also for precise returns.

At a fitting moment you will let the Duke of Ragusa know how much I am offended by his inexplicable conduct in not waiting two days for succours from the armies of the Centre and of the North.

I am anxiously expecting the arrival of the King's aide-de-camp, that I may obtain some real information; what the King has written is of little value.

[764.] NAPOLEON TO CLARKE.

Ghiast, Sept. 2, 1812.

M. le Duc de Feltre,—I think it advisable to put the Duke of Ragusa's justification into the 'Moniteur.' You must also insert the staff officer's report, describing the subsequent state of things, and an article, with the date of the day on which the King with his troops reached Olmedo, and that on which the cavalry from the army of the north arrived.

Ask General Clausel also to send you a detailed report, to be inserted in the 'Moniteur,' with some passages softened. The public will thus understand what has happened, and will see that the check which the Duke of Ragusa has sustained does not prevent our affairs in Spain from being prosperous, as our armies are excellent, and our losses are about equal to those of the enemy.

[765.] NAPOLEON TO CLARKE.

Moscow, Sept. 12, 1812.*

M. le Duc de Feltre,—I think General Reille the man best fitted to command the army of Portugal. If nothing has occurred to the contrary, I think that you will do well to give him that command.

[766.] NAPOLEON TO CLARKE.

Moscow, Oct. 19, 1812.†

M. le Duc de Feltre,—An aide-de-camp from the King of Spain has brought letters to me dated the first week in September. You are aware that at this distance I can do nothing for the armies of Spain.

Let the King of Spain and the Duke of Dalmatia know how little help they are to expect, and how necessary their present situation makes it that they should unite, and diminish as much as is in their power the disasters caused by a pernicious system; that it was very absurd in the King to allow 400 men to be taken at Guadarrama, and 1300 at the Retiro; these men were of use against the town and the guerillas, but were incapable of making a defence against any other enemy; that it is grievous that the Duke of Ragusa permitted garrisons to be taken at Salamanca, Toro, Zamora, &c. Such events are calamities.

Write to the King that I desire that such things may not recur; that Lerida, Tarragona, and the other fortresses in Catalonia must be blown up; that if we are to lose this frontier, it must not be left in a state in which it would be difficult to take it again. I have given this order repeatedly.

Let the cohort of La Rochelle and the other cohorts in the interior advance towards the frontier to defend it.

They should not pass beyond the frontier, but remain there to prevent invasion.

* This date is erroneous. The advanced guard of the French army did not enter Moscow until the 14th of September.—Tr.

† If the date of this letter be correct, it must have been written as Napoleon was in the act of quitting Moscow. He marched out before daybreak on the 19th of October.—Tr.

[767.] NAPOLEON TO CLARKE.

Bienitza, Dec. 5, 1812.*

M. le Duc de Feltre,—I have read with interest the journal of the siege of the castle of Burgos; I think that it ought to be put into the 'Moniteur.'

Let me have a draft of a decree for rewarding General Dubreton and the officers and soldiers who distinguished themselves in that defence.

[768.] NAPOLEON TO CLARKE.

Paris, Dec. 24, 1812.

M. le Duc de Feltre,—I wish your relations with the army of Spain to remain unaltered. You will insert in the 'Moniteur' whatever you think proper.

* On the night of the 5th of December Napoleon left the Grand Army, having previously dictated the 29th bulletin. He reached Paris on the 18th.—TR.

CHAPTER XIX.

THIS chapter embraces the first six months of the year 1813. Napoleon passed a small part of that year in France. He left Paris on the 15th of April; he returned on the 9th of November. During his absence he appears to have paid little attention to the affairs of Spain, and when he returned he found his armies driven across the frontier of France, and Joseph quietly established as a country gentleman at Mortefontaine.

I have translated an interesting letter from Desprez, Joseph's aide-de-camp, describing his interview with Napoleon a few hours before the commencement of the retreat from Moscow, and the retreat itself up to Wilna.

I have also translated four letters from Clarke to Joseph, the only ones which seem to have been dictated by Napoleon.

Others appear to have been written. In a letter dated the 11th of July, Joseph alludes to orders of Napoleon's dated the 8th, and to a letter dated the 9th, and he afterwards refers to one of the 16th.

None of these documents are inserted by M. du Casse, nor is their absence explained.

[769.] DESPREZ TO JOSEPH.

Paris, Jan. 3, 1813.

Sire,—I have already had the honour of announcing to your Majesty my arrival in Paris; but as the express was my means of communication, I was forced to use the utmost discretion

The Queen having advised me to write to you in detail, and offered to send my letter by the first courier whom she despatches, I take the opportunity of giving an account to your Majesty of the result of my mission, and of some of the events which I have witnessed.

I arrived at Moscow on the evening of the 18th of October. The Emperor had just heard that the advanced guard, under the command of the King of Naples, had been attacked, and forced to retreat with only part of their artillery. The withdrawal of the troops was already decided upon, and they had begun to put themselves in motion. My arrival was announced to his Majesty, who returned at first an answer which was but little favourable. However, in the middle of the night I was called. I delivered to the Emperor the despatches with which your Majesty had intrusted me, and, without opening them, he questioned me as to the contents; he then made upon the campaign some of the reflections which your Majesty anticipated.

He said that your march to assist the army of Portugal was commenced too late; that it might have been made a month sooner; that he himself had dictated the course to be adopted under such circumstances when, in 1808, he had left Madrid without hesitation to march upon the English who had advanced as far as Valladolid. I replied that your Majesty set off a few hours after the arrival of Palombini's division, that you were obliged to wait for this division in order to carry to the army of Portugal such a reinforcement as to put success beyond a doubt; that you thought it less necessary to hasten the movement as Marshal Marmont had frequently written to say that he considered himself too weak to engage the English without assistance; that he had the power of choosing his own time; that he was not beaten in his position on the Douro, but on a field of battle, on which his presence was uncalled for. The Emperor then observed that, on hearing of the loss of the battle of Salamanca, your Majesty should have proceeded towards the Douro to join yourself to the army of Portugal. I reminded him of your march from the Guadarrama on Segovia, and of the critical position in which you were left by the Duke of Ragusa, who himself had proposed this manœuvre.* The Emperor said that he was well aware of all the reproaches which might be addressed to Marshal Marmont on this subject. He added that, having effected a retreat upon Madrid, the army of the centre ought to have held the defiles of the Guadarrama for a longer time; that they crossed the Tagus too soon; that, at any rate, when this retreat was resolved on, the garrison should have been withdrawn from the Retiro, all the gun-carriages broken up, the eagles carried off, and the clothing burnt; that he never had considered this post as fit for more than to keep down the people of Madrid; that, as the enemy was master of the field, it should have been abandoned to him; and that of all the faults of the campaign this was the one which he least understood. I answered these remarks in the manner agreed upon with your Majesty.† The Emperor then proceeded to the Duke of Dalmatia's letter; he told me that it had already reached him through another channel, but that he had attached no importance to it; that Marshal Soult was in error; that he could not attend to such trifles while he was at the head of 500,000 men and engaged in enormous undertakings —these were his expressions; that, however, the Duke of Dalmatia's suspicions did not much surprise him; ‡ that they are shared by many generals belonging to the army of Spain, who think that your Majesty prefers Spain to France; that he was convinced that you had a French heart, but that those who judged

* Joseph had advanced to within two marches of Salamanca when he heard of Marmont's defeat, and retreated across the Guadarrama pass towards Madrid. Letters from General Clausel induced him to suspend his retreat, to cross again the Guadarrama, and march to Segovia, where he hoped to join Clausel. He waited for Clausel four days, and, finding that he was marching on Burgos, returned himself to Madrid, remained there from the 2nd to the 10th of August, and then retired to Valencia.—TR.

† What this answer was does not appear, nor is it easy to conjecture it. The reader will probably agree with Napoleon, that Joseph's conduct in this matter was inexplicable.—TR.

‡ Soult had written to Napoleon to express his suspicions that Joseph was betraying the French cause, in the hope of pleasing the Spaniards, getting rid of the French, and retaining his throne through the allies. Joseph had required that Soult should be recalled and punished.—TR.

you by your public speeches might think otherwise. He added that Marshal Soult's was the only military head in Spain; that he could not withdraw him without endangering the army; that, on the other hand, he was perfectly easy as to Marshal Soult's intentions, as he had just learnt from the English newspapers that the Marshal was evacuating Andalusia, and joining the armies of the centre and of Aragon; that this junction will make them strong enough to take up the offensive; that he had no orders to send; that it was impossible to give orders from such a distance; that he did not disguise from himself the extent of the evil; and that he more than ever regretted that your Majesty had not followed his advice not to return to Spain.*

He added that it was useless for me to return; that I should stay with the army, where employment would be given to me. I entreated then to be sent back to your Majesty in a manner which seemed to make some impression on the Emperor; and he ended by telling me that I should be sent back, but that it was impossible just at present; that, as I was in want of rest, I should remain at Moscow; and that, since I was an engineer, I should be charged with the direction of the works and defence of the Kremlin, under the command of the Duke of Treviso. I received, in consequence, an order written by the Prince of Neufchâtel. When, after the complete evacuation of Moscow, Marshal Mortier's corps rejoined the army, I asked and obtained permission to remain attached to it till I was sent back. I feared that, if I stayed at head-quarters, new duties, which might prevent my return, would be assigned to me, and that perhaps they would avoid sending to your Majesty an eye-witness of the events which were taking place, and I remained with Marshal Mortier, waiting for an opportunity of returning. Having reached Wilna a short time after the Emperor left it, I obtained the Duke of Bassano's permission to proceed to Paris and wait there for orders. In a former letter I had the honour of announcing to your

* It is difficult to suppose that this advice was not actually given, when we find it thus referred to by Napoleon. But there is no trace of it in the Correspondence, and Joseph's supposed refusal to follow it is inconsistent with his constant and earnest entreaties to be allowed to quit his Spanish throne.—TR.

Majesty that the state of my health forced me to postpone my return to Spain.

The army, when I quitted it, was in the most horrible misery. For a long while previously the disorder and losses had been frightful; the artillery and cavalry had ceased to exist. The different regiments were all mixed together; the soldiers marched pell-mell, and sought only how to prolong mechanically their existence. Although the enemy was on all sides of us, thousands of men strayed every day into the neighbouring villages, and fell into the hands of the Cossacks. Nevertheless, large as is the number of prisoners, that of the dead exceeds it. It is impossible to describe the famine; during more than a month there were no rations; dead horses were the only resource, and even the marshals were frequently in want of bread. The severity of the climate rendered hunger more fatal; every night we left at the bivouac several hundred corpses. I think that I may, without exaggeration, estimate those who have been lost in this manner at 100,000—the truth is best expressed by saying that the army is dead. The young guard, which formed part of the corps to which I was attached, was 8000 strong when we left Moscow; at Wilna it scarcely numbered 400. All the other corps are reduced in the same proportion; and as the flight did not end at the Niemen, I am persuaded that not 20,000 men reached the Vistula. It was believed in the army that a great many soldiers were on in front, who would rally when it was possible to suspend the retreat. I convinced myself of the contrary; at 5 leagues from head-quarters I met no more stragglers, and I was then aware of the extent of the calamity.

A single fact may give your Majesty an idea of the state of things. Since crossing the Niemen a corps of 800 Neapolitans, the only corps which has preserved any sort of order, formed the rear-guard of a French army the strength of which once amounted to 300,000 men. It is impossible to say how contagious was the disorder: the corps of the Dukes of Belluno and Reggio amounted together to 30,000 men when they crossed the Beresina; two days afterwards they had melted away like the rest of the army. Sending reinforcements only increased the losses, and at last we became aware that fresh troops must not be allowed to come in contact with a disorderly multitude which could no longer be called an army. The King of Naples declared that, in delegating the command to him, the Emperor exacted the greatest possible proof of his devotion. Both the moral and physical strength of the Prince of Neufchâtel were completely exhausted. If your Majesty were now to ask me when the retreat is to end, I can say only that it depends on the enemy. I do not think that Prussia will make much effort to defend her territory. M. de Narbonne, whom I saw at Berlin, and who was the bearer of letters from the Emperor to the King of Prussia, told me that both the King and his prime minister were favourably disposed, but that he was aware that the feeling of the nation was different. Already several brawls had taken place between the citizens of Berlin and the soldiers of the French garrison; and when I passed through Prussia I had opportunities of convincing myself that no trust could be placed in our recent ally.

It seems also that in the Austrian army the officers declaim openly against the war.

Sad as this picture is, I believe it to be painted without exaggeration, and that my observations have been made with impartiality. My estimate of the extent of the evil is the same now as it was when I was nearer to the scene of action.

[770.] CLARKE TO JOSEPH.

Paris, Jan. 4, 1813.

Sire,—I have laid before his Imperial Majesty the letters which your Majesty did me the honour of writing to me from Arevalo on the 30th of November, and from Madrid on the 4th of December.

The Emperor assumes that the 29th bulletin* has informed your Majesty as to the affairs of the north, and shown that they require all our cares and all our efforts, and that Spanish questions must be subordinate to them. In these circumstances the

* The celebrated bulletin, announcing the destruction of the French army in Russia.—TR.

Emperor thinks that your Majesty should move with your head-quarters to Valladolid, and let Madrid be occupied only by one of the extremities of your line. The communication between your head-quarters and France will thus be shorter and safer, and the north will be better protected. When your Majesty is in this new position, the Emperor hopes that you will turn to account the inactivity of the English by pacifying Navarre, Biscay, and Santander. The increase of the guerrillas in this direction has rendered Caffarelli unable to perform all his duties. Forced as he is to escort convoys, to protect communications, to guard our portion of the coast, and to collect contributions and subsistence, he ought also to retake the posts seized by the enemy, and to drive them from Santander, Castro, Bermeo, and Bilbao. The support and the reinforcements which your Majesty can give will afford the means, and the tranquillity of the north of Spain will be the result. As to the various demands contained in your Majesty's letter, I will answer them successively, and I trust that you will rely on my eagerness to comply with them.

[771.] CLARKE TO JOSEPH.

Paris, Feb. 12, 1813.

Sire,—I had the honour of writing three times to your Majesty during January, to transmit the Emperor's wishes on the management of Spanish affairs, and, as my despatches were, at the least, triple, I trust that they reached their destination. I received to-day a duplicate of your Majesty's letter of the 8th February, the first not having arrived, which shows the continuing difficulty of communication. The inconvenience becomes more sensible as the prompt execution of the Emperor's orders becomes more urgent. His Majesty is most anxious to know what has been done in Madrid in pursuance of his instructions; and his constant disappointment leads him to dread that the precious period of two months, during which the English have been inactive, has been lost. He trusts that, at latest, the 29th bulletin has shown to your Majesty the necessity of opening and securing by every possible means your communication with France. This can be done only by throwing the forces in your

Majesty's hands on the line of communication between Bayonne and France, and by sending into Navarre and Aragon troops sufficient to destroy the bands which lay waste those provinces.

The army of Portugal, acting with that of the North, is sufficient for these purposes, and the armies of the Centre and the South can hold in check the English until circumstances change. The Emperor commands me to reiterate to your Majesty that the use of Valladolid, as a residence and as head-quarters, is an indispensable preliminary. From thence must be directed on the Burgos road, and on the other fit points, the troops which are to reinforce or to second the army of the North. Madrid, and even Valencia, form parts of this system, only as posts to be held by your extreme left, not as places to be kept by a concentration of forces. Valladolid and Salamanca are now the essential points between which the troops that are to be ready to take the offensive against the English, and to defeat their plans, are to be distributed. The Emperor hears that they are strengthening themselves in Portugal, and appear to intend either to enter Spain or to send from Lisbon an expedition of 25,000 men, English and Spanish, to invade the French coast while we are fighting in the north. To prevent this we must always be ready to move forward, and to threaten a march on Lisbon, or the conquest of Portugal. At the same time the communication with France must be easy and safe, which, as I have already stated to your Majesty, can be effected only by employing the time while the English are inactive, to pacify Biscay and Navarre.

As the Emperor's anxiety respecting the affairs of Spain has led me to reproduce his wishes on several occasions, and in different forms, I now recapitulate the most important suggestions which I have had the honour of making to your Majesty.

To occupy Valladolid and Salamanca, to use the utmost exertion to pacify Navarre and Aragon, to keep the communication with France rapid and safe, to be always ready to take the offensive—these are the Emperor's instructions for the campaign, and the principles on which all its operations ought to be founded. I need not add that, if the French armies in Spain are inactive, and allow the English to invade our coasts, the tranquillity of

France will be endangered, and the ruin of our cause in Spain inevitable.

[772.] CLARKE TO JOSEPH.

Paris, Feb. 26, 1813.

Sire,—After I had written to your Majesty on the 12th of February, in reply to your letter of the 8th of January, I received a further letter from your Majesty of the same date. The latter part of it is a copy of the letter which I have answered. The earlier part is a statement of the wants of the army of Spain and of your Majesty.

I have laid both letters before the Emperor. His Majesty commands me to send to you by General Lucolle a copy of my last letter, and to repeat his wishes respecting the conduct of the war.

I trust that General Lucolle will find the head-quarters at Valladolid, and troops sent to pacify Navarre and Aragon. Madrid will be held by a moveable corps, and the Emperor wishes Salamanca and Leon to be so held. His Majesty thinks that all the hospitals ought to be in Valladolid, Burgos, Vittoria, Tolosa, and Pampeluna. He also wishes a siege-train to be prepared at Burgos, to threaten Ciudad Rodrigo, and make the English fear the invasion of Portugal. This measure will check them, and must be immediately adopted.

His Majesty commands me also to say that it is important to lay heavy contributions on Madrid and Toledo, and to exact their full payment. Circumstances require this manner of providing for the army and for your Majesty's immediate wants.

His Majesty also requests your Majesty to make dispositions for receiving twice a week a courier from Bayonne. The interruption of our communications is always mischievous, sometimes alarming and may become fatal. It is necessary that it be seriously attended to, and made not only safe but expeditious, by making the couriers, escorted by infantry, travel between Bayonne and Valladolid at least a league per hour without interruption.

Such are His Majesty's wishes, and I cannot insist too much

on their prompt execution. Your Majesty will perceive their importance, and I trust that they will not meet with any of the obstacles of which you have had to complain. I hope that I shall hear quickly that these instructions have been followed, and that a freer and more rapid communication will inform me more regularly as to all that concerns your Majesty.

[773.] CLARKE TO JOSEPH.

Paris, April 29, 1813.

Sire,—The Emperor, on returning to me your Majesty's despatches of the 1st and 3rd of April, ordered me to answer them in such a manner as shall put an end to all uncertainty, and to the conflict of authorities of which your Majesty has long had to complain. The Emperor desires me to say that, having given to your Majesty the chief command of his armies in Spain, he is surprised that complaints so often reach him of want of obedience on the part of the generals: the Emperor thinks that this is caused by the view which your Majesty takes of your position, which leads you to confuse the King of Spain with the commander-in-chief of the French armies. The Emperor has no intention that his armies should, under any circumstances, be under the orders of the Spanish ministers, in whom he has reasons for placing no confidence, and whom he believes to be indifferent to the welfare of his soldiers; but whenever it pleases your Majesty to give any orders to the French generals, they will always be punctually executed, if, with regard to military operations, they are transmitted through Marshal Jourdan, and, respecting the commissariat, through Commissary-general Mathieu Favier. The Emperor will not allow O'Farill or any other minister to be employed by your Majesty in your relations with the French armies, the Emperor's fixed determination being that his troops shall never depend on Spanish administrations. To carry out this principle it is necessary for your Majesty to strike off from your general orders everything which puts the supplies of the French troops at the disposal of the Spanish agents. Commissary Mathieu Favier alone must be intrusted with transmitting orders relating to the commissariat. The Emperor cannot make him *intendant-général*, but he is the commissary-general. All the other commissariat officers belong only to the different corps which are under the orders of your Majesty. There is nothing, therefore, to prevent arrangements being made for establishing, according to your Majesty's desire, the magazines which your Majesty finds to be necessary at Burgos. The Emperor wishes this to be done at Santona, and wherever your Majesty thinks it advisable. There ought to be no difficulty in attaining this object, and, the better to secure its execution, I am writing to General Clausel, and to all the other generals belonging to the army, acquainting them, in precise terms, with the Emperor's wishes. Notice will be given to all of them that your Majesty's orders for securing the communications and directing the movements of the armies will be transmitted to them through Marshal Jourdan, and those concerning the commissariat through Commissariat-general Mathieu Favier, the Emperor's desire being that all orders transmitted through this channel be executed without delays or difficulties.

But while giving these orders, the Emperor directs me to announce to your Majesty that, in the present state of France, you are to expect nothing from him, with the exception of the portion of pay which is provided for by the budget. This circumstance must influence your Majesty's measures, and they must be in the spirit of the Imperial orders which I have already had the honour of transmitting to you.

The Emperor desires me likewise to remind your Majesty that, in order to command an army properly, it is necessary to be incessantly employed on it, to provide for every emergency, and to be ever hunting for intelligence.

The Emperor is sorry to see that this is not the conduct which has been pursued during the last four months. The troops have been kept inactive, while they might have been occupied in re-establishing order in Navarre and in the rear of the army. By this time all this might have been finished, and the troops now engaged in the north would long ago have become available against the English. It is essential that your Majesty should now obtain news every day from Bayonne, for which purpose the couriers should be required to travel at the rate of a league an hour. The Emperor thinks that this might be easily done by establishing a succession of posts, and that Valladolid might then communicate with Bayonne in four days. The Emperor attaches great importance to this measure, and orders me particularly to recommend its execution to your Majesty.

[774.] JOSEPH TO QUEEN JULIE.

Yrursun, June 23, 1813.*

My dear Friend,—The day before yesterday the army was attacked in its position at Vittoria, before General Clausel could join it with the troops from the army of Portugal, and after it had been weakened by having to furnish escorts to two immense convoys. The battle was fierce, and lasted the whole day. The killed and wounded on each side were about equal, but the state of the roads occasioned us to lose all our baggage and artillery; the teams only were saved. The force of the enemy doubled ours, as they had been joined by all the guerrillas of the province, and we had not the army of Portugal.

If the Emperor has returned, tell him as soon as I have placed my army on the frontier, and united it to those of the North and of Aragon, I shall repair to Mortefontaine, as I told you, at the time, that I ought to have done after Salamanca. Let me have the Emperor's answer. Whatever it be, I shall go home. I can do no good here.

Tell Clary to transmit, through James and Brocq, 100,000 francs to my secretary, M. Presle. Among the killed were M. Thibaud defending my treasure, and poor Alphonse,† whom I loved, though I scolded him.

Send me back the courier. I shall not stop at Paris, but at Mortefontaine, whether you are there or at a watering-place. Kisses to you and to the children.

* I have inserted this letter, as it closes Joseph's royal career. He left Spain five days after its date.—TR.

† He was left on the field for dead, and taken prisoner. He afterwards 'oined Joseph in America.—ED.

CHAPTER XX.

The letters contained in this chapter extend from the 29th of December, 1813, to the 9th of February, 1814.

They relate to what may be called the first act of the great drama of 1814.

In the beginning we find Napoleon preparing for his final struggle, sadly but resolutely. He feels that all Europe is in arms against France, and still more against himself. His illusions are gone. He rebukes Joseph for calling himself King of Spain. He is not without the hope that he shall repel the invaders, but he contemplates only two results as possible—his success or his death.

As the brothers, from the time of their reconciliation at the end of December until the 25th of January, when Napoleon took the command of his army at Châlons, both inhabited Paris, few letters passed between them. After the 29th of January, when the battle of Brienne was fought, their correspondence became incessant, particularly during the week which Napoleon spent at Troyes and at Nogent, watching Blucher, who was advancing from the north-east, and Schwartzenberg, who was marching from the south-east, and ready to spring on the one who was the most vulnerable or the most dangerous. Schwartzenberg seemed to be the most exposed, and Napoleon was tempted to select him for attack, especially as the Emperor Alexander was at his head-quarters. But Blucher was nearest to Paris; and the bold scheme of leaving Paris to defend itself while he attacked the invaders in their rear had not at this time suggested itself to his daring imagination. The first blow, therefore, fell upon Blucher, and the last of his letters contained in this chapter was written while his horse was waiting to carry him to Sézanne, from whence he commenced the great manœuvres and actions which drove back the army of Silesia from Montmirail to Châlons.

[775.] JOSEPH TO NAPOLEON.

Dec. 29, 1813.

Sire,—the violation of the Swiss territory has laid France open to the enemy.

In this state of affairs I am anxious that your Majesty should be persuaded that my heart is wholly French. Recalled by circumstances to France, I should be glad to be of some use, and I am ready to undertake anything which may prove to you my devotion.

I am also aware, Sire, of what I owe to Spain; I see my duties, and wish to fulfil all of them. If I make claims, it is only for the purpose of sacrificing them to the general good of mankind, esteeming myself happy if by such sacrifices I can promote the peace of Europe.

I hope that your Majesty may think fit to commission one of your ministers to come to an understanding on this subject with the Duke of Santa Fé, my minister for foreign affairs.

[776.] NAPOLEON TO JOSEPH.

Dec. 1813.

My Brother,—I have received your letter of the 29th of December. It is far too clever for the state of my affairs. I will explain it in two words. France is invaded, all Europe is in arms aganst France, and above all against me. You are no longer King of Spain. I do not want Spain either to keep or to give away. I will have nothing more to do with that country except to live in peace with it, and have the use of my army.

What will you do? Will you, as a French Prince, come to the support of my throne? You possess my friendship and your apanage, and will be my subject as prince of the blood. In this case you must act as I have done,—announce the part which you are about to play, write to me in simple terms a letter which I can print, receive the authorities, and show yourself zealous for me and for the King of Rome, and friendly to the regency of the Empress. Are you unable to do this? Have you not good sense enough for it? Then retire to the obscurity of some country-house 40 leagues from Paris. You will live there quietly if I live; you will be killed or arrested if I die. You will be useless to me, to our family, to your daughters, and to France; but you will do me no harm, and will not be in my way. Choose quickly the line which you will take.

[777.] JOSEPH TO NAPOLEON.

Mortefontaine, Jan. 1, 1814.

Sire,—I beg your Majesty to accept my best wishes that the year which is commencing may be happy both for you and for your subjects.

I hope that the year which has just finished has exhausted all your ill-fortune. Zenaïde, who came in just now, bringing some presents from the Empress, was nearly burnt close to the fire in my room; she was saved, and is quite well. This accident prevents my writing as well as usual, as I can use only two fingers. I entreat your Majesty not to doubt my complete and affectionate devotion.

[778.] NAPOLEON TO JOSEPH.

Paris, Jan. 1, 1814.

My Brother,—I thank you for your good wishes, and for the sentiments which you express on the occasion of the new year. I am also glad that my niece's accident has been followed by no bad effects.

[779.] NAPOLEON TO JOSEPH.

Paris, Jan. 10, 1814.

My Brother,—I have inserted in the regulations of the palace that you are in future to be announced under the title of *King Joseph*, and the Queen under the title of *Queen Julie*, with the honours due to the French princes of the blood. I send to you a pamphlet which I have just received from London, and which is circulated by the British government. I authorise you to take the uniform of the grenadiers of my guard, which is what I wear myself. I do not think that you ought to use any foreign decoration; you should wear only the French order. Forward to me a list of the persons of whom you wish to compose your household as well as that of the Queen, and tell me on what day you will receive the court and the authorities.

[780.] NAPOLEON TO JOSEPH.

Brienne, Jan. 31, 1814.

You write to me that General Ornano has no money. The paymaster told me that the 12th million advanced to the guard from my treasury had been distributed since my departure in the following manner:—400,000 francs to the cavalry, 250,000 to the foot grenadiers, 250,000 to the foot chasseurs, 70,000 to the artillery, and 30,000 to the train. Baron de la Bouillerie, as he received the order for this distribution, ought to have executed it. If, by any chance, the order did not reach him, you will present this letter to La Bouillerie, who will pay the million in the manner above described. Propose to me the distribution of a 13th million; but give notice to Ornano that he must look after his quartermasters: I suspect that they rob me.

P.S.—The 13th million has just been distributed by General Drouot.

[781.] NAPOLEON TO JOSEPH.

Brienne, Jan. 31, 1814, in the evening.

The bulletin will have informed you of the events which have taken place. The engagement at Brienne was very hot. I have lost 3000 men, and the enemy's loss amounts to between 4000 and 5000.* I pursued him half-way to Bar-sur-Aube. I have repaired the bridges over the Aube which were burnt. In another instant General Blücher and the whole of his staff would have been taken. The nephew of the Chancellor of Hardenberg, who was close to them, *was* taken. They were on foot, and did not know that I was with the army.

Since the battle of Brienne the allies have had great respect for our armies. They did not believe that we had any. I have reason to think, although I am not certain, that the Duke of Vicenza has reached the Emperor's head-quarters at Chaumont. This affair of Brienne, the position of our armies, and the opinion which is entertained of them, may hasten the peace. It is advisable that the newspapers should describe Paris as determined to defend itself, and should announce large numbers of troops as arriving from every quarter.

I have ordered a column of from 1000 to 1200 horses belonging to the guard, 2 pieces of cannon, 3 or 4 infantry waggons, and between 3000 and 4000 men of the young guard, altogether a column of from 4000 to 5000 men to leave Paris. To these should be joined a company of the baggage-train belonging to the guard, if there is one ready. This column is to proceed towards Nogent and Fismes, where it will wait for further orders. The Duke of Treviso had evacuated Troyes in order to advance upon

* The first and indecisive battle of Brienne was fought on the 29th of January. Napoleon, having failed in preventing the junction of Blücher and Schwartzenberg, remained at Brienne until the 1st of February, when he was attacked by a superior force of the allies under Blücher, and forced, after a battle which lasted from about one in the afternoon till midnight, to retreat towards Troyes, with the loss of between 4000 and 5000 killed and wounded, 3000 prisoners, and several guns. This second battle of Brienne is called by the French historians the battle of La Rothière, a village a few miles to the east of Brienne, in which Napoleon's advanced guard was posted.—TR.

Arcis-sur-Aube; but I desired him to return to Troyes, and he arrived there this evening at seven o'clock. It is very important to reinforce as soon as possible the division which is at Troyes.

[782.] NAPOLEON TO JOSEPH.

Piney,* Feb. 2, 1814.

It seems that the allies have fixed the 3rd of February for opening the congress at Chatillon; that Lord Castlereagh and half a dozen other Englishmen will negotiate for England, M. de Stadion for Austria, M. de Humboldt for Prussia, and Rasumowski for Russia. It appears that the allies feared lest the arrival of the Duke of Vicenza at their head-quarters might develop and mature the seeds of disunion already existing amongst them. They preferred to hold the congress at a distance from their head-quarters. I shall be at Troyes to-morrow.

[783.] NAPOLEON TO JOSEPH.

Troyes,† Feb. 3, 1814.

My Brother,—I have received your letter of the 1st of February. I wish that you had sent to me a return of the troops which you had at parade on the 31st, infantry and cavalry, both the guards and the line. Before I give battle I wait to be reinforced by the divisions from Spain, which I have ordered to proceed towards Nogent-sur-Seine.

[784.] JOSEPH TO NAPOLEON.

Paris, Feb. 5, 1814.

Sire,—I have received your letter of the 3rd. The march of Leval's division has been delayed; it is expected to-morrow at Versailles. I inspected to-day 5000 infantry and 1200 horses belonging to the guard, and 600 horses from the depôt at Versailles. I have retained here only 1000 foot and 400

* Piney is a village half-way between Brienne and Troyes. Napoleon slept there on the 2nd of February, on his retreat to Troyes.—TR.

† Napoleon remained three days at Troyes, and on the 7th continued his retreat to Nogent-sur-Seine.—TR.

horse. The public mind was depressed to-day, and I had great trouble in keeping up the spirts of many people. I have seen the Empress twice, and when I left her last night she was more composed; she had just received a letter from your Majesty in which you mention the congress.

If your Majesty should meet with serious reverses, what form of government ought to be left here in order to prevent intriguers from putting themselves at the head of the first movement? Jérôme asks me what should be his conduct in such a case? Men are coming in, but we want money to clothe them. Count Daru can obtain only 10,000 fr. a day from the Treasury; this delays terribly the departure of the troops. There are here two battalions of National Guards.

[785.] NAPOLEON TO JOSEPH.

Troyes, Feb. 6, 1814.

My Brother,—I received your letter of the 5th of February at Troyes. The Duke of Ragusa has reached Nogent with his corps to hold the enemy in check. I have decided on reconnoitring his position this morning, to proceed thither with the army, and to quit Troyes. It seems to me that the only person to be left in Paris, should anything extraordinary take place, would be an Imperial commissioner. Think over the persons among whom I must choose; consult on the subject the Arch-Chancellor and the Ministers of Finance, of the Treasury, and of the Interior. I suppose that it would not do to leave any of the ministers (but I hope that nothing of the sort will take place).

[786.] NAPOLEON TO JOSEPH.

Troyes, Feb. 6, 1814, 3 P.M.

My Brother,—Your courier has just arrived. I shall reach Nogent early to-morrow; the Duke of Ragusa has been there since the 5th. I am in a position therefore to cover Paris. Let me know the exact route of all the troops and of the second division from Spain, as well as the information which you possess as to the road to Châlons through Épernay, and that to Vitry through Sézanne. The Minister of War must immediately send muskets and cartridges to Montereau, to La Ferté, and to Meaux, to arm the national guards. I am very much annoyed by these arrangements, for I wished to attack Bar-sur-Seine to-morrow, in order to beat the Emperor Alexander, who seems to have made false dispositions; but I sacrifice everything to the necessity of covering Paris. Send officers along the two roads which I have just mentioned to you, that I may obtain precise information. Send the Duke of Valmy to Meaux; he will correspond with me by way of Sézanne. The plan of placing Paris under King Louis, in any unforeseen event seems to me good. You remember all that I said to you about the Princesses. However, the course which I am about to pursue will prevent your coming to that. Take away from Fontainebleau all valuables, and above all everything which might serve as a trophy, without, however, unfurnishing the château too much; it is useless to leave in it plate or anything that can be easily removed. I am writing to La Bouillerie to desire him to hold a million francs at your disposal, to hasten the clothing and equipment of the troops.

[787.] NAPOLEON TO JOSEPH.

Nogent-sur-Seine, Feb. 7, 1814.

My Brother,—From the return of the guard which I have before me, of the 5th of this month, it seems that there are 700 of the Old Guard in Paris; they may be divided into two battalions of great value to lead a column or form a reserve. From the same return it appears that there were already 5000 voltigeurs or tirailleurs. Of these 5000 General Ornano sends off 1000 to-day; there will remain therefore only 4000, but at least 6000 ought to arrive on the 6th, 7th, 8th, 9th, and 10th; I reckon therefore on 10,000 men at the depôts of the guard in Paris on the 10th. There are in Paris 20 or 22 cadres of battalions; this would produce 20 battalions, 500 men in each, which may be formed into two divisions, each of 5000 men. As the conscripts arrive, the battalions must be completed to 800 men each. In the course of to-morrow it will be advisable to distribute the 6000 or 7000 conscripts in the depôts of the guard of

Paris among the different cadres. It is better to have many companies of 60 men than a few companies of 120 men. I reckon therefore that to-morrow evening you will be able to pass in review two divisions forming four brigades, consisting of from 22 to 24 battalions, forming 5000 or 6000 present under arms, which will be added to every day.

There are 1200 cavalry; the artillery has 22 pieces of cannon; clothing cannot long be wanting. There is in Paris a large provision of great-coats, cartouch-boxes, and shakos: great-coats must be given to some, and coats to others, in order that these men may be of use immediately; and you will distribute the 1000 or 2000 men who will arrive every day among the 24 battalions.

You must order General Boyer to travel post to take command of the 2nd division. General Charpentier will command another division. There are cadres at Lille and at Amiens; if necessary, they can be sent by post to Paris. I am therefore inclined to hope that between the 10th and 12th you will have in Paris two fine battalions of the Old Guard, two squadrons of horse, and 22 pieces of artillery, altogether 22,200 men. Order these men to fire at a mark every day, that they may learn how to use their muskets. As for the line, I am absolutely ignorant as to what it can furnish you, but I assume that it can give you 20 battalions of from 300 to 400 men. You must act on the same principle. As we are too much pressed to have time to teach them, two companies of 50 men each are better than one of 100. If the line can give you 20 battalions of 300 men each, this will be a reserve of 6000 men. You may distribute them in two divisions, and give them four batteries, served by sailors from Cherbourg or by the youths of the *École Polytechnique.* You will thus have in hand by the 10th four divisions, 60 guns, and 2000 cavalry, making an army of more than 30,000 men. The national guards of Soissons and Meaux must amount to 6000 men. With them you would have five divisions and one division of cavalry; altogether 40,000 men,—which would be great.

Call in Generals Hullin and Gérard to consult as to what is

possible. As soon as I hear that this reserve has been formed, I will name a marshal to command it. In my calculations as to conscripts I hope that the line may give me as many as the guard, that is, from 20 to 30 battalions of from 300 to 500 men. Great-coats, shakos, &c., are to be found at the war-office, and with common activity 3000 or 4000 great-coats may be made every day, and you may give, as I have already remarked, a great-coat to one and a coat to another. Write to me on this subject in detail. Nothing is done except under the master's eye. If you do not enter into all these details, you will have a crowd of men wasting their time in the depôts, who might defend the capital. I shall order General Bourdesoulle to return to Paris to command all the cavalry which you can collect at Versailles. Let a copy of this despatch be sent to the Minister of War. I repeat that your battalions ought to be small, in order to make use of all the cadres. In this army my battalions are very small, and every day they do for me as much as the large battalions used to do. Forty men per company are quite enough. If they are conscripts that is twice too many.

I reckon on receiving your answer to-morrow evening, and that it will give me positive information as to your resources.

[788.] NAPOLEON TO JOSEPH.

Nogent-sur-Seine, Feb. 7, 1814.

My Brother,—I wrote to you this morning respecting an army of reserve of from 30,000 to 40,000 men, which it might be possible to form by exhausting all the depôts, and to have ready in Paris on the 10th. I think that 100 guns might be provided for this reserve. If horses are wanting, 2000 could easily be furnished, on demand, by Paris. If men are wanted to drive them, the public must send grooms with their horses.

[789.] NAPOLEON TO JOSEPH.

Nogent-sur-Seine, Feb. 7, 1814.

My Brother,—You tell me in your letter of the 5th that you have sent 600 cavalry to Meaux, but you do not tell me in what brigade or under what general these men are to be found. You give me no details as to their composition; yet it is necessary that I should know all this. General St. Germain has at Meaux 300 horse; I have desired him to reconnoitre La Ferté-sous-Jouarre.

[790.] NAPOLEON TO JOSEPH.

Nogent-sur-Seine, Feb. 7, 1814.

My Brother,—I received your two letters of this morning at one in the afternoon. I do not believe that the enemy has reached La Ferté-sous-Jouarre, nor do I think that he has reached Meaux; these are false alarms. Marshal Macdonald wrote to me from Châlons, on the 5th, that he covered the roads of Épernay, Montmirail, and Sézanne. At this instant I am sending 2000 men to occupy Sézanne; I shall proceed thither to-night* with a sufficient force to beat and drive off all that may intercept this line of communication. From thence I shall move rapidly towards Meaux. I think that by my manœuvres I have forced the main army of the enemy to move from before Troyes to Bar-sur-Aube, and that I have gained two marches upon it. Leval's division has reached Provins. You must give me more precise military details: you have sent two battalions to Meaux, but you do not tell me which they are. I ought to know, in order to collect my troops. As you are sending a detachment of cavalry to me, tell me from what corps. I give you no orders for La Bouillerie,† as I do not think it necessary. At all events, he will be

* Napoleon did not in fact move on Sézanne until the afternoon of the 9th.—TR.

† The treasure in the hands of M. de la Bouillerie was gradually accumulated by Napoleon out of the contributions which he imposed on conquered towns, and out of the sale or the revenues of the domains belonging to the sovereigns whom he deposed or robbed. It was completely at his disposal, but was employed by him only for military purposes. Not much is known as to its extent, or as to the mode in which it finally disappeared; but the general opinion is, that at the beginning of 1814 it amounted to about 150 millions of francs, and that about 110 millions of it were spent on the army before the expulsion of Napoleon. When that event happened about 40 millions of this treasure are supposed to have remained. It fell into the hands of the government which succeeded him, but was never accounted for; one or two of the great fortunes of the Restoration are suspected to have been created out of it.—TR.

able in six hours to load all that he has in 15 carriages, and to draw it, with horses from my stables, in the first instance to Rambouillet. But I do not think that we have come to that yet. I do not fear the enemy; I am full of hope as to the result.

Hold firmly the barriers of Paris. Place two guns at each barrier. Post there the national guards who have muskets or fowling-pieces; above all, take care that the Minister of War sends muskets to Montereau and to Meaux. I intend to leave a battalion of national guards at Soissons, and to send the others by post to Meaux. Send the Duke of Valmy to Meaux to correspond with me, and to superintend all these details. As I shall depend on you for news, keep me well informed in every respect. Watch the three roads from Épernay to Meaux, from La Ferté-sous-Jouarre to Montmirail, and from Meaux to Sézanne. Besides the soldiers who ought to be placed there by the Minister of War, the police must have secret agents, for knowledge of the enemy's movements is one of the great elements of perfect success.

There should be at each of the principal barriers 50 men armed with muskets, 100 armed with fowling-pieces, and 100 armed with pikes; altogether 250 men. You must form every day a reserve of from 400 to 500 men armed with muskets, twice as many armed with fowling-pieces, and one-third armed with pikes, composing a reserve of 2000 men, to proceed whithersoever they may be wanted, with the mounted batteries of the guard and the *Ecole Polytechnique.*

[791.] NAPOLEON TO JOSEPH.

Nogent-sur-Seine, Feb. 7, 1814, 4 P.M.

My Brother,—I have received news from the Duke of Taranto, dated the 6th, at 3 o'clock in the afternoon. His rear-guard was still between Épernay and Châlons, about as far as Cherville, but he was unable to send any troops to occupy the road leading to Montmirail or that to Sézanne. In two hours the road to Sézanne will be occupied, as the Duke of Ragusa started at noon to march upon that town. Thence we shall endeavour to advance upon Montmirail. As a courier takes only four hours between La

Ferté-sous-Jouarre and Paris, you ought to have early information of what goes on towards Montmirail. If there should happen to be one battalion at La Ferté-sous-Jouarre and a few pieces of cannon to check the advance of the enemy's light troops, they will not reach Paris; my manœuvre will surround them.

[792.] NAPOLEON TO JOSEPH.

Nogent-sur-Seine, Feb. 7, 1814, 5 P.M.

My Brother,—Put into the 'Moniteur' of to-morrow that on the 5th the Duke of Vicenza gave a dinner to Lord Castlereagh, the English Minister for Foreign Affairs; to Lord Cathcart; to Lord Aberdeen, Plenipotentiary for England at the Congress; to Count Stadion, the Austrian Plenipotentiary; to Count Rasumowski, Plenipotentiary for Russia; and to Baron Humboldt, Plenipotentiary for Prussia; and that negotiations appear to be actively carried on. This article should be inserted under the head, not of *Paris*, but of *Châtillon-sur-Seine.*

[793.] NAPOLEON TO JOSEPH.

Nogent-sur-Seine, Feb. 7, 1814, 7 P.M.

My Brother,—I have received your letter of the 6th, but I think that it reached me after your letter of the 7th, which I have already answered. The state of things in Paris is not as bad as their fears have made it. I am surprised that the ministers of war and of police do not obtain three times every day news from the roads about which they are uneasy. People lose their heads, and in consequence do nothing useful. The Duke of Taranto was not at Épernay on the 4th, as he was at Châlons on the 5th. He was still only at a distance of one league from Châlons at 3 o'clock in the afternoon of the 6th. As his couriers have passed through La Ferté, I scarcely think that any detachment of the enemy has appeared before it. It seems, however, that the Duke of Taranto has not been able to protect the road to Montmirail: this is unlucky. If it had been known, 300 men and some guns might have been sent to La Ferté-sous-Jouarre, so as to provide for every emergency.

I have written to you at length on the resources of Paris. I conclude that there are arms enough for the troops, as the Minister of War has promised to provide 60,000. I have as yet no news of the Duke of Ragusa, but I shall fall fiercely upon the enemy in the direction of the Meaux and Châlons roads. The alarm will then, perhaps, spread towards Sens; but General Pajol is making preparations there. I think that a battery of artillery had better be sent to him. As soon as I have an answer to the general orders which I have given for the formation of four divisions, I will point out the positions which they are to occupy on the different roads. The Empress thought of visiting St. Geneviève. I fear that this would produce only a bad result.

Without doubt this is a difficult moment, but since I left Paris I have met with nothing but success. The bad spirit of such men as Talleyrand, who endeavoured to paralyse the nation, prevented my having early recourse to arms, and this is the consequence. In our circumstances the qualities wanted are confidence and audacity.

It is possible that parties of cavalry may actually threaten Soissons. The enemy has an immense cavalry, which he pours over France. A few towns, such as Châlons-sur-Saône, have resisted; Lyons has secured itself; but those who are at the head of the Government have given a false direction to public opinion. I presume that the Minister of War has given positive orders for the defence of Soissons. I cannot think why your letters requiring immediate attention are not sent to me by extraordinary expresses; they would arrive at least three hours before the couriers. It is, however, useful to send from time to time intelligent and safe men as couriers, because I put questions to them, and you may likewise do so. When there is urgent business tell Lavalette to send your letters by extraordinary express.

P.S.—Keep the Empress in spirits. She is dying of grief.

[794.] JOSEPH TO NAPOLEON.

Paris, Feb. 7, 1814.

Sire,—Our affairs are becoming more and more serious.

I have asked the Minister of War to order General Maurice Mathieu to join me as chief of my staff. General Hullin is so much occupied with the fortification of Paris that important movements may escape his notice, and I require a general always by my side. Maurice Mathieu will arrive with the first division. He will execute what is to be done under my eyes, and will give orders to General Hullin, who is full of willingness and zeal. Major Allant's relations with me continue unaltered; he has much to do, and does it well. I consider myself lucky in having such a man; but he himself, as well as the minister, has urged me to keep with me an experienced general. I have sent an officer to the Duke of Taranto to know what he is doing. I am assured that on the 4th he was at Épernay. I have ordered General Hullin to send a brigadier-general, with 1400 men, to La Ferté-sous-Jouarre, to correspond with Marshal Macdonald, watch all the roads, and report the enemy's movements. General Leval set off to-day, with 700 horses, from the depôt of Versailles. Conscripts are flowing in at the rate of 2000 a day. Your Majesty knows what it is that we unfortunately want. The national guard stands in the same need. It is this deficiency of arms, Sire, which alone can give a chance to the enemy. As for men, your Majesty may have as many as can be required. I despatched yesterday a courier with a letter to your Majesty; I beg you to send me the instructions which I have asked for on several important subjects. M. de la Bouillerie is pressing for a decision.*

The unhappy evacuation of Châlons by the Duke of Taranto struck Paris with consternation, which was a little relieved by the article in the 'Moniteur' on the negotiations and the plenipotentiaries. Soissons is threatened. Detachments have presented themselves near Montargis. At one o'clock the Minister

* He wished to be authorised to remove from Paris the treasure, which it required twenty-four hours to pack.—TR.

of War sent me word that the enemy had appeared at Maison Rouge. La Ferté-sous-Jouarre is threatened. The general in command of the camp at Meaux writes to me that the town is crowded with artillery and carriages on their way from Châlons. He has with him only 300 men with arms, the remainder are without them. He entreats for cavalry. In this state of things, as I have no cavalry here, and can hope for none from Versailles under several days; as I am ignorant if the detachment which has appeared before La Ferté be formidable or not, and whether Marshal Macdonald is or is not on that road, I have decided, though with great regret, on ordering the 600 or 700 horses which started this morning* to proceed to-morrow to Meaux; they will be followed by three battalions. As soon as I obtain precise information I shall desire these horses to go on to Nogent. The state of the public mind to-day is such as to make it of the first importance to prevent our receiving any affront on the approaches to the capital.

[795,] NAPOLEON TO JOSEPH.

Nogent, Feb. 8, 1814, 4 A.M.

My Brother,—The enemy has never been at Montmirail; consequently he cannot have reached La Ferté-sous-Jouarre. On the 7th he had not got farther than Châlons. The Duke of Ragusa has entered Sézanne, thus closing up the third road.† At Sézanne the enemy never had more than a few detachments of cavalry. I once more request you to let me have a return of all the troops whom you have sent to Meaux. Scattered forces are useless. I shall then send them orders to collect together.

P.S.—Insert in the 'Moniteur' an article, headed Châtillon-sur-Seine, saying that on the 6th the members of the Congress dined with the Duke of Vicenza; that it is remarked that all the ambassadors are on terms of the greatest politeness, especially those of France and England, who are full of attentions for each other.

* Mentioned before as accompanying General Leval.—TR.

† The three roads alluded to are probably those by Château Thierry, Montmirail, and Sézanne.—TR.

[796.] JOSEPH TO NAPOLEON.

Paris, Feb. 7, 1814, 11 P.M.

Sire,—I have received your Majesty's two letters of yesterday. I have seen and written to the Duke of Valmy. He starts to-night for Meaux. He showed me a letter from the Duke of Taranto, dated the 6th. He was still at Épernay, and had heard nothing from your Majesty for four days. He had abandoned Châlons after defending it for some time. The artillery was directed on Meaux. The enemy had entered Sézanne. The intendant and the public treasure had escaped falling into the hands of the enemy.

I enclose the exact route of the 9th infantry division of the army of Spain.

I have sent an aide-de-camp along the Châlons road by way of Vitry. I have desired the Minister of War to despatch another on the road to . . . .*

The Minister of War tells me that he sent 2000 muskets to Montereau this morning.

I wrote to him from . . . .* this evening. I have spoken to Louis about leaving him here; he has written to me a long letter on the subject. I have determined on forwarding it to your Majesty. I believe that your Majesty told me that the princesses were to accompany the Empress. If this should not be the case, I ought to have positive orders on the subject. I am most anxious that the departure of the Empress should not take place. We cannot disguise from ourselves the fact that the consternation and despair of the people may lead to sad and even fatal consequences. I think, and so do all persons whose opinion is of value, that we should be prepared to make many sacrifices before resorting to this extremity. The men who are attached to your Majesty's Government fear that the departure of the Empress will abandon the people of Paris to despair, and give a capital and an empire to the Bourbons. Although I express the fear which I see on every face, your Majesty may rest assured that your orders will be faithfully executed by me as soon as I receive them.

* Illegible.—ED.

I have spoken to General Caffarelli on the subject of Fontainebleau, and to M. de la Bouillerie about the million for the war and the removal of the treasure. I do not know how far your Majesty may approve of my observations, but I must say that I think it important to pay a month's salary to the great dignitaries, ministers, conseillers d'état, and senators. Several have been mentioned to me who are really in distress, and, in the event of their departure becoming expedient, it is thought that many will be detained in Paris for want of the means of travelling.

Marshal Brune has called on me; I was not able to see him. I have no doubt that he came to offer his services. I should like to know your Majesty's wishes on the subject.

Jérôme is annoyed that your Majesty has not yet explained your intentions as to the request which I made for him in two of my former letters.*

I am told that M. de la Fayette was one of the first grenadiers of the national guard on duty at the Hôtel de Ville.

The barriers will be completely fortified to-morrow, and we shall begin to send artillery thither.

General Caffarelli answered to the Duke of Conegliano that he had not yet received a reply from the Grand Marshal of the Palace to his request for permission to place 25 national guards at the Tuileries.

P.S.—I have received your Majesty's letter, dated to-day, from Nogent. I have already ordered its directions to be followed, and I will keep your Majesty informed during the progress of their execution.

The courier Remy will be the bearer of this letter.

[797.] NAPOLEON TO JOSEPH.

Nogent, Feb. 8, 1814, 11 A.M.

My Brother,—I have received your letter of the 7th, 11 P.M. It surprised me extremely. I have answered you on the event

* Joseph had proposed that he should be employed.—TR.

of Paris,* that you may not ask me any more about what is to follow it,—a matter which interests more persons than me. When that happens I shall be no more, consequently it is not for myself that I speak. I told you that the movements of the Empress and the King of Rome, and the rest of our family, must be governed by circumstances, and you have not understood me. Be sure that, if the event takes place, what I have prophesied will certainly follow; I am persuaded that she herself has the same expectation.†

King Louis talks of peace. His advice is ill-timed; in fact, I can understand nothing in your letter. I thought that I had explained myself to you, but you never recollect anything, and you are of the opinion of the first comer and of the last speaker.

I repeat, then, in two words, Paris will never be occupied while I am alive. I have a right to be believed if I am understood.

I will add that if, through unforeseen circumstances, I should march towards the Loire, I should not leave the Empress and my son at a distance from me, because, whatever happened, they might both be carried off to Vienna; this would be still more likely to take place if I were not alive. I cannot make out how, with all these intrigues going on around you, you can bestow such imprudent praise upon the proposals of traitors, who are incapable of giving honourable advice: never employ them, even in the most favourable circumstances. Besides, no one is bound to do what is impossible. I can no longer pay any of my officers: I have nothing.

* If Napoleon refers to any of the letters now published, they must be the two of the 6th February. But neither of these letters mentions the Empress or the King of Rome. Perhaps he refers to *vivâ voce* instructions.

It is to be observed that he never mentions the capture of Paris in direct terms. Here he alludes to it as "l'évènement de Paris." In his first letter of the 6th he calls it "Dans des moments extraordinaires;" in the second, "Dans tout évènement imprévu."—TR.

† This seems to be an allusion to something that passed in conversation.—TR.

I own that I am annoyed by your letter of the 7th, 11 P.M. because I see that there is no coherence in your ideas, and that you allow yourself to be influenced by the chattering and the opinions of a set of people who never reflect. Yes, I will talk to you openly. If Talleyrand has anything to do with the project of leaving the Empress in Paris in case of the approach of the enemy, it is treachery. I repeat, distrust that man. I have dealt with him for the last 16 years; once I even liked him; but he is undoubtedly the greatest enemy to our house since it has been abandoned by fortune. Keep to my advice. I know more than all those people. If we are beaten and I am killed, you will hear of it before the rest of my family. Send the Empress and the King of Rome to Rambouillet; order the senate, the conseil-d'état, and all the troops, to assemble on the Loire: leave in Paris a prefect, or an imperial commission, or some mayors.

I have told you* that Madame † and the Queen of Westphalia ‡ may remain in Paris in Madame's house. If the Viceroy has returned to Paris, he may also stay there; but on no account let the Empress and the King of Rome fall into the hands of the enemy.

Be certain that, from that moment, Austria, the band which connected her with France being broken,§ would carry her off to Vienna and give her a large apanage; and on pretence of securing the happiness of the Empress, the French would be forced to do whatever England and Russia might dictate. Every [national] party would thus be destroyed, for . . . ||; instead of which, in the other case, the national feelings of the numbers whose interest it would be to rebel, make it impossible to foresee the result.¶

* Apparently in conversation.—TR.

† Napoleon's mother.—TR.

‡ Jerome's wife.—TR.

§ The words of the text are, "l'Autriche étant désintéressée." I think that this is their meaning.—TR.

|| Illegible.—ED.

¶ The loss of the first part of this sentence renders the second part obscure.—TR.

However, it may happen that I beat the enemy on his approach to Paris, and that none of these things may take place. It is also possible that I may make peace in a few days. But, at all events, it appears from your letter of the 7th, 11 P.M., that you have no means of defence. Your judgment in these matters is always at fault; your very principles are wrong.* It is for the interest even of Paris that the Empress and the King of Rome should not remain there, because its welfare depends on their safety; and since the world has existed I have never heard of a sovereign allowing himself to be taken in any open town. This would be the first instance.

The unfortunate King of Saxony has just reached France; he is beginning to lose his happy illusions.

In difficult and critical circumstances a man does his duty, and leaves the rest to take its course. If I should happen to live, I ought to be, and I have no doubt that I shall be, obeyed; if I die, my son as sovereign, and the Empress as regent, must not, for the honour of the French, allow themselves to be taken; they must retreat to the last village.

Remember what was said by the wife of Philip V. What, indeed, would be said of the Empress? That she had abandoned our throne and that of her son. Nothing would better please the allies than to make an end of everything by carrying them off prisoners to Vienna. I am surprised that you do not see this. I see that fear has turned all your heads in Paris.

The Empress and the King of Rome once at Vienna, or in the hands of our enemies, you and all others who attempted a defence would be rebels.

As for me, I would rather they would kill my son than see him brought up at Vienna as an Austrian prince, and I think well enough of the Empress to believe that she is of the same opinion, as far as that is possible to a woman and a mother.

I have never seen Andromaque acted without pitying the fate of Astyanax in surviving the rest of his house, nor without think-

* In the original, "Pour comprendre ces choses, je trouve toujours votre jugement faux; c'est enfin une fausse doctrine"—a sentence not easily intelligible.—TR.

ing that it would have been a blessing for him if he had died before his father.

You do not understand the French nation. It is impossible to foresee the ultimate result of such great events as these.

As for Louis, I think that he ought to follow you.

[798.] NAPOLEON TO JOSEPH.

Nogent, Feb. 8, 1814, 11 A.M.

My Brother,—I think that attention must be paid especially to the neighbourhoods of Sens and of Pont-sur-Yonne.

It seems that it is Wittgenstein and York who attack towards Châlons. In the course of the day I shall have troops on the road to Montmirail.

[799.] NAPOLEON TO JOSEPH.

Nogent, Feb. 8, 1814, 3 P.M.

My Brother,—I have sent to the Empress an article for the 'Moniteur.' If you receive this letter before 5 o'clock to-morrow morning, and if it be possible to withdraw the article, I should like to delay its insertion for 48 hours, because it would inform the enemy too soon as to my plans and position, which is always inconvenient.

[800.] NAPOLEON TO JOSEPH.

Nogent, Feb. 8, 1814, 6 P.M.

My Brother,—I have just written to the Minister of War about the evacuation of Italy, and as to King Ferdinand. Send for the minister; he will show you my letters. All the correspondence with M. de Laforest relating to the affairs of Spain will be carried on by M. d'Hauterive, whom you will also send for.

[801.] MARIE LOUISE TO JOSEPH.

Paris, Feb. 8, 1814.

My dear Brother,—I received last night a letter from the Emperor, dated the 6th. He tells me that he is well, and that circumstances, although they are difficult, have improved during the last week. He desires me not to be anxious: you know that this is impossible. If you have any details, it will be very kind in you to send them to me. You see, my dear brother, from my teasing you in this way, the confidence which I have in your friendship and patience. I entreat you to believe in the friendship of your affectionate sister.

[802.] NAPOLEON TO JOSEPH.

Nogent, Feb. 8, 1814, 6 P.M.

My Brother,—Let this letter be delivered to the Empress Josephine in person. It is to tell her to write to Eugène. You will ask her to send to you her letter, which you will despatch by an express.

[803.] JOSEPH TO NAPOLEON.

Paris, Feb. 8, 1814, noon.

Sire,—I have received your letter of the 7th. I have sent that which treats of the army of reserve to the minister. I am perpetually tormenting him for muskets. I shall see him again immediately, and I will let your Majesty know the result.

I have written to the Duke of Conegliano to reinforce the posts of the national guards at the barriers. They have already begun to serve. Muskets are what they want, or even fowling-pieces. The troops which are gone to La Ferté-sous-Jouarre are commanded by General Minot: they consist of the 6th battalion of the 86th of the line, the 1st and the 28th light infantry, and the 4th and 70th of the line; in the whole 2000 men. General St. Germain was at Compiègne; he has just been ordered to Meaux. Soissons is threatened. I have desired General Hullin to send thither a battalion. I have written to General Berruyer to defend the place; I am repeating the order to him. It seems that the national guards at Soissons have no muskets. I send back to your Majesty the aide-de-camp whom I despatched to the Duke of Taranto, and who met General Minot and his troops last night near La Ferté-sous-Jouarre. I will see directly the

Minister of War and the Minister of the Administration of War, to deliver to them your Majesty's orders; but I must tell you beforehand that the Minister of War has repeated to me a hundred times that he has not 5000 muskets at his disposal, and that the governor of Vincennes told me yesterday that he had 30,000, but out of repair.* Since yesterday I have written to desire the minister to hasten these repairs by every means in his power, and to let me know how many it is possible to have ready by the 20th and by the 30th of this month. That I may not delay the officer's departure, I will write no more to your Majesty at present.

The bearer of this letter is my equerry, M. Monval.

[804.] JOSEPH TO NAPOLEON.

Paris, Feb. 8, 1814, 10 P.M.

Sire,—I have put at the disposal of the Minister of the Administration of War the amount of the credit which your Majesty has granted me upon your treasury, at the rate of 100,000 francs a day. I have seen the Minister of War: M. Gérard is employed in forming the four divisions. I will transmit to your Majesty the report of what has been done as soon as I receive it. I have given similar orders to General Ornano. The Minister of War assures me that he now has 11,000 muskets at Vincennes fit for use. The artificers have arrived from Charleville; workshops are being constructed for them. We are expecting some likewise from St. Étienne. I have ordered General Hullin to appoint an officer of the line to command each of the barriers which is to be held. General Hullin will place this evening at each of the principal barriers, especially on the right bank of the

* The historical importance of these figures cannot be exaggerated. The want of muskets in Paris was the principal cause of its capture. If all who asked for arms could have been supplied, the defence might have been prolonged for some hours, the Emperor would have had time to arrive with a portion of the guard, and the whole state of things would have been changed. The war with Russia, and that of 1813, had occasioned an enormous consumption of arms, and there had not been time to replace them. A natural consequence of previous events has been called treachery.—ED.

Seine, 100 soldiers of the line, and Marshal Moncey 150 of the national guard, armed with muskets and fowling-pieces. I have ordered General Ornano to put six pieces of artillery belonging to the guard at the disposal of General Hullin.

There are at Vincennes nearly 2000 artillery waggons and 700 guns without harness. I sent to you this morning a list of the troops who are gone to Meaux. The Minister of War has just told me that two battalions of national guards from Lille have been sent thither; so that there must now be at La Ferté five battalions of infantry, and nearly 800 cavalry, 300 of whom, belonging to General St. Germain's division, went from Compiègne, and 500 from the depôt at Versailles.

I have asked the Ministers of War and of Police to send officers on the roads to Sézanne and La Ferté. Arms have been sent to 2000 of the national guards at Soissons; General Berruyer was in the town in a state of great anxiety. He has written to ask the Minister of War to let the 2000 men for whom the arms are intended remain at Soissons; they will be of more use there, as they will be armed, than at Meaux, where there are troops without muskets. Your Majesty will see by the annexed letters that detachments of the enemy have appeared at Montmirail and Vieux-Maisons. Your Majesty's letter reached me this morning. I am glad to hear that the Duke of Ragusa has entered Sézanne. The Minister of War assures me that he sends punctually to your Majesty all the reports which he gives to me of the movements of the troops in the 1st division. He tells me to-day that General Treilhard's 1st brigade * will reach Montmirail on the 10th, 15th, 17th, and 19th, each regiment marching separately.

[805.] JOSEPH TO NAPOLEON.

Paris, Feb. 8, 1814, midnight.

Sire,—I have desired M. de la Bouillerie to make arrangements which will enable him, if I desire him to leave Paris with the treasure, to set off in six hours after receiving the order. He has therefore been obliged to load some fourgons and to house

* A brigade of dragoons from Spain.—ED.

them in the court of the Grand Écuyer on the Carousal. This was effected in the night, and the officers on guard in the palace alone can have been aware of it. The director of the Museum came to-day to tell me that it ought to be shut up, and the things of most value sent out of Paris, unless I gave him orders to the contrary. As your Majesty has given none to me, I could give none to him. If I should receive any from your Majesty, I will communicate them without delay.

It appears to me, Sire, that the proposed solemnity at St. Geneviève will not have a good effect. The public is already so depressed, and so inclined to trust to accidents for its defence, that we ought not to increase its inactivity by telling it to hope for safety from religious intercession. I may add, that to the incredulous these prayers would be a mere ceremony, or an avowal of danger and of distrust in our own exertions. With respect to the good Catholics, your Majesty may rest assured that the government will obtain nothing from them till you are publicly reconciled to the Vicar of Jesus Christ. No, Sire, in France none are truly religious but those who acknowledge the Pope as their spiritual head. The rest are not Catholics, but unbelievers or Protestants. Therefore, till I see in the 'Moniteur,' "The Pope has returned to Rome; the Emperor has ordered him to be properly escorted and received there," I do not think that any religious ceremony would produce an impression on the Catholics in your Majesty's favour. This, Sire, is the truth. The Empress is in better spirits to-day. I have passed the day in sustaining the hopes of people who have much less self-possession than belongs to her Majesty.

[806.] NAPOLEON TO JOSEPH.

Nogent, Feb. 9, 1814, 3 A. M.

My Brother,—I have received your letter written at noon on the 8th of February, which was brought to me by your aide-de-camp. You tell me that at La Ferté-sous-Jouarre General Minot is in command of a column consisting of the 6th battalion of the 86th, of the 1st of the 8th light infantry, and the 4th of the 70th, altogether 2000 men. The Minister of War composes this column differently, of the 6th battalion of the 86th, and the 1st and 2nd of the national guards of the North. What is the cause of this discrepancy?

I have written to the Minister of War that the battalions must be composed of only 400 or 500 men each, because we have more cadres than there are conscripts to fill them; and it is better to have six battalions of 400 men than three battalions of 800. I think, indeed, that they are twice as useful, that is to say, that three battalions of 400 conscripts will do nearly as much work as three battalions of 800. I am surprised that there are not enough men in Soissons to hold it. Six battalions, or 4000 men, must be there. It would have been better, therefore, to have sent thither 1000 muskets than more troops. It seems, from the Minister of War's report, that to-morrow the 10th, a division of national guards, consisting of from 8000 to 9000 well-armed men, will reach Meaux. Urge the Minister of War to send thither majors to command the regiments, captains to act as adjutant-majors, and officers to serve in the cadres. This division will be a great resource. A general of division and two brigadiers will be required. Cartridges must likewise be sent thither, that the troops may practise every day at a mark. The divisions of Soissons and of Montereau, which are exercised every day, will also be of great use. Paris was to furnish Montereau with two battalions; have they started? The Duke of Ragusa reached Champ-Aubert on the road to Montmirail early yesterday, on his way to Épernay; my guard, both horse and foot, are at Sézanne, in order to support him. I am expecting every instant to receive news which will carry me thither myself; I consider the diversion in favour of the Duke of Taranto as already made, and that the enemy will have to fall back upon Châlons.

[807.] NAPOLEON TO JOSEPH.

Nogent, Feb. 9, 1814, 11 A.M.

My Brother,—I had so much to do all last night, that I was not able to start for Sézanne. The Duke of Ragusa *has reached Champ-Aubert. General Sacken, with* 15,000 *men, was at Montmirail. His park passed by Champ-Aubert on the* 8*th,* *coming from Châlons.** I intend to attack him to-morrow. Besides this, detachments have shown themselves towards Coulommiers, and in other directions; they are mere marauders, and are of no consequence.

[808.] NAPOLEON TO JOSEPH.

Nogent, Feb. 9, 1814.

My Brother,—*Unless you had some reason which is unknown to me, you were wrong in placing* 8 *guns belonging to the guards, at the disposal of General Hullin.* There are plenty of guns at Vincennes, and plenty of means of transport for them in Paris. Let General Ornano, therefore, retain these guns. *The guard forms a special corps.* Nothing of theirs must be taken *for the line.* If you do not *give* the guns belonging to the guard to General Hullin, he *will set to work to provide for himself; the national guards must be accustomed to do duty at the barriers by themselves, otherwise, when the troops of the line are moved on from Paris,* the national guards will think that they are lost. You may place a much smaller guard at the unimportant barriers, which are not threatened. Desire the Minister of War to fill up all the companies of gunners, to send for their cadres from the depôts, and to complete them with conscripts. I ought to have 30† gunners in Paris; they can serve more than 200 guns, which *are absolutely necessary.*

I am of your opinion about the prayers at St. Geneviève; I think that it would do no good; it was only a piece of devotion on the part of the Empress. Hold the 22 guns belonging to the guard, the 1200 horse, the 24 battalions of the guard, 500 strong, ready to start at a moment's notice. I intend to station them halfway. Do not include them in the defence of Paris. Send to Compiègne a battalion of the guard from 200 to 300 strong, to be increased to 500, with 2 pieces of cannon to defend the town and palace against the enemy's partisans. Send another battalion

* The italics in this and in the following letter are in Napoleon's hand. —ED.

† This must be a mistake. Perhaps the figures ought to be 300.—TR.

of the guard to Fontainebleau for the same purpose. The officers whom you send to command in those towns will organise the national guards so that they may assist in the defence of the palaces, which the towns will be willing enough to do, as the palaces may be said almost to belong to them. Tell Demazis to remove from Compiègne and Fontainebleau the plate, and everything that might serve as a trophy. There are portraits of all my ministers and of my family at Compiègne. This must be done without disturbance or attracting attention.

[809.] NAPOLEON TO JOSEPH.

Nogent, Feb. 9, 1814.

My Brother,—I have received your courier of the 8th at 11 at night. The Minister of Police gives you false information. I think that he does not know how to ask questions. He says that M. Bonne, a superior officer of the corps of geographical engineers, saw the enemy at La Ferté-sous-Jouarre. Send for him, and he will tell you that he did not see them; but that he was told that the enemy was approaching, which is a very different affair. The same thing with regard to Vieux-Maisons. I have always found the police doing great harm by their want of judgment: they alarm without informing. I gave to them a printed list of questions, providing for every case: this prevented their blundering. Order the police to give these printed papers to their agents in order to direct their inquiries.

[810.] NAPOLEON TO JOSEPH.

Nogent, Feb. 9, 1814, 2 P. M.

My Brother,—I am setting off for Sézanne, and I hope to attack the army of Silesia to-morrow. I have ordered General Minot, whom you sent to La Ferté-sous-Jouarre, to push on to Montmirail, where General Sacken is, with 15,000 men. I shall advance upon him by way of Sézanne and Champ-Aubert. If this manœuvre should meet with complete success, it may decide the fate of the campaign.

These are my dispositions; it is important that you should

know them. I leave at Nogent the Duke of Belluno, with his own two divisions, General Gérard's division, and General Milhaud's 5th cavalry corps. These will form a corps of infantry, cavalry, and artillery, amounting to between 14,000 and 15,000 men. His orders are to defend the heights of Pont-sur-Seine and the town of Nogent, which I have barricaded; and, finally, if the whole of Schwartzenberg's army should fall upon him so as to prevent his defending Nogent, to blow up the bridge, and to take up his position on the right bank. The great park of artillery, the head-quarters of the Intendant, and the greater part of my household, will be placed at Provins, escorted by a division of the young guard commanded by General Rothenbourg. The Duke of Reggio commands the 7th corps, composed of twenty battalions from Spain and Bourdeaux. One of his divisions is at Provins, his head-quarters; this evening and to-morrow it will be at Nangis. Rothenbourg's division, with the head-quarters under its protection, the division of national guards which is at Montereau and at Sens, General Pajol, who defends the Seine between Nogent and Bray, Pont-sur-Yonne, Sens, and in the 2nd line, Moret, Nemours, and Montargis, up to the Loire, are under the orders of the Duke of Reggio. I reckon that the two Spanish divisions, increased by the battalions from Bourdeaux, will amount to 12,000 men. General Pajol must have 2000 cavalry, the national guards of Montereau ought to amount to 6000; Rothenbourg's division consists of 4000. The Duke of Reggio has therefore about 25,000 men. If Schwartzenberg's army, which is at Troyes, should march upon Sens and Pont-sur-Yonne without attacking Nogent, or only masking it; or if he storms the place and throws the Duke of Belluno on the right bank; in either case the Duke of Reggio, supported by the Duke of Belluno, will proceed, if the enemy's manœuvre be of importance, towards Yonne and Montereau, where he will concentrate all his troops. If you have notice that the enemy is about to make his great attack upon Fontainebleau, you will have time enough to arm the bridges of Corbeil and Choisy, and to despatch our reserves to Moret and the Loing. If I succeed, in the course of the next two or three days, in crushing the army of Silesia, I shall debouch upon Nogent or Montereau. With the reserves I may have 80,000 men, and give an unexpected turn to affairs.

My army is thus divided into three corps:—

One which is acting under my orders: it is composed of two divisions of the old guard (8000 men); two divisions of the young guard who are with the Prince of Moskowa (6000 men); of the Duke of Ragusa's corps (6000 men)—in the whole 20,000 infantry; of the cavalry of the guard (6000 men); of the 1st corps of cavalry (2000 men); of General Defrance's cavalry (2000 men)—in the whole 10,000 cavalry. I have, therefore, under my orders 30,000 men, and about 120 guns. The forces of Generals York, Blücher, and Sacken, are valued at from 40,000 to 45,000; but the Duke of Taranto must find employment for at least 5000 of them. I shall therefore have 30,000 against 40,000: this proportion gives me hopes of success. The point of support of my corps to-night will be Sézanne; its line of march will be by the roads to Montmirail and Château-Thierry. Centre: the Duke of Belluno, as I have said already, with 14,000 men. Right wing: the Duke of Reggio, as before, with 25,000 men. This is my whole force, consisting of from 60,000 to 70,000 men, including all arms, even the engineers and artillery.

I estimate the enemy's forces at 45,000 of the army of Silesia, and 150,000 of Schwartzenberg's army, but including Bubna and the Cossacks; so that, if I succeed in beating the army of Silesia, and rendering it incapable of action for a few days, I may turn round upon Schwartzenberg with 70,000 or 80,000 men, including the reinforcement which you will send to me from Paris, and I do not think that on a single point he will be able to oppose to me more than from 110,000 to 120,000 men. If I am not strong enough to attack, I may at least hold him in check, and harass him for a fortnight or three weeks, which will give opportunities for new combinations.

It is essential that Albert should take this letter to the Ministers of War and of the Administration of War, that they may each be well aware of what they have to do. If the enemy should push on to La Férte or Meaux, there will be no occasion for alarm, as to-morrow I attack his rear. I have not counted among my resources the division of the national guard of Meaux, which I hope will soon amount to between 8000 and 10,000 men. I have ordered St. Germain, who, with 800 horse, is at Meaux, to proceed to La Ferté-sous-Jouarre: the division which has been armed of the national guard may also be sent thither.

[811.] JOSEPH TO NAPOLEON.

Paris, Feb. 9, 1814, 4 A. M.

I have received your Majesty's letter desiring me to postpone the insertion of the article in the 'Moniteur.' I have sent my aide-de-camp to the Duke of Cadore; I hope that he will have arrived in time. The annexed letter* will acquaint your Majesty with the state of affairs towards Laon.

I have not yet received the report of Gérard, of the war-office; but my last night's letter will have already informed your Majesty that the Minister of War reports, after careful investigation, that he has only 11,000 muskets, which he reserves for the Imperial guard.

[812.] JOSEPH TO NAPOLEON.

Paris, Feb. 9, 1814, 4 A. M.

Sire,—I have received your letter of yesterday of 11 A. M., in answer to mine of the 7th, 11 P. M.

Your Majesty may be assured that, so far as depends on me, your wishes will be complied with. Circumstances may occur in which this expression of them may contribute to such a result. My letter may thus have been useful by eliciting this written manifestation of your will, which will decide the conduct of many persons now unresolved.

[813.] JOSEPH TO NAPOLEON.

Paris, Feb. 9, 1814, 11 A. M.

Sire,—I have received your letters of the 8th at 8 P. M. I have sent the one to the Empress Josephine, and I am expecting an answer by Tascher. After the cabinet council I will see MM.

* This letter does not appear.—TR.

de Feltre and d'Hauterive. The Minister of War has written to me a letter which I send on to your Majesty; you will see that our muskets are reduced to 6000. It is, therefore, useless to expect to form a reserve of from 30,000 to 40,000 men in Paris. Things are stronger than men, Sire; and when this is clearly proved, it seems to me that true glory consists in preserving as much as is possible of one's people and one's empire; and that to expose a precious life to such evident danger is not glorious, because it is against the interests of a great number of men whose existence is attached to your own. Your Majesty may rest assured that I shall faithfully execute your commands, whatever they may be. No one here has anything, directly or indirectly, to do with what I am writing to your Majesty in perfect openness, just as it occurs to me.

I see so much depression, that I fear that it is useless to expect an army of reserve, or any extraordinary effort to be made in Paris: you must therefore submit with fortitude to necessity; whether you are permitted to make a great nation happy, or you are forced to yield, there being no choice left except between death and dishonour; and, at this juncture, I see no dishonour for your Majesty unless you abandon the throne, because in this case you would ruin a number of individuals who have devoted themselves to you. If it be possible, then, make peace at any price; if that is impossible, when the hour comes we must meet death with resolution, as did the last Emperor of Constantinople.

Should this occur, your Majesty may be persuaded that I shall in every respect follow out your wishes, and that I shall do nothing unworthy either of you or of me.

CHAPTER XXI.

THE letters contained in this chapter extend from the 10th to the 18th of February, 1814.

They were nine days of victories. Napoleon had been posted for some days at Nogent, on the Seine, between the army of Silesia, and the allied grand army. The army of Silesia, commanded by Blücher, was advancing on Paris from Châlons by two roads, one down the Marne by Épernay and Château-Thierry, the other across a difficult and marshy country by Vertus, Étoges, Vauchamps, Champ-Aubert, and Montmirail; the two roads meeting at La Ferté-sous-Jouarre on the Marne.

The allied grand army, under Schwartzenberg, was marching towards Paris by the valley of the Seine, its head-quarters being at Troyes. The reader has seen, by Napoleon's last letters, that on the 9th he intended to make a flank movement by cross-roads to Sézanne, in order to attack the Silesian army, which was marching in 4 divisions, under Sacken, York, Alsufief, and Blücher. He found, what he does not seem to have expected, a part of the Silesian army at Baye, between Nogent and Sézanne, beat it, and reached Sézanne on the 9th. The next day, the 10th, he beat Alsufief at Champ-Aubert; on the 11th he defeated Sacken at Montmirail; on the 12th he defeated York at Château-Thierry; and, finding that Blucher was advancing, he turned back to Montmirail, and on the 14th defeated him with great loss at Vauchamps, a village between Montmirail and Étôges, and drove him back through Étôges to Châlons.

But Schwartzenberg was profiting by Napoleon's absence to march on Paris by the Seine. He drove Victor out of Nogent, occupied Montereau, and penetrated beyond Nangis to Mormant, a village not more than 25 miles from Paris. Three marshals, Oudinot, Victor, and Macdonald, were opposed to him with a force of about 47,000 men, but they appear to have expected defeat, and earnestly implored Napoleon's presence. Napoleon left Montmirail on the 15th, a few hours after he had defeated Blücher, reached Meaux the same day, and on the 16th joined his marshals at Guignes, a small town at the intersection of the roads from Meaux to Melun and from Paris to Nogent. On the 17th he drove the Russians, under Count Pahlen, from Mormant, and entered Nangis, and on the 18th he drove the Prince of Würtemberg out of Montereau, and marched on Troyes, from whence the allied sovereigns and Schwartzenberg fled in terror, and scarcely paused until they found themselves more than 100 miles off at Langres. In nine days he gained seven victories, made nine marches in the depth of winter, most of them over cross-roads, such as the cross-roads of France then were, and drove away or frightened away two armies, each much larger than his own.

It is not surprising that such wonderful success, immediately following two years of almost uninterrupted disaster, somewhat intoxicated him, and led him to believe that the chances were again in his favour, and even to imagine that the allies themselves had little hope of escaping with many of their troops from France.

[814.] BERTHIER TO JOSEPH.

Feb. 10, 1814.

The Emperor left a great part of his army at Pont and Nogent, and made a long flank march yesterday to attack Blücher, who is taking the Montmirail raod with a considerable portion of the army of Silesia. When we reached Pont St. Prix we found that the enemy was in position at Baye to cover the road to Sézanne. It was Sacken's corps. He was attacked in flank, broken, and retreated on Champ-Aubert, followed by our cavalry. Marshal Ney's corps and a part of the guard arrived opportunely. The enemy is cut in two—one portion is in the direction of Montmirail, the other is falling back on Châlons.

[815.] NAPOLEON TO JOSEPH.

Sézanne, Feb. 10, 1814, 10 A.M.

My Brother,—Your two letters of the 9th have reached me. Your aide-de-camp must have taken my yesterday's letter to you. I reached this place yesterday evening. I am mounting my horse to advance on Champ-Aubert. I am much impeded by the state of the roads: they are horrible; there are six feet of mud. I am assured this morning that the enemy has begun to retire from Montmirail to Vauchamps.* I cannot understand why the Duke of Taranto is retreating so rapidly. As the shortest way of communicating with him is through Paris, send him word that to-day, the 10th, at 11 A.M. I was at Champ-Aubert, on the rear of the enemy's column, which is at Montmirail.

[816.] NAPOLEON TO JOSEPH.

Champ-Aubert, Feb 10, 1814, 10 P.M.

My Brother,—I attacked the enemy to-day at Champ-Aubert. His force consisted of 12 regiments and 40 pieces of cannon. I have taken the Commander-in-Chief Alsufief, with all his generals, colonels, officers, guns, waggons, and baggage.

* This was not true. Blucher was not aware of Napoleon's march.—TR.

We have 6000 prisoners, 40 guns, and 200 carriages. The rest were driven into a lake, or killed on the field. This corps is entirely destroyed. We are marching towards Montmirail, and shall be there this evening at 10 o'clock. I shall reach it in person to-morrow morning before daybreak, to march with 20,000 infantry upon Sacken at La Ferté-sous-Jouarre. I am treading close upon the enemy's heels. The Duke of Taranto has between 8000 and 10,000 men, with the national guard of Meaux, and all that you can spare from Paris. [This force] alone will be sufficient to hold the enemy in check. I am in great hopes that Sacken is lost, and, if fortune continues to second us as she has done to-day, the state of affairs will be changed in an instant; for the whole strength of the Russian army consists in Sacken's corps which contains 10 divisions, or 60 regiments. Blücher is cut off from Sacken; he has 2 divisions; he is 8 leagues off on the Bergères road. He will be held in check during my march. I do not think that we have lost 200 men.

[817.] NAPOLEON TO JOSEPH.

Farm of Epine-aux-Bois, between Montmirail and Vieux-Maisons,
Feb.11, 1814, 8 P.M.

My Brother,—Berthier despatched a courier to you from the field of battle. Since that time I sent off young Montesquiou to you. It is eight o'clock, and before bed-time I wish you to have these two lines to let you know that to-day has been decisive. The army of Silesia has ceased to exist; I have completely routed it. We have carried off all their guns and baggage, and we have taken several thousand prisoners, perhaps more than 7000, and they continue to arrive every instant; 5000 or 6000 of the enemy are left on the field. All this has been done, although only half of my old guard were engaged; they did more than one has any right to expect from men. The enemy fled disbanded towards Château-Thierry. I presume that the Duke of Treviso pursued them to La Ferté-sous-Jouarre and Château-Thierry. These two days have entirely

* This was a mistake.—TR

changed the state of affairs. Sacken was killed,* many of their generals are prisoners, some are wounded, and several left on the field. Here then are 10 Russian divisions, forming 60 regiments, almost annihilated. I think that in the night we engaged York's corps, which arrived on the field. He shared the fate of the Russians. I have desired the Empress to fire a salute of 60 guns. Our loss is slight. General Michel of the guard is wounded in the arm. I do not think that I have lost more than 1000 men. My foot-guard, my dragoons, and horse-grenadiers performed miracles. I hope to be to-morrow in communication with La Ferté-sous-Jouarre. I think then that these two days place Paris completely out of danger, for the army of Silesia was the best that the allies had. Tell me what is going on towards Sens and Montereau. I must know, in order to arrange my further operations.

[818.] JOSEPH TO NAPOLEON.

Paris Feb. 11, 1814, 7 A.M.

Sire,—I did not receive your letter dated Sézanne, the 10th, 10 A.M., till to-day at seven. I have despatched a courier to inform Marshal Macdonald of your Majesty's arrival at Champ-Aubert, on the rear of the enemy's column then at Montmirail.

Nothing remarkable is going on here. The public mind continues in the same state. The wives and children of many of the principal public functionaries have left the capital. The rise in the funds which took place yesterday is attributed to a letter from the Duke of Vicenza, giving hopes of the negotiations terminating favourably. Every one is persuaded that our affairs can be re-established in no other way; the state of the exchequer and the arsenals is known to all the world; and whatever prodigies may yet be expected from the experience and skill of your Majesty, it is not thought possible that you can struggle alone against numbers and circumstances. The ministers have doubtless already informed your Majesty that one of the Bourbons has joined Lord Wellington's army, and that another is in Holland. Many sick have arrived here.

Money is wanting to pay the troops; they commit in consequence all sorts of irregularities, which exasperate the inhabitants to such a degree (I can speak chiefly of those of Versailles, Compiègne, and Senlis), that it is not uncommon to hear it said publicly, "The enemy could not do worse."

I do not write these disagreeable truths to your Majesty for the sake of persuading you to make peace—I know that you desire it more than any other person—but in order to console you, if you should be forced to submit to conditions to which France would not be reduced, if the strength of mind of all her people were in proportion to that of her sovereign. I entreat your Majesty to believe that my language to the rest of the world is very different; but I am obliged to own that there is no salvation for us but in the speediest peace, on whatever conditions. I know no one who is of a contrary opinion. Your Majesty's most faithful servants are chiefly distinguished by their profound conviction that, with peace, your Majesty will find in your own genius, and in the confidence of the nation, means to restore our affairs.

[819.] NAPOLEON TO JOSEPH.

Faubourg de Château-Thierry, Feb. 12, 1814.

My Brother,—I am in the suburb of Château-Thierry. I pursued the enemy's rear-guard; as I had cut him off from Châlons, his army was obliged to cross the Marne to gain the road to Soissons. I carried off the whole rear-guard, which consisted of four Russian battalions, three Prussian battalions, and three pieces of cannon. I took them all, even the Russian general who was in command; 2000 prisoners were made to-day. The Duke of Ragusa is about to march from Etoges upon Epernay and Châlons. If Marshal Macdonald had manœuvred on the right bank of the Marne, as I hoped, not one man would have escaped. We have, however, taken between 8000 and 10,000 prisoners, among whom are five or six generals; they start to-morrow for Paris. We have taken almost all the enemy's artillery and baggage, and killed immense numbers. His force, which was 35,000, does not amount to-day to 12,000, and they are in horrible confusion. If the movements of the Austrians do not recall me towards the Seine, I shall seize the enemy in the rear. Considering the great results, I engaged very few troops; my guard, both horse and foot, has covered itself with glory.

[820.] JOSEPH TO NAPOLEON.

Paris, Feb. 12, 1814, 10 A.M.

Sire,—The funds set apart for the use of the guard are exhausted. We have no credit, and General Ornano urges me to obtain from your Majesty another million, to be divided equally between the cavalry and the infantry. If we have no money, both horses and men must remain in the state in which they now are. There are 1500 men who want clothing. Your Majesty is aware that between 1000 and 1500 recruits arrive every day for the guard. A remount of 1000 horses is also required, otherwise the cavalry must remain here idle. I send a return of the guard to your Majesty; I intend to inspect it at noon to-day. Marshal Macdonald tells me that he has heard nothing directly from your Majesty. He has received the intelligence which I sent to him yesterday of the action of Champ-Aubert. He heard a loud cannonade in the direction of Montmirail. He despatched thither General St. Germain with 300 horse, who captured a few horse-soldiers at St. Fiacre. A great mistake was made in blowing up the bridge of Trilport; an officer whom I sent yesterday to Meaux assures me that they are preparing the means of crossing the river on rafts. He thinks that the enemy's artillery will not be able to retire, as the bridges towards La Ferté-sous-Jouarre have been cut.

[821.] NAPOLEON TO JOSEPH.

Farm of Lumeron, near Château-Thierry,
Feb. 13, 1814, 10 A.M.

My Brother,—During the whole of the 11th the enemy attacked the town of Nogent. The Duke of Belluno had passed over to the right bank with all his troops, and had left in the town only 1200 men, under the command of General Bourmont. (This Bourmont is the famous chief of the Chouans; I am extremely pleased with him.) The enemy tried to enter in close columns, and was shot down from the houses and barricades. In short, he was repulsed in three successive assaults, and lost, as was to be expected in such fighting, between 2000 and 3000 men. General Bourmont was wounded, but in other respects our loss was slight. The enemy, enraged, then brought forward howitzers and set fire to the town, but with no effect; and on the 12th, our men were ready to give the enemy a similar reception. It is said that General Schwartzenberg, with all his army, was watching this operation. I have heard nothing from Montereau since the 11th. General Pajol was at Fossart, near Montereau. I have ordered the Duke of Reggio to proceed to Montereau with Rothenbourg's division and the 9th division from Spain. But this division, which was to have arrived on the 9th, was not here yesterday evening, the 10th. The Minister of War ought to know the cause. This division should be sent to Montereau. I ordered Leval's division to join me; but as I do not want it, this has become a false march. By the return which General Ornano has sent to me, I see that the guard has 2000 cavalry and 8000 infantry under arms, altogether 10,000 men, and 22 pieces of cannon. I have ordered two more batteries to be added, so that they will have 32 pieces.

The Minister of War writes reports and waits for my approbation before executing my orders. This is not the way to act at this juncture; it did very well when I was in Paris. You must immediately place at General Ornano's disposal the two companies of artillery from Spain with 16 pieces of ordnance. They alone will form a good reserve corps. Let it march towards Fontainebleau. Generals Charpentier and Boyer should go with them. Some brigadier-generals will be required; the Minister of War must appoint them. These troops, however, must not be sent to a distance from Paris; instead of cantoning them on the roads to Meaux and Villette, they must be placed near Charenton, Villejuif, and Essonne, and one division always kept in Paris. The Minister of War has also sent to me a report on the formation of two divisions of reserve for the line; I have not yet read it with attention. The chief thing is to act, and not to forget that with conscripts it is better to have battalions of only 300 men than that they should be more numerous. Send a courier to Soissons to obtain news of the enemy, and let the commandant of that town hold to the death; for the enemy will be considerably embarrassed if he cannot enter Soissons. I do not think that Schwartzenberg will entangle himself with Fontainebleau as long as we remain masters of the bridge of Nogent. The Austrians are too well acquainted with my mode of action, and bear its scars too deeply, to doubt that, if they suffer us to retain possession of the bridge of Nogent, I shall fall upon their rear, as I did here.

However, if the enemy were to bring together a considerable force and make a decided movement, I should desire the Duke of Belluno to proceed from Nogent to Montereau to support the Duke of Reggio. He will have orders to blow up the bridge of Nogent, and to leave on the opposite right bank troops sufficient to prevent the enemy from rebuilding it. I have not yet settled my plan of operations for to-day, but if it be necessary I shall march rapidly towards Montereau, accompanied by the Duke of Belluno's corps, the Duke of Reggio, and Ornano's reserve, and my force will be strong enough to hold Schwartzenberg in check. I tremble lest those rascally Russians should retaliate by setting fire to Fontainebleau. I hope in the course of the day to rebuild the bridge over the Marne at Château-Thierry; I shall then fix my plans. What I hear from Sens proves that General Allix has repulsed the enemy; he held his ground on the evening of the 11th. He had obliged the enemy to open trenches. All the cavalry which arrives from Spain ought to proceed, as I have already ordered, to Montereau, to be under the command of General Pajol and the Duke of Reggio.

[822.] NAPOLEON TO JOSEPH.

Château-Thierry, Feb. 13, 1814.

My Brother,—General Drouot tells me that he has distributed the 14th million. I have received your letter of the 12th at 10 A.M. I enclose a letter from the Duke of Treviso; you may insert an extract from it in some of the smaller newspapers. Everything which I hear here proves to me more and more the extent of the enemy's disaster. The inhabitants assure me that of that immense army not 12,000 came back. I hear nothing more of the 2nd division of the line. I told you to forward a division of the guard in the first place to Essonne; those whom you have sent to Fontainebleau will do instead. I sent to you this morning my orderly officer, Gourgaud. If Soissons hold out, the enemy will be extremely embarrassed. They endeavoured to retreat upon Reims, and tried in vain to find a road. Whatever happens, despatch an officer to desire Berruyer to hold out. The bridge at Château-Thierry is not yet rebuilt.

[823.] NAPOLEON TO JOSEPH.

Château-Thierry, Feb. 13, 1814, 2 P.M.

My Brother,—The chief of the staff will communicate to you the dispositions which I have made for the defence of Montereau. As soon as you are acquainted with them, forward them by express to the Duke of Reggio. You must send off immediately General Charpentier with two batteries of foot artillery, and a division of the guard consisting of 12 battalions. He may reach Essonne to-morrow. He will occupy Corbeil, La Ferté-Alais, and all the little bridges across the Essonne. You must give him 1000 horses belonging to the guard. The other division, also with 1000 horses, will be cantoned at Charenton and in Paris, and will hold themselves ready to take up a position on the Yères, if it should be required. I do not know to what extent your regiments of the line are organised. If you have a division ready, send it to Villeneuve-sur-Seine, and let me know the state of the Paris reserve. It is probable that the news of the disasters of Sacken and of York may stop the enemy's movements. The police and the war-office should send agents to discover the effect which has been produced upon them. All these divisions must be properly provided with artillery. I have just ordered the available part of the national guard, which is at Meaux, to proceed to Montereau under the orders of the Duke of Taranto.

[824.] NAPOLEON TO JOSEPH.

From the Lumeron Farm, near Château-Thierry,
Feb. 13, 1814.

My Brother,—I have seen the officer whom you sent to me. I am told that he is an excellent man, but he has neither the education nor the talents which ought to belong to your aide-de-camp. He talked nothing but nonsense to me about Nogent and Provins. You should choose men of more acuteness, information, and cleverness to be your aides-de-camp. This man, who was a very good captain of grenadiers, would perhaps be useful at the head of a battalion.

[825.] MARIE LOUISE TO JOSEPH.

Paris, Feb. 13, 1814.

My dear Brother,—I have received two letters from the Emperor: he is well. He overtook yesterday and routed the rear-guard of the enemy, and General Sacken, who was in command, was killed. If you have any further information, pray, my dear brother, pass it on to me. When I see you this morning, I shall ask you to help me to decipher my letters, for I am to put the Emperor's news into the 'Moniteur' under the head of Paris. I entreat you to believe in my sincere friendship.

[826.] NAPOLEON TO JOSEPH.

Château-Thierry, Feb. 14, 1814, 3 A.M.

My Brother,—It is 3 o'clock in the morning. The Duke of Treviso crossed yesterday the bridge of Château-Thierry at 5 in the afternoon, and followed up the pursuit. The enemy became entangled in the cross-roads between this place and Reims, through Fère en Tardenois, and abandoned there the remainder of his carriages. The Duke of Ragusa was yesterday at Etoges, and fell back upon Fromentiers, on seeing Blücher, with, as he supposed, a superior force, ready to fall upon him. I am just starting; by 8 o'clock I shall be there. I intend to attack the enemy, and I hope to beat him thoroughly in the course of the day, and thus destroy another of his corps; this corps seems to be Wittgenstein's.* As it appears that the enemy will not pass by Soissons, I have ordered the Duke of Treviso, as soon as he has covered the town, to withdraw some of the troops and national guards who are there, in order to reinforce his corps, leaving, however, a few troops to defend the town. Let the Minister of War order the fortifications of this important post to be gone on with.

I have received your undated letter, apparently of the 13th. Inspect the national guards; hasten their preparations. I think that the Minister of the Interior should send a conseiller d'état or some other official to report on the crimes committed by the enemy in the places which he has evacuated, and of the conduct of the inhabitants. His report should be inserted in the 'Moniteur.'

The Duke of Belluno writes to me, dated yesterday, the 15th, at noon, that he has blown up the bridge of Nogent, and fallen back on Provins, to be nearer to Montereau. His motive was that he heard that the enemy was strengthening his forces to attack Montereau, and was threatening Paris from Fontainebleau. I have ordered the Duke of Taranto to proceed towards Montereau with all his troops, which amount to more than 16,000 men, including the national guard of Meaux. The Duke of Reggio ought to be there with General Rothenbourg's division and the 9th division from Spain, which, as the Minister of War assures me, arrived there on the 12th.

The troops at Montereau may, therefore, be stated as follows: the Duke of Belluno, 10,000 infantry and 3000 cavalry, with 40 pieces of cannon; the Duke of Reggio, 15,000 infantry, including the division of the national guard of Montereau; 4000 cavalry under Bourdesoulle and Roussel, and 50 pieces of cannon; the Duke of Taranto 12,000 infantry, 3000 cavalry, and 40 pieces of cannon. Here, then, is a force of between 50,000 and 60,000 men,† without including the Paris reserve.

If, as I hope, to-day turns out well, and I succeed in ridding myself of this corps, which I suppose to be Wittgenstein's from

* It was Blucher's.—TR.

† 47,000.—TR.

the Rhine, I may go immediately in person to Montereau, unless the enemy should have ceased to act on the offensive.

Order the Minister of the Interior to have the bridge at Trilfort repaired in 24 hours, as well as that at La Ferté-sous-Jouarre. If the bridges cannot be repaired, let them make bridges of boats, so that I may be able to cross. Desire the Minister of War to send to La Ferté-sous-Jouarre a commandant with a battalion, and to send anothor to Meaux. Tell the Minister of the Interior to write to the Mayor of Meaux that I am not satisfied with the conduct of the inhabitants: they must behave so as not to oblige me to make examples.

[827.] NAPOLEON TO JOSEPH.

Montmirail, Feb. 14, 1814.

My Brother,—It is 9 o'clock in the evening. I write a line to acquaint you with the happy result of the battle of Vauchamps.

Blücher's head-quarters were at Vertus.* He had been joined by Kleist from Germany with 24 battalions, and by a new Russian corps of 12 battalions, in all 20,000 men, but was separated from the rest of his army. On the 13th he moved on Étoges and Champ-Aubert. The Duke of Ragusa retired without fighting. I left Château Thierry at 3 this morning, and reached Montmirail as the enemy was just at its gates. He took up his position at the village of Vauchamps. I beat him, took 8000 prisoners, 10 colours, and three guns, and drove him back, fighting up to the gates of Etoges. His loss in killed and wounded must have been more than 4000 men. My killed and wounded were not 300.

The means by which I obtained these great results were that he had little cavalry, while I had from 6000 to 8000, and very good, with which I kept outflanking and surrounding him; and that he could use few of his guns, for fear of losing them, while I crushed him all day with grape-shot from 100 pieces of cannon. My three household squadrons covered themselves with glory.

* A village about half-way on the road between Châlons and Montmirail. —TR.

I had them always in hand, made them charge repeatedly, and they took 1000 prisoners. I think that I mentioned to you yesterday that the Duke of Treviso is closely pursuing the shattered remains of Sacken and York by the cross-road to Reims.

[828.] NAPOLEON TO JOSEPH.

Montmirail, Feb. 15, 1814, 3 A.M.

My Brother,—I have received your letter of the 14th, which was brought to me by young Montesquiou. I shall start as soon as the day breaks, and I shall reach La Ferté-sous-Jouarre early with my guard; thence I shall proceed in person towards Meaux. I cannot understand why the Duke of Reggio did not defend the bridge of Bray.

Yesterday, the 14th, the Dukes of Belluno, Reggio, and Taranto were to join between Nangis and Guignes. I have no doubt that I shall soon learn what has taken place. In the article which you will insert in the 'Moniteur' on the battle of Vauchamps, you must mention as prisoners Prince Woronzow, Russian general of division, and a Russian brigadier-general. Their corps acted as rear-guard during the night, was charged and routed; 1200 prisoners and four pieces of cannon were taken.

It seems that the enemy's operations are confined to the right bank of the Seine. The cavalry from Spain might therefore have assembled at Fontainebleau; as the bridges of Melun and Montereau are cut off, it can join us only by the bridge of Corbeil. It appears that there still are 1000 men of the national guard of Montereau without arms, and that they are all in want of camp-utensils. Order them to be properly provided. Send General Radet's gendarmes (which ought to reach Paris to-day) to meet the 7000 or 8000 prisoners who are about to start from hence. The peasants have picked up here on the battle-fields more than 40,000 muskets, which the rapid movements of our troops prevented us from collecting. Perhaps the national guard of Paris might obtain many of them by sending agents among the country people. As the enemy is manœuvring on the right bank of the Seine, and has partisans on the left bank, it is important to reinforce the cordon which protects Paris on that side.

[829.] NAPOLEON TO JOSEPH.

La Ferté-sous-Jouarre, Feb. 15, 1814, 2 P.M.

My Brother,—Your letter of the 14th reached me at 5 o'clock. I am surprised that by that time you had not received the courier whom the chief of the staff sent to you from the field of battle, at one in the afternoon. I shall be at Meaux early this evening with my guard. I do not know whether the whole of my foot-guard will be able to get so far, but I hope that it will march beyond La Ferté this evening. It will be difficult therefore for the foot-guard to reach Guignes* before to-morrow afternoon. The wisest plan will be† to retire behind the Yères, and to avoid engaging the enemy. If this position is such as to make it impossible for the enemy to attack the army to-morrow, it should remain there. If, on the contrary, an attack should be feared, the army, leaving a light corps to protect the road from Brie, might fall back upon Fontenay, on the road to Meaux, and meet me. The great park, after passing Brie-Comte-Robert, should move to the road between Fontenay and Paris. However, I shall probably before night receive news of the army, and I shall then give positive orders; I shall be at Meaux this evening in person. At any rate I will not lose a moment in informing you of my intentions. I presume that the barricades towards the Jardin des Plantes are finished, and that you have placed there troops and guns. A commandant must also be appointed for Bicêtre, and a battalion and some guns placed there: this advanced post sweeps the whole road. If the enemy, notwithstanding the checks which he has experienced, should persist in his advance, which would probably occasion his

* A village to the south of Meaux, between Paris and Sens. The Yères runs to the north of Guignes.—TR.

† This advice is given to the army consisting of three corps, amounting in the whole to about 47,000 men, under the command of Oudinot, Victor, and Macdonald. Napoleon was now marching to join this army.—TR.

total ruin, all our forces, artillery, infantry, and cavalry, should be brought together by the bridge of Corbeil or by that of Choisy. These bridges must be held, not destroyed; they are necessary to me in order to manœuvre on both banks; for as soon as the enemy begins to retreat in good earnest I shall cross over to the other bank to pursue and to surround him. For this purpose I must use the bridges of Corbeil and Choisy, as those of Melun and Montereau are destroyed. The Yères has overflowed and is not fordable; it will protect the army for at least three days. On the 17th I shall be ready to attack.

[830.] NAPOLEON TO JOSEPH.

Meaux, Feb. 15, 1814, 7 P.M.

My Brother,—I have just arrived; my guard will be with the army to-morrow.*

[831.] NAPOLEON TO JOSEPH.

Meaux, Feb. 15, 1814.

My Brother,—It is useless to build a bridge at Villeneuve-St.-Georges, as that at Choisy will do for me: nor do we want a new bridge at Charenton. A stone bridge fit to gallop over, and wide enough for two carriages abreast, is enough, especially as I have that of St. Maur. To build these new bridges would therefore alarm Paris unnecessarily and occasion useless expense.

[832.] JOSEPH TO NAPOLEON.

Paris, Feb. 15, 1814, 5 A.M.

Sire,—General Bordesoulle has arrived with two letters which I send on. He says that it is absolutely necessary that your Majesty should determine which of the three marshals is to command. All are anxious to see your Majesty at their head; they certainly will be attacked to-morrow, and they appear to have little confidence in one another. I am writing to the Minister of War to request him to send all the cavalry from the depôt of Versailles,

* The rest of the letter is scratched out.—ED.

that is disposable, towards Brie-Comte-Robert. The Imperial guard which was in Paris will also take part in this decisive battle, so that if we are beaten I shall have no escort for the Empress and the King of Rome. No one doubts that your Majesty's presence would weigh immensely in our favour; and as the safety of the capital, perhaps of the empire, may depend on our success, I have no doubt that you will endeavour to reach this army, whatever be the state of things on the Marne.

[833.] JOSEPH TO NAPOLEON.

Paris, Feb. 15, 1814, 10 A.M.

Sire,—I have no news of your Majesty, or of the Dukes of Reggio, Belluno, and Taranto, since your Majesty's last letter from the field of Vauchamps. I have written to your Majesty in duplicate, and I wait in the utmost anxiety for your orders to the corps of the Dukes of Belluno, Reggio, and Taranto. I need not say how indispensable your Majesty's presence is, on the eve of a battle on which the fate of the empire may rest.

I hear again from General Bordesoulle that the Dukes of Reggio and Belluno were to march at 9 last night towards the small river Yères, resting their left on Remy and the forest of Crécy. I requested Bordesoulle to entreat them merely to keep the enemy in check until the arrival of your Majesty.

[834.] NAPOLEON TO JOSEPH.

Meaux, Feb. 16, 1814, 8 A.M.

My Brother,—It is 8 o'clock; I start for Guignes. I shall attack to-morrow. Send by diligences all the men belonging to the old guard; I hear that you have 800 of them in Paris. Send also all the men of the old horse-guard to repair the losses which it has sustained. The Duke of Treviso is manœuvring between Soissons and Reims. Do not send any cavalry either to Rambouillet or to Chartres, but direct it all on Fontainebleau. As soon as I have accomplished my march, the enemy will disperse. I missed yesterday a splendid opportunity: 6000 Bavarians were two leagues off from me, near Montmirail, in the cross-road. The enemy manœuvres with such ignorance that I hope to do great things in the next few days.

[835.] NAPOLEON TO JOSEPH.

Guignes, Feb. 16, 1814, 4 P.M.

My Brother,—I received your letter of to-day, 9 A. M. I reached this place at 3 in the afternoon. I shall put the army in motion immediately. It will take its position to-night, so as to reach Nangis by daybreak to-morrow. I shall also have Melun occupied, and the bridge repaired. I have sent to know what is going on at Fontainebleau. If anything new had occurred there, you would have heard of it and have let me know. Send all the available cavalry to join us by Brie-Comte-Robert. I have ordered the parks to come back. The préfet of Melun was away; if he is in Paris, tell him to return to Melun directly. There are many national guards dispersed in different directions; the Minister of War must make a return of them, and let them all join and reinforce our army. There is no objection to your placing your aide-de-camp Lecapitaine in the young guard; send him off immediately.

[836.] NAPOLEON TO JOSEPH.

Guignes, Feb. 16, 1814, 6 P.M.

My Brother,—I have received your letter of the 16th, 11 A.M. I think that no troops are wanted near Rambouillet. My present manœuvre will recall all the enemy's parties. The Duke of Treviso has orders to watch Soissons and Reims. He has two divisions of cavalry and one of infantry. The Minister of War must write to him, and keep him informed as to all the parties which approach Paris. The remounts at Versailles must be kept up as actively as possible. Recall the detachments from Rambouillet and keep them in reserve. They may be sent if necessary towards Soissons and Villers-Cotterets. General Dombrowski, who is in the neighbourhood of Compiègne, should remain there Let the Duke of Treviso know that General Dombrowski is under his orders.

[837.] NAPOLEON TO JOSEPH.

Guignes, Feb. 17, 1814, 4 A.M.

My Brother,—I send to you a report from the Minister of War addressed to La Bouillerie. You will see by it that I have put two millions at the disposal of the Minister for the Administration of the War for the remounts at Versailles, and that of these two millions 500,000 francs were paid before my departure; and yet they complain of want of money. It seems that the depôt for remounts makes no progress. Make them give you an account of the horses which have been bought in the public markets and elsewhere. I wish to employ these two millions in remounts, but I want cavalry directly. It appears that up to the present time very few horses have been purchased.

[838.] NAPOLEON TO JOSEPH.

Guignes, Feb. 17, 1814, 5 A.M.

My Brother,—The Duke of Treviso was yesterday evening at Villers-Cotterets. He tells me that the enemy have evacuated Soissons, and recalled all the detachments which they had sent out in the direction of Compiègne. Their defeat has so terrified them, that the Duke of Treviso thinks that they are retreating as fast as possible to the Ardennes. They have marched by Fismes;* so you see that you are safe in that quarter. Write to the Minister of War to assist the Duke of Treviso's operations. On the evening of the 14th, at about 8 o'clock, the Duke of Ragusa attacked again the Russian army at Etoges, and did them much more harm than appears by the bulletin, as he took nine pieces of cannon, and left the field covered with dead. The enemies are extremely worn out and frightened. Collect all the scattered battalions.

[839.] NAPOLEON TO JOSEPH.

Guignes, Feb. 17, 1814, 6 A.M.

My Brother,—Paris is no longer threatened on any side, since the Duke of Treviso is at Villers-Cotterets. I do not approve of the Minister of War sending battalions to Meaux, Lagny, and

* On the road from Soissons to Reims.—TR.

other places; he should keep all these resources to form the 1st and 2nd divisions of the Paris reserve.

I see that the 1st brigade of the 1st division, under the command of the Duke of Padua, is organised. I have ordered it to Villeneuve-St.-Georges. See that it is immediately provided with eight pieces of cannon.

The Duke of Padua must establish his head-quarters at Villeneuve to-day, and the brigade must have its artillery, as the Duke of Padua may receive orders in the course of the day. The Duke of Padua must make sure that each soldier has his four packets of cartridges. The 2nd brigade ought to be formed immediately, and brought together, with its six pieces of artillery, at Charenton. I wish it to be there to-morrow, ready for service. There is at Corbeil a battalion of the 65th, which may form part of this division. Other battalions may be collected, which have been improperly scattered. I have ordered General Charpentier to proceed to Melun, and from thence to Fontainebleau. I have desired General Boyer, who is at Charenton, to take General Charpentier's place at Corbeil and Essonne. It is possible that I may give him definite orders to-morrow. Organise quickly, therefore, the 2nd division of the Paris reserve. Once more, pray tell the Minister of War to make a return of all the detachments, and recall every one of them. Send off a battery of horse-artillery to join General Charpentier; let it proceed along the right bank to Meaux. This battery may nearly reach Melun to-day.

[840.] NAPOLEON TO JOSEPH.

Nangis, Feb. 17, 1814, 3 P.M.

My Brother,—I ordered 1000 muskets to be sent to-night from Vincennes to Brie-Comte-Robert for the national guard; but as they were able to arm themselves on the field of battle, I think that the minister should desire these muskets to be returned to Paris. All this grand army, Austrian, Russian, Bavarian, and Wurtembergian, is recrossing the Seine in every direction, and with the utmost precipitation. By to-night there will probably be not one man left on this side; but time, which is of the utmost importance to me, will be lost while I am repairing the bridge at Montereau.

[841.] JOSEPH TO NAPOLEON.

Paris, Feb. 17, 1814, 10 A.M.

Sire,—I have received your Majesty's letter of yesterday, 6 P.M. The national guard will escort the prisoners only within the walls of Paris. As up to this time it has been impossible to furnish it with muskets, it is irregularly armed; and to have permitted several hundreds of the national guard to leave Paris would have hindered the equipment and arming of several thousands. The institution of the national guard has singularly quieted the public mind: it is likewise very useful as a municipal force; but we should lose all these advantages if we treated it as a force capable of acting beyond the walls. My opinion is shared by all the higher authorities.

[842.] NAPOLEON TO JOSEPH.

Nangis, Feb. 18, 1814.

My Brother,—Prince Schwartzenberg has at last shown signs of life. He has just sent a flag of truce to ask for a suspension of hostilities. It is hard to be dastardly to such a degree. He constantly, in the most insulting terms, rejected every species of suspension of arms or armistice; and after the capitulation of Dantzic and that of Dresden he refused even to receive my flags of truce, a barbarity of which there are few examples in history. On the first repulse these wretches are on their knees. Happily the Prince of Schwartzenberg's aide-de-camp was not allowed to come within our posts. I received only his letter, which I shall answer at my leisure. I shall not grant any armistice till I have cleared my territory of them. From what I hear, the allies seem to have quite changed their minds. The Emperor of Russia, who, a few days ago, broke off the negotiations because he wished to impose upon France worse conditions than those of our ancient limits, wishes now to renew them; and I hope that I may soon attain a peace rounded on the terms of Frankfort, which are the lowest that I could accept with honour.* Before I began my last operations, I offered to sign on the basis of the ancient limits, provided they would cease hostilities immediately. This proposal was made by the Duke of Vicenza on the 8th. They refused. They said that even the signature of preliminaries would not put a stop to hostilities; that the war should last till all the articles of peace were signed. They have been punished for this inconceivable answer, and yesterday, on the 17th, asked for an armistice!

You may well imagine that on the eve of a battle† which I was resolved to win, or to perish, when, if I failed, my capital was taken, I would have consented to anything rather than run so great a risk. I owed this sacrifice of my pride to my family and to my people. But since they refused these terms; since the danger has been encountered; since everything has returned to the ordinary risks of war; since a defeat no longer exposes my capital; since all the chances are for me, the welfare of the empire and my own fame require me to make a real peace. If I had signed on the terms of the ancient limits, I should have rushed to arms in two years, and I should have told the nation that I had signed not a peace, but a capitulation. I could not say this in present circumstances, for, as fortune is again on my side, I can impose my own conditions. The enemy is in a very different position from that which he occupied when he made the Frankfort propositions; he must now feel almost certain that few of his troops will recross the frontier. His cavalry is worn out and low; his infantry is exhausted by marches and countermarches; he has lost all heart. I hope, therefore, to make a peace such as will satisfy a reasonable man; and I wish for no more than the conditions of Frankfort. Whisper that the enemy,

* The terms offered by the allies from Frankfort were what the French have called the "natural limits" of France, namely, the Alps, the Pyrenees, and the Rhine.

The term "ancient limits" signifies the frontier of France before 1789, and, with slight modifications, her present frontier.—TR.

† Napoleon uses the word battle to signify his whole connected operations against Blücher.—TR.

finding himself embarrassed, has asked for an armistice, or a suspension of hostilities, which was absurd, as it would have deprived me of the fruit of my operations: add that this shows how thoroughly he is disheartened. Do not let this be printed, but let it be repeated in every quarter.

[843. JOSEPH TO NAPOLEON.

Paris, Feb. 18, 1814, 11 P.M.

Sire,—I have received the letter in which your Majesty does me the honour of announcing to me the enemy's request for a suspension of hostilities, and your Majesty's determination to grant nothing until peace is signed. It is certain that they have been treating long enough to be ready to sign the preliminaries without delay; and as they themselves proposed the Frankfort conditions before crossing the Rhine, those conditions may well be accepted by both parties. With regard to your Majesty, it signifies little whether, at the time of signature, the enemy have recrossed the Rhine or not, if what he signs on this side of the river is what was proposed when he was on the other side. Such a signature will prove that he was wrong in not adhering to the terms which he had been the first to offer, and I consider the honour of France secured by the signatures of the conditions proposed at Frankfort, whether they be signed here or there, provided that the natural limits be recognised. It is plain that the enemy, confused by your Majesty's manœuvres, wishes for a suspension of hostilities to have time to look about him and to collect his scattered troops, and that your Majesty is right in refusing it. I have represented things as they really are; and however eager, however devouring be the thirst for peace, every one will acknowledge the wisdom of your Majesty's conduct in requiring the immediate signature of the peace which was offered by the enemy at Frankfort.

CHAPTER XXII.

THE letters contained in this chapter extend from the 19th to the 26th of February inclusive. During these seven days Napoleon made only three marches, from Montereau to Nogent, from Nogent to Châtres, and from Châtres to Troyes, and fought no battle, except a hot skirmish with Blücher on the 23rd at Mery, between Châtres and Troyes, which seems to have been an accident, neitheir party being aware of the neighbourhood of the other.

His activity was probably relaxed by the prospect of peace, which at this time seemed not improbable, and might certainly have been attained if success had not raised his hopes and his demands, still more than failure depressed the allies. And the violent exertions of the previous nine days must have made some repose necessary.

[844.] NAPOLEON TO JOSEPH.

Surville, opposite to Montereau, Feb. 19, 1814, 3 A.M.

My Brother,—I beat yesterday two divisions of the reserve under the Austrian General Bianchi, and the Würtemberg troops. Their loss in men was great; we took their colours, and from 3000 to 4000 prisoners; but the real subject of congratulation is, that I had the good fortune to carry the bridge before they could cut it.

I have sent back the Duke of Belluno on account of his extreme slowness and carelessness.* I am glad that 1200 horses have left the depôt at Versailles. All the men belonging to the 1st cavalry corps, which is under the Duke of Ragusa, must be kept, as I intend them to remain on the Châlons road. They must all be sent from Versailles or —— † towards Meaux, to reinforce him. I think that you were wrong in permitting the Danish officer ‡ to communicate with his minister. You should have waited for my orders, and I should not have given them quickly. Even now I do not choose that he should go away without my express permission. I may keep him for a long time. All the men belonging to the guard of honour, and to the 10th hussars, must be forwarded to Compiègne to reinforce the Duke of Treviso's corps.

Surville, 8 A.M.

All the available soldiers of the old guard should be sent to the Duke of Treviso. Form a column of 1200 men, cavalry, infantry, and artillery, of the troops which belong to that Marshal, and send it to him.

[845.] NAPOLEON TO JOSEPH.

Château de Surville, Feb. 19, 1814, 9 P.M.

My Brother,—It has taken us the whole day to pass the horrible defile of Montereau. I have just thrown a bridge over the Seine, and another over the Yonne. General Roussel and his

* The bridge alluded to was the bridge over the Seine at Montereau. Victor had been ordered to seize it on the 17th, but had lost time in resting his men, and had found it occupied by the Würtemberg troops. Napoleon ordered him to leave the army. Victor answered that he would carry a musket. Napoleon, relenting, gave him a command in the guard. In the attack on Montereau on the 18th, both Victor and Napoleon exposed themselves like common soldiers. Napoleon resumed his earliest profession, and himself pointed many of his guns.—TR.

† Illegible.—ED.

‡ Joseph had allowed a Dane, carrying despatches from his Court to the Danish Minister, to enter Paris, accompanied and watched by a French officer.—TR.

cavalry, and General Gérard with the 2nd corps,* have reached Pont-sur-Yonne. General Allix is on his way to Nemours; General Charpentier is at Montereau. I suppose that General Boyer will reach Melun this evening, with a division of the guard, and that one of his brigades will be at Fontainebleau. My advanced guard is at Bray.

The Emperor of Russia and the King of Prussia were at Bray. As soon as they heard that I had forced the bridge of Montereau, they ran away as fast as they could. Their whole army is terrified. The three sovereigns spent a few days at Pont, with Madame. They intended to reach Fontainebleau to-morrow, and in a very few days Paris: they cannot understand what is taking place. To-day we have snow, and the weather is rather severe. I am sending an article for the 'Moniteur' to the Empress, but you may put into the 'Moniteur,' as well as into the other newspapers, under the head of Provins, a notice of the precipitation with which the sovereigns quitted Bray. The Austrians protected my palace at Fontainebleau from the Cossacks. We have taken several convoys of baggage, and some carriages going towards Bray. Several hundred Cossacks have been taken in the forest of Fontainebleau. My advanced guard will reach Bray to-morrow.

Try to hasten the supplies of artillery horses. Ammunition must likewise be provided more quickly. They have only 40,000 rounds more at Vincennes. What is that if I fight a great battle? I shall consume between 80,000 and 100,000! The Duke of Ragusa is at Montmirail; the Duke of Treviso at Villars-Cotterets; General Grouchy is still at La Ferté-sous-Jouarre, with from 6000 to 7000 men. The Duke of Castiglione's corps must by this time amount to 15,000 men.† I conclude that he is about to march. Tell the minister to write to him

* The corps which had been Victor's.—TR.

† This alludes to Augereau's army at Lyons.—TR.

Augereau at this time, and for some days longer, may be said to have held in his hands the destinies of France. He disobeyed the repeated orders of the Emperor to attack the enemy in flank, and march on Geneva. He was one of the causes of the failure of the campaign.—ED.

again: it is in his power to do the enemy great harm. I could not be better pleased than I am with the spirit both of the towns and of the country, and in fact, of all my people. I am much grieved at General Château's wound; he was an officer of promise: I was told this morning that it was fatal, but this evening they say that it is not. I am not satisfied with General Maison; he gives no proof of the talents which I supposed him to possess. I have ordered him to collect the garrisons of the different places in Flanders; to march towards Antwerp, and resume operations.

[846.] JOSEPH TO NAPOLEON.

Paris, Feb. 19, 1814.

Sire,—The Minister for the Administration of War has informed your Majesty that the hospitals in Paris already contained more than——.* The Minister of the Interior proposes to make use of the "Invalides" for the reception of the sick, and to place the invalids in private houses. Others think rather of using the great Courbevoie barrack, which is nearly empty. The guard might select their conscripts at the Ecole Militaire, instead of, as at present, at Courbevoie. In my opinion, Sire, the "Invalides" should not be touched. I see fewer objections to using the Courbevoie barrack. At any rate, I thought that I ought to ask your Majesty for orders. Letters from the South incline me to think that Lord Wellington is meditating an attack upon the army of Spain. Every person whom I have seen has spoken in terms of the highest praise of your Majesty's conduct in insisting on a speedy and lasting peace, and refusing a suspension of hostilities, which would be employed by the enemy in assembling his troops, collecting his resources, and postponing peace indefinitely. I have sent an officer to obtain news of the Duke of Ragusa.

[847.] NAPOLEON TO JOSEPH

Chateau de Surville, Feb. 20, 1814, 6 A.M.

My Brother,—I do not approve of more than 12,000 sick and wounded being admitted into Paris. 12,000 more may easily be

* Four or five lines almost obliterated, evidently relating to the number of sick in the hospitals.—ED.

distributed between Versailles, Rouen, Evreux, St. Germain, Chartres, and other places. It is not advisable to put too many sick in a large town. If hospital fever were to spread, it might destroy the population of Paris. You must not place the sick in slaughter-houses.

[848.] NAPOLEON TO JOSEPH.

Nogent, Feb. 20, 1814, 6 P.M.

My Brother,—I have just reached Nogent. From Montereau the enemy fell back upon Troyes with the greater part of his army. He has been fortunate in a frost, which has enabled him to go across country, otherwise half of his baggage and artillery would have been taken. We are inconvenienced too by this severe frost. The enemy has committed crimes which cannot even be mentioned, at Montereau, Bray, and Nogent: they ought to be known in Paris. The Emperor of Austria has not left Troyes. From Bray the Emperor of Russia has sent to mark his apartments at Fontainebleau. On the 18th he was forced to run away by the shortest road.

[849.] NAPOLEON TO JOSEPH.

Nogent, Feb. 20, 1814, 9 P.M.

My Brother,—The Duke of Bassano will forward to you a copy of the proposals of the Allies. It will prove to you how out of place your sermons are, and that I do not require to be lectured into signing an honourable peace, if it be possible. I shall also send to you an intercepted letter from the Duke of Angoulême; you will take advice as to whether printing it would produce a good effect upon Belgium.

Adieu, dear friend, adieu.

The Emperors had fixed their head-quarters at Fontainebleau for the 18th; on that very day they were forced to quit Bray in desperate haste for Troyes, where the allied armies have taken refuge.

[850.] NAPOLEON TO JOSEPH.

Nogent, Feb. 21, 1814.

My Brother,—You need not be uneasy about Orleans or Montargis. The movement which I am about to make will draw off the enemy immediately; his different corps will be glad to be able to fall back as soon as they can. I think that it would produce a good effect if the Empress were to write to the town of Orleans in nearly these terms:—"I hear that the town of Orleans is threatened by 1500 of the enemy's skirmishers. What! the town of Orleans, which contains 40,000 inhabitants, is afraid of 1500 horsemen! Where then is the energy of France? Organize your national guard; form a company of gunners; take from your own stables the horses which are required. I have ordered the Minister of War to furnish you with 12 pieces of cannon and five howitzers, to enable you to defend your town and your property. The enemy who ravages our country and plunders our towns is as implacable as he is faithless. To arms then, inhabitants of Orleans! and let your conduct confirm the opinion which I have of you, and of the energy of the French nation!"

Such letters, signed by the Empress, will be more effective than if they were signed by me. Let this letter be sent with one from the Minister of the Interior. The municipal authorities should meet to receive it, and then organize the national guard, form a company of gunners, prepare teams, and place the town in a state of defence. A deputation to the Empress should give an account of the measures which they have taken.

The Duke of Treviso has cut the bridge at Soissons. The Minister of the Interior must write to Soissons to desire the national guard to be organised and the town placed in a state of defence. I think that the Empress should write to Lille, Valenciennes, Cambrai, and to the other large towns on the northern frontier, in nearly the same terms as to the town of Orleans, varying the expressions according to circumstances, and the proofs which these towns gave of their zeal during former wars. These letters ought to be in the Empress's own handwriting. I think also that a proclamation made by the Empress, as

Regent, to Belgium, would be of use. This proclamation might be drawn up in the form of a letter addressed to the Mayor of Brussels, the Mayors of Ghent, of Bruges, Mons, &c. The Empress should acquaint them with my victories, and tell them that the English wish to separate them from France, and place them under the yoke of a prince who has always been hostile to their country and to their religion: and assure them that the enemy will soon find that no peace will be signed unless the natural limits of France are admitted. These letters to the mayors may be varied in their expressions so as to make as many different proclamations. Write to Montargis and Nemours to form the national guard. Let the Minister of War send pikes everywhere. Order the national guard of Beauvais to be organised, and above all take care to let all this make a great noise in the newspapers.

The enemies have committed all sorts of horrors in every direction. The Minister of War must send good reporters to the towns which they have occupied, to draw up narratives of the atrocities which have been committed. These reports are to be inserted in the 'Moniteur.' I wish also the towns of Nogent, Provins, Nangis, Bray, Montereau, Sens, Epernay, Château-Thierry, Reims, Soissons, &c., to acquaint the municipality of Paris with all that they have suffered, and these letters to be placarded in every direction; for, in short, one must not deceive oneself as to the fact (and you ought to say so) that the Russians intended to sack and burn Paris. It is therefore the duty of the government to convince the inhabitants of this. I even think that it would be well if deputations from these towns came to read their addresses to the conseil-général of Paris. It can only do good if the Parisians hear on all sides,—"It is you who were attacked; it is you whom they intended to pillage."

Put into the newspapers a detailed account of the noble conduct of the brave Admiral Verhuel,* and let it be known that the squadron and the key of Holland are still ours. Speak to the Minister for Marine Affairs on the subject.

* Though deserted by his Dutch sailors, he seized, with his French marines, the fort of the Helder, and held out against the Prince of Orange.—TR.

The Duke of Taranto's head-quarters to-day are at St. Martin de Bosnay and Romilly. The advanced posts are at Châtres and Méry. General Gérard is at Sens, and his advanced posts at Villeneuve-l'Archevêque. My head-quarters remain for to-day at Nogent. The bridge is so broken that it will be very difficult to repair it. I have established a bridge of boats. The route of the army will be in future by Nangis to Nogent.

[851.] NAPOLEON TO JOSEPH.

Nogent, Feb. 21, 1814.

My Brother,—These are my intentions with respect to the King of Westphalia. I allow him to wear the uniform of the grenadier guard, and I grant the same permission to all the French princes. (You will inform King Louis of this.) The king is to dismiss all his Westphalian household. They are free either to return home or to stay in France. The King will immediately propose for my approbation three or four French aides-de-camp, one or two equerries, and one or two chamberlains, all French, and two or three French ladies-in-waiting for the Queen. She will put off to some future time appointing her lady-in-waiting. All the Westphalian pages must be placed in the Lycées, and will wear the uniform of the Lycées. They will be educated at my expense. One-third will be placed in the Lycées of Versailles, one-third in that of Rouen, and the remaining third in the Lycée of Paris. The King and Queen will then be presented to the Empress; and I authorise the King to occupy Cardinal Fesch's house (since it appears that it belongs to him), and to establish his household there. The King and Queen will continue to bear the title of King and Queen of Westphalia, but they are to have no Westphalians in their suite.

[852.] JOSEPH TO NAPOLEON.

Paris, Feb. 21, 1814.

Sire,—The Empress held a council to-day to settle the best plan for obtaining the 2000 horses for which your Majesty has asked the Minister of War. M. d'Hauterive tells me that M. de St. Charles has received orders to join your Majesty's head-quarters. You will find annexed a paper which will prove to your Majesty that it is useless to rely on the princes;* they will never be able to do anything for you. The bulletin of to-day was not very well received; some passages were interpreted as raising doubts as to the success of the negotiations. Every one agrees that your Majesty would have done wrong in granting a suspension of hostilities. Peace with the natural limits is desired by all. No one now would accept the ancient limits.

[853.] JOSEPH TO NAPOLEON.

Paris, Feb. 22, 1814.

Sire,—The annexed extract from a letter from M. Bastarrèche of Bayonne, which has been forwarded to me by the Duke of Conegliano will acquaint your Majesty with the state of the Duke of Dalmatia's army. The Ministers of the Interior and of the Police and the Arch-Chancellor have just left me; they have given me a most deplorable picture of the state of things at Toulouse and Bourdeaux. The spirit of these towns is very unfavourable; a Bourbon appearing there would be well received. Your Majesty will be astonished at the behaviour of the Duke of Dalmatia, unless he retreated by your orders. He is the only man in authority whose intentions I could venture to suspect.

Another report, which I annex (No. 2), lends some probability to a rumour, just communicated to me by the Minister, that the enemy has entered Amiens. The two ministers assured me that the Russian proclamations in favour of the Bourbons have fouud an echo. I suppose that we are on the eve of a battle. Whatever may be the result, the present state of things cannot last. The Ministers declare to me, in the presence of the Arch-Chancellor, that the administration is everywhere falling to pieces, that money is wanting, and that the system of requisition ends by alienating all hearts, and leaving the government to stand alone. However hard these truths may be, as they cannot reach your Majesty through your ministers, I fulfil without hesitation the painful duty of acquainting you with them.

* I cannot explain this allusion.—TR.

[854.] JOSEPH TO NAPOLEON.

Paris, Feb. 22, 1814.

Sire,—I enclose the rough drafts of two letters which the Empress is ready to sign, should they meet with your Majesty's approbation. I have seen the Minister of the Interior: he is writing to your Majesty. The plan of sending deputations from the different towns to the Council-General of Paris seems to him to be open to some objections. I share in this opinion, and I am sure that, if your Majesty had time to think again on the subject, you would relinquish the idea.

The Ministers and the Duke of Conegliano are also of opinion that it would be impossible to double the national guard without changing its nature. Besides, there still remains the unconquerable difficulty of the want of arms. The Minister of War has been asked . . . . . .* As to the national guard, as it now stands, it is a safeguard against anarchy; it is well disposed; it enters into the views of the government; it was electrified by the account of the prodigies which have been performed by your Majesty in such a short time; it wishes for peace to restore you to your capital; its attachment for you is equal to its admiration. The capital shares in these opinions; but to say more, Sire, would be to deceive oneself as well as your Majesty. The people of Paris, hostile to the government a month ago, touched by your Majesty's confidence in trusting your wife and your son to them, encouraged and astonished by your Majesty's successes, are yet not in a state in which more than mere fidelity and obedience can be expected. They admire your genius, but they can be excited only by the hope of a speedy peace, and they are by no means inclined to oppose any effective resistance to a hostile army, or to send detachments of the national guard beyond the walls. This, Sire, is the exact truth. Your Majesty must not rely on an exertion greater than can fairly be expected from a population so disposed.

* Illegible.—ED.

[855.] NAPOLEON TO JOSEPH.

Châtres, near Méry, Feb. 23, 1814, 2 P.M.

My Brother,—I have received your letters of the 22nd.* I am sorry to see that you continue to conjure up phantoms. The greater number of the facts contained in your letters are untrue. The enemy is not at Amiens; the Duke of Dalmatia has not commenced his retreat. It is an old story that the Comte d'Artois is at Basle; it is not certain, nor does it much signify, whether there be, or be not, 300 rebels in Le Comtat Veñaissin: at all events, courage, patience, and presence of mind can overcome everything. But you will do nothing if you collect together all sorts of reports, and excite your imagination by working them up into striking pictures. You will be cowed and hopeless.

My advanced guard by this time ought to have reached Troyes, where I shall be myself in two hours. The allies are retreating to Vandœuvre.† Prince Schwartzenberg has again asked for an armistice. He wishes commissioners from both parties to meet.‡ They seem to fear a general action and its consequences. Winzingerode, Sacken, York, and Blücher have crossed the Aube, and are all to meet at Vandœuvre; Marmont herefore has no one before him.§

I do not deny that the state of affairs is very serious. Do not fancy that I am ill-informed; ministers generally want presence of mind. Placards of addresses from the different villages which

* The two last letters.—TR.

† A village on the cross-road between Troyes and Bar-sur-Aube.—TR.

‡ They did meet; Lamartine tells the story thus:—"Napoleon appointed the village of Lusigny, between Vandœuvre and Troyes, as the scene. He sent thither one of his most brilliant officers, M. de. Flahault. General Duca represented Austria, General Schuwaloff Russia, and General Rauch Prussia; but the result was only some hours of conversation."—*Histoire de la Restauration*, vol. i. pp. 113–126.—TR.

§ This was a mistake, as Napoleon found a few hours later. Blücher, who, after his defeat at Vauchamps, on the 14th, had recovered himself almost miraculously, was then at Méry, a few miles from Châtres, and on this very day fought a sharp, indecisive action with Napoleon. In the night of the 23rd he marched northward to attack Marmont at Sézanne.—TR.

have been invaded by the enemy will produce an excellent effect. There is no objection to the council of the municipality of Paris receiving deputations and hearing what they have to say. Let their addresses be full of facts, and placard them immediately. The inhabitants of Paris will see that they are threatened with rape, pillage, and fire. As to the notion of doubling the national guard, as you disapprove of it, I give it up. If I had listened to the Ministers, I should not have formed a national guard, and I should have distrusted Paris. If skilful use be made of these addresses from the invaded towns, they will, I repeat, produce an excellent, and incalculable effect. When the towns tell of all the fine promises which the enemy made on arriving, and of his behaviour afterwards, it will rouse general indignation. Give the greatest possible activity to the communication between Paris and the districts which have been occupied by the enemy.

The placards may be headed thus:—

"The deputies of Sens were admitted to the sitting of the council of the municipality, and presented the following report, &c."

This report must also be inserted in the newspapers. The result will be that fear will teach the Parisians what they have to do.

I am badly served in the north. General Maison is a man of narrow understanding and of little energy. Let the Minister of War repeat the instructions to him to issue from the fortified places, and to attack the enemy by falling in detail upon his quarters. The Duke of Treviso must return to Château-Thierry, to draw nearer to me, and to set the Duke of Ragusa free.

I have written to the Duke of Castiglione. I have told the Empress to speak to his wife. I think that you ought to speak to her also, and make the ladies of the court do the same. He must advance, take example by me, and do himself honour.

The enemy sets fire to everything, and appears to have given up all thoughts of Paris. The Prince of Schwartzenberg's aide-de-camp, Prince Lichtenstein, with whom I have just conversed for some time, let it drop that they were very much alarmed by this movement of the Duke of Castiglione. I will send to you from Troyes the letter which I have written to the Emperor of Austria.

Well, we have thrown back the enemy's armies nearly to Langres. As I foretold, Montargis and Orleans are relieved; the Cossacks are flying as fast as they can in every direction. I have written to Borghese to order him to send 6000 men from his division to Chambéry;* let the Minister of War reiterate this order. Desire the Minister of War likewise to repeat to the Duke of Dalmatia the order not to retreat without fighting.

[856.] NAPOLEON TO JOSEPH.

Faubourg des Noirs, before Troyes, Feb. 23, 1814, 7 A.M.

My Brother,—I am at Troyes. The enemy besieges me with flags of truce demanding a suspension of hostilities. We shall perhaps settle upon granting one this morning; but only if the negotiations at Châtillon proceed on the basis of the conditions of Frankfort. This evening all my troops will be at Châtillon-sur-Seine.

I have had several cavalry actions; I have taken 2000 prisoners and 8 pieces of cannon. I have written to the Empress to fire a salute of 30 guns to celebrate not only these smaller successes, but also the deliverance of the capital of Champagne. I could have entered Troyes yesterday evening, but I must have sacrificed the town, the enemy insisting upon holding out in order to remove their baggage. If I had had 20 boats to cross the Seine where I wanted, the Austrian army would have ceased to exist: at any rate terror reigns in the ranks of the enemy.

A few days ago they thought that I had no army; now their imagination sticks at nothing: 300,000 or 400,000 men are not enough for them. They fancied that I had none but recruits; they now say that I have collected all my veterans, and that my

* To meet Augereau, who was to have marched from Lyons towards Geneva, to cut off the communications of the allies.—TR.

armies consist of picked men; that the French army is better than ever, &c. See what is the effect of terror. The Parisian newspapers must confirm their fears. Newspapers are not history, any more than bulletins are history: one should always persuade the enemy that one's forces are immense.

I do not agree with the remarks which have been made on the communications between the country and Paris; I wish my orders on the subject to be executed. The Minister of the Interior is a coward: he has absurd ideas about men. Neither he nor the Minister of Police knows more of France than I do of China. When the deputies from the country show the letters which they have received, the préfet must assemble the notables to hear them read. This is not a got-up thing nor an imposture: the enemy has committed such atrocities that the whole of France will be indignant. Here, on the spot, the most moderate people speak of them with rage. If the French were as contemptible as the Minister of the Interior believes them to be, I myself should blush to be a Frenchman. With regard to the project of doubling the national guard, I yield to your observations the more readily as the measure does not appear to be necessary.

[857.] NAPOLEON TO JOSEPH.

Troyes, Feb. 25, 1814, 4 P.M.

My Brother,—My troops have entered Bar-sur-Seine and Vandœuvre. It seems that the enemy is retreating towards Langres. General Blücher, after crossing the Aube and advancing on Méry, recrossed it yesterday the 24th, and marched upon Anglure with between 8000 and 10,000 men, the remainder of the corps which he commanded.* The Duke of Ragusa reconnoitred him yesterday, the 24th, but was not strong enough to

* Napoleon, fatally for himself, miscalculated the force of Blücher. Baron von Muffling [1] shows that Blücher's army, at this instant, consisted of 53,000 men. He estimates the allied grand army at 71,000, and the army under Napoleon at Troyes at 62,000. It is not probable that Marmont thought of attacking Blücher.—TR.

[1] Life and writings, p. 453.

attack him. The Duke of Padua is at Nogent; the Duke of Belluno at Méry. As soon as I see what Blücher intends to do, I shall try to fall upon his rear and to cut him off.

I have written to the Minister of War that General Maison does not know what he is about; that he ought to march out of his fortresses, collect all the garrisons of Antwerp, &c., and fall upon the rear of the enemy.

I have told the Minister of War to transmit similar orders to the commandant of Metz. He should also try to convey orders to the same effect to Mayence, where the commandant has allowed himself to be blockaded by a mob. The commissioners discussing the armistice are still sitting at Lusigny. It is said that the Crown-Prince of Sweden is at Cologne. Could you not, on your own responsibility, send some one to make him sensible of his folly, and persuade him to alter his conduct? Try, but do not implicate me.

[858.] JOSEPH TO NAPOLEON.

Paris, Feb. 25, 1814.

Sire,—I regret that I have to report to you that there is a perceptible diminution in the arrival of conscripts. The imperial guard has received 2236 between the 17th and 23rd instant inclusive. Yesterday it was joined by only 95. The line has received, between the 17th and 22nd inclusive, only 604. On the 23rd only 25 arrived. By the line I mean the general depôt of Paris, under the inspection of General Fririon.

[859.] NAPOLEON TO JOSEPH.

Troyes, Feb. 26, 1814.

My Brother,—It seems that the allies have not yet ratified the treaty with the King of Naples.* Despatch by a courier, with the utmost haste, a letter to the King, in which you will frankly point out to him the iniquity of his conduct, offering to

* The treaty by which Murat joined the coalition, and Austria in return guaranteed to him the throne of Naples, was dated the 11th of January, 1814.—TR.

mediate for him if he will return to his duties. Tell him that this is his only hope; that if he take any other course he must be destroyed either by France or by the allies. I need not point out all that you may say. Even the English do not recognise him as king. There is still time to save Italy and to replace the Viceroy on the Adige. Write also to the Queen on her ingratitude, which revolts even the allies. Say that, as no battle has yet taken place between the French and Neapolitan troops, all may be arranged; but there is not a moment to lose. As Senator Fouché* is still in those parts, you may write to him to converse with your messenger on these subjects.

[860.] JOSEPH TO MURAT.

Paris, Feb. 28, 1814.

My dear Brother,—I sent long ago an answer to the letter which you had the kindness to write to me on the 31st of December.

I find that it has not reached you, and I am anxious to atone for my apparent neglect, and to repeat to you my gratitude for all the friendliness and affection contained in your letter. This was the only subject of my answer; but I now think it my duty both towards you and towards your family, to express to you my opinions and my feeelings on the grave circumstances in which we are placed. I will not enter into political discussions, but what strikes *me*, as well as every other Frenchman, is that it is impossible that you should be happy if France is miserable, or if you are her enemy. I am either mistaken in your character, or you will never be able to play the hateful part of an enemy to the very country to which you owe your glory. You are too good and too honest not to lament during the whole of the remainder of your life any success opposed to the welfare of France.

Moreover the fact is that in the long run you have nothing to hope either from the English or from the allies; your head therefore may follow the suggestions of your heart: it is not too late,

* Fouché, then at Rome and in disgrace, is said to have given Murat advice unfavorable to Napoleon.—TR.

since no battle as yet has been fought. I shall esteem myself doubly fortunate if I can restore the good understanding which ought always to subsist between the Emperor and yourself, for the sake of France, of your subjects, and of our family. I entreat you therefore to place me in a position to prove to you, at this crisis of your fate, that I am really your friend.

I have conversed frequently with M. Faypoult, who possesses all my confidence, and who deserves yours. I hope that you will place sufficient reliance in him to trust him with your wishes, and that you will empower me to attain the end which we ought both of us to desire. . . . Among those who serve you how few there are whose interests are the same as your own! Look closely into them, and you will see how little they deserve to be trusted. The enemies of France and the enemies of the Emperor are your enemies.

[861.] NAPOLEON TO JOSEPH.

Troyes, Feb. 26, 1814, 6 P.M.

My Brother,—I have received your letter of the 25th, 9 P.M.

The Austrian commandant of Châtillon-sur-Seine quitted the town yesterday. I have ordered the duty to be performed by the national guard of Châtillon, not choosing to place there troops of the line, as it would have been a waste of two battalions, added to which, in honour of the Congress, they must have been grenadiers. In the mean while the Congress is in our hands, which proves how completely the plans of the enemy have been frustrated. Lord Castlereagh asked if he were safe, considering that he is not actually an ambassador; of course there can be no question: all that appertains, directly or indirectly, to the Congress, is protected by the law of nations. Our troops were to enter Bar-sur-Aube this evening. Guns were heard yesterday in the direction of Sézanne: it seems that Blücher, who was slightly wounded in the action at Méry, is manœuvring there. The Prince of Moskowa has crossed the Aube at Arcis, in order to fall upon his rear.

CHAPTER XXIII.

THE letters contained in this chapter extend from the 27th of February to the 10th of April, 1814.

This was the third act of the tragedy of 1814.

No portion of Napoleon's military life, except perhaps his first Italian campaign, has been so praised as the campaign of 1814. The portion of it to which the letters in the last chapter relate deserves all the admiration which it has received. Nothing could be more masterly than the vigour, the precision, and the force of the blows with which in ten days he drove back and broke Blücher to the north of Paris, and Schwartzenberg to the east. But all the remainder of his operations were unsuccessful, and, if an unprofessional writer may venture to criticise so great a general, unskilful. His attempt at the beginning of the campaign to prevent the junction of Blücher and Schwartzenberg failed. The battle of Brienne was undecisive; in that of La Rothière he was beaten. And although the destruction of the allies in those two battles probably exceeded that of the French, yet the loss of 5000 men to Napoleon was more injurious than that of 10,000 to his enemy.

The success, the skill, and the decision of Napoleon in the last part of the campaign may be estimated from the following summary:

On the 27th of February Napoleon broke up from Troyes and marched northward to attack Blücher, leaving Oudinot and Gérard in Bar-sur-Aube to keep Schwartzenberg in check.

On the 28th he was at Sézanne.

On the 1st of March at Jouarre.

On the 2nd at Jouarre.

On the 3rd at La Ferté-sous-Jouarre, where he crossed the Marne: in the mean time Oudinot and Gérard had been driven out of Bar-sur-Aube, and Schwartzenberg entered Troyes on the 4th.

On the 4th of March Napoleon was at Fismes. Blücher's army had retreated before him with some loss, and Napoleon believed that Marmont was before it at Soissons, and that it might be attacked from the front as well as from the rear. Soissons, however, had surrendered on the 2nd, and Blücher had passed through it on his march to the strong position of Laon.

The 5th Napoleon remained at Fismes. He ordered a *levée en masse.*

On the 6th he crossed the Aisne at Béry-le-Bac, having failed in an attack on Soissons.

On the 7th he attacked Blücher at Craonne. The loss on each side was great: the only result was that Blücher retreated a few miles to Laon.

On the 8th, 9th, and 10th he attacked Blücher in the formidable position of Laon, was repulsed, and retreated to Chavignon.

He slept on the 10th at Chavignon.

On the 12th at Soissons.

On the 13th, 14th, 15th, and 16th at Reims.

The attack on Blücher had failed, except in driving him back to Laon; and Schwartzenberg had established himself within four days' march of Paris.

Napoleon now thought it time to turn on Schwartzenberg. He marched

On the 17th to Épernay;

On the 18th to Fère-Champenoise;

On the 19th to Plancy-on-the-Aube; and

On the 20th to Arcis-sur-Aube.

Here he was attacked by Schwartzenberg, whom his advance had, as he expected, recalled from Troyes, and repelled the attack with difficulty, and with the boldest personal exposure.

On the 21st he left Arcis. Between him and Paris were Blücher and Schwartzenberg. Instead of attacking either, he turned to the north-east towards Luxemburg or Lorraine.

On the 22d he was at Olcomte on the road to Vitry, which was held by the allies. He summoned in vain the commandant to surrender it, and

On the 23rd reached St. Dizier.

On the 24th and 25th, he remained at Doulevent, in the neighbourhood of St. Dizier.

On the 26th he returned to St. Dizier, and skirmished, without much result, with the corps of Winzingerode; which had been left to watch him.

On the 27th he made another unsuccessful attempt to frighten the Prussian commandant of Vitry into a surrender, and then fell again on Winzingerode, and beat him.

On the 28th his advanced guard had proceeded a further march to the eastward, and reached Bar-le-Duc in Lorraine.

It is supposed that on that day he heard that the allied armies, having left only Winzingerode's corps to watch him, were marching direct on Paris.

He returned to Doulevent, and

On the 29th reached Troyes, having marched 50 miles in one day.

On the 30th he started from Troyes early in the morning with what remained of his guard, left them behind him at the first station, and in a light carriage, with Berthier and Caulincourt by his side, passed through Sens at midnight, where he ordered rations to be prepared for 150,000 men, who, as he said, were following him, and reached the post-house of La Cour de France, about 10 miles from Paris, at about four in the morning of the 31st.

On that morning the allies entered Paris.

Now, if one of the Marshals had been in command,—if he had had to report that such had been the employment of the last army, and the last month, of the empire,—what would have been the storm of reproach and invective with which he would have been assailed by Napoleon!

The ill-success of the first fortnight may be excused. In his desperate state Napoleon was forced to run great risks, and the defeat of Blücher would have been a glorious prize. But from the time that he marched eastward, to the rear of Schwartzenberg, he seems to have wandered without any definite plan, at least without any definite military plan. He relied on the terror of his name. He had so often repeated that "in war moral force is everything," that he seems to have believed it to be literally true. He believed that all the armies that were advancing on Paris would turn back as soon as they found that he was in their rear, and would follow him till he could be succoured by his garrisons on the Rhine. In this expectation he marched and countermarched, approached Vitry on the 22nd, was in St. Dizier on the 23rd, left it on the 24th, returned to it on the 26th, tried Vitry again on the 27th, and awoke from his dream on the 28th to find that, while he was in Lorraine, the allies were within a march of Paris.

There is a wonderful resemblance between the conduct of Napoleon at the close of his struggle against the allies and that of Turnus, when, in the last battle before his capital, he left its front unprotected in order to fall on the rear of the invaders:—

Interea extremo bellator in æquore Turnus
Palantes sequitur paucos, jam segnior, atque
Jam minus atque minus successu lætus equorum.
Attulit hunc illi cæcis terroribus aura
Commixtum clamorem, arrectasque impulit aures
Confusæ sonus urbis et illætabile murmur.
——————— Medios volat ecce per hostes.
Vectus equo spumante Saces, adversa sagittâ
Saucius ora, ruitque implorans nomine Turnum—
"Turne in te suprema salus, miserere tuorum,
Soli pro portes Messapus et acer Atinas
Sustentant aciem. Circum hos utrinque phalanges
Stant densæ strictisque seges mucronibus horret
Ferrea, *tu currum deserto in gramine versas.*"

[862.] NAPOLEON TO JOSEPH.

Troyes, Feb. 27, 1814, A.M.

My Brother,—I am moving to Arcis-sur-Aube to attack the corps which is advancing on La Ferté-Gaucher. The greater part of the army remains at Bar-sur-Aube.

[863.] NAPOLEON TO JOSEPH.

Arcis-sur-Aube, Feb. 27, 1814, 5 P.M.

My Brother,—I am at Arcis. I intend to sleep at Herbisse; to-morrow at 9 A.M. I shall reach La Fère-Champenoise; thence, according to circumstances, I shall march either on Sézanne or on La Ferté-Gaucher. I shall thus be in the rear of the whole of the enemy's army. Give notice of this to the Duke of Ragusa, who to-day, the 27th., ought to be between La Ferté-Gaucher and La Ferté-sous-Jouarre. The Duke of Treviso sends me word that he was to join him yesterday evening, the 26th; that they are pressing on the enemy, and preventing him from turning upon me with his whole force. As your courier may be captured, write in cipher, and select an intelligent man who will carry your orders in his head. I hope that my courier will reach you to-morrow before 3 A.M., and that the Duke of Ragusa will receive your letter before nine o'clock. The main body of the Austrian army continues to retreat upon Langres. I have recalled none of my troops from Bar-sur-Aube.

I have received some engravings of the King of Rome. I wish you to change the inscription, "May God watch over my Father and France," to this, "I pray to God for my Father and for France;" it is simpler. I also wish some copies to be struck off representing the King in the uniform of the National Guard.

[864.] NAPOLEON TO JOSEPH.

Herbisse, Feb. 28, 1814, 2 A.M.

My Brother,—To-day I shall be near La Ferté-Gaucher. Tell the Dukes of Ragusa and Treviso that they may manœuvre accordingly.

[865.] NAPOLEON TO JOSEPH.

Sézanne, Feb. 28, 1814, 3 P.M.

My Brother,—The Prince of Moscow is by this time halfway to La Ferté-Gaucher, which we shall reach to-morrow in good time. A division of Cossacks and of light troops under Tetenborn were driven out of La Fère-Champenoise. The Duke of Ragusa ought to know this. Write to him. If the enemy have taken up his position at La Ferté-Gaucher, we shall attack him to-morrow; the marshals must, therefore, act with a view to this.

[866.] JOSEPH TO NAPOLEON

Paris, Feb. 28, 1814.

Sire,—The Duke of Ragusa has sent word to-day to the Minister of War that a superior force of the enemy advancing from Reims has forced him to retreat on Jouarre, whence he goes on this morning to Meaux. The Duke of Treviso has joined him, and does the same.

The Duke of Ragusa believes that the enemy is marching on Paris: he implores reinforcements, and I have little to give.

I am preparing to guard the bridges of Lagny, St. Maur, and Charenton, and to form a small reserve.

[867.] NAPOLEON TO JOSEPH.

Jouarre, March 1, 1814, 8 P.M.

My Brother,—Your three letters of the 28th reached me at 9 A.M., at noon, and at 1 P.M.

I have not yet communicated with the Duke of Ragusa, and know nothing of the events of yesterday. I am at Jouarre; I have taken La Ferté-sous-Jouarre, and at the same time I cut off the bridges which the enemy had placed across the Marne. I captured some baggage, and took between 300 and 400 prisoners. The whole of the enemy's army is thrown upon the right bank of the Marne. By Préval's report I see that the Poles are to start to-morrow, the 2nd: send them to La Ferté-sous-Jouarre. Order all the cavalry which is on its way to the Duke of Ragusa, and which does not belong to him (that is to say, to the 1st cavalry corps), to proceed to Meaux; I shall then send them to their different corps, for the great thing is to keep all the cavalry together. Let me have a return of the troops at St. Maur and at Lagny. Besides the 600 Poles who are coming, 1200 more ought to be ready; they are my Cossacks. I wish them to start soon. General . . . . . . * has obtained from me a decree, putting 150,000 francs, which were in General Dombrowski's chest, at the disposal of his regiment. Write to General Préval to watch this operation, and let these men join me without delay. I have left the Duke of Tarento, the Duke of Reggio, and General Gérard upon the Aube, between Bar-sur-Aube and Vandœuvre. I have placed General Sebastiani in Troyes as governor. Send an officer to find out what is going on there. It seems to me that General Ornano is not sufficiently active in re-organising the cavalry of my guard. He has 2200 men ready and 1400 horses; why has he not as many more in preparation? Let him bestir himself a little more, for I am anxious to keep at a high complement the cavalry of my guard, as in these forced marches many men are

* Illegible.—ED.

lost. In all the reports which have reached me of conversations among the officers in Blücher's army, he is spoken of as a madman, and his manœuvre blamed. The express which should have left Paris yesterday morning with my newspapers has not yet arrived.

[868.] NAPOLEON TO JOSEPH.

Jouarre, March 2, 1814.

My Brother,—On the receipt of the present letter I wish you to call together, in presence of the Regent, the high dignitaries, my ministers, and the President of my Conseil d'Etat, and to read to them the note of the allies, containing their proposals; my letter to the Emperor of Austria; the letter from Prince Schwartzenberg to the chief of the staff, with his answer; and the draft of a note which I have just dictated to be presented by the Duke of Vicenza to the Congress; in short, the different papers which give information as to the state of the negotiation for the armistice,—in order that the proper councillors of my government may know how the question stands. The Duke of Cadore will take down all that each of them says. I do not ask for formal advice, but I wish to know different people's impressions.

[869.] NAPOLEON TO JOSEPH.

La Férte-sous-Jouarre, March 2, 1814, P.M.

My Brother,—Up to this time nothing has reached La Ferté from Paris through Meaux, yet I despatched to you yesterday evening a courier by the direct road. Desire Lavalette to regulate the posts properly. The bridge of La Ferté will be repaired this evening. At midnight I shall be in pursuit of the enemy; it is said that his movements are considerably embarrassed by the mud. We may possibly meet with great success. I have ordered Prince Borghese, through the minister of war, to send from 6000 to 8000 men, with horse artillery, to Chambéry: repeat this order. Converse sometimes with the Ministers of War and of the Interior. I think that Gantheaume should be recalled; he is a pessimist. The National Guard of Toulon alone would render what he fears improbable,* still more the addition of 8000 or 10,000 men from the squadron. Reiterate the order for all the disposable men in the 7th and 8th divisions to repair to Lyons; it is there that troops are required. I have desired that the pontoon-train, which, as I hear, left Paris to-day, may travel night and day till it reaches me—it is my greatest want. If I had had one at Méry I should have cut to pieces Schwartzenberg's army, and this morning I should have destroyed Blücher. I am preparing to carry the war into Lorraine,† where I shall collect all the troops which are in garrison on the Meuse and the Rhine. There are many soldiers in Paris; I see in the return that there are a number ready for service. Why are they not sent off?—more activity is required. It is necessary to organise as soon as possible the 4th provisional division of the guard, to remount 2000 cavalry, and to form the 4th division of the line, in order that you may always have troops at hand in Paris.

[870.] JOSEPH TO NAPOLEON.

Paris, March 2, 1814, 5 P.M.

Sire,—We hear to-day that the commissioners for the armistice have separated. The ministers held a council to-day. It seems that, in every respect, we are at the end of our resources. I have sent 700 men to Lagny. They are old soldiers picked up in the hospitals, left when Laval's division marched. They are to join their corps.

[871.] JOSEPH TO NAPOLEON.

Paris, March 3, 1814, 6 A.M.

Sire,—I have received your letter from La Ferté-sous-Jouarre, dated on the evening of the 2nd of March. I have

* Napoleon alludes to the fears expressed by Admiral Gantheaume and Masséna of the English effecting a landing at Toulon, where Gantheaume commanded the fleet and Masséna the district.—ED.

† This is the first notice of the march on the rear of the allies, leaving them between himself and Paris, which Napoleon effected three weeks afterwards. —TR.

desired M. Lavalette to send his couriers by the most direct road. I have written to the minister to remind Prince Borghese to send troops to Chambéry. He tells me that this order has been executed; and with respect to placing a proper garrison in Alexandria, that the order was despatched long ago. I have sent to ask if the pontoon-train has started. I was not aware that one was to be sent. If what we hear of Schwartzenberg's movements be true, it seems to me that it will be difficult for your Majesty to quit the neighbourhood of Paris. General Hullin has no soldiers who can be sent out of Paris, unless the veterans are included. I have already written to your Majesty that, in order to form the 4th provisional division of the guard, we want conscripts, arms, and money. It shall be formed as soon as we have men and arms, if your Majesty consents to the distribution of the 17th million. To mount 2000 men, it would be necessary to begin to spend an 18th million. With regard to the 4th division of the line, similar obstacles exist; they shall be surmounted as quickly as possible. Until the division of the guard is formed, that of the line cannot be, as the guard, anxious to fill up its ranks speedily, spares few men to the line. I have not yet received the papers relating to the negotiation, which your Majesty has desired me to read.

[872.] NAPOLEON TO JOSEPH.

La Ferté-sous-Jouarre, March 3, 1814.

My Brother,—The cavalry has been filing off since 10 o'clock this morning. By this time it must have reached the parks of artillery. I go myself to Montreuil.* One of our columns has gone to Château-Thierry to repair the bridge. I have heard nothing to-night from the Duke of Ragusa. I think that we shall have news from him before long. Yesterday evening he was in the neighbourhood of Gesvre and Crouy.† The enemy was yesterday opposite to Mareuil.

* A village three or four miles from La-Ferté-sous-Jouarre, on the road to Château-Thierry.—TR.

† Five or six miles to the north of Meaux.—TR.

P. S.—Send some officers to Troyes to learn what is going on. The papers which were mentioned in last night's despatches are annexed. There are six.

[873.] NAPOLEON TO JOSEPH.

Bezu, March 4, 1814.

My Brother,—The prefect of Melun's news is false.* Desire Count Lavalette to punish his agents who spread such mischievous reports. In fact, Bar-sur-Aube was not a position which could be held. It was necessary either to advance or to retreat. In consequence of my manœuvre on the Marne, it was advisable to retreat. We had an action in which we lost from 700 to 800 men; but our enemy's loss was double, and we did not evacuate the town till night. There are more than 3000 unattached men in Paris; but General Hullin is by no means active in filling up his cadres. You should appoint a general who has no other duty. The 2nd division of reserve ought to have been ready, and to have marched to Meaux to the assistance of the Duke of Ragusa. I say again, all these men are scattered among the five battalions which are in the 1st military division. Desire the minister for Marine Affairs to answer Admiral Verhuel that he is to hold out to the last gasp; that the loss of two frigates and 500 or 600 men is not to be thought of in comparison with the advantage of keeping for five or six months Holland in blockade, by holding Fort Lasalle.

[874.] NAPOLEON TO JOSEPH.

Fismes, March 4, 1814.

My Brother,—I have reached Fismes. The enemy has been driven back in every direction. We have taken 2000 prisoners, and between 400 and 500 baggage and ammunition carts. The Duke of Ragusa must be at Soissons, and my skirmishers before Reims. The enemy seems to be moving towards Laon and

* It does not appear what this news was. Oudinot and Gérard were driven out of Bar-sur-Aube by Schwartzenberg on the 27th of February. —TR.

Avesnes, he is in the greatest confusion. He has sustained an immense loss in men, horses, and carriages.

Send one of your officers to Troyes, to tell the Dukes of Taranto and Reggio that I may possibly manœuvre by Vitry, St. Dizier, and Joinville, on the enemy's rear, which will set them free, as the enemy will be forced to abandon the Seine to fly to the assistance of his rear. One advantage of this operation will be the raising the blockade of my fortresses, whence I shall draw large garrisons and reinforcements. I am writing by express to the Minister of War to say that I am displeased with General Maison, who commits blunders. Let the Minister of War order him, in my name, to collect the garrisons of the different fortresses, the garrison of Antwerp, and part of that of Ostend, and to fall upon the enemy's rear. It is a fact that I have more troops in those posts than the enemy, but General Maison's inexperience and timidity render them inactive. Tell the Minister of War to forbid him, in my name, to enter any fortress; he must place himself at the head of all his troops, and march, either by Antwerp on the enemy's rear, or on the rear of his line of operations, which is by Avesnes and Mons. This general, who formerly distinguished himself, has not fulfilled my expectations, or deserved the trust which I placed in him. I am, however, still willing to suspend my judgment. The Minister of War will write to him that he must show more energy, boldness, and intrepidity. The Minister of War should also send word to the Duke of Castiglione that he is to advance; that, with the troops which he has, he is able to beat double the enemy's force, if he will be the most constant and the most forward under fire.*

[875.] JOSEPH TO NAPOLEON.

Paris, March 4, 1814, 6 P.M.

Sire,—I have had no letter from you since the one of yesterday from La Ferté-sous-Jouarre. The Empress held to-day the

* On that very day the Duke of Castiglione, who had under his command 20,000 old soldiers from the armies of Spain, gave up his march on Geneva, which had caused so much uneasiness to the allies, and fell back upon Macon. Little desirous to head his troops in the field, and tired of war, he spoke of the Emperor in terms of bitter reproach.—ED.

special Council ordered by your Majesty. I read the papers which you sent to me. All the members of the council seemed to be of one mind: the enemy's proposals were considered most unjust, and perfect confidence was expressed in whatever commands your Majesty may think fit to give to your plenipotentiary, in order to enable France to benefit immediately by the enormous sacrifices which are exacted of her. They are all convinced that your Majesty will never consent to such sacrifices, unless driven to them by absolute necessity, and that your Majesty is a better judge of this necessity than any one else can be.

But they almost unanimously agreed in thinking that it would be better to accept conditions, reducing France to her limits in 1792, than to expose the capital.* The occupation of the capital is dreaded as the end of the present state of things, and the commencement of great misfortunes. The whole of Europe joins in wishing to reduce France to what she was in 1792. Let it therefore be the foundation of a treaty which is rendered imperative by circumstances, but let the country be evacuated immediately.

To sum up: an immediate peace, whatever may be the terms, is indispensable. It will be a truce lasting for two or three years; but, whether it be favourable or not, we must have peace. The Emperor will obtain the best terms that he can. At this juncture it is sure to do good, as it will enable the Emperor to pay exclusive attention to the interior, and a wise system of administration may place him in a position to regain what has been unjustly demanded and wisely yielded. The natural limits would be a real boon both for France and the rest of Europe: we might then hope for a lasting peace; but impossibility relieves from every obligation. Peace now is indispensable; it may be broken on the day when France is able to re-assert her rights. Make then what in your breast you will consider as a mere truce, since the enemy's injustice will not permit you to make an equitable peace, and the state of public feeling and of public affairs does not allow you to hope from France efforts proportionate to the end to be attained.

* It is said that Comte Lacuée de Cessac was the only member of the Council who dissented.—TR.

Your letter to the Emperor of Austria was thought full of dignity and good sense. France will still possess *you;* you will possess her as thoroughly as when she astonished Europe; and you, who have already delivered her once, will rescue her a second time, and also rescue yourself, by signing an immediate peace. Make England recognise you, deliver France from the Cossacks and Prussians, and France will make up to you in blessings what superficial persons may think that you have lost in glory. But I perceive that I am growing diffuse. Whether your Majesty be victorious or not, you must turn your thoughts to peace. This is the summary of all that is spoken here, and thought here.

[876.] NAPOLEON TO JOSEPH.

Fismes, March 5, 1814, 11 A.M.

My Brother,—Put the following notice into the 'Moniteur:'—"His Majesty the Emperor and King fixed his head-quarters on the 5th at Béry-au-Bac on the Aisne. The enemy's army, under Blücher, Sacken, York, Witzengerode, and Bülow, was in retreat. Had it not been for the treachery of the commandant of Soissons, who abandoned his post, that army would have been lost. General Corbineau entered Reims on the 5th at four in the morning. We beat the enemy at Lizy-sur-Ourcq and at May. We have taken in the different actions 4000 prisoners, 600 baggage-waggons, and many guns, and have delivered Reims."

[877.] NAPOLEON TO JOSEPH.

Fismes, March 5, 1814.

My Brother,—I thought that the Duke of Ragusa would have been yesterday at Soissons; but the commandant basely evacuated the town without firing a shot. He retreated, with all his troops, with the honours of war and six pieces of cannon; he is at Villers-Cotterets. I have ordered the Minister of War to have him arrested, brought before a court-martial, and shot. He must be executed in the Place de Grève, with the utmost publicity. The sentence must be printed, and its grounds well stated.

Five generals must be appointed to try him. This business has done us incalculable harm. I should have reached Laon to-day, and I have no doubt that the enemy would have been routed and cut to pieces. I must now manœuvre and lose time in constructing bridges. See that at least an example is made.

I attacked Reims at 3 A.M. We took 2000 prisoners; more that 100 of them were officers, among whom are several colonels; and we captured a great quantity of baggage. I am writing to the regent to fire a salute.

[878.] NAPOLEON TO JOSEPH.

Béry-au-Bac, March 6, 1814, noon.

My Brother,—If the Duke of Taranto is ill, he must give up the command to the Duke of Reggio, and place General Sebastiani at the head of the 11th corps. I am assured that Troyes has just been evacuated; I cannot believe in such incapacity. There can be no finer position than Troyes, where the enemy is forced to manœuvre upon both banks. I am going to drive the enemy to-day towards Laon. I shall then march upon Châlons and Arcis. It is indispensable to hold the Seine for five or six days at Nogent, Bray, and Montereau. I could not be worse seconded than I am. I left a splendid army and excellent cavalry at Troyes; but the soul is wanting. I am sure that this army is stronger in the field than any which Prince Schwartzenberg can oppose to it. Consult the Minister of War: a sick general is worse than any thing. The Minister of War will give the command to the Duke of Reggio, and the Duke of Taranto's corps to General Sebastiani.

[879.] JOSEPH TO NAPOLEON.

Paris, March 7, 1814.

Sire,—I enclose to you the duplicate of a letter from the Duke of Taranto to the chief of the staff; I hope that the original will have reached you two hours earlier, and I have no doubt that the army is marching to the assistance of Paris. The Minister of War has received intelligence that the Duke of Taranto is perfectly well, and able to retain the command. . . . .* De la Bouillerie up to now. . . . .* A debt of 200,000 francs for the requirements of the guard has been covered by the funds which your Majesty placed subsequently at the disposal of the generals. M. de la Bouillerie has warned me to-day to trust no longer to this resource, unless your Majesty will give an express order. The Duke of Conegliano having informed me that he has been unable to obtain the pikes which he asked the Minister of War to give to him for the use of the national guard, I have authorised him to have some made, as well as to purchase 3000 muskets, which he hopes to find means of doing in Paris. The municipality of Paris will defray these expenses, which may amount to from 200,000 to 300,000 francs. In order not to lose time, I have promised to pay him to-morrow 50,000 francs in advance, for which I shall be reimbursed by the municipality. I depend, however, on M. de la Bouillerie's kindness for this purpose. Nothing can now be done here on credit.

[880.] NAPOLEON TO JOSEPH.

L'Ange-Gardien,* March 8, 1814, 11 A.M.

Yesterday, the 7th, I beat Witzingerode, Langeron, and Woronzow, with the remains of Sacken's corps. I captured 2000 prisoners, took some of their guns, and drove the enemy from Craonne to l'Ange-Gardien. The battle of Craonne was glorious. The Duke of Belluno and General Grobier are wounded. My killed and wounded amount to between 700 and 800: the enemy has lost from 5000 to 6000. My advanced guard is before Laon. Send everything by way of Soissons: convey this news to the Duke of Taranto. I have heard nothing from you since the 6th. I am well although the weather is cold. My love to you and to your wife.

P.S.—Put the news contained in this letter into the 'Moniteur.'

* Illegible in MS.—ED.

* A small inn between Craonne and Laon.—TR.

[881.] JOSEPH TO NAPOLEON.

Paris, March 8, 1814.

Sire,—I have had no letter from you since that of the 6th at noon. I wrote to you this morning. The news from the Duke of Dalmatia's army increases our alarm.

We already see the English at Bourdeaux; nor do we see how their progress is to be arrested, unless it be opposed by the Duke of Dalmatia in the centre of France. The Austrian army is on the Seine, and we are uneasy that your Majesty should be at such a distance from us. The Dukes of Taranto and Reggio do not agree; no good can come of the combined services of these two marshals.

It is most important that your Majesty should proceed instantly to the Seine and the neighbourhood of your capital: considering what is passing on the Garonne, the consequences of the occupation of Paris are to be feared; and if . . . .* and therefore our hopes . . . .* repeat the same things.

[882.] JOSEPH TO NAPOLEON.

Paris, March 9, 1814, 11 A.M.

Sire,—I have received your letter from l'Ange-Gardien of the 8th at 11 A.M. I had had none since that of the 6th at noon. I have communicated to the Duke of Taranto the victory of Craonne. I presume that Soissons is ours, and that you are drawing nearer to Paris in that direction. This is indispensable. The Duke of Taranto's army seems to have been outflanked on the left; detachments of the enemy having entered Sézanne, and even advanced as far as Coulommiers. The funds fell yesterday to 51. The Duke of Dalmatia's movements cause the greatest anxiety with respect to Bourdeaux, which might easily become a hot-bed of civil war. After your recent victory, you may honourably sign a peace on the ancient limits. Such a peace would restore the prosperity of France after the long struggle which began in 1792; and there could be nothing dishonourable to her in it, as she would lose no portion

* Illegible.—ED.

of her territory, and has arranged her affairs at home as she thought fit.*

As for you, Sire, who have been so repeatedly victorious, I am convinced that you possess all the qualities which might make the French forget, or rather might recall to them, the best features of the reigns of Louis XII., Henri IV., and Louis XIV., if you will make a lasting peace with Europe, and if, returning to your natural kindness and renouncing your assumed character and your perpetual efforts, you will at last consent to relinquish the part of the wonderful man for that of the great sovereign.

After having saved France from anarchy within, and from all Europe without, you will become the father of your people, and you will be adored as much as Louis XII., after having been admired more than Henri IV. and Louis XIV.; and in order thus to accumulate every species of glory, you have only to will your own happiness, as well as that of France.

[883.] JOSEPH TO NAPOLEON.

Paris, March 9, 1814, midnight.

Sire,—I have the honour of transmitting to your Majesty, 1st, a report from General Préval, who asks for 2,200,000 francs to mount 6000 men in the course of this month; 2ndly, a summary from the return of the 1st military division on the 8th instant. Your Majesty will see that throughout the empire there are only 7575 disposable men. There are no longer any in Paris, as they have all been sent in succession to Meaux, and thence to Moret.

[884.] NAPOLEON TO JOSEPH.

Chavignon, March 10, 1814.

My Brother,—I have received your letter of the 9th. The army which I beat at Craonne was the Russian army, commanded by Sacken, united to Witzingerode; they have sustained a

* In allusion to the threats of the allies in 1792, if France dethroned the Bourbons.—TR.

great loss, and have retreated to Laon, where they have joined the Prussian army, consisting of the corps of Bulow, York, and Kleist. As they are strongly posted, I was satisfied yesterday with observing and reconnoitring them. Paris is in greater danger from this army than from that of Schwartzenberg. Nevertheless I will draw near to Soissons, in order to be more within reach of Paris; but until I have been able to obtain another victory over this army, I can hardly proceed elsewhere. The detachments which Schwartzenberg's army has sent to its rear have considerably diminished its strength, and it seems to fear to venture crossing the Seine.

The Duke of Ragusa has marched from Béry-au-Bac to the neighbourhood of Laon. He had driven the enemy before him; but in the night, as he was taking up his position, he was suddenly attacked, and his infantry fell into confusion. His soldiers lost their heads, and he was obliged to fall back for several leagues somewhat in disorder, and to abandon a few pieces of cannon. This is only one of the accidents of war, but it is very annoying just now when I am in want of success. It has determined me not to engage the enemy to-day, although I had already made arrangements for a vigorous attack, however superior might be his numbers.

I think that you ought to assemble the ministers to consult as to the means of raising 30,000 men from among the masses who have taken refuge in Paris, and the workmen who are without employment. This levy should be called the levée en masse of the national guard. As you have muskets, you will have no difficulty.* All the workmen who have nothing to do will thus be well provided for. This measure seems to me to be indispensable. The national guard ought to co-operate in it, as by this means the mob will be used to protect the town instead of threatening an insurrection against property. See what you can do.

* This remark of Napoleon's would appear very extraordinary, after all Joseph's letters, if there had not been already frequent opportunities for observing that the Emperor often chose not to understand what was written to him, especially on the subjects of money, arms, and materials.—ED.

[885.] NAPOLEON TO JOSEPH.

Chavignon, March 11, 1814.

My Brother,—I have reconnoitred the position of the enemy at Laon; it was too strong to be attacked without severe loss. I have therefore determined on returning to Soissons. It is probable that the enemy would have evacuated Laon in the fear of an attack if it had not been for the skirmish with the Duke of Ragusa, whose behaviour was that of an ensign. The enemy's loss has been immense; he attacked yesterday the village of Clary five times, and was each time repulsed.

My young guard melts away like a snowball; the old guard is still in good order. My horse-guard also disappears rapidly. It is essential that General Ornano should take every means for remounting the dragoons and chasseurs, beginning with the old soldiers. Préval shall have the two millions for which you have asked me; order them to be given to him, and let some of the public works which are wanted in Paris be made as a means of giving charity. I think that some redoubts on the heights would be of use, especially with regard to their moral effect. Let some be immediately constructed at Montmartre.

[886.] JOSEPH TO NAPOLEON.

Paris, March 11, 1814, 10 P.M.

Sire,—I have received your letter from Chavignon. I have assembled the Ministers; those of the Interior and of the Police were of opinion that it was utterly impossible to find 1000 men who would leave Paris to join the army; the Minister of War has given me a return of our arms, of which I annex a copy. The result is that, far from having 30,000 muskets, there are not 6000 fit for service, and that these 6000 are for the daily use of the battalions of the line and of the imperial guard.

The result of all that I hear from the Ministers, from the chief officers of the national guard, from all the persons whom I know to be attached to the present order of government, is, that circumstances render peace imperative. There is not one individual in Paris who would not loudly ask for it if it were not for the fear of offending you; and, in truth, none but your enemies can endeavour to persuade you to refuse a peace with the ancient limits.

The spirit of the Duke of Taranto's army is very bad. The annexed letter * will acquaint you with the situation of the Duke of Dalmatia's army, and of the departments south of the Garonne. Unpleasant reports, tending to diminish the popularity of your Majesty, are beginning to circulate in the capital For instance, it is said that the Duke of Conegliano, who is liked, is about to be recalled; that he is to be replaced by General Sebastiani, who has been here for the last five days; that the Duke of Padua will shortly arrive; that he is to be employed in Paris, and that Paris is to be defended. The month of March is slipping away, yet the fields are not sown. It is however superfluous to enter into further details. Your Majesty must feel that there is no longer any remedy but peace, and an immediate peace. Every day that is lost is mischievous to our personal popularity. Individual distress is extreme; and on the day when it is believed that your Majesty has preferred prolonging the war to making even a disadvantageous peace, there is no doubt that disgust will incline the public mind in another direction. If Toulouse or Bourdeaux should set up a Bourbon, you will have civil war, and the immense population of Paris will support the side which promises to give them peace soonest.

Such is the state of opinion; no one can change it. This being the case, the only way is to submit. If the peace be unfavourable, it will be no fault of yours, as all classes here insist upon it. I cannot be mistaken, as my view is that of all the world. We are on the eve of total destruction; our only hope is in peace.

I was with the Empress when she received a letter from her father. From what she told me, he appears to be well-disposed. It seems that he has answered your letter. I earnestly hope that his reply was in favour of a speedy termination.

* It does not appear.—TR.

1060 men, who have been mounted at the Versailles depôt, are to sleep to-night in Paris, and start to-morrow morning for Soissons. I have just received the minutes of proceedings in council to-day, which I annex.

[887.] JOSEPH TO NAPOLEON.

Paris, March 12, 1814.

Sire,—I have written to General Préval to tell him to be, if possible, doubly active in obtaining remounts; and that he may depend upon receiving the two millions. Your Majesty orders works of defence, which are to be at the same time works of charity, to be constructed on the heights above Paris beginning at Montmartre. The committee for the defence of the city has sketched a plan; its execution is stopped only by the want of funds. In my letter of the 5th, when I proposed to your Majesty to levy a contribution of from 400,000 to 500,000 francs upon the city of Paris,* I proposed at the same time that you should order M. de la Bouillerie to pay this sum in advance, because I foresaw the delays which would take place in levying a contribution which must first be resolved on in the municipal council, then in the conseil d'état, &c. In your letter of yesterday your Majesty orders me to commence these works. I have written to M. de la Bouillerie to know whether he is authorised to advance the sum. If your Majesty has not yet written to him for this purpose, it is indispensable that you should do so immediately if you wish these works to be executed without loss of time.

[888.] NAPOLEON TO JOSEPH.

Soissons, March 13, 1814.

My Brother,—Before commencing the fortifications of Paris, I must see the plan; the one which was sent to me seems to me to be very complicated; I want something simple. The people complain everywhere of the mayors and authorities who prevent them from defending themselves. I see that in Paris it is just the same. The people possess energy and good faith. I fear greatly

* No such letter appears.—TR.

that the difficulty consists in the unwillingness to fight of certain principal personages, who will be confounded, after the event has taken place, by finding what will be their own fate.

[889.] JOSEPH TO NAPOLEON.

Paris, March 13, 1814, 11 P. M.

Sire,—The person* whom I sent to the Crown-Prince of Sweden returned to-day; he left the Prince at Liége on the 10th ult. If your Majesty would like to question him, your orders will find him at the quarters of the Prince of Neufchâtel, for whom I shall give him a letter. This person is a Frenchman, formerly Bernadotte's physician, and his wife's secretary for the last eight years; he is somewhat slow, but very sensible. If your Majesty should think fit to see him, he can give you important military details as to the country which he has passed through. I hasten to communicate to your Majesty the news of a sortie effected by General Carnot; he drove the enemy back to Mechlin, and re-entered Antwerp with provisions and 600 prisoners. The Prince of Sweden talks openly and perpetually about the Bourbons; he says that he is temporising to give you an opportunity for making peace; he is anxious for it in order to return home. . . . . †

[890.] NAPOLEON TO JOSEPH.

Reims, March 14, 1814.

My Brother,—Yesterday I reached Reims, which was occupied by the commander-in-chief St. Priest, with three Russian divisions, and a new Prussian division coming from the blockade of Stettin. I beat them, retook the town, captured 20 pieces of cannon, a quantity of baggage and ammunition waggons, and 5000 prisoners. General St. Priest is mortally wounded, one of his thighs has been amputated. The extraordinary part of the affair is that the gun was fired by the artilleryman who killed General Moreau; it seems really like a stroke of Providence.

* M. de Franzemberg.—ED. † Several lines illegible.—ED.

[891.] NAPOLEON TO JOSEPH.

Reims, March 14, 1814,

My Brother,—I have received your letter of the 12th of March.* I am sorry that you repeated to the Duke of Conegliano what I had written to you. I do not like all this gossip. If it suited me to remove the Duke of Conegliano, all the idle talk of Paris would have no effect. The national guard of Paris is a part of the people of France, and, as long as I live, I will be master everywhere in France. Your character is opposed to mine; you like to flatter people and to yield to *their* wishes; I like them to try to please me, and to obey *my* wishes. I am as much a sovereign now as I was at Austerlitz. Do not permit any person to flatter the national guard, nor Regnaud or any one else, to set himself up as their tribune. I suppose, however, that they see that there is some difference between the time of La Fayette, when the people ruled, and the present time, when I rule.

I have issued a decree for raising 12 battalions in Paris out of the *levée en masse.* On no pretext must the execution of this measure be delayed. I have written my wishes on this subject to the Ministers of the Interior and of the Police. If the people find that, instead of doing what is for their good, one is trying to please them, it is quite natural that they should think that they have the upper hand, and that they should entertain but a mean opinion of those in authority over them.

[892.] NAPOLEON TO JOSEPH.

Reims, March 16, 1814.

In accordance with the verbal instructions which I gave to you, and with the spirit of all my letters, you must not allow, happen what may, the Empress and the King of Rome to fall into the hands of the enemy. The manœuvres which I am about to make may possibly prevent your hearing from me for

* I am inclined to think that the letter, to which this is an answer, is that of the 11th of March.—TR.

several days. If the enemy should march on Paris with so strong a force as to render resistance impossible, send off towards the Loire the Regent, my son, the great dignitaries, the ministers, the senators, the President of the Conseil d'Etat, the chief officers of the crown, and Baron de la Bouillerie, with the money which is in my treasury. Never lose sight of my son, and remember that I would rather know that he was in the Seine than that he was in the hands of the enemies of France: the fate of Astyanax, prisoner to the Greeks, has always seemed to me to be the most lamentable in history.

[893.] JOSEPH TO NAPOLEON.

Paris, March 16, 1814, 5 P. M.

Sire,—General Ornano has just told me that the Imperial Guard set off this morning in consequence of your Majesty's orders. The arms of the National Guard, including muskets, fowling-pieces, and pikes, are sufficient now for 12,000 men.

[894.] NAPOLEON TO JOSEPH.

Reims, March 17, 1814, noon.

My Brother,—I have seen the person attached to Madame Bernadotte's service whom you sent to me. He gave me some important intelligence, as well as some which was false. If you can trust him, I think that it would be useful to send him back again, and to depute others, if it were only for the purpose of acquiring information as to those provinces. The Duke of Bassano has written to desire Count d'Hauterive to send to you a copy of the declaration of the allies at Châtillon, that they four intend to treat for all the other powers. You may forward this paper confidentially to the Crown-Prince, and advise him to endeavour to have a minister at the congress; for it cannot possibly be for the interest of Sweden that this Quadrumvirate should take possession of the whole of Europe. She must continue to do what she has always done, watch over her own affairs herself. Before you send the person in question, make sure that he is not a traitor, and intreat him to be perfectly discreet.

[895.] NAPOLEON TO JOSEPH.

Épernay, March 17, 1814, P. M.

My Brother,—I reached Epernay this evening. To-morrow at daybreak I shall resume my march towards Arcis-sur-Aube, which I shall reach by noon on the 19th. I shall construct three bridges, and proceed, according to circumstances, either towards Méry or towards Troyes, to fall upon the rear of the enemy. The Duke of Taranto must therefore dispute every foot of ground. To-morrow night, at 10 o'clock, my dispositions will have already begun to take effect, for the enemy will then become aware of my manœuvre, and it will influence all his operations. The Duke of Ragusa remains at Béry-au-Bac; the Duke of Treviso is at Reims; General Charpentier is at Soissons. I have desired the Minister of War to send a brigadier-general to Compiègne. I shall leave Brigadier-General Vincent at Epernay; he has a few detachments of cavalry, and is charged with superintending the leveés en masse.*

I do not think that Blücher, who has suffered considerably, will be able to move for the next few days. He will then have to cross the Aisne, and the Dukes of Ragusa and Treviso will dispute every inch of ground with him. I expect great things from my manœuvre, which will throw the rear as well as the head-quarters of the enemy into the utmost disorder and confusion. If the enemy should still be at Troyes, you must despatch couriers to me by way of La Ferté-sous-Jouarre, and thence, through Epernay or Montmirail, to Arcis-sur-Aube. Desire the Ministers of War and of Police to say nothing which is unnecessary, and to write the important parts in cipher, until I have re-established the communication through Nogent. Send an officer to Compiègne, to Soissons, to Reims, and to Epernay. I have ordered a division of 12,000 men, whom I am collecting together at Metz, to repair to Châlons; I do not know whether this order will reach them; it would be a great piece of good fortune.

* Napoleon, while at Reims, issued a decree ordering a levée en masse against the invaders.—TR.

[896.] NAPOLEON TO JOSEPH.

Épernay, March 18, 1814.

My Brother,—I have received no letter of yesterday from Paris; I conclude that the express continues to make the détour by Soissons. All my army is in motion, in order to sleep to-night on the other side of Fère-Champenoise, thence to advance upon Arcis and the bridges held by the enemy; I am in communication with my garrisons at Verdun and Metz. I am expecting a division of 12,000 men, which I draw from all those fortresses. It seems that the enemy has left Noyon, which sets Compiègne free; that town has behaved perfectly well.

[897.] NAPOLEON TO JOSEPH.

Épernay, March 18, 1814, noon.

My Brother,—I have received your letter of the 17th. General Préval has still 450,000 frs. in hand, besides the 500,000 frs. which remain to his account with M. de la Bouillerie from the two millions. There are consequently 900,000 frs. still to spend; he therefore does not require 2,200,000 frs., but 1,700,000 frs. As soon as he has exhausted his present credit, I will open for him a further credit for 1,700,000 frs.

[898.] NAPOLEON TO JOSEPH.

Plancy, March 20, 1814, 6 A. M.

My Brother,—I crossed the Aube yesterday at Plancy. I immediately advanced on Méry. I attacked the town, and took possession of it at 7 P. M. My cavalry forded the Seine, turned the bridge of Méry, and cut off the road between Nogent and Troyes. The chasseurs of the guard carried off a quantity of baggage and an excellent pontoon-train. The Emperor Alexander reached Arcis on the 18th. He remained there only an hour; we found ourselves nearly face to face. He returned to Troyes, which their head-quarters quitted immediately after. We constantly pick up prisoners; the enemy is flying in every direction.

The enemy began to retreat early on the 17th, as soon as he

found out that I had retaken Châlons, and that I was marching on his rear. Put the annexed article into the 'Moniteur.'*

[899.] BERTHIER TO JOSEPH.

Arcis-sur-Aube, March 21, 1814.

Sire,—The Emperor reached Arcis yesterday before his advanced guard. General Wrede's corps endeavoured to take Arcis by assault. He was repulsed, and 400 of his men taken prisoners. He captured two of our guns, and we took two of his. In the night he retired. Prince Schwartzenberg's army seems to be retreating upon Brienne. The Emperor has recrossed the Aube, and is advancing upon Vitry. We lost no person of importance in yesterday's action. His Majesty is in excellent health. Our communication at present is through Coulommiers, La Ferté-Gaucher, and Sézanne.†

[900.] JOSEPH TO NAPOLEON.

Paris, March 22, 1814, 11 A.M.

Sire,—The march of Blücher on Reims and Fismes, and that which the Dukes of Treviso and Ragusa have been ordered to make on Châlons, lay open Paris. This was remarked by the Duke of Treviso himself to the officer by whom I sent the order. As your Majesty is kept by the Duke well informed, I have no doubt that you will give such orders as the circumstances require.

[901.] JOSEPH TO CLARKE.

Paris, March 24, 1814.

Monsieur le Duc,—The appearance of the enemy on the banks of the Oise makes necessary immediate means of resistance.

As the feelings of the country people are good, and require only to be directed, a general officer should be sent to Senlis, if

* This is the last of Napoleon's letters before the battle of Paris. The manœuvre upon Vitry took place almost immediately, and the communications with the capital were entirely cut off.—ED.

† This was the beginning of the march upon Vitry and St. Dizier, which nearly saved, but, as things turned out, in reality lost Paris.—ED.

there be not one there already, to call out the national guards or the levée en masse, to raise some works which may prevent the town from being taken by assault, and to occupy and defend the bridges of Creil and Pont St. Maxence, and the heights of Verberie.

If it were possible to send some troops of the line to those points, to head the national guards and the armed inhabitants, they would be very useful.

The same remarks apply to Pontoise. Pray give the necessary orders. These measures appear to me to be urgent.

[902.] JOSEPH TO CLARKE.

Paris, March 25, 1814.

Monsieur le Duc,—The reports of several commandants of fortresses, and especially that of the Commandant of Meaux, prove that a great number of soldiers are without arms. It seems to me that it is urgent to find out the cause of this state of things, and to apply an immediate remedy. I am convinced that posts such as La Ferté, Meaux, &c., are worse defended by 2000 men, half of whom are unarmed, than by 1000 with arms: and that the remaining 1000 who are without arms would do better in Paris, where their comrades could not be demoralized by their example, as they would not be in presence of the enemy; nor would they desert so readily as if they were in the field and felt their helplessness. This leads me to the importance of knowing day by day the number of arms which can be distributed in Paris. It seems to me indispensable—1st. To give arms to the troops engaged in active service and who require them; 2ndly. After this has been done, if there should be any arms left, to insist upon the completion and arming of the two battalions of national garde mobile which Paris is bound to supply. Other measures may then be proposed for arming the soldiers. I intend to advise the Regent to neglect no measures for attaining an object so important to the public safety. The first thing to be done is to have a double return—1st, of the troops without arms; and 2nd, of the arms which have not been distributed for want of soldiers. I have written to Count Daru to supply the shoes which are wanted here.

[903.] JOSEPH TO NAPOLEON.

Paris, March 26, 1814.

Sire,—I have no letters since that from Arcis-sur-Aube of the 21st. The Empress has received one of the 22nd. To-morrow a column will move on the Oise, where the inhabitants are in arms to repel the enemy's parties. The spirit of Paris is good. We are at work on the outer posts.

[904.] JOSEPH TO CLARKE.

Paris, March 27, 1814.

Monsieur le Duc,—Before I received your letter of yesterday I directed General Hullin to send the 11th marching cavalry regiment with the column which is on its way to the Oise. There remains for to-day's inspection only the 12th marching cavalry regiment, which may after the inspection move towards its destination, which I suppose to be Meaux. Pray let me know.*

[905.] JOSEPH TO NAPOLEON.

Paris, March 28, 1814, 9 A.M.

Sire,—I have announced to you the arrival of the Dukes of Treviso and Ragusa at Provins.† Troops have gone from hence towards Claye,‡ to assist the garrison which has marched out of Meaux. Soissons held out on the 26th. No letters from your Majesty since those of the 21st. One from M. Fain to M. Lavalette is the only one which has reached us. We wait impatiently for the news of your return to the capital.

* Thus, on the 28th of March, there would have been no troops left in Paris; and if the troops of Marshals Marmont and Mortier had not retreated on the capital, the only force to resist the enemy would have been the reserves of the guard under General Ornano.—ED.

† About fifty-five miles from Paris on the road to Troyes. This letter does not appear.—TR.

‡ A village about fifteen miles from Paris on the road to Meaux.—TR.

[906.] MARIE LOUISE TO JOSEPH.

Rambouillet, March 29, 5¼ P.M.

My dear Brother,—I have this instant reached Rambouillet, very sad and very harassed. It would be very kind if you would let me know what is going on, and whether the enemy has advanced. I wait for your answer before I decide whether I ought to go farther or to remain here. If I ought to move I beg you to tell me what place you think would be best and safest for me. I earnestly wish that you could write to me to return to Paris; it is the thing of all others which would give me most pleasure. A thousand remembrances to the Queen. Pray believe in the sincere friendship with which I am your most affectionate sister.

[907.] JOSEPH TO CLARKE.

Paris, March 29, 1814.

Monsieur le Duc,—To prevent misapprehension as to that we have agreed on, I think that I ought to remind you to order the Duke of Treviso to move to-night with his corps to La Villette, where he will take the command of the troops under General Ornano. The Duke of Ragusa will join in the neighbourhood of Pantin the corps of General Compans, and take it under his command.

Thus the Duke of Treviso is charged with the defence of Paris from La Villette to St. Denis inclusively; the Duke of Ragusa from La Villette to Charenton. At daybreak to-morrow I shall be at Montmarte to watch the movements of the enemy and give orders in consequence.

[908.] JOSEPH TO QUEEN JULIE.

Montmartre, March 30, 1814, 8 A.M.

My dear Friend,—There has been firing for the last two hours; as yet nothing is serious, but we are only beginning the day. I think that if your health will permit, you should set off with the children, Miot, Presle, and any other people whom you may like to take. If not, you must send on our children with

Miot and Madame Danneri. Your sister's house is your best refuge; but I hope that you will be able to start. Let Maillard return with your verbal answer as soon as possible.

[909.] JOSEPH TO THE GREAT JUDGE

Paris, March 30, 1814.

Monsieur le Comte,—I think that you should give notice to the Ministers that it is advisable that they should follow the Empress in her retreat. Tell this to the Senators, the Conseillers d'Etat, &c.

[910.] JOSEPH TO THE HIGH TREASURER.

March 30, 1814.

Monsieur l'Architrésorier,—I think that the high dignitaries should follow the Empress in her retreat from Paris towards Chartres.

Have the kindness to communicate with the other high dignitaries.

[911.] JOSEPH TO THE ARCH-CHANCELLOR.

Chartres, March 31, 1814.

Monsieur l'Archichancelier,—I have received a letter from the Emperor, from the post-house of La Cour de France, dated four this morning.

The Emperor met the armies of the Dukes of Ragusa and Treviso, which are to join our other armies near Fontainebleau.

I propose to set out myself to-morrow at daybreak.

[912.] JOSEPH TO NAPOLEON.

Chartres, March 31, 1814, 5 P.M.

Sire,—I wrote to you this morning by a courier in disguise. I have your Majesty's letter of this morning.* I have sent on to the Empress the one which was addressed to her. I shall set off this evening to follow the Empress. She intended to proceed

* This letter does not appear.—TR.

first to Tours. In obedience to your Majesty's wishes she will go to Blois with all the members of the government. The ministers who are here agree in thinking this course the best; they will start this evening. The Empress and the King of Rome are well, I saw them this morning; they will reach Châteaudun this evening.

The Ministers of War, of the Administration of War, of Finance, of the Treasury, of the Interior, and of Marine Affairs are here. Your Majesty must be already acquainted with all that has passed from the Marshals' reports, and from what I told to M. Déjean, your Majesty's aide-de-camp. The enemy's force was very large; the corps of the Dukes of Treviso and of Ragusa could not possibly make head against it.

[913.] NAPOLEON TO JOSEPH.

Fontainebleau, April 2, 1814.

I desired the Grand Marshal to write to you on the necessity of not crowding into Blois.* Let the King of Westphalia go to Brittany or towards Bourges. I think that Madame had better join her daughters at Nice, and Queen Julie and your children proceed to Marseilles. The Princess of Neufchâtel and the marshals' wives should go and live on their estates. It is natural that King Louis, who has always liked hot climates, should go to Montpellier. As few persons as possible should be on the Loire, and let every one settle himself quietly, without attracting attention. A large colony always excites a sensation in the neighbourhood. The Provence road is now open—it may not remain so for one day. Among the other ministers you do not mention the Minister of Police. Has he reached you? I do not know whether the Minister of War has his cipher. I have none with you, and as this is the case I cannot write to you on important subjects.

Advise everybody to observe the strictest economy.

* This letter was not received.—ED.

[914.] JOSEPH TO BERTHIER.

Vendôme, April 2, 1814.

I have received your letter of the 31st of March from Fontainebleau. We shall be at Blois this evening. The Ministers of the Interior and of War are answering your Highness. The want of arms remains an insurmountable difficulty. The other ministers will not reach Blois before to-morrow. The Empress has already started, and will be there to-night; she wishes to rest there to-morrow. When I reach Blois, I hope to receive letters from your Highness with the Emperor's final decision as to the destination of the court and the government. I entreat your Highness to believe in my constant and long existing friendship. In two words, the wish of all here is for repose. If it be possible to treat, it should be done at any price. The royalists begin to raise their heads. Peace, on whatever terms, would quell a party which the war, if it continues, will render more than threatening.

[915.] JOSEPH TO NAPOLEON.

Blois, April 3, 1814.

Sire,—I have received your letter of the 2nd. Mamma and Louis are ready to fulfil your wishes. Mamma is in want of money; six months of her pension is due. Neither has Jérôme any money. My wife has no longer any friends at Marseilles. What occasions our train to appear so large is the number of empty state-carriages belonging to the court. I have received no letter from the Grand Marshal on this subject or on any other. The Minister of Police has returned hither from Tours. The council to-day was unanimous in its opinions and wishes. We are waiting for your Majesty's decision as to the place of residence. May the fears which have been excited by the Duke of Vicenza's report never be realised! The Minister of War has no cipher with your Majesty, nor have I. The Ministers of the Treasury and of Finance know no longer how to discharge their duties. M. de la Bouillerie asks for orders to ensure the safety of his convoy. One of his fourgons, containing two millions, has reached

Orleans—it was left in Paris when the Empress went away. Might not Jérôme be sent to command the army of Lyons?

[916.] JOSEPH TO NAPOLEON.

Orleans, April 10, 1814.

Sire,—I wrote to you yesterday that we should be here to-day, and here we actually are. General Schuwaloff, aide-de-camp to the Emperor of Russia, accompanied the Empress. He came to Blois yesterday with M. de Saint-Aignan, who said nothing on the subject of his mission. If what is reported should prove true, and the Bourbons should be called to the throne, I am most anxious not to be obliged to ask anything from them. I could not possibly live in France, nor could I take my wife and children to the island of Elba. If sad necessity should force your Majesty thither, I will go to visit you, and to prove to you my attachment; but it will not be until I have placed my wife and children in safety on the continent.

All that takes place, Sire, justifies my old and fatal predictions. You must take a decided course, and put an end to this cruel agony. Why not appeal to Austria if necessary? Your son is the grandson of Francis. Why not speak the truth openly to France, and at length proclaim peace, abolish the conscription and the droits réunis, issue a general amnesty, and adopt a real constitutional monarchy? France wishes for peace and a liberal monarchy, but she does not wish for Bourbons. She prefers them to perpetual war, but she receives them only as a punishment, to which she resigns herself because she is beaten.

M. Faypoult has just returned from Italy; the army there is in excellent order; the Viceroy is quietly at Mantua; the King of Naples prays for your success, if you desire universal peace and the independence of Italy. A single effort might perhaps extricate France from the abyss into which she is falling. An immediate decision with regard both to military affairs and to politics may perhaps repair all in favour of your son; be bold enough to try. Save the state from imminent danger by getting rid of princes who will revive old hatreds and inflict a fresh injury upon the country by internal disturbances, brought on by the pride of the old nobility and the vanity of the new, and the character of the people raised by the revolution to a level at which we may lament that it was not left.

The Cossacks have appeared on the road from Beaugency to Orleans, and robbed some of the carriages belonging to the convoy.

CHAPTER XXIV.

THE letters from Napoleon contained in this chapter extend from the 22nd of April to the 16th of June, 1815. I have added one from Fain, one from Soult, and three from Bertrand. They were necessary to complete Napoleon's autobiography, as sketched in this Correspondence. I have added in an appendix a letter from Prince Louis Napoleon, which does not properly form a part of this work; but its intrinsic interest, and the great position now held by its author, tempted me to insert it.

[917.] NAPOLEON TO JOSEPH.

Paris, April 22, 1815.

My Brother,—I send the plan of a constitution for your private consideration. If you have any improvements to suggest, you can bring them to me this evening.

[918.] NAPOLEON TO JOSEPH.

Paris, May 2, 1815.

My Brother,—It is necessary to organise the Spaniards who are in France. A junta must be created composed of five members from the most active and enterprising. They will reside here, and correspond with the Minister of Foreign Affairs. The existence of this junta must be kept secret. It must have agents on the principal points of our frontier on the Pyrenees. The agents must be known to our civil and military officers, and their correspondence with the junta be post free. The business of the junta will be to edit in Paris a Spanish newspaper, to appear every two days, and to be circulated by these agents through every channel and in every part of Spain. The objects of the newspaper will be to enlighten the Spaniards, to make known to them our constitution, and to induce them to rebel and to desert. A further duty of the junta will be to raise guerillas, and to introduce them into Spain. The president of the junta will be accredited to the Minister of Foreign Affairs. All the pecuniary assistance afforded to the Spaniards, at the rate of 120,000 francs a month, will be distributed by the junta.

[919.] NAPOLEON TO JOSEPH.

Paris, May 19, 1815.

My Brother,—I wish to create a house of peers, and to appoint at first eighty members. As I desire to profit by the advice of those in whom I place confidence, I ask you to present to me on Sunday a list of 120 persons, whom you will select as if their nomination depended upon you. If there are any among them with whom I am not acquainted, please to add notes to their names. This list will remain a secret between you and me. You do not require to be told that no one need know that I have asked you for it.

I have despatched a similar letter to each of my ministers, and to other persons on whose judgment and attachment I can depend.

[920.] NAPOLEON TO JOSEPH.

Paris, June 2, 1815.

My Brother,—Having resolved to assemble the House of Peers on Saturday next at 3 o'clock, in the room which we have appointed for its sittings, our wish is that you be there, and that you take your place, that by your influence you may contribute to the good of the state and the consolidation of our Imperial authority. As this letter has no other object, I pray God, &c.

[921.] NAPOLEON TO JOSEPH.

Avesnes, June 14, 1815.

My Brother,—I shall carry my head-quarters this evening to Beaumont; to-morrow, the 15th, I shall march upon Charleroi, where the Prussian army is, the consequence of which will be either a battle or the retreat of the enemy. My army is excellent, and the weather tolerably fine; the country is perfectly well-disposed. I will write to you this evening as to whether the communications should be made on the 16th.* In the mean while preparations must be made. Adieu.

[922.] NAPOLEON TO JOSEPH.

Beaumont, June 15, 1815, 3 A.M.

My Brother,—As the enemy has made an aggressive movement, I am advancing to meet him. Hostilities will therefore commence to-day. Consequently I wish you to publish the declaration which has been prepared.

[923.] BARON FAIN TO JOSEPH.

Charleroi, June 15, 1815, 9 P.M.

Monseigneur,—It is 9 o'clock. The Emperor, who has been in the saddle since three in the morning, has just come in, overpowered by fatigue. He will throw himself on his bed to sleep for a few hours, and get on horseback again at midnight. As his Majesty is not able to write to your Highness, he has desired me to send to you the following intelligence.

The army forced the passage of the Sambre, near Charleroi, and placed advanced guards half way between Charleroi and Namur, and between Charleroi and Brussels. We have taken 1500 prisoners and six pieces of cannon. Four Prussian regiments are destroyed. Few of our men were killed, but the Emperor has sustained a loss which grieves him deeply: his aide-de-camp, General Letort, was killed on the table-land of Fleurus as he was leading a charge of cavalry. It is impossible to describe the

* The declaration of war.—ED.

enthusiasm of the inhabitants of Charleroi, and of all the country through which we have passed; the feeling is the same as it was in Burgundy. The Emperor, Monseigneur, wishes you to communicate this news to the ministers, and to make any use of it which you may think proper. An action of the utmost importance may take place to-morrow.

[924.] NAPOLEON TO JOSEPH.

Charleroi, June 16, 1815.

My Brother,—The bulletin will acquaint you with what has passed. I am carrying my head-quarters to Fleurus. The whole of the army is in motion. I regret deeply General Letort. Our loss yesterday was small; it fell almost entirely on the four squadrons of household troops.

P.S.—Letort is better.

[925.] SOULT TO JOSEPH.

Ligny, June 16, 1815, 8·30 P.M.

Monseigneur,—The Emperor has just obtained a complete victory over the Prussian and British armies, united under the command of Lord Wellington and Marshal Blücher. The army is advancing in pursuit of the enemy through the village of Ligny beyond Fleurus. I hasten to announce this happy news to your Imperial Highness.*

[926.] BERTRAND TO JOSEPH.

Isle of Aix, July 14, 1815.

Prince,—The Emperor communicated this morning with the British cruisers. The admiral's answer has not reached us, but the captain † is ordered by his government to receive the Emperor, if he should present himself, with the persons composing his suite. The captain is not acquainted with the further intentions of his government, but he does not doubt that the Emperor will

* This letter was the last which Joseph received from the army.—ED.

† Captain Maitland of the Bellerophon.—TR.

be well treated; for even if the government should wish to act otherwise, public opinion in England will, he thinks, force them to behave as they ought to do on such an occasion. M. de Las-Cases has returned on board,* and to-morrow morning the Emperor will repair thither. His Majesty desires me to give you this information.

[927.] BERTRAND TO JOSEPH.

London, Sept. 10, 1821.

Prince,—I write to you for the first time since the awful misfortune which has been added to the sorrows of your family. Uncertain whether a letter would reach you, as I was not quite sure of your address, I hoped that a letter from you or from Rome would acquaint me with it. I have decided on depositing this letter with Messrs. Baring, and I hope that you will receive it.

Your Highness is acquainted with the events of the first years of this cruel exile; many persons who have visited St. Helena have informed you of what was still more interesting to you—the manner of living and the unkind treatment which aggravated the influences of a deadly climate.

In the last year of his life, the Emperor, who for four years had taken no exercise, altered extremely in appearance: he became pale and feeble. From that time his health deteriorated rapidly and visibly. He had always been in the habit of taking baths; he now took them more frequently and stayed longer in them: they appeared to relieve him for the time.

Latterly Dr. Antomarchi forbad him their use, as he thought that they only increased his weakness.

In the month of August he took walking exercise, but with difficulty; he was forced to stop every minute. In the first years he used to walk while dictating; he walked about his room, and thus did without the exercise which he feared to take out of doors lest he should expose himself to insult. But latterly his strength would not admit even of this. He remained sitting nearly all day, and discontinued almost all occupation. His health declined sensibly every month.

* Of the Bellerophon.—TR.

Once in September, and again in the beginning of October, he rode out, as his physicians desired him to take exercise; but he was so weak, that he was obliged to return in his carriage. He ceased to digest; his debility increased. Shivering fits came on, which extended even to the extremities; hot towels applied to the feet gave him some relief. He suffered from these cold fits to the last hour of his life As he could no longer either walk or ride, he took several drives in an open carriage at a foot-pace, but without gaining strength. He never took off his dressing-gown. His stomach rejected food, and at the end of the year he was forced to give up meat; he lived upon jellies and soups. For some time he ate scarcely any thing, and drank only a little pure wine, hoping thus to support nature without fatiguing the digestion; but the vomiting continued, and he returned to soups and jellies. The remedies and tonics which were tried produced little effect. His body grew weaker every day, but his mind retained its strength.

He liked reading and conversation ; he did not dictate much, although he did so from time to time up to the last days of his life. He felt that his end was approaching, and he frequently recited the passage from 'Zaïre' which finishes with this line:—

A revoir Paris je ne dois plus prétendre.

Nevertheless the hope of leaving this dreadful country often presented itself to his imagination; some newspaper articles and false reports excited our expectations. We sometimes fancied that we were on the eve of starting for America; we read travels, we made plans, we arrived at your house, we wandered over that immense country, where alone we might hope to enjoy liberty. Vain hopes! vain projects! which only made us doubly feel our misfortunes.

They could not have been borne with more serenity and courage, I might almost add gaiety. He often said to us in the evening, "Where shall we go? to the Théâtre Français, or to the Opera?" And then he would read a tragedy by Corneille, Voltaire, or Racine; an opera of Quinault's or one of Molière's comedies. His strong mind and powerful character were perhaps even more remarkable than on that larger theatre where he eclipsed all that is brightest in ancient and in modern history. He often seemed to forget what he had been. I was never tired of admiring his philosophy and courage, the good sense and the fortitude which raised him above misfortune.

At times, however, sad regrets and recollections of what he had done, contrasted with what he might have done, presented themselves. He talked of the past with perfect frankness; persuaded that on the whole he had done what he was required to do, and not sharing the strange and contradictory opinions which we hear expressed every day on events which are not understood by the speakers. If the conversation took a melancholy turn, he soon changed it; he liked to talk of Corsica, of his old uncle Lucien, of his youth, of you, and of all the rest of the family.

Towards the middle of March fever came on. From that time he scarcely left his bed, except for about half an hour in the day; he seldom had the strength to shave. He now, for the first time, became extremely thin. The fits of vomiting became more frequent. He then questioned the physicians on the conformation of the stomach, and about a fortnight before his death he had pretty nearly guessed that he was dying of cancer. He was read to almost every day, and dictated a few days before his decease. He often talked naturally as to the probable mode of his death; but when he became aware that it was approaching, he left off speaking on the subject. He thought much about you and your children. To his last moments he was kind and affectionate to us all; he did not appear to suffer so much as might have been expected from the cause of his death. When we questioned him, he said that he suffered a little, but that he could bear it. His memory declined during the last five or six days; his deep sighs, and his exclamations from time to time, made us think that he was in great pain. He looked at us with the penetrating glance which you know so well; we tried to dissimulate, but he was so used to read our faces that no doubt he frequently discovered our anxiety. He felt too clearly the gradual decline of his faculties not to be aware of his state.

For the last two hours he neither spoke nor moved; the only

sound was his difficult breathing, which gradually but regularly decreased; his pulse ceased; and so died, surrounded only by a few servants, the man who had dictated laws to the world, and whose life should have been preserved for the sake of the happiness and glory of our sorrowing country.

Forgive, Prince, a hurried letter, which tells you so little, when you wish to know so much, but I should never end if I attempted to tell all.

You are so far off, that I know not when I shall have the honour of seeing you again. I must not omit to say that the Emperor was most anxious that his correspondence with the different sovereigns of Europe should be printed; he repeated this to us several times. In his will the Emperor expressed a wish that his remains should be buried in France; however, in the last days of his life he ordered me, if there was any difficulty about it, to lay him by the side of the fountain whose waters he had so long drank.

APPENDIX.

PRINCE LOUIS NAPOLEON TO JOSEPH.

New York, Apri 22, 1837.

My dear Uncle,—On my arrival in the United States I hoped to find a letter from you. I own that your displeasure grieved me; knowing, as I do, your good sense and your kindness, it surprised me. Indeed, uncle, my conduct must have been strangely misrepresented to you before you could have been induced to repel as enemies the men who sacrificed themselves for the empire. If, having succeeded at Strasbourg (and I very nearly did so), I had marched on Paris, followed by a people fascinated by the recollections of the empire, and, arriving in the capital as Pretender, I had seized the government, then to disavow me and to break with me might have been noble and magnanimous! But when I attempt one of the bold enterprises which alone could bring back what twenty years of peace have effaced; when I offer to it the sacrifice of my life, persuaded that even my death would be of use to our cause; when against my will I escape from the bayonet and the scaffold to a foreign shore, I find there only contempt and disdain on the part of my family!

If my respect and esteem for you were less sincere I should not be so sensitive, for I venture to say that the public will never allow that there can be a schism between us. None will believe that you repudiate your nephew because he has perilled his life for your cause; no one will believe that you can treat as enemies men who have exposed their lives and their fortunes to replace the eagle on our standards; any more than it would have been believed that

Louis XVIII. had repulsed the Prince de Condé or the Duc d'Enghien because they failed in their enterprises.

I know you too well, dear uncle, to doubt your affection, and not to hope that you will in time do justice to me, and to others who have compromised themselves for our cause. As for me, however you may treat me, my behaviour will not alter; the general sympathy, the tranquillity of my conscience, and, above all, the persuasion that, if the Emperor looks down on me, he approves me,—these are the considerations which compensate for the many mortifications and injuries which I have endured. My attempt failed, it is true; but it proved to France that the family of the Emperor is not yet extinguished, that it possesses devoted friends; in short, that its pretensions are not to reclaim a few pence from the government, but to re-establish in favor of the people what the foreigners and the Bourbons have destroyed. This is what I have done; is it for you to reproach me?

I annex the account of my removal from the prison of Strasbourg, in order that you may be acquainted with all my proceedings, and that you may be convinced that I have done nothing unworthy of the name which I bear.

I beg you to present my respects to my uncle Lucien; I trust my cause to his judgment and to his affection.

Pray, dear uncle, do not be offended at the brevity with which I represent facts as they really stand. Never doubt my unalterable attachment.

Your affectionate and dutiful nephew,

Napoleon-Louis.

P. S. I have delayed writing because you left my letters from Europe unanswered. I own that in this respect I was wrong.

On the 9th of November, towards 8 o'clock in the evening, Director Lebel came to tell me that I was to be removed from prison. Immediately afterwards the door was opened and I was desired to enter a carriage where were already General Voirol and the prefect. Believing at first that I was to be transferred to another prison, I entreated General Voirol to leave me in the same place with the other prisoners. On reaching the court of the Prefecture we got out of the carriage; I then perceived two post-chaises with horses. Fancying that I was to be taken from Strasbourg, I urged General Voirol to let me remain in prison. Soon afterwards I was placed in a carriage with three persons whom I did not know, and who informed me that they had orders to take me to Paris.

I then understood that I was to receive a special pardon; and, unable to restrain my tears, I explained to the officers who accompanied me how painful to me was the thought of a pardon which might make me pass for a coward, and would deprive me of the means of dissipating the calumnies by which my intentions had been misrepresented to the country.

M. Cugnat and M. Thibautot, whose consideration and attention I cannot sufficiently praise, tried to console me by saying that my removal might be useful to my companions in misfortune.

We reached Paris on the 11th at two in the morning. I was taken to the Prefecture, where I found M. Delessert, who is the only person whom I saw while I was in Paris. He informed me that my mother had come to France to ask my pardon of the King, and that I was to be taken to Lorient, and thence transported to the United States of America.

I expostulated once more with the Prefect on my removal, adding that my absence would deprive my fellow-sufferers of much evidence in their favour. The Prefect answered, "When you reach Lorient you may make in writing any depositions which you think proper." Was he aware that Commandant Cugnat had express orders not to let me write one word before I embarked?—orders so strict that, when I wrote to Madame Laity, through the Prefect of Lorient, to give her news of her son, the government telegraphed to M. Cugnat that he was to execute precisely the orders which he had received.

My fate being irrevocably fixed, there remained only to do all that I could to be useful to my friends. I wrote to the King to say that life was a small favour, since I had renounced it when I planted my foot on French ground; but that, if he would pardon my companions in misfortune, I should be eternally grateful. At four in the morning I quitted Paris. On reaching the citadel of Port-Louis I wrote secretly to M. Odillon Barrot a letter in which, taking all blame upon myself, I endeavoured to clear my friends of acting with premeditation.

On the 21st we sailed from Lorient, imagining that we were going to New York. When we reached latitude 32°, the captain of the frigate opened sealed orders, in the handwriting of the Minister for Marine Affairs, which enjoined him to take me to Rio-Janeiro; to allow me to speak to nobody; to remain there only long enough to take in water, and then to sail for New York. As the frigate had no business in the Brazils, she must have been ordered out of her way in order to prevent me from communicating with the prisoners at Strasbourg until the trial was over.

THE END.

D. APPLETON & COMPANY'S PUBLICATIONS.

Captain Canot; or, Twenty Years of an African Slaver: being an Account of his Career and Adventures on the Coast, in the Interior, on Shipboard, and in the West Indies Written out and Edited from the Captain's Journals, Memoranda, and Conversations. By BRANTZ MAYER. 1 vol. 12mo. With eight Illustrations. Price, $1 25.

The Preservation of Health and Prevention of Disease: including Practical Suggestions on Diet, Mental Development, Exercise, Ventilation, Bathing, Use of Medicines, Management of the Sick, etc. By B. N. COMINGS, M. D. 1 vol. 12mo. 75 cents.

The Youth of Madame de Longueville; or New Revelations of Court and Convent in the Sixteenth Century. From the French of Victor Cousin. By F. W. RICORD. 1 vol. 12mo. $1 00.

Emmanuel-Philibert; or, the European Wars of the XVIth Century. By ALEXANDER DUMAS. 2 vols. 12mo. Price, paper covers, $1; cloth, $1 25.

The Nursery Basket: a Hand-Book of Practical Directions for Young Mothers, including the Preparation of Infants Wardrobe, the Choice and Making-Up, the Child's Bath, Out-of Door Dress, Worsted Knitting, Flannel Embroidery, the Clothes of Older Children, etc., etc. 1 vol. square 16mo. 37½ cents.

The Iron Cousin; or, Mutual Influence. By MARY COWDEN CLARKE, author of "The Concordance to Shakspeare," etc. 1 vol. 12mo. Price, $1 25.

The Chemistry of Common Life. By JAMES W. JOHNSTON, M. A., F. R. S., etc., author of "Lectures on Agricultural Chemistry and Geology." Parts 1 to 4 now ready. Price 25 cents each.

Johnson's Treatise on Words. 1 volume, 12mo. Price, $1 00.

Thiers' French Revolution. New edition. With Steel Engravings. 4 vols. 8vo. Price $5 00.

The Great Work on Russia.

Fifth Edition now ready.

RUSSIA AS IT IS.

By Count A. de Gurowski.

One neat volume 12mo., pp. 328, well printed. Price $1, cloth.

CONTENTS.—Preface.—Introduction.—Czarism: its historical origin—Th Czar Nicholas.—The Organization of the Government.—The Army and Navy.—The Nobility.—The Clergy.—The Bourgeoisie—The Cossacks.-The Real People, the Peasantry.—The Rights of Aliens and Strangers. —The Commoner.—Emancipation.—Manifest Destiny —Appendix.—The Amazons.—The Fourteen Classes of the Russian Public Service; or, the Tschins.—The Political Testament of Peter the Great.—Extract from an Old Chronicle.

Notices of the Press.

"The author takes no superficial, empirical view of his subject, but collecting a rich variety of facts, brings the lights of a profound philosophy to their explanation. His work, indeed, neglects no essential detail—it is minute and accurate in its statistics—it abounds in lively pictures of society, manners and character. * * Whoever wishes to obtain an accurate notion of the internal condition of Russia, the nature and extent of her resources, and the practical influence of her institutions, will here find better materials for his purpose than in any single volume now extant."—*N. Y. Tribune.*

"This is a powerfully-written book, and will prove of vast service to every one who desires to comprehend the real nature and bearings of the great contest in which Russia is now engaged."—*N. Y. Courier.*

"It is original in its conclusions; it is striking in its revelations. Numerous as are the volumes that have been written about Russia, we really hitherto have known little of that immense territory—of that numerous people. Count Gurowski's work sheds a light which at this time is most welcome and satisfactory."—*N. Y. Times.*

"The book is well written, and as might be expected in a work by a writer so unusually conversant with all sides of Russian affairs, it contains so much important information respecting the Russian people, their government and religion."—*Com. Advertiser.*

"This is a valuable work, explaining in a very satisfactory manner the internal conditions of the Russian people, and the construction of their political society. The institutions of Russia are presented as they exist in reality, and as they are determined by existing and obligatory laws."—*N. Y. Herald.*

"A hasty glance over this handsome volume has satisfied us that it is one worthy of general perusal. * * It is full of valuable historical information, with very interesting accounts of the various classes among the Russian people, their condition and aspirations."—*N. Y. Sun.*

"This is a volume that can hardly fail to attract very general attention, and command a wide sale in view of the present juncture of European affairs, and the prominent part therein which Russia is to play."—*Utica Gazette.*

"A timely book. It will be found all that it professes to be, though some may be startled at some of its conclusions."—*Boston Atlas.*

"This is one of the best of all the books caused by the present excitement in relation to Russia. It is a very able publication—one that will do much to destroy the general belief in the infallibility of Russia. The writer shows himself master of his subject, and treats of the internal condition of Russia, her institutions and customs, society, laws, &c., in an enlightened and scholarly manner."—*City Item.*

Songs and Ballads of the American Revolution.

LOYAL AND WHIG. WITH NOTES AND ILLUSTRATIONS.

BY FRANK MOORE.

"More solid things do not show the complexion of the times as well as *Ballads and Libels.*"—*Selden.*

1 vol. 12mo., with two illustrations by Darley. Price $1.

(*Extract from Editor's Preface.*)

This volume presents a selection from the numerous productions, in verse, which appeared during the war of the American Revolution. Many of them are taken from the newspapers and periodical issues of the time, others from original ballad, sheet, and broadsides; while some have been received from the recollections of a few surviving soldiers, who heard and sang them amid the trials of the camp and the field.

Nearly every company had its "smart one," a poet who beguiled the weariness of the march or the encampment, by his minstrelsy, grave or gay, and the imperfect fragments which survive to us, provoke our regret that so few of them have been preserved.

(*From the Boston Evening Transcript.*)

It is a curiosity of literature, a patriotic treasury of quaint, yet honest verse, an antiquarian gem, a native and primitive fruit—in short, a delectable book for the curious in literature, and the lovers of the native muse, in her rude infancy. The notes indicate patient research, and give historical value to the work. * * * The verses to the memory of Hale are mournfully graphic; and, as we take up the book, fresh from Irving's page, it seems to transport us to hamlet and bivouac, and reproduce the life of the people, when the events of the Revolution were gradually unfolding.

(*From the Albany Morning Express.*)

The real life of a people may be found in its songs and ballads. The prosaic pen of the historian gives only an outline of the picture; the true color and complexion of the times are preserved in those traditionary legends and songs, which conceived on the impulse of the moment, inspired by the time and the occasion, and the absorbing scenes of heroic action, are handed down from father to son, and cling to the very heart of the people. Mr. Moore's collection has been long needed, and is a valuable contribution to our national literature.

(*From the Criterion.*)

Mr. Moore has done a real service to the country, not only in a literary, but a historical point of view; and no library or private collection, of any pretension or value, can be without this volume of poetical history. Moore's collections of the BALLADS AND SONGS OF THE REVOLUTION must fill the same place in the literature of this country that is filled in Great Britain by SCOTT'S MINSTRELSY OF THE SCOTTISH BORDER.

(*From the Transcript and Eclectic.*)

The work fills a void in our national and historical literature; and also addresses itself especially to the tastes and comprehension of the masses of the people.

(*From Correspondent of Boston Post.*)

I regard this volume as an exceedingly valuable contribution to our historic literature. * * * With the rude effusions here first collected, was born American liberty; and the harp of Homer or Milton could not have been tuned to a nobler resolve than that which called them forth.

(*From the N. Y. Entr' Acte.*)

Mr. Moore has done for his country what Herder did for the Jewish nation—what Goethe and Schiller labored to perform for Germany, early in the last century—namely, to give to the land of his birth a ballad literature; not, indeed, created by his own genius, but collected from among those emanations which were called forth when the forefathers of our country were upon the battle-field, in defence of human rights, and with arms in their hands. The fruits of his labors will be received with enthusiastic delight. His work breathes of Bunker Hill, of Concord, and Lexington. Its poetic productions are associated with that struggle, which is among the most noble in history—American Independence. And every American will read it.

www.ingramcontent.com/pod-product-compliance
Lightning Source LLC
LaVergne TN
LVHW020124110826
845151LV00001B/263

* 9 7 8 1 4 2 5 5 4 1 5 4 5 *